The Structural Evolution of Morality

It is certainly the case that morality governs the interactions that take place between individuals. But what if morality exists because of these interactions? This book argues for the claim that much of the behavior we view as "moral" exists because acting in that way benefits each of us to the greatest extent possible, given the socially structured nature of society. By drawing upon aspects of evolutionary game theory, the theory of bounded rationality, and computational models of social networks, this book shows both how moral behavior can emerge in socially structured environments, and how it can persist even when it is not typically viewed as "rational" from a traditional economic perspective. Since morality consists of much more than mere behavior, this book also provides a theory of how moral principles and the moral sentiments play an indispensable role in effective choice, acting as "fast and frugal heuristics" in social-decision contexts.

J. McKenzie Alexander is Reader in Philosophy in the Department of Philosophy, Logic and Scientific Method at the London School of Economics and Political Science.

The Structural Evolution of Morality

J. McKENZIE ALEXANDER
London School of Economics and Political Science

CAMBRIDGE
UNIVERSITY PRESS

CAMBRIDGE UNIVERSITY PRESS
Cambridge, New York, Melbourne, Madrid, Cape Town, Singapore, São Paulo

Cambridge University Press
The Edinburgh Building, Cambridge CB2 8RU, UK

Published in the United States of America by Cambridge University Press, New York

www.cambridge.org
Information on this title: www.cambridge.org/9780521870320

First published 2007

Printed in the United Kingdom at the University Press, Cambridge

A catalogue record for this publication is available from the British Library

ISBN   978-0-521-87032-0 hardback

Contents

Preface

The central claim of this book is that morality provides a set of heuristics that, when followed, serves to produce the best expected outcome, for each of us, over the course of our lives, given the constraints placed by other people. That's quite a mouthful, but the basic idea is straightforward. Each of us has goals we would like to attain and ends we wish to achieve. However, your ability to attain your goals and achieve your ends is constrained by the fact that you are a social being. You live in a society where *other* people are trying to attain *their* goals and achieve *their* ends and, on some occasions, their goals and ends are incompatible with yours. The heuristics embedded within moral theories prescribe ways of acting so that the majority of people wind up sufficiently satisfied with their lot in life the majority of the time.

That description, while accurate as it stands, still leaves out one key aspect of the account developed in this book: societies have *structure*. The structure of society is composed of social relations, friendship networks, kinship networks, professional networks, and so on. The structure of society constrains how people interact, how people learn, and what people do in order to attain their goals. Social structure proves to be a powerful influence and is, I shall argue, the main reason why our moral theories have the form that they have.

What does evolution have to do with all of this? Plenty, although I must admit that the kind of evolution I am primarily concerned with is *cultural* evolution rather than *biological* evolution. The few places I will talk about biological evolution are places where – curiously enough – models of cultural evolution and biological evolution have the same form.

By cultural evolution, I mean nothing more than change in belief over time. Sometimes the social structure of society is causally efficacious in how belief changes over time. For example, we learn new things all the time, but we learn new things more frequently from our friends and acquaintances than from a randomly selected individual from the society in which we live. Because our network of friends plays a causal role in determining (or, at the very least, influencing) what we learn, this is an example of what I call *structural evolution*.

All of these ideas, plus a few more, are covered at length in chapter 1. That chapter sets the stage for the rest of the book by introducing the core concepts of the book: bounded rationality, strategic choice, and evolutionary game theory. It also provides an argument for why one should adopt bounded rationality and evolutionary game theory as the core tools for studying the evolution of society.

Chapter 2 provides a detailed introduction of the evolutionary models covered in this book. I discuss several models of cultural evolution, arguing that an agent-based approach provides the most empirically satisfactory way to proceed. Although it is a bit abstract, this material provides the necessary foundation for making sense of the next four chapters.

The bulk of the book (chapters 3–6) considers the evolution of cooperation, trust, fairness, and retribution, using a number of well-known games. Since all of these games are elementary two-player games, chapter 7 considers what happens when we approach the question of the evolution of cooperation, trust, and fairness in an environment where groups matter. The moral of the story – in all of these chapters – is that social structure often favors the evolution of what we typically take to be the "right thing to do" in these games.

The final chapter broaches a number of philosophical questions concerning what, exactly, these evolutionary results imply for our understanding of morality. It would be hubristic to think that an actual solution has been provided. I do hope, though, to have achieved a bit more than an extended exercise in hand-waving. But only a bit.

A good friend who had the wherewithal to read through this manuscript suggested that I include a note identifying the target audience. The answer, I'm afraid, is that this book is aimed at anyone interested in the evolution of morality from both a philosophical and a social-scientific perspective, and who also possesses that ill-defined quality known as "mathematical sophistication" but no particular pre-requisites. Where possible, I have flagged slightly more mathematical passages that can be skipped at no loss with a vertical line in the left margin.

Acknowledgements

Elephants have a gestation period of approximately twenty-two months. Although I do not know what it is like to be a bat, I now have some idea of what it is like to be an elephant. In the time I have been working on this book, a very determined elephant could have produced half a football team.

Given this, the number of people I have to thank for their help and support over these years is considerable. I owe the most to Brian Skyrms, whose initial encouragement to work on the ideas contained in this book saved the world from having a very bad philosopher of mathematics added to its ranks. I also would like to thank Jeff Barrett, Cristina Bicchieri, Ken Binmore, Luc Bovens, Richard Bradley, Helena Cronin, Joshua Epstein, Allan Gibbard, Patrick Grim, Stephan Hartmann, Jim Joyce, Christian List, Ned McClennen, Alex Rosenberg, William Rottschaefer, Peter Vanderschraaf, Alex Voorhoeve, and H. Peyton Young for a number of stimulating discussions that informed the present work. Portions of the manuscript were presented at meetings of the Choice Group at the London School of Economics, and the criticism received was very valuable in influencing the overall form of the argument. Alex Voorhoeve, Luc Bovens and two anonymous referees were also kind enough to provide comments on portions of the manuscript, for which I am most grateful.

Then there are the personal debts. First and foremost, my parents, Jack and Patricia Alexander, provided unwavering support and encouragement through a very trying time. I am also indebted to Stephanie Bauer, for innumerable conversations that ultimately led to my becoming a philosopher; Royce Williams, whose good cheer could always be counted upon to pull me out of the doldrums; Brian Eno, whose brilliant album *Music for Airports* has effectively been on loop play the entire time; and all of those friends whose good wishes and interest were instrumental in helping see the project to fruition. Last, but not least, I would like to thank the barstaff at my local, the Greenman & French Horn, who can pull a pint of Old Peculier like no one else.

1

Introduction

1.1 Darwin's decision problem

On a list of history's great romantics, Darwin is an unlikely candidate for inclusion. He was a man unusually devoted to the study of barnacles and, when the time came for him to decide whether to marry, he divided a sheet of paper into two vertical columns and listed the reasons for and against marriage:

MARRY

Children—(if it please God)—constant companion, (friend in old age) who will feel interested in one, object to be beloved and played with—better than a dog anyhow—Home, and someone to take care of house—Charms of music and female chit-chat. These things good for one's health. Forced to visit and receive relations *but terrible loss of time.* My God, it is intolerable to think of spending one's whole life, like a neuter bee, working, working, and nothing after all.—No, no won't do.— Imagine living all one's day solitarily in smoky dirty London House.— Only picture to yourself a nice soft wife on a sofa with good fire, and books and music perhaps—compare this vision with the dingy reality of Grt Marlboro' St.

Not MARRY

No children, (no second life) no one to care for one in old age . . . Freedom to go where one like—Choice of Society *and little of it.* Conversation of clever men at clubs.—Not forced to visit relatives, and to bend in every trifle—to have the expense and anxiety of children—perhaps quarrelling.

Loss of time—cannot read in the evenings—fatness and idleness—anxiety and responsibility—less money for books etc—if many children forced to gain one's bread.—(But then it is very bad for one's health to work too much)

Perhaps my wife won't like London; then the sentence is banishment and degradation with indolent idle fool—

At the bottom of the sheet of paper, Darwin concluded that he should indeed "Marry—Marry—Marry." Whether his closing remark was intended to be tongue-in-cheek or as a serious comment on these reflections is difficult to say: Darwin signed off on these deliberations with "Q.E.D." An interesting proof indeed (Barlow, 1987).

I suspect few people would recommend basing one's decision to marry on the outcome of such workmanlike calculations and comparisons of pros and cons. Yet the hope that such calculations could be applied to all matters of importance – including questions underlying lifelong happiness – drove the early Utilitarians. If a "hedonic calculus" could be found, it would be a relatively simple task, they thought, to achieve the greatest good for the greatest number. One such process is in fact suggested by Darwin's decision procedure: in order to select the best outcome from a set of alternatives, simply pick any two from the set at random, determine the better of the two, discard the inferior option, and then draw a new option from the (now slightly smaller) set. Repeat this procedure until only one option remains. At the end of the process, through a simple algorithm involving only pairwise comparisons, the best of all possible options has been found.[1] Had Bentham's notion of utility values corresponded to some real, measurable quantity, they could have been used by a social planner to chart the future course of society.

Utility does not exist – at least not in the objective, measurable sense supporting the interpersonal comparisons needed for a hedonic calculus of the Benthamite kind. Hence Bentham's dream, and with it the Utilitarian project in its purest form, failed. We do not have a prudential calculus for settling important problems and, in the absence of such a calculus with methods for quantitatively comparing the real values of alternatives, Darwin's decision procedure seems to illustrate only a mere choice heuristic. Some will, no doubt, find Darwin's use of this heuristic unsettling when applied to the marriage question. Mere heuristics seem appropriate when little is at stake – such as choosing an entrée at dinner or a film to see – but for important decisions our intuitions suggest that other procedures, ones more appropriate for treating the weighty matters at hand, should be used. An appropriate procedure would give due consideration to all of the important and relevant factors of the problem at hand, such as personal values, moral principles, individual goals, and the likely causal consequences stemming from the action chosen. *These* are the factors one ought to consider when choosing, rather than merely tabulating salient features of the situation. The intuition is that serious thought and rational reflection are necessary in order to make the right decision; methods that skimp on the amount of reflection are less likely to identify the right choice. In cases where much is at stake, like marriage for example, one should think long and hard about what to do. This strikes us as common sense.

Love and marriage are difficult topics to think about from the point of view of proper decision procedures. Let us turn our attention to a subject where the

---

[1] One complication exists if two options may be equally good. In this case, the procedure can be extended by including a randomization device, such as a coin, to choose between two equally good options.

connection between choice and outcome is clear, unlike love and marriage, but which some people care for almost as much: chess. The game of chess has been viewed as a metaphor for life – it has three main outcomes: Win, Lose, and Draw. If one keeps score by counting the value of pieces, you can even Win Big or Lose Badly. More importantly, from our point of view, the game of chess has an optimal strategy. It can be proven that either White has a winning strategy, or Black has a winning strategy, or that each player has a strategy which guarantees at least a draw.

Chess thus seems the perfect arena in which to observe people engaged in rational, deliberative calculations that approach the ideal standard. If a perfectly rational player knew the optimal strategy to employ when playing chess, he or she would always win, or at least force a draw. Hence, one might think that the closer a player approached the ideal, deliberative standard, the better they would be at playing chess. Or, stating the connection the opposite way, one might think that the better a person is at playing chess, the closer they approach the ideal, deliberative standard. If by "ideal deliberative standard" one means a careful consideration of all the available alternatives, combined with an assessment of the respective merit of each alternative, there turns out to be very little correlation between the strength of a chess player and the breadth of their search. Although it *is* true that chess players "spend much of their time searching in the game tree for the consequences of the moves they are considering," it is also true that "the search is highly selective, attending to only a few of the multitude of possible continuations" of play (Newell and Simon, 1972, p. 750).

The author of one particular study (de Groot, 1965) attempted to measure the number of positions typically considered by grandmasters in the course of determining their next move. Surprisingly, the number of positions considered ranged between only 20 and 76, even though many more moves were possible. The narrowness of this search becomes all the more remarkable in light of the fact that, until relatively recently, people were *consistently* better chess players than computers, the very model of the "ideal, deliberative agent" which exhaustively examines all possible positions (to the extent of the computer's ability, at least). Consider the following: Gary Kasparov can evaluate roughly three chess positions a second, whereas IBM's Deep Blue can evaluate 200 000 000 a second. In the first game of the 1997 match between Kasparov and Deep Blue, each player was given three minutes per move to think. In this time, Deep Blue could examine and evalute 36 000 000 000 moves compared with Kasparov's 540. Yet Kasparov won the first match.[2]

---

[2] Kasparov lost the overall tournament. The results of the six-game match were as follows: Kasparov, Deep Blue, draw, draw, draw, Deep Blue.

If human chess players fall so short of the ideal deliberative standard, why do they do so well? Newell and Simon note several key differences between how people play chess and how computers play chess. First, people tend to re-define the problem they are considering.[3] Although the human player attempts to choose the best possible next move, he typically conceives of the task quite differently. Instead of simply choosing the best next move with the intention of forcing checkmate, the human player will choose the best next move which, for example, "strengthens my defensive position on the right side of the board." This ties into a second, related point: people describe and analyze chess positions using classificatory terms that are rich in their implications. The meaning attached to these classificatory terms, such as a particular board position's "vul-nerability," are difficult to operationalize and translate into computational terms.

Another reason offered by Newell and Simon for the success of human chess players actually *credits* the use of heuristics. In a different experiment, Newell and Simon had players from a wide range of abilities assess a given board configuration in order to determine the future course of play. Even though the players differed greatly in their abilities and were tested separately, the set of possible moves considered tended to have considerable overlap. In particular, "the seven moves mentioned by the largest number of subjects (16 to 6) accounted for about two-thirds $\left(\frac{62}{94}\right)$ of all mentions" (Newell and Simon, 1972, p. 757). To explain this overlap, Newell and Simon speculated as follows.

> How are we to account for this high degree of consensus? First, we may look at it from a sociological standpoint. All the players, even the weakest of those studied, belong to a common chess culture. This culture is transmitted in across-the-board play, in conversation among chess players, and in writing on chess (move-by-move reports and analyses of games among grandmasters, books on chess strategy and tactics) . . . Thus, all of these players know . . . substantially all the heuristic principles that have been incorporated in existing chess programs and a great many more. They approach the position, therefore, with a common body of beliefs acquired through participation in a common culture. The beliefs are not identical, of course—else all the players would be grandmasters—but their commonality in terms of the task requirements is substantial.
>
> *(Newell and Simon, 1972, pp. 757–758)*

Players tend to focus on the same set of possible moves because they use shared heuristics to determine what the set of possible moves should be. These heuristics incorporate "a common body of beliefs acquired through participa-tion in a common culture." Since these beliefs are based on analyses of past games, move-by-move reports, and so on, this common body of beliefs has

---

[3] See Newell and Simon (1972), p. 753.

considerable evidence supporting it, which justifies the adoption of that common body of beliefs. We might then refer to "common knowledge" acquired by participation in the common culture instead of just "common beliefs." Heuristics encapsulate this common knowledge in comprehensible, and readily apprehended, forms, which can then be applied in contexts different from the one in which it was originally acquired.

Life is not chess, but decision procedures used by humans in chess mimic decision procedures used by humans in life, at least in the following sense: many of the decision problems we face in real life have determinate, optimal solutions in terms of maximizing our expected payoff. If we were perfectly rational machines equipped with unlimited computational capacity, we would have little difficulty in choosing the best action to take. Since we are not these machines, we instead muddle our way through life relying on less-than-perfect calculations derived from heuristics and rules of thumb.

Given our unavoidable reliance on heuristics, any project that attempts to explain and predict individual choice in decision contexts by positing man as a perfectly rational agent appears misguided. Nevertheless, the model of man as a perfectly rational agent, the *homo economicus* so beloved by economic theorists, has been adopted by many as the standard model of the rational agent. Not everyone finds this model satisfying. In the late nineteen fifties, Herbert Simon introduced the concept of *bounded rationality* in direct opposition to the concept of perfect rationality then so commonly assumed:

> The alternative approach [to economic man] . . . is based on what I shall call the *principle of bounded rationality*:
>
> > *The capacity of the human mind for formulating and solving complex problems is very small compared with the size of the problems whose solution is required for objectively rational behavior in the real world—or even for a reasonable approximation to such objective rationality.*
>
> If the principle is correct, then the goal of classical economic theory—to predict the behavior of rational man without making an empirical investigation of his psychological properties—is unattainable. For the first consequence of the principle of bounded rationality is that the intended rationality of an actor requires him to construct a simplified model of the real situation in order to deal with it. He behaves rationally with respect to this model, and such behavior is not even approximately optimal with respect to the real world.
>
> *(Simon, 1957, pp. 198–199)*

Rejecting *homo economicus*, Simon sought to introduce a new conception of rationality, more applicable to real people, which, at the same time, improved our ability to predict the choices people make.

Simon is perhaps too pessimistic in claiming that bounded rationality is not even approximately optimal with respect to the real world. If by "approximately optimal" one means "likely to identify the optimal choice, or a nearly optimal choice," in the case of chess, human behavior is approximately optimal. We can, and do, divide human chess players into ranked levels of ability, where a player belonging to level N can generally beat a player belonging to level $N - 1$, and the probability that a player belonging to level N_+ will beat a player belonging to level N_-, where $N_+ > N_-$, rapidly converges to 1 as the distance between N_+ and N_- increases. A grandmaster will *always* beat a neophyte. Since a perfectly rational player would have the strategy that allowed him to win (or draw) regardless of his opponent, and a grandmaster can always win (or draw) when he plays people of significantly lesser ability, the heuristics used by the grandmaster are, in this sense, "approximately optimal."

Bounded rationality, in Simon's sense, means that individuals should be thought of as *satisficing* rather than *optimizing* agents. Each individual has a given *aspiration level* he wishes to attain and will take action believed to be conducive to meeting his aspiration level. Consider the problem of selling a house: the seller selects a price that she wishes to obtain, and as soon as an offer that exceeds her set price arrives, she agrees to sell the house. However, since people presumably adjust the price of a house up or down on the basis of the nature of the market, Simon allowed for the possibility that individual aspiration levels may vary in light of recently acquired information. Thus, Simon's conception of bounded rationality also includes a dynamic aspect in which people's aspiration levels vary over time.

Conceiving of people as boundedly rational agents, in Simon's sense, makes for a more descriptively accurate theory, and may even describe Darwin's deliberation reasonably well. Seeking to attain a certain level of happiness in the future, Darwin considers two courses of action and, after due deliberation, chooses marriage as more likely to make him happy. Moreover, his deliberation involves appeal to general principles best viewed as rules of thumb: he believes that marriage generally requires forced family visits and leads to a loss of time in the evenings. Even though these general principles are based on a simplified model of the real situation, Darwin entrusted his happiness to them.

The greater descriptive accuracy of bounded rationality does not mean that all vestiges of the perfectly rational agent have been removed from the theory. Gigerenzer *et al.* (1999) rightly point out that Simon omits an account of how a boundedly rational agent chooses his initial aspiration level, or how a boundedly rational agent should adjust his aspiration level in light of new evidence. In part, this is understandable since the exact procedures of adjustment will presumably be both context- and agent-dependent. One concern, though, is that many procedures for selecting an appropriate aspiration level, and for modifying the aspiration level in light of new evidence, will assume a level of rationality that again overshoots the meagre cognitive abilities of ordinary individuals.

In order to avoid commitment to assumptions of perfect rationality, Gigerenzer *et al.* espouse a theory of "fast and frugal heuristics"[4] that downplays talk of aspiration levels and their dynamic adjustment. Rather, they argue, the heuristics people use for making decisions and taking action are efficient, easy to implement, and require minimal cognitive abilities – hence the name "fast and frugal." Such heuristics often work because they take advantage of certain structural features of the problem. As an example of such heuristics in action, consider the problem faced by a baseball outfielder who wishes to catch a fly ball in a baseball game. It seems that catching the ball requires a great deal of cognitive machinery, for the outfielder needs to infer where the ball will land given its initial trajectory and then move to that location. Determining where the ball will land, given its initial conditions, requires solving a problem in multivariable calculus. This must be done extremely quickly and accurately in order for the outfielder to have time to be at the proper location when the ball lands. As we may expect, a simpler and equally effective heuristic exists. Gigerenzer notes that, if the outfielder simply runs toward the ball so as to maintain the angle of his gaze constant, he will reach the point where the ball hits the ground at the same time as the ball arrives. This simple heuristic is extremely efficient, effective, and widely used. Gigerenzer, along with others from the Center for Adaptive Behavior and Cognition at the Max Planck Institute in Berlin, have found numerous instances in which people use other fast and frugal heuristics to reduce complex decision problems to manageable levels, many of which work surprisingly well.

In most cases, unlike the example of the outfielder and the fly ball, the heuristics provide no guarantee that the "right" answer or "best" outcome will be achieved. Each heuristic works well for a certain class of problems whose structure satisfies certain necessary conditions required for the reliable functioning of the heuristic. A heuristic recommending that an individual, when faced with a choice problem, should choose the option most recently encountered in the past will work well only when there is a correlation between the most recently encountered option and the optimality of that option. An attempt to apply such a heuristic to a new problem, for which no such correlation holds, means that, in those problem instances, the misapplied heuristic will likely perform no better than randomization, and may in fact do worse. Heuristics belong to an "adaptive toolbox" (Gigerenzer and Selten, 2001) and, just like

---

[4] See also Gigerenzer and Selten (2001).

tools, are guaranteed to work well only for the set of tasks they were constructed to do well. A hammer serves as a paperweight just as well as it drives nails, but the fact that the hammer performs the former function well is by accident, not design.

People are cognitively limited beings and, as such, often make choices using heuristics that *homo economicus* would scoff at. When possible, we do engage in rational deliberation, but only to the extent of which we are capable, given the limits on our abilities and the information we possess. If Gigerenzer *et al.* are correct in claiming that (1) people *do* use fast and frugal heuristics for many, if not most, of their decisions; and (2) Simon's conception of bounded rationality as satisficing requires a higher degree of rationality than does the use of fast and frugal heuristics, we should revise our reaction to Darwin's decision procedure accordingly. By approaching the marriage question as a problem of *satisficing*, we might say that Darwin did, in fact, show due respect for the solemnity of marriage. After all, he used a decision procedure that requires a higher degree of rationality than the fast and frugal heuristics he employed in other decision contexts.

1.2 Parametric and strategic choice

A careful reader, attuned to modern sensibilities, will detect an important omission from Darwin's deliberation. Whereas a great deal is made about the costs and benefits of attendant social obligations and the virtues of having children, virtually no thought is given to the possible responses by the prospective Mrs. Darwin to the marriage offer. Darwin's deliberation concerns the expected value of outcomes – Marry, Not Marry – with little regard for the connection between his choosing to get married and the actual occurrence of marriage. In short, Darwin's decision problem is one of *parametric* choice. If Darwin decides that he wants to marry, he will; if he decides that he does not want to marry, he won't. Whether the future Mrs. Darwin will accept the marriage offer, what Darwin might need to do to increase the probability of his offer's acceptance, and how the burden of these negotiations affects the overall expected benefit of being married are not subjects of consideration.

In retrospect, Darwin's framing of the marriage problem as one of parametric choice might make sense. In Victorian England few women had opportunity for meaningful careers outside of the home. For many women, ensuring a comfortable existence meant marrying well and, Darwin's love of barnacles notwithstanding, he could reasonably assume that an offer of marriage would not be turned down, provided that it was made to a woman of comparable status. Therefore, an offer of marriage would likely lead to marriage, and so the problem really was one of parametric rather than strategic choice.

Darwin's decision problem is not ours. We live in a world where people's reactions to our choices can have a significant effect on the resulting outcome. If we recognize this, and take it seriously when deciding what to do, we soon find ourselves engaging in spiraling calculations of the form "I think that you think that I think that . . . "[5] Decision methods that work well for problems of parametric choice do not adapt well to problems of strategic choice. This point is important because problems of strategic choice tend to characterize better the choice problems faced by people in social contexts. The fact that Darwin could reasonably conceive of the marriage problem as one of parametric choice derives from peculiarities of Victorian culture more than from the nature of interdependent choice in society. Most interdependent choice problems in society have the structure of the modern marriage problem, where the outcome reflects a mutual agreement among rational persons.

The expression "a mutual agreement among rational persons" suggests the outcome of a process of rational deliberation in which all parties negotiate a settlement. Negotiating a settlement is a complex process, with many considerations by each party. Such considerations include whether one should state everything one wants from the agreement at the beginning of negotiations or refrain from stating these wants until later. The best course of action for each person depends upon what everyone else does. Interdependent decision problems of this type fall within the scope of that branch of mathematics and decision theory known as game theory.

Game theory was developed to analyze interdependent decision problems.[6] However, even though interdependent decision problems occur in many different social contexts, game theory has been, for the most part, a tool of analysis used almost solely by economists. Given the prevalence of interdependent decision problems, it is well worth asking why other disciplines have been reluctant to adopt the formal tools of game theory. I suspect part of the reason for game

---

[5] For example, consider the following game: members of a group of people are told to guess a number between 0 and 1, and the person whose guess is closest to the *mean* guess of the group will win $100. In the case of a tie, the money is split between those who tie. What number should a player P guess? P's guess depends upon what P thinks each other player will guess. But every other player's guess depends on what they think that P will guess. Reiterating these kinds of strategic reflections gives rise to expressions of the form "I think that you think that I think that . . . "

[6] It originated in von Neumann's seminal work on the theory of games published in 1928, and was later developed at length by von Neumann and Morgenstern in *Theory of Games and Economic Behavior* (1944). Significant resources were poured into game-theoretic research by the RAND corporation at the beginning of the Cold War. After all, what is global thermonuclear war but a game in which the only winning move is not to play?

theory's predominant confinement to economics stems from the model of the individual it employs.[7] Game theory assumes a perfectly rational agent who possesses an amazingly complete and consistent set of preferences, as well as usually perfect information about the game and the preferences of her fellow agents (although this need not always be the case). The model of man as *homo economicus* underwrites all results in game theory.

It has already been noted how real people are boundedly rational and rely on heuristics. Even with this difference between *homo economicus* and real people, one could argue that there was good reason for studying *homo economicus* as a model of real people. After all, relying on heuristics to cope with cognitive limitations effectively is a rational response. Real people might not be *homo economicus*, but they might approximate *homo economicus* in their behavior. Yet even this attempted justification for the use of *homo economicus* as a model of man faces problems, because people fail to conform to the assumptions of *homo economicus* in several important ways.

For one, people in experimental settings frequently violate the Sure Thing principle, which orthodox game theory assumes. In essence, this principle states that if a, b, and c denote possible outcomes, then one's choice between the sets $\{a, c\}$ and $\{b, c\}$ is determined solely by one's preference for a or b. On the surface, this seems plausible enough; since one gets the "sure thing" c regardless of what one chooses, it should not affect the choice.

Suppose that you are a contestant on a television game show and are told that you will play two games. The games are very simple and require no particular talent or ability. You are told that the game show's host will roll a fair, 100-sided die to determine what prize you win, and the only thing you have to do is choose what reward scheme you want before each roll of the die. That is, the choice is among reward schemes that map outcomes of the roll of the die onto personal payoffs. Suppose that, for the first game, you must choose between the following reward schemes:

p_1: receive $100 no matter what the roll is;
p_2: receive $0 if the host rolls a 1, $100 if the host rolls 2–90, and $500 if the host rolls 91–100.

For the second game, you have the following choice:

q_1: receive $0 if the host rolls 1–89 and $100 if the host rolls 90–100;
q_2: receive $0 if the host rolls 1–90 and $500 if the host rolls 91–100.

---

[7] It must be noted that evolutionary game theory – of considerable theoretical interest in evolutionary and population biology – adopts a very different model of the individual from that in traditional game theory, which in part explains its increasing use.

Marcias Allais, who introduced this scenario in 1953, speculated that most people would choose p_1 and q_2. His speculation has since been confirmed by experiment – most people *do* choose p_1 and q_2. This violates the Sure Thing principle.

One can see that this pattern of choice violates the Sure Thing principle by comparing the two choices as follows. Suppose that, in the first game, one prefers p_1 to p_2. This game can be written in the following equivalent form.

p_1': receive $100 if the host rolls 1, $100 if the host rolls 2–90, and $100 if the host rolls 91–100.

p_2': receive $0 if the host rolls a 1, $100 if the host rolls 2–90, and $500 if the host rolls 91–100.

All we have done is rewrite the payoff options of p_1 in an expanded form. Now, let c denote "Lose $100 if the host rolls 2–90." According to the standard theory of expected utility, if one prefers p_1 to p_2, then one prefers p_1 and c to p_2 and c. These outcomes are the following.

p_1' and c: receive $100 if the host rolls 1, $100 if the host rolls 2–90, $100 if the host rolls 91–100, and lose $100 if the host rolls 2–90.

p_2' and c: receive $0 if the host rolls a 1, $100 if the host rolls 2–90, and $500 if the host rolls 91–100, and lose $100 if the host rolls 2–90.

Receiving a payoff of $100 in addition to losing $100 is the same as receiving nothing, so these outcomes can be simplified further.

p_1' and c: receive $100 if the host rolls 1, $0 if the host rolls 2–90, and $100 if the host rolls 91–100.

p_2' and c: receive $0 if the host rolls a 1–90, and $500 if the host rolls 91–100.

Receiving a payoff of $100 if the host rolls a 1 or 91–100, and nothing if the host rolls 2–90, is equivalent (in terms of expected payoff) to receiving $100 if the host rolls 90–100 and nothing if the host rolls 1–89. So from the point of view of expected payoffs, p_1' and c is equivalent to q_1, and p_2' and c is equivalent to q_2.

The fact that most people choose p_1 and q_2 is known as "Allais's Paradox." See Allais (1953a, 1953b, 1953c) and Allais and Hagen (1979). One implication of Allais's Paradox is that, if most people's considered preferences are such that they really do prefer p_1 and q_2, then people's preferences do not conform to the pattern required of *homo economicus*. The preferences of *homo economicus* must conform to the axioms of the standard theory of expected utility, one of the main tools used by game theory to analyze problems of strategic choice.

We can incorporate additional assumptions into the theory of expected utility such that the new theory can explain the phenomenon of preference reversal (of which Allais's Paradox is an instance). But is the standard theory of expected utility worth preserving? If we take seriously the point made by advocates of bounded rationality – namely, that people are limited in their cognitive ability, then we should dispense with the standard theory of expected utility on descriptive grounds because many of the assumptions it makes are incompatible with the conception of people as boundedly rational individuals.

The standard theory of expected utility constructs a utility function for an individual that maps outcomes of choice onto numerical values by considering that individual's particular preferences. Initially, one might not think that defining a utility function for an individual would require terribly strong rationality assumptions. If you ask someone to develop a procedure for constructing utility functions from individual preferences, one natural method that occurs to most people is the following: present the subject with every possible pair of goods and ask him to identify which of the two goods in the pair he prefers, if any. If the expressed preferences form a linear ordering,[8] the notion of a "utility function" can be defined by mapping the goods over which those preferences exist onto numbers that preserve that ordering. For example, suppose that a subject prefers three goods in the order $g_1 \precsim g_2 \precsim g_3$, where "$x \precsim y$" indicates that the subject either prefers or is indifferent to y over x. One "utility function" compatible with this preference ordering assigns g_1 a utility of 0, g_2 a utility of 1, and g_3 a utility of 2.

Although this approach assigns numerical values to particular goods, it suffers from one important problem: the actual values assigned are meaningless. *Any* function that assigns numbers so as to preserve the relative ordering of the goods will suffice. Instead of assigning the values 0, 1, and 2 to g_1, g_2, and g_3, we could have assigned the values -100, $\sqrt{\pi}$, and π instead. Both "utility functions" reflect the preference ordering for the individual in that the more-preferred goods receive a higher numerical value.

The following example reveals why this method of constructing utility functions is fundamentally inadequate. Suppose that Joe prefers g_3 to g_2 and g_2 to g_1. Two "utility functions" compatible with Joe's preference ordering, and derived using the above method, are the following:

1. $f_1(g_1) = 0$, $f_1(g_2) = 1$, $f_1(g_3) = 2$;
2. $f_2(g_1) = 0$, $f_2(g_2) = 1$, $f_2(g_3) = 10$.

Furthermore, suppose that Joe is given a choice of playing one of two lotteries. Lottery 1 rewards g_1 with probability $\frac{7}{12}$, g_2 with probability $\frac{1}{6}$, and g_3 with

---

[8] A subject's preferences are linearly ordered if they satisfy reflexivity, antisymmetry, transitivity, and comparability. That is, for any goods A, B, and C, A is weakly preferred to A; if A is weakly preferred to B and B weakly preferred to A, then the subject is indifferent between A and B; if the subject weakly prefers A to B and B to C, the subject weakly prefers A to C; and, lastly, either A is weakly preferred to B or vice versa.

probability $\frac{1}{4}$. Lottery 2, on the other hand, rewards g_1 with probability $\frac{1}{3}$, g_2 with probability $\frac{1}{2}$ and g_3 with probability $\frac{1}{6}$. Which lottery will Joe prefer to play? If we take f_1 as the description of Joe's preferences, lottery 1 gives Joe an expected utility of $\frac{1}{6} + \frac{1}{2} = \frac{4}{6}$ and lottery 2 gives Joe an expected utility of $\frac{1}{2} + \frac{1}{3} = \frac{5}{6}$, so Joe would prefer to play lottery 2. However, if we take f_2 as the description of Joe's preferences, lottery 1 gives Joe an expected utility of $\frac{1}{6} + \frac{10}{4} = \frac{32}{12}$ and lottery 2 gives Joe an expected utility of $\frac{1}{2} + \frac{10}{6} = \frac{13}{6}$, so Joe would prefer to play lottery 1. The two "utility functions" lead to different predictions as to which lottery Joe would play.

The problem, of course, is that one cannot meaningfully speak of expected utility if our utility theory gives us utility functions whose only meaningful properties concern the ordering. In order to speak of expected utility, we must be able to compute the average utility of various outcomes. This requires us to be able to add and multiply the resultant values of the utility function – operations that are meaningful only if the utility values themselves have meaning beyond their ordinal properties.

Modern utility theory allows one to speak meaningfully of the notion of expected utility. This is achieved by restricting the set of possible functions that might serve as an individual's utility function. It requires the individual to have a complex set of preferences (more complex than the naïve example above) because that allows us to restrict the range of possible utility functions. If an individual has a sufficiently rich set of preferences, it becomes possible to define a utility function for the individual such that the numerical values have meaning beyond their ordinal properties.

> The key requirement is that the subject must have preferences over all possible pairs of lotteries defined over the basic goods. What does it mean to require that our subject be able to specify preferences over all possible pairs of lotteries? Consider our subject with his preferences over the goods g_1, g_2, and g_3, and consider a lottery awarding g_1 with probability p and g_3 with probability $1 - p$. Now suppose that our subject can choose between determinately receiving g_2 or participating in the lottery. If p is very large and our subject knows this, he should prefer receiving g_2 with certainty to participating in the lottery, since he has a very slim chance of being awarded g_3. On the other hand, if p is very small (but not 0), most people would choose the slight uncertainty of the lottery over receiving g_2 with certainty because the lottery, though the outcome is not determinate, still favors their attaining their most desired good. This suggests that, at some intermediate value of p, our subject should be indifferent between the choice of receiving g_2 with certainty and participating in a lottery between the goods g_1 and g_3.
>
> For sake of completeness, I will run through a formalization of the standard theory of expected utility to highlight its underlying assumptions. (The axioms cited are taken from Luce and Raiffa's classic 1957 text, *Games and Decisions*.) The point

I wish to call attention to is that, although many of the axioms have considerable intuitive appeal, they commit one to a conception of individuals as highly rational beings. Thus the standard theory of expected utility stands in stark contrast with the view of people as, at best, only boundedly rational.

To begin, assume that a rational agent has preferences defined for every possible pairwise combination of basic goods. This means that, whenever an agent faces a choice between two goods, she can either identify which of the two goods she prefers, or will admit to being indifferent between the two. In addition, assume that a rational agent's preferences are transitive, so that if she prefers A to B, and prefers B to C, then she prefers A to C. If we denote the preference or indifference relation by $\precsim$, then the first axiom can be stated.

Axiom 1 (Ordering of alternatives). For any g_i and g_j, either $g_i \precsim g_j$ or $g_j \precsim g_i$; and if $g_i \precsim g_j$ and $g_j \precsim g_k$, then $g_i \precsim g_k$.

Since all of the basic goods are comparable and the preference relation is transitive, it is possible to reindex the set of basic goods $\{g_1, \ldots, g_n\}$ as $\{g_{i_1}, \ldots, g_{i_n}\}$ so that $g_{i_1} \precsim g_{i_2} \precsim \cdots \precsim g_{i_n}$. Since the particular index assigned to a good does not matter, we can assume without loss of generality that $g_1 \precsim g_2 \precsim \cdots \precsim g_n$.

A *compound lottery* is a lottery over a set of lotteries. Imagine, as an example, a coin toss for which one receives a certain lottery ticket if the coin lands heads, and a different lottery ticket if the coin lands tails. The thought is that the "rewards" of a compound lottery are not basic goods, but rather are themselves lotteries.

Now, given knowledge of the probability calculus, one might think that it should be possible to eliminate compound lotteries by replacing each compound lottery with an equivalent ordinary lottery, namely one having the appropriate probabilities. For example, consider the following compound lottery (call it C): a coin is flipped and, if it lands heads, you have a 10% chance of getting X and a 90% of getting Y; if it lands tails, you have a 33% chance of getting X and a 67% chance of getting Y. How should you, as a rational agent, feel about the choice between C and the ordinary lottery which gives you a 21.5% chance of getting X and a 78.5% chance of getting Y? There is a strong intuition that you should be *indifferent* between C and the ordinary lottery because, regardless of which you choose, you have the same chance of receiving X or Y. The following axiom formalizes this intuition.

Axiom 2 (Reduction of compound lotteries). Any compound lottery is indifferent to a simple lottery with $g_1, g_2, \ldots, g_n$ as goods, their probabilities being computed according to the ordinary probability calculus. In particular, if

$$L^{(i)} = (p_1^{(i)} g_1, p_2^{(i)} g_2, \ldots, p_n^{(i)} g_n), \quad \text{for } i = 1, 2, \ldots, s$$

then

$$\left(q_1 L^{(1)}, q_2 L^{(2)}, \ldots, q_s L^{(s)}\right) \approx (p_1 g_1, p_2 g_2, \ldots, p_n g_n)$$

where

$$p_i = q_1 p_i^{(1)} + q_2 p_i^{(2)} + \cdots + q_s p_i^{(s)}.$$

Consider the following scenario: suppose that we have a set of basic goods that contains one hundred items, where g_1 is a bowl of mud and g_{100} is a brand-new Ferrari. (I assume, for the sake of argument, that we strictly prefer the brand-new Ferrari to the bowl of mud.) Let us also assume that g_{17} is a brand-new laptop computer.

Let $L = ((1 - p)g_1, pg_{100})$ denote the lottery which awards the bowl of mud with probability $1 - p$ and the Ferrari with probability p. The following choice behavior seems highly plausible: when $p = 0$, so that L awards the bowl of mud with certainty, if we are given the choice between L and the laptop, we will always choose the laptop. However, when $p = 1$, so that L awards the Ferrari with certainty, we will always choose the lottery L over the laptop. For values of p between 0 and 1, it also seems clear that the same choice behavior will hold for values very close to 0 and values very close to 1. For intermediate values of p, though, it's less clear what will happen. It seems plausible that, for *some* value of p, given a choice between L and the laptop, we will be perfectly *indifferent* between the two. The following axiom formalizes this intuition.

Axiom 3 (Continuity). Each good g_i is indifferent to some lottery involving just g_1 and g_n. That is to say, there exists a number u_i such that g_i is indifferent to $(1 - u_i)g_1, 0g_2, \ldots, 0g_{n-1}, u_i g_n)$. For convenience, we write $g_i \approx ((1 - u_i)g_1, u_i g_n) = \widetilde{g_i}$.

It seems that part of what it means to say that one is *indifferent* between two things is that the things can be interchanged in certain contexts without affecting a person's behavior. Given this, it seems plausible that, if we are truly indifferent between $\widetilde{g_i}$ and g_i, then we should be able to interchange the lottery for the basic good in certain contexts. The following axiom states one particular context in which such interchanges are allowed.

Axiom 4 (Substitutability). In any lottery L, $\widetilde{g_i}$ is substitutable for g_i, that is,

$$(p_1 g_1, \ldots, p_i g_i, \ldots, p_n g_n) \approx (p_1 g_1, \ldots, p_i \widetilde{g_i}, \ldots, p_n g_n).$$

The next axiom says that the preference relation over lotteries behaves much like the preference relation over basic goods.

Axiom 5 (Transitivity). Preference and indifference among lotteries are transitive relations.

Recall that, under our indexing scheme, g_1 is either the least-preferred good or one of the least-preferred goods. Likewise, g_n is either the most-preferred good or one of the most-preferred goods. When should we prefer the lottery $((1 - p)g_1, pg_n)$ to the lottery $((1 - p')g_1, p' g_n)$? Simply when our chance of receiving g_n in the first lottery is greater than the chance of receiving g_n in the second lottery. This is the intuition behind the following axiom.

Axiom 6 (Monotonicity). A lottery $((1 - p)g_1, pg_n)$ is preferred or regarded indifferently to $((1 - p')g_1, p' g_n)$ if and only if $p \geq p'$.

Given a subject whose preferences satisfy the above six axioms, the existence of a utility function defined over all possible lotteries over the set of basic goods can be proved. To see this, notice that axioms 1 through 5 provide a way of reducing two lotteries L and L' (complex or not) to the canonical form mentioned in axiom 3. Call the reduced forms of these lotteries $\hat{L}$ and $\hat{L}'$, respectively. Axiom 6 provides a method of comparing the reduced lotteries $\hat{L}$ and $\hat{L}'$, and axiom 4 allows us to transfer the resulting comparison back to the original lotteries L and L'. One can then prove the following theorem (see Luce and Raiffa, 1957, p. 29).

Theorem 1. If the preference or indifference relation $\precsim$ satisfies axioms 1 through 6, there are numbers u_i associated with the basic goods g_i such that for two lotteries L and L' the magnitudes of the expected values

$$p_1 u_1 + p_2 u_2 + \cdots + p_n u_n \qquad \text{and} \qquad p'_1 u_1 + p'_2 u_2 + \cdots + p'_n u_n$$

reflect the preference between the lotteries.

Some variant of the above theory of expected utility underwrites all contemporary work in traditional game theory and formal decision theory. Such schemes assume the following.

1. Any two goods are comparable (this is explicitly assumed in axiom 1).
2. Only the basic goods matter (this is implicitly assumed in axiom 2).

   Compound lotteries can be reducible to ordinary lotteries only if people do not feel "differently" about receiving a lottery as a prize rather than receiving an ordinary good as a prize.
3. People have an uncountably infinite set of preferences (this is implicitly assumed in axiom 2).

   If there are at least two basic goods, there is an uncountably infinite number of compound lotteries[9] and each compound lottery must be equivalent to some lottery defined over basic goods. Each person's preference set must be such that this equivalence of lotteries is recognized by the indifference relation, which implies that each person must have an uncountably infinite set of (coherent) preferences.
4. People's preferences are transitive (this is explicitly assumed in axioms 1 and 5).

The crucial question is that of how likely it is that real people have preferences that are "sufficiently rich" in the way needed for one to be able to define a utility function. Consider the fact that the standard theory of expected utility requires that any two goods need to be comparable. *Are* any two goods always comparable? It would seem not. Do you prefer the life of your mother over the life of your father? The lives of five randomly chosen children over the life of your mother? The lives of five randomly chosen mothers over the life of your child? Ten billion dollars over the life of 10 000 children?[10] These are not intended to be read as merely rhetorical questions, for it is quite possible that a person may be able to answer them. If one can, it is worth reflecting on whether these express actual *preferences* or the conclusion of an *argument* that

---

[9] For any two basic goods g_1 and g_2, there is a lottery $L_p = (pg_1, (1-p)g_2)$ for each p in [0, 1]. Given p, q, r in [0, 1], the lottery $\mathfrak{L}(p, q, r) = (pL_q, (1-p)L_r)$ is a compound lottery. There is an uncountably infinite number of such lotteries.

[10] Think of how much good one could do with ten billion dollars. One could easily save the lives of one million children from less-developed countries – and this includes giving each and every one of them a college education.

one has constructed for rationalizing the choice, in the event that one should encounter such a choice situation.[11] If the latter, it seems that the standard theory of expected utility assumes too much, for you did not *actually* have a *preference* for one of the pair of goods prior to engaging in some serious (and perhaps troubling) reflection. The conclusion to draw is twofold. First, while many goods *are* comparable, many goods are not. Second, even among those goods which are comparable, we might not have well-defined preferences until we are actually presented with a choice situation in which we have to choose among them, in which case we come to realize what our preference is, or come to form that preference in the first place.

The assumption that, for any choice problem, only the basic goods matter, is a point which Allais's Paradox calls into question. If only the basic goods matter, then the Sure Thing principle seems eminently plausible. The fact that people choose the way they do in Allais's Paradox-type situations suggests that the way in which the choice is presented has an important effect on the resultant choice.[12] If so, then more is factored into people's preferences than just the basic goods.

However, the most important assumptions to focus on concern the possession of an uncountably infinite set of preferences and the transitivity of the preference relation. It is unlikely that cognitively limited individuals would have an uncountably infinite set of preferences, much less a *coherent* uncountably infinite set of preferences. Given this, there is a fundamental conflict between the conception of individuals as boundedly rational and the standard theory of expected utility assumed by traditional game theory.

This poses a problem. If interdependent decision problems are an inescapable feature of individual choice in social situations, we need to be able to analyze them. Yet, if the proper analysis of interdependent decision problems requires that they be viewed as problems of strategic choice, and the traditional theory of games is incompatible with a conception of people as boundedly rational, how is one to analyze them?

1.3 Evolutionary game theory

One important characteristic, perhaps *the* most important characteristic, about decision problems occurring in social contexts is that they recur. Social agents

---

[11] Also, realize that, if it is the latter, there is now a nontrivial question as to whether your preference set is consistent. Many of the choices involve moral questions. Is the moral theory on which you based your argument consistent?

[12] A point reflected both in prospect theory and in regret theory (see Bell, 1982; Loomes and Sugden, 1982).

play the same game over and over again, often against the same individuals. The one-shot games played between anonymous individuals that have been so heavily studied provide a poor account of the decision problems faced by real social agents. A better approach would study repeated games. An ideal approach would combine a study of repeated games with a model of man as boundedly rational. Such is the approach of evolutionary game theory.

Evolutionary game theory originated in the work of R. A. Fisher[13] in his attempt to explain the approximate equality of the sex ratio in mammals. The puzzle Fisher faced was this: why is it that the sex ratio is approximately equal in many species in which the majority of males never mate? In these species, the non-mating males would seem to be excess baggage carried by the rest of the population, having no real use. Fisher realized that, if we measure individual fitness in terms of the expected number of grandchildren, then individual fitness depends on the distribution of males and females in the population. When there is a greater number of females in the population, males have a higher individual fitness; when there are more males in the population, females have a higher individual fitness. Fisher pointed out that, in such a situation, the evolutionary dynamics lead to the sex ratio becoming fixed at equal numbers of males and females.[14] The fact that individual fitness depends upon the relative frequency of males and females in the population introduces a strategic element into evolution. Equality of the sex ratio is a Nash equilibrium in this game of fitness: provided that everyone else does not change their behavior, you do not increase your expected fitness by changing yours.

The concept of a Nash equilibrium is the central solution concept used in traditional game theory. However, in the case of the equality of the sex ratio among mammals, the Nash equilibrium emerges not by being selected by perfectly rational agents, through a process of rational deliberation, but rather as a consequence of the invisible hand of natural selection. The agents participating in this evolutionary process are very far removed from being perfectly rational agents. Nonetheless, the outcome is precisely that which one would expect to occur if this "game" of the sex ratio were played by perfectly rational agents, interested in maximizing their expected fitness, and capable of freely choosing what strategies they will play.

In the social world, we do not typically make choices with the explicit intent of maximizing Darwinian expected fitness. Although there is some correlation between the strategies people employ in choice problems in social settings and those adopted by their offspring, this is not the primary mechanism determining

---

[13] See *The Genetic Theory of Natural Selection* (1930).
[14] Modulo several important assumptions that I shall not discuss here.

how people respond to choice problems in society. Nonetheless, as we will see in greater detail in chapter 2, certain processes of imitative learning allow us to formulate models of individual choice in repeated decision problems that are worthy of the name "evolutionary" in every respect. The "evolution" in this new setting is *cultural* rather than biological evolution.

Ever since Dawkins first introduced the idea of a "meme," the unit of cultural inheritance, in *The Selfish Gene* (1976), some have been reluctant to talk of cultural evolution. Whereas we typically think that we have a good idea of what we mean by a gene,[15] the concept of a meme lacks a similar degree of clarity. What are memes made of? How are memes transmitted from one person to another? Talk of memes, and with it talk of cultural evolution, seems mysterious.

Yet cultural evolution is not mysterious. It is not magical. One does not need to invoke "memes" in order to speak of cultural evolution. Cultural evolution, as I understand the term, means nothing more than change in belief over time. The change in belief may occur as a result of a combination of factors: experimentation with new behaviors or strategies (the cultural analogue of mutation), conscious imitation of another person's behavior or strategy (the cultural analogue of reproduction), deliberate instruction of one's children (another cultural analogue of reproduction), the random fluctuation of beliefs that do not have significant impact on people's well-being (the cultural analogue of genetic drift), and the introduction or elimination of beliefs from a population through immigration or emigration of the holders of those beliefs. None of these factors requires strong rationality assumptions, and all of them are present in real populations.

1.4 The evolution of morality

Darwin's approach to his decision problem nicely illustrates one of the many possible procedures that a boundedly rational creature may use when confronted with a difficult decision. Taking the boundedly rational nature of man as given, we then saw that evolutionary game theory provides a better way of analyzing the interdependent decision problems that occur in human society than traditional game theory. Darwin, evolution, game theory – what, if anything, does all this have to do with the origins of morality?

---

[15] Yet even this concept proves particularly difficult to make sense of. See Sarkar (1998), Falk (2000), and Moss (2003) for a discussion of some of the difficulties encountered in reconciling the concept of a gene with our contemporary understanding of molecular biology.

Darwin's thoughts on the connection between man's social nature and the origin of the moral sense are recorded in *The Descent of Man* (2004). It is worth quoting at length.

> The following proposition seems to me in a high degree probable – namely, that any animal whatever, endowed with well-marked social instincts, the parental and filial affections being here included, would inevitably acquire a moral sense or conscience, as soon as its intellectual powers had become as well, or nearly as well developed, as in man. For, *firstly*, the social instincts lead an animal to take pleasure in the society of its fellows, to feel a certain amount of sympathy with them, and to perform various services for them. The services may be of a definite and evidently instinctive nature; or there may be only a wish and readiness, as with most of the higher social animals, to aid their fellows in certain general ways. But these feelings and services are by no means extended to all the individuals of the same species, only to those of the same association. *Secondly*, as soon as the mental faculties had become highly developed, images of all past actions and motives would be incessantly passing through the brain of each individual; and that feeling of dissatisfaction, or even misery, which invariably results, as we shall hereafter see, from any unsatisfied instinct, would arise, as often as it was perceived that the enduring and always present social instinct had yielded to some other instinct, at the time stronger, but neither enduring in its nature, nor leaving behind it a very vivid impression. It is clear that many instinctive desires, such as that of hunger, are in their nature of short duration; and after being satisfied, are not readily or vividly recalled. *Thirdly*, after the power of language had been acquired, and the wishes of the community could be expressed, the common opinion how each member ought to act for the public good, would naturally become in a paramount degree the guide to action. But it should be borne in mind that however great weight we may attribute to public opinion, our regard for the approbation and disapprobation of our fellows depends on sympathy, which, as we shall see, forms an essential part of the social instinct, and is indeed its foundation-stone. *Lastly*, habit in the individual would ultimately play a very important part in guiding the conduct of each member; for the social instinct, together with sympathy, is, like any other instinct, greatly strengthened by habit, and so consequently would be obedience to the wishes and judgment of the community.

Darwin's argument for the inevitable appearance of the moral sense is grounded on the feeling of sympathy. Sympathy inclines one individual to perform "various services" for another. If one does not follow the inclinations of sympathy, these feelings of sympathy will reappear to haunt one later, as some apparent precursor to the conscience. Yet sympathy is not the only cornerstone on which the structure of morality is built. Culture, in the form of common opinion, plays an important role. Here we see the first appearance of the importance of strategic thinking. If I seek approbation and wish to avoid disapprobation, when choosing to act I need to reflect upon what reaction you will have to what I do. The first link of the "I think that you think that I think . . . " chain has thus been forged.

From these humble beginnings, the moral sense eventually produces morality. However, one should not confuse Darwin's intuition that all sufficiently intelligent social animals will inevitably acquire *a* moral sense with the Kantian conclusion that all sufficiently intelligent social animals will inevitably acquire the *same* moral sense. Darwin explicitly disavows the latter claim:

> It may be well first to premise that I do not wish to maintain that any strictly social animal, if its intellectual faculties were to become as active and as highly developed as in man, would acquire exactly the same moral sense as ours. In the same manner as various animals have some sense of beauty, though they admire widely different objects, so they might have a sense of right and wrong, though led by it to follow widely different lines of conduct. If, for instance, to take an extreme case, men were reared under precisely the same condition as hive-bees, there can hardly be a doubt that our unmarried females would, like the worker-bees, think it a sacred duty to kill their brothers, and mothers would strive to kill their fertile daughters; and no one would think of interfering. Nevertheless, the bee, or any other social animal, would gain in our supposed case, as it appears to me, some feeling of right or wrong, or a conscience.

How does this feeling of right or wrong affect the actions of the social animal?

> [A]n inward monitor would tell the animal that it would have been better to have followed the one impulse rather than the other. The one course ought to have been followed, and the other ought not; the one would have been right and the other wrong . . .

Darwin's account of the origin of the moral sense is a fascinating, speculative Just So Story[16] wrapped in enough naturalistic clothing to be plausible – but only barely. From a contemporary point of view, it would be imprudent to attribute too much of a theory of moral sentiments to sympathy, especially since it remains an open question just how much sympathy – in a robust, biological sense – really does influence our choices and actions. However, Darwin's identification of the importance of culture and habit (although perhaps not the *reasons* why culture and habit are important) seems spot on, and this allows us to thread together all of the notions discussed thus far.

Look again at Darwin's explanation for how the "inward monitor" is supposed to work. It tells the animal that it would have been "better" to do *X*

---

[16] The name "just so story" is taken from the title of Rudyard Kipling's 1902 book, *Just So Stories*. Because that book provides fantastic "causal" explanations of how various phenomena originated (like how the camel got its hump), the term now refers to any evolutionary explanation that lacks any empirical evidence.

rather than Y. But *better* in what sense? There are two ways of reading this. One way is that it would be "better" in that the moral sense would have made the animal *feel better* about doing X rather than Y. Another way is that it would have been "better" for the animal to do X rather than Y because doing X serves to maximize the individual's expected fitness. The animal need not – and presumably doesn't – know this, but that doesn't change the fact that it *would have been better*, in a very real, objective sense, for the animal to have done X rather than Y.

I would like to suggest the following connection between the inward monitor and heuristics. Ordinary people and ballplayers alike catch fly balls in more or less the same way: they run to the ball, keeping the angle constant. Few people are aware that their success in catching fly balls depends upon such a heuristic; fewer could explain why such a heuristic works. Perhaps the inward monitor, our conscience, morality, and social norms in general, function similarly. When each individual in society follows their inward monitor and behaves morally, each person *does better* from the point of view of maximizing satisfaction of his or her personal preferences over the long run of their life.

Notice that I have explicitly shifted the focus from maximization of Darwinian expected fitness or maximization of expected utility to maximizing satisfaction of our personal preferences. This was deliberate. I don't wish to make any specific claims about how following moral principles serves to maximize our fitness. I wish to avoid this because I suspect that relatively little of our current behavior is explicitly done *because* it maximizes our expected fitness. If the evolutionary psychologists are correct, some of our behavior was selected for because it served to maximize our expected fitness *at one time*; however, such behaviors needn't maximize our expected fitness in any meaningful sense now. I also wish to avoid talk of maximization of expected utility because, keeping with the general view that humans are boundedly rational, we fail to satisfy the conditions required for ascribing utility functions to individuals. (If it *is* possible to define utility functions for individuals, I view this as a happy accident; there's nothing that precludes a boundedly rational individual from forming preferences in such a way that permits defining a utility function – just imagine a boundedly rational individual who is indifferent among every possible outcome – but it is too much to assume that *every* bounded rational individual has a set of preferences that permit the definition of a personal utility function.) Speaking of maximizing the satisfaction of our personal preferences avoids both sets of problems. However, because old habits die hard, I will on occasion speak of maximizing expected utility in the remainder of the book. This talk should always be understood as *really* referring to maximizing the satisfaction of one's personal preferences.

The core idea which I will explore in this book is the following: morality comprises a set of heuristics that govern behavior in interdependent decision contexts that work to the benefit of each person in society when followed. That is, acting in accordance with those heuristics serves to maximize satisfaction of each person's preferences, as much as is possible, given the constraints placed upon satisfaction of our preferences by the fact that many people's preferences are in conflict. The reason why such heuristics (moral norms) work in this way derives from the social structure of the interdependent decision problems whose choices they regulate. The fact that most people (perhaps all people) do *not* know why or how the heuristics work is of no real consequence: most people cannot explain, or justify, the functioning of the heuristic they use to catch fly balls.

The remainder of this book offers a preliminary argument for the claim that many of the norms governing behavior, in particular, certain primitive moral principles, can be understood as general heuristics whose adoption insures that an individual will generally *do better* if they are followed than if they are not followed. These social norms exist as a culturally evolved response to repeated interdependent decision problems that occur in a socially structured environment. The exact meaning of *doing better* referred to above depends upon the particular interdependent decision problem, and hence is context-sensitive.

The claim that people will generally do better following moral norms than not should not be confused with the similar-sounding claim that people have deliberately *chosen* to adopt those norms *on the grounds that* acting in accordance with them serves to maximize their individual expected "utility."[17] However, it would be accurate to say that *whenever* individuals choose to act in ways that accord with the various social norms examined here, acting in that way serves to maximize their individual expected "utility" over the long run.

Another misinterpretation should be cautioned against. Often in speaking of a social norm one means that violators of the norm suffer sanctions imposed by the rest of society. In this environment, one could argue that complying with the norm serves to maximize an individual's expected "utility" because failure to comply results in the imposition of sanctions. This is not the sense in which I mean to say that individual expected "utility" is maximized. Individual expected "utility" is maximized in the sense that the environment in which the norm is generally followed tends to maximize an individual's expected "utility" given the set of possible payoffs for the interdependent decision problem at hand.

---

[17] I use scare quotes here to indicate that such talk of "utility" needs to be understood very loosely, since the boundedly rational nature of individuals does not guarantee that we can define a utility function for them.

The argument I offer is a preliminary one simply because it would be impossible to demonstrate, for each social norm, that the appropriate relation between acting in accordance with that norm and long-term maximization of expected "utility" holds. I merely wish to demonstrate that this relationship holds for a small but important subset of our moral norms: whether one ought to cooperate in certain strategic situations, whether one ought to trust other players in other situations, how one ought to distribute resources in still other strategic situations, and, lastly, whether one ought to retaliate, or take punitive action, in yet other strategic situations. While these four problems are obviously important, they do not by any means exhaust the space of strategic situations that are socially and morally revelant. However, they are problems of sufficient importance and generality that, if we can establish my primary claim in these cases, we have reason to hope that a similar kind of explanation can be advanced in other cases. Much more work remains to be done at the end of the day, regardless. In addition, it will almost always be assumed[18] that none of these strategic situations overlap: individuals who face problems of cooperation are not simultaneously facing resource-allocation problems. This assumption is not just implausible, it is false. But it serves to keep the scope of the discussion manageable. If one cannot tell a plausible story of the kind I wish to tell in such simple, artificial contexts, what hope is there for telling a plausible story in more complicated contexts? But, if we can tell a plausible story in such simple, artificial contexts, we have reason to broaden our search, and push onwards to more complicated contexts.

---

[18] The one exception will be cases involving norms of retaliation, retribution, and punishment. Although it is possible to study the emergence of a norm of cooperation by considering individual behavior in certain isolated interdependent decision problems (such as the prisoner's dilemma), this cannot be done for norms of retaliation, retribution, and punishment. Such norms exist for the sole purpose of influencing individual behavior in *some other* context, and hence the strategic problem framing punitive behavior has to be imposed on top of something else.

2

Types of evolutionary models

All evolutionary models contain at least two things: a representation of the state of the population and a specification of the dynamical laws that tell how the state of the population changes over time. Since one cannot specify the dynamical laws without referring to some representation of the population, the choice of representation constrains the set of possible dynamical laws. Even so, given a particular representation, it is usually the case that many different sets of dynamical laws are compatible with that representation.

The main choice that exists regarding the representation of the population is whether to model it using continuous or discrete methods. Continuous, or aggregative, models represent the population using global statistics concerning the distribution of genotypes or phenotypes in the population. The most commonly studied aggregative model is the replicator dynamics, which represents the state of the population by the frequency with which certain genotypes or phenotypes occur. Notice that aggregative models necessarily assume that questions such as *which* individual in the population has a particular phenotype or genotype are unimportant, since all differences between individuals are lost when one uses frequency data to represent the population state. In contrast, the discrete method known as agent-based modeling keeps track of the identities of individuals of the population, where the identity of an individual includes information such as its genotype/phenotype, together with additional properties, such as its spatial position, location in a social network, and so on.

The primary trade-off between the two approaches exchanges mathematical tractability for computational complexity. The replicator dynamics (see section 2.1) expresses the evolutionary dynamics as a set of differential, or difference, equations.[1] One virtue of using the replicator dynamics, as in Skyrms (1996), is that the art of solving and analyzing systems of differential and difference equations has been pursued for years and, for many systems of interest, exact solutions can be found and expressed in terms of familiar mathematical functions. When no such solutions exist, there are well-known methods for generating numerical solutions to arbitrary precision. On the other hand, no analytical techniques of comparable sophistication and generality exist for agent-based models. Although some results can be established analytically, one usually relies on computer simulation and Monte Carlo methods to demonstrate the existence of tendency laws and long-term convergence behavior.

However, another more important trade-off exists. Aggregative models, by their very nature, cannot represent the *structure* of society and social interactions. Representing social structure requires one to specify the relations that individuals stand in and, because aggregative models collapse differences between individuals through the use of statistics to represent the population state, one cannot differentiate between two individuals who are identical with respect to their genotype or phenotype. This can have important consequences, for it has been known for a long time that structured interactions between individuals can give rise to outcomes very different from those of unstructured interactions (see Nowak and May, 1992).

These different outcomes come about, in part, because the replicator dynamics assumes that individuals engage in random interactions. That is, when individuals meet to play a two-player game, the probability of any two individuals in the population meeting is equally likely. While this assumption is plausible for certain biological systems – such as large populations of bacteria in continuously mixed environments – it is generally false for human interactions. In human society, our interactions are constrained according to some preexisting network of social relations, or the kinds of tasks we undertake during the course of a given day. One tends to interact with one's friends more often than with total strangers and, more importantly, the *significance* accorded to interactions with one's friends and acquaintances is generally greater than that accorded to interactions with total strangers. Interactions with friends typically influence future behavior more readily than interactions with strangers.

Of course, merely identifying an assumption as false does not mean that the model derived from that assumption is inaccurate or useless. There is a long

---

[1] The difference between the two depends on whether one assumes that the state of the population changes continuously from one time to another, or in discrete "jumps." The two formulations can disagree in their predictions regarding long-term convergence. See Weibull (1995) for a detailed discussion of when the two approaches agree and disagree.

tradition of instrumentalism in the social sciences, whose definitive statement can be found in Friedman (1953), wherein the value of an assumption, or theory, is to be measured solely in terms of its predictive power.[2] Oversimplified models derived from false assumptions often have great instrumental value, and the replicator dynamics is no different. The relevant question, from our point of view, is whether the absence of structure in aggregative models makes a real difference in the predictions and analyses those models provide, and whether including structure leads to the generation of models whose predictions and analyses more closely agree with the observed behavior of individuals.

Including structure in evolutionary game-theoretic models makes a real difference in the long-term behavior of the model (see Durrett and Levin, 1994; Alexander and Skyrms, 1999; Skyrms, 2003). Population states that are unstable in the replicator dynamics can be stable in structured agent-based models. Moreover, as we will see in later chapters, incorporating structure into agent-based models enables us to model situations whose long-term convergence behavior more closely approximates the behavior found in real human populations. For example, evolutionary game-theoretic models incorporating structure allow cooperation to persist in the prisoner's dilemma, selection for universal stag hunting in the Stag Hunt, fair division in the Nash bargaining game, and – under certain circumstances – retribution in the ultimatum game. The fact that a single family of evolutionary models accounts for such a wide variety of human behavior, much of it in violation of the "predictions" of standard game theory, is telling, especially considering that incorporating structure seems to be a necessary requirement for this outcome, since many of these results are not obtainable under the replicator dynamics. The structure of evolution plays an important part in the evolution of social norms.

In what follows, I discuss several different classes of evolutionary game-theoretic models that will be considered at length in subsequent chapters. Beginning with the simplest aggregative model of interest, the replicator dynamics, I then turn to agent-based models possessing an elementary social structure defined by a social network. (Such models are also known as local-interaction models in the evolutionary game-theoretic literature.) Since real social networks feature a variety of topologies, we need to be sensitive to such concerns. Much

---

[2] In Popperian spirit, Friedman claims that, "Viewed as a body of substantive hypotheses, theory is to be judged by its predictive power for the class of phenomena which it is intended to 'explain.' Only factual evidence can show whether it is 'right' or 'wrong' or, better, tentatively 'accepted' as valid or 'rejected.'... [T]he only relevant test of the validity of a hypothesis is comparison of its predictions with experience. The hypothesis is rejected if its predictions are contradicted ('frequently' or more often than predictions from an alternative hypothesis); it is accepted if its predictions are not contradicted; great confidence is attached to it if it has survived many opportunities for contradiction."

of the literature on local-interaction models – and, for that matter, many of the agent-based models considered in the Artificial Life literature – suffer from the shortcoming of assuming that the only relevant topology is that of a ring or a two-dimensional lattice. These structures are important, especially for certain applications of evolutionary game theory to biology, such as the competition between types of bacteria on plates of agar, but their importance should not be overstated. One also needs to consider other categories of social networks: such as "small-world" networks,[3] social networks in which the number of relations each person has falls between a lower and upper bound, random hierarchical structures, and, in general, random social structures. Lastly, another family of evolutionary models employs a generalized social network in which the edges represent the probability of two individuals interacting (see Skyrms and Pemantle, 2000). This family of models neatly bridges random-mixing models, like the replicator dynamics, and agent-based models defined on social networks, showing how an initially unstructured population may develop structure over time.

2.1 The replicator dynamics

Although the replicator dynamics cannot model social structure,[4] it does have the virtue of being completely neutral as to whether it models biological or cultural evolution. The replicator dynamics was first introduced as a model of biological evolution (Taylor and Jonker, 1978) and was later realized to admit a cultural-evolutionary interpretation as well.

The simplest form of the replicator dynamics states that the frequency of a strategy in a population increases or decreases according to how the expected fitness of a person who uses that strategy compares with the average fitness of the population. It is easier to express this idea mathematically, and we just need a little notation to do so. Let s_i denote the frequency of strategy i in the population, and denote the expected fitness of i in the population by $F(i|\vec{s})$. (The "$\vec{s}$" symbol stands for the vector of strategy frequencies in the population.) Then the replicator dynamics says that the instantaneous rate of change for s_i is

$$s_i\big(F(i|\vec{s}) - F(\vec{s}|\vec{s})\big), \tag{2.1}$$

where $F(\vec{s}|\vec{s})$ denotes the average fitness of the population.

---

[3] Networks in which the mean distance between any two nodes is surprisingly low, given how few edges exist.

[4] More precisely, the replicator dynamics cannot model social structure beyond the relatively crude form of interactions between groups. Multipopulation, or multigroup, forms of the replicator dynamics do exist and can capture social structure at one level.

When the expected fitness of strategy i equals the average fitness of the population, there will be no change in how many people use i. (The rate of change of s_i equals zero, in this case.) However, when the expected fitness of i is greater than the average fitness, more people will employ strategy i in the future than are doing so now. (The rate of change of s_i is greater than zero, in this case, which means that s_i is *increasing*, i.e., more people will use i in the future than are doing so now.)

Let's consider the biological derivation of the replicator dynamics. Suppose that we have a large population of agents. Each agent has a certain phenotype, which we denote by σ. For simplicity, assume that there are only finitely many phenotypes, say $\sigma_1, \ldots, \sigma_m$. Without loss of generality, we can simply use the integer i to refer to the phenotype σ_i.

Let n_i denote the total number of agents in the population with the phenotype i, with the total size of the population given by $N = \sum_{i=1}^{m} n_i$. If the only thing that matters about each agent is their phenotype, all of the relevant information about the population is contained in the state vector $\vec{s} = (s_1, \ldots, s_n)$, where $s_i = n_i/N$ for all i. Each s_i denotes the proportion of the population with phenotype i.

As time passes, the proportion of agents having certain phenotypes will change. Let the growth rate of the ith phenotype be r_i and assume that the rate of change in the number of agents with phenotype i is proportional to the number of individuals with phenotype i in the population, i.e.,

$$\frac{dn_i}{dt} = r_i n_i. \tag{2.2}$$

Given this expression for the rate of change of phenotype i, we calculate the rate of change for the total population as follows:

$$\frac{dN}{dt} = \frac{d}{dt}\left(\sum n_i\right) = \sum \frac{dn_i}{dt} = \sum r_i n_i = \sum r_i s_i N = \bar{r} N, \tag{2.3}$$

where the constant $\bar{r}$ is defined to be $\sum r_i s_i$.

Equation (2.3) provides an expression for the total change in the population over time, but what we are really interested in is how the relative frequencies of each phenotype change over time. Determining this means that we need to calculate the rate of change of s_i:

$$\frac{ds_i}{dt} = \frac{d}{dt}\left(\frac{n_i}{N}\right) = \frac{N\frac{dn_i}{dt} - n_i\frac{dN}{dt}}{N^2} = \frac{r_i(s_i N)N - \bar{r}(s_i N)N}{N^2} \tag{2.4}$$
$$= s_i(r_i - \bar{r}).$$

Assuming that the current growth rate of n_i is approximately equal to the expected fitness of phenotype i, equation (2.4) may be rewritten as

$$\frac{ds_i}{dt} = s_i(F(i|\vec{s}) - F(\vec{s}|\vec{s})), \tag{2.5}$$

where $F(\vec{s}|\vec{s})$ denotes the average fitness of the population, i.e., $\sum_{i=1}^{m} s_i F(i|\vec{s})$.

Table 2.1. *The payoff matrix for the*
Hawk–Dove game

	Hawk	Dove
Hawk	$\frac{1}{2}(V - C)$	V
Dove	0	$V/2$

Equation (2.1) describes the continuous replicator dynamics, which assumes that the increase or decrease of the phenotype frequencies occurs without well-defined generational breaks; that is, it assumes that there is not a well-defined notion of "the next generation" applying to the population. If the measure of fitness is that of the expected number of offspring, we obtain the biological interpretation of the replicator dynamics using Darwinian fitness.

How does one calculate the expected fitness for a given phenotype in a population? One way conceives of the number of offspring as payoffs in a game that each individual plays with the rest of the population (Maynard Smith, 1982). Each phenotype corresponds to a strategy in the game. The expected fitness of an individual in a population, then, is simply the expected payoff of that individual's strategy in the corresponding game.

The classic example (see Maynard Smith and Price, 1973) is the Hawk–Dove game.[5] Two animals compete for a fixed amount of resources V, and each animal follows one of two strategies: *fight* or *yield*. A "Hawk" always fights and a "Dove" always yields. If a Hawk meets a Dove, the Dove yields and so the Hawk gets to keep all of the resource. If two Doves meet, they share the resource evenly. If two Hawks meet, they fight it out until one becomes injured and retreats. If the cost incurred by an injured Hawk is C, and the probability of each Hawk getting injured when they fight is equally likely, the payoff matrix for the Hawk–Dove game is that listed in Table 2.1. If the number of offspring that an animal has is directly proportional to the amount of the resource it receives, the expected payoffs in the Hawk–Dove game correspond to expected fitness.

> The cultural evolutionary derivation of the replicator dynamics is a bit more complicated. In this section, I discuss the derivation from Weibull (1995) and Björnerstedt and Weibull (1999); there are other derivations of the replicator dynamics for cultural evolutionary contexts as well.

---

[5] Which was initially called the "Hawk–Mouse" game. Price's religious commitments were such that he objected to that symbolic use of the dove.

Suppose that we have a population of boundedly rational agents who repeatedly interact and play the game G, with strategies $1, \ldots, m$. In addition, let us suppose that each agent wants to maximize their payoff from the game G, and so they will change their strategy from time to time if they believe that they are not doing sufficiently well.

More precisely, let's suppose that each agent periodically *reviews* her strategy. At the end of each review process, depending on the outcome, she may adopt a new strategy. Although, in principle, each agent might review her strategy at her own unique rate, let us assume that each agent following strategy i reviews her strategy at the same rate r_i.

When an individual reviews her strategy, what strategy will she adopt? There are many heuristics a boundedly rational individual may use for selecting a new strategy. Without worrying about the specific heuristic, at this time, let us simply denote the probability that an individual following strategy i will switch to strategy j by p_i^j.

Can we say anything more specific about the way in which an individual reviews her strategy? We can, if we make the following assumptions.

1. The number of times an agent reviews her strategy between time t and $t + \Delta t$ does not affect the number of times that she reviews her strategy during another interval, between t' and $t' + \Delta t'$. Let us call this the "no-burnout condition" because it implies that the number of times an agent reviews her strategy in the past has no effect on the number of times she will review her strategy in the future.

2. The average rate at which she reviews her strategy remains constant.

3. Each agent must finish reviewing her strategy before beginning to review it another time.

The "no-burnout" condition is the most suspect of the above assumptions. However, making them allows us to say something useful about the rate at which strategy reviews and strategy switches occur in the population as a whole. These three assumptions imply that the review time of each individual is a Poisson process. Poisson processes have a number of useful properties, including that the aggregate of a number of statistically independent Poisson processes is itself a Poisson process, and the rate of the aggregate process is the sum of the individual rates.

If each individual strategy review and strategy switch is independent of every other strategy review and strategy switch, and if the population is sufficiently large (a euphemism for saying that we are really looking at the infinite limit), we can express in a compact form the proportion of the population that reviews and switches its strategy at any given time. In this limiting case, let us denote the proportion of the population following strategy i that chooses to review it by $s_i r_i$. Similarly, let us denote the proportion of the population following strategy i that switches to another strategy j, after review, by $s_i r_i p_i^j$. Hence the total rate at which people start using strategy i is

$$\sum_{j \neq i} s_j r_j p_j^i$$

and the total rate at which people stop using strategy i is

$$\sum_{j \neq i} s_i r_i p_i^j.$$

The overall rate of change for the frequency of strategy i is just the difference of these two:

$$\frac{ds_i}{dt} = \left(\sum_{j \neq i} s_j r_j p_j^i\right) - \left(\sum_{j \neq i} s_i r_i p_i^j\right).$$

A more useful form can be obtained by rearranging the expressions slightly.

$$\frac{ds_i}{dt} = \left[\left(\sum_j s_j r_j p_j^i\right) - s_i r_i p_i^i\right] - \left[\left(\sum_j s_i r_i p_i^j\right) - s_i r_i p_i^i\right]$$

$$= \left(\sum_j s_j r_j p_j^i\right) - s_i r_i p_i^i - \left(\sum_j s_i r_i p_i^j\right) + s_i r_i p_i^i$$

$$= \left(\sum_j s_j r_j p_j^i\right) - s_i r_i \sum_j p_i^j.$$

Since $\sum_j p_i^j = 1$, the rate of change of strategy i in the population is thus

$$\frac{ds_i}{dt} = \sum_{j=1,\ldots,m} s_j r_j p_j^i - r_i s_i. \tag{2.6}$$

Provided that the review rates r_i and the probabilities p_i^j of individuals switching strategies are Lipschitz continuous (see Weibull, 1995, pp. 153 and 232), equation (2.6) gives a well-defined set of dynamical laws for the cultural evolution of the population. The evolution is "cultural" in the sense that the strategy an individual follows is presumably determined by various beliefs she holds and, as those beliefs change, so does her strategy. Hence change in the frequency of strategies in population corresponds to change in the beliefs held by individuals – not to any substantive biological change.

Equation (2.6) provides a set of dynamical laws, but it doesn't yet have the form of the replicator dynamics. This is because we have yet to specify exactly how people review and switch strategies. This makes sense: obtaining the replicator dynamics as a model of cultural evolution should require one to make certain assumptions about how people review and switch their strategies. A population in which everyone believed that the best way to change their strategy was to roll an m-sided die and adopt whatever strategy corresponded to the outcome of the toss would *not* change their beliefs in a way described by the replicator dynamics. The replicator dynamics state that the future strategy frequencies are a nonrandom function of the present strategy frequencies, and this is patently *not* true for a culture in which everyone changes their beliefs by tossing a die.

One can derive the replicator dynamics from equation (2.6) by assuming that the review rates and the change probabilities have a particular form. It is worth noting that the form required is not at all unnatural: good reasons exist for thinking that people do, at least some of the time, behave in the way required.

Gigerenzer *et al.* (1999) discuss a particular heuristic they call "take the last." According to this heuristic, a boundedly rational individual chooses the last option they've encountered. In our model, this means that an individual will adopt the strategy held by the last person they've encountered from the population. If people mix randomly, the probability that a person following strategy i will adopt strategy j is just the frequency of strategy j in the population, i.e.,

$$p_i^j = s_j. \tag{2.7}$$

This provides a precise value for the probability that an individual will switch from strategy i to strategy j, a quantity left unspecified until now.

Björnerstedt (1993) observed that, if the review rate decreases linearly with the individual's payoff (which means that individuals review their strategy less often as their payoff increases), then equations (2.6) and (2.7) give the replicator dynamics. The particular review rate Björnerstedt suggested had the following form:

$$r_i = a - bG(i|\vec{s}),$$

where $G(i|\vec{s})$ denotes the expected payoff of strategy i in the population $\vec{s}$, $a, b \in \mathbb{R}$ with $b > 0$, and $a/b \geq G(i|\vec{s})$.

From this, it follows that

$$
\begin{aligned}
\frac{\mathrm{d}s_i}{\mathrm{d}t} &= \sum_j s_j r_j p_j^i - r_i s_i \\
&= \sum_j s_j \big[a - bG(j|\vec{s})\big]s_i - \big[a - bG(i|\vec{s})\big]s_i \\
&= \sum_j \big(s_j s_i a - s_j s_i bG(j|\vec{s})\big) - s_i\big[a - bG(i|\vec{s})\big] \\
&= s_i a \sum_j s_j - s_i b \sum_j s_j G(j|\vec{s}) - s_i a + s_i bG(i|\vec{s}) \\
&= s_i a - s_i bG(\vec{s}|\vec{s}) - s_i a + s_i bG(i|\vec{s}) \\
&= bs_i(G(i|\vec{s}) - G(\vec{s}|\vec{s})).
\end{aligned}
$$

That is, a population of boundedly rational individuals who (a) choose to review their strategies with a frequency according to their level of dissatisfaction, and (b) adopt new strategies using the "take the last" heuristic, evolves – in the cultural evolutionary sense – according to a rescaled version of the continuous replicator dynamics. Since the constant b is a free parameter, setting $b = 1$ gives the continuous replicator dynamics exactly.

2.2 Agent-based models on a social network

The replicator dynamics assumes that the population was infinite and that all pairwise interactions were equally likely. The first assumption justified representing the population state by the vector of strategy frequencies $\langle s_1, \ldots, s_m \rangle$ and allowed us to obtain a set of deterministic dynamical laws for the population as a whole from stochastic dynamics at the level of the individual.

The second assumption, that the population mixes at random, allowed us to identify the probability that an individual who follows strategy i will interact with an individual following strategy j to be s_j.[6] Both play crucial roles in the derivation of the replicator dynamics.

Taken together, there is a fundamental tension between these two assumptions, at least from the point of view of modeling human interactions. Real human populations are very far away from being "essentially infinite." More significant, though, is the fact that the random-mixing hypothesis is false, *especially* in the case of large populations. In London, simple geographic and social constraints prevent all pairwise interactions from being equally likely. The probability of East End boys and West End girls getting together is greater in song than in reality.

Agent-based models differ from replicator dynamic models of cultural evolution by dropping the assumption of essentially infinite populations. Agent-based, social-network models further improve upon the replicator dynamics by dropping the assumption of equiprobable pairwise interaction. The net effect increases the level of realism present in the model. Of course, not all increases in a model's level of realism necessarily count as an improvement: replacing the continuous fluid dynamics underlying aerodynamic theory by a discrete-particle model provides one example where an increased level of realism imposes an undue cost. Any possible benefits of using a discrete-particle model for aerodynamics are outweighed by the additional computational cost imposed by the size of the system. Modelers should strive for additional realism if and only if the sum total of accrued benefits outweighs the cost. Consider some of the benefits of using agent-based, social-network models.

Small populations.   The model population of rational actors may range in size from very small to the size of any real, existent social group. Contrast this with aggregate models like the replicator dynamics in which the population must be exactly one size: infinite. It must be admitted that, because agent-based models are typically studied computationally (due to a lack of good general analytical techniques), in principle an upper limit on the size of the model exists. In practice, this limit rarely presents a problem. Moreover, some

---

[6] Note that here, too, is another case in which we need an infinite population. Suppose that agent A follows strategy i. What is the probability that A will interact with another agent following strategy i? Suppose that we have a finite population consisting of N agents in total, n_i of which follow strategy i. If all pairwise interactions are equally likely, the probability that A interacts with another person following strategy i is $(n_i - 1)/N$, since A cannot (presumably) interact with herself. The frequency of strategy i in the population, s_i, is defined to be n_i/N. Although it is true that n_i/N and $(n_i - 1)/N$ will agree in the infinite limit, the difference can be very great for small populations.

agent-based models have properties that are scale-invariant; in these cases one can reliably infer the behavior of large models from smaller models. (See, for example, the lattice models in chapters 3 through 6.)

Constrained interactions. Interactions between rational agents are said to be *constrained* if the probability that any two agents selected at random from the population will interact is not constant across the population. Agent-based, social-network models provide a natural and general framework for handling constrained interactions between rational agents.

Key agents. A *key agent* is one whose adoption of a different strategy sparks a large-scale shift in the strategy frequencies found in the population. A key agent occupies an Archimedean point, enabling her single action to alter radically the future state of society. Such agents are the formal analogue of a Napoleon, Caesar, or Ghandi – a single individual who, through particular circumstantial effects applying uniquely (or almost uniquely) to himself or herself, exerts a significant effect on the final long-term state of the population. Understanding the effects that key agents may have on the long-term dynamics of a social system, and what circumstances are conducive to the creation of key agents, is crucial to our understanding of social systems in general, and social norms in particular. (Consider, for example, how many existent moral norms stem from the work of a single key agent such as Jesus, Mohammed, or Buddha.)

Despite the importance of key agents in social systems, the replicator dynamics cannot model them. Within the formalism of evolutionary models, a key agent results from "mutation," an unpredicted adoption of a particular strategy, perhaps one that is utterly novel, by that agent. In an infinite population, though, a single mutation does not change the strategy frequencies for that population since a single mutation in an infinite population introduces only an infinitesimal change. Since the replicator dynamics operates deterministically on the strategy frequencies, the evolutionary path traced out by a population after a single mutation is the *same* as it would have been had that mutation never occurred.[7] Yet modeling key agents requires that this at least exist as a *possibility*.

---

[7] Another way of putting the point is as follows: all mutation in the replicator dynamics occurs by shifting the population from its current point to some other point in a sphere of radius ε centered around its original position. Since the population is continous, the only possible interpretation of the effect of the mutation is that a subgroup (consisting of many more than one individual) switched strategies in unison, where the size of the sphere reflects the size of the subgroup. A mutation by a single individual corresponds to an infinitesimal change but, from the point of view of the replicator dynamics, $x + dx$ is treated in the same way as x.

Requiring that an evolutionary model be able to represent key agents sounds akin to requiring that the model demonstrate sensitive dependence on initial conditions, yet it is a strictly stronger criterion. Skyrms (1992, 1993) describes cases of chaotic dynamics (and, hence, sensitive dependence on initial conditions) for the replicator dynamics. Since we have just argued that the replicator dynamics cannot model key agents, the two notions, though related, should not be conflated. A key agent can be thought of as the limiting case of sensitive dependence on initial conditions for finite models since, according to the informal definition of a key agent, a key agent corresponds to the smallest possible change in the modeling conditions.

Viewed this way, we can see why continuous, deterministic dynamical systems cannot model key agents, even if they exhibit sensitive dependence upon initial conditions. Sensitive dependence upon initial conditions means that the evolutionary trajectory of two initial points x_1 and x_2 that are close (but not identical) in state space diverge exponentially. However, continuity requires that, as x_1 approaches x_2, the amount of time that it takes for the evolutionary trajectories to diverge significantly increases. As x_1 converges to x_2, the evolutionary trajectory beginning at x_1 eventually converges to the evolutionary trajectory beginning at x_2. This is exactly the opposite of the behavior that should occur in a model permitting key agents: part of the idea of a key agent is that the smallest possible change permitted in the system should have sudden and dramatic effects. Not only do continuous, deterministic dynamical systems lack a well-defined concept of "smallest possible change," but also they lack the possibility of sudden and dramatic changes occurring independently of the magnitude of the change.

Nondeterminism. As previously noted, the replicator dynamics provides a deterministic dynamical model of cultural evolution. Although deterministic dynamics provides reasonable approximations of certain biological phenomena (such as the *in vitro* growth of bacteria or fungi), it is inappropriate for cultural evolutionary models. The natural method of incorporating slight amounts of nondeterminism into the replicator dynamics[8] involves mutation: at each generation some fraction ε of the population undergoes mutation. Given the infinite-population assumption, this means that in each generation an infinite number of agents undergo mutation, provided that $\varepsilon > 0$.

---

[8] Recall the derivation of the replicator dynamics from the cultural evolutionary point of view. The primary reason for considering the limit as the population grew without bound was to *wash out* stochastic effects occurring on the individual level. There is something perverse, then, about *reintroducing* stochastic effects into the system afterwards.

Heterogeneity. Another shortcoming of the replicator dynamics that is sel-dom discussed in the surrounding literature concerns its requirement that agents be homogeneous, except for their strategy; see, for example, the derivation of the replicator dynamics in a cultural context by Bögers and Sarin (1993), as well as the derivation above. One way to remove the homogeneity assumption introduces several disjoint populations of individuals who do not interbreed, yet repeatedly interact and receive payoffs according to some common game (see Gale *et al.*, 1995). This solution seems *ad hoc*.

The requirement of homogeneity is also problematic if we seek an em-pirically adequate model of cultural evolution. Since differences in learning rules, interaction styles, and the like exist in real populations, we must take this heterogeneity seriously. Whether heterogeneity results in any significant dynamical effects depends, of course, on the model under consideration. How-ever, given the complexity of social-network models, and the possibility that heterogeneity may result in effects that we might not be able to predict ahead of time (such as the emergence of feedback loops in which different types of agent play off one another's presence in unexpected ways, as in the autocatalytic sets of Kauffman (1993)), it does not seem unreasonable to suggest that, if a model indicates the emergence of certain effects from homogeneous populations, we should view these results with caution until it can be shown that the occurrence of such behavior does not depend on the assumption of homogeneity.

Whereas the above list primarily contains properties possessed by agent-based models that are not shared by the replicator dynamics, there are two important senses in which agent-based models and the replicator dynamics are similar. Both model interaction between boundedly rational individuals and both can be interpreted as models of cultural evolution. These similarities allow us to view agent-based models as a natural refinement of the replicator dynamics. Indeed, one can show that, under certain circumstances, agent-based social-network models converge in the limit to the replicator dynamics (Skyrms, 2003).

Many of the above remarks argued that, in one way or another, agent-based models, particularly ones situated on a social network, are preferable to aggregate models. However, it should be noted that the models developed below clearly fail to do justice to many of the complex features present in, and driving, human social interaction. It would be a mistake to view these models as offering anything more than a modest improvement over the replicator dynamics. However, even with these limitations and inadequacies, the following models are worthy of study in their own right for two reasons. First, the slight improvement they offer improves our understanding of the process of cultural evolution. Second, the structural approach discussed below has the advantage of providing a single formalism that is sufficient for modeling a number of different cultural phenomena, one phenomenon for each possible interpretation of the "connection" relation in the social network. Regarding the proper interpretation of this relation, I shall remain silent.

2.2.1 Agent-based, social-network models

An agent-based model contains a finite population $P = \{a_1, \ldots, a_N\}$ of agents. A social network is a relation, or set of relations, defined on the population that serves to constrain the possible interactions between agents. We denote the _social network_ (sometimes also called a _population structure_ or a _local-interaction structure_) specifying the set of possible interactions by a connected, undirected graph (P, E), where E denotes the set of edges of the graph.

We assume that the social network is connected simply because this rules out the possibility of having two noninteracting groups inside a population, although in some cases we will allow for the possibility of unconnected social networks. Considerations of simplicity also underlie the assumption that the network is undirected, i.e., that, if a can interact with b, then b can interact with a. There is no _a priori_ reason why this has to be true, but it provides a natural starting point. Since considering evolutionary models defined on connected, undirected social networks already introduces a host of complexities, I shan't pursue anything further at this time.

The _neighborhood_ of an agent a, denoted v_a, is the set of all agents b such that an edge connects a to b. That is, $\{a, b\} \in E$. The members of v_a are known as the _neighbors_ of a. One useful visualization of a social network represents it in the following way: each agent corresponds to a vertex of the graph. The entire population can thus be represented by a number of circles arranged in a ring, each circle representing a vertex of the graph, and hence a single agent. The edges of the graph, representing various social relations that determine who interacts with whom, are indicated by lines connecting the vertices. Two vertices are connected by a line if and only if the corresponding agents stand in the relevant social relation to each other. Figure 2.1(a) illustrates a social network consisting of thirty agents and figure 2.1(b) shows the neighborhood of one particular agent.

The social network enters into the evolutionary dynamics in several ways. To begin, as before, we assume that there is some particular game that the agents play when they interact. The only restrictions placed on the nature of the game are that it be noncooperative and have at most a finite number of strategies, say m.

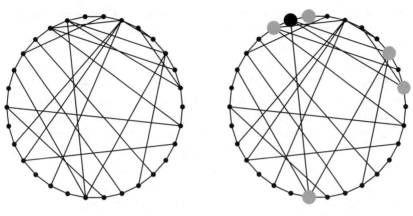

(a) A thirty-agent social network (b) A node and its neighbors

Figure 2.1 Network and neighborhood. The large gray circles are the neighborhood of a randomly selected agent, indicated by the large black circle.

In each round of play, each agent a interacts with every player in his neighborhood v_a, receiving a total score equal to the sum of payoffs from each individual game. At the end of each round of play, every agent engages in a review process, comparing his score with the score of each of his neighbors. If an agent's score is lower than that of at least one of his neighbors, that agent will switch strategies by adopting one of his neighbors' strategies. For all models except that of section 2.2.5, an agent's score is not cumulative; high scores obtained at earlier stages in the game play no role in determining what agents will do in the future.

If an agent judges his current strategy to be inferior, according to some criteria, how does he select a new strategy to adopt? Just as real people can use a number of different heuristics to solve problems, depending on the context, there are various update, or *learning*, rules that an agent may use. We will consider four different rules, three based on imitation and one based on a version of best response tailored to boundedly rational individuals. Each rule has a certain degree of intuitive plausibility, and each corresponds to a good heuristic for certain classes of problems.

Imitate the best neighbor. This is a very natural and common learning rule in the modeling literature; for a brief sampling, see Nowak and May (1992, 1993), Lindgren and Nordahl (1994), Huberman and Glance (1993), and Epstein (1998), among others. According to this rule, at the end of each generation, every agent surveys the scores of her neighbors and adopts the strategy of the one who did the best, where "best" means "earned the highest score." We also assume, here and elsewhere, that an agent will not switch strategies unless she has some incentive to do so; if the highest scoring neighbors of an agent still managed to earn lower scores than her, the agent will not switch strategies.

There is one minor detail that needs to be mentioned. For some games and some networks, it is possible that, when an agent goes to update her score, several of her neighbors may have tied for first place. In this case, how does the agent choose a strategy to adopt? We need to specify a tie-breaking rule that selects a unique strategy in such circumstances. In general, whenever this happens we assume, unless noted otherwise, that a strategy is chosen by rolling a weighted die. The weights on the die reflecting the number of times the strategy tied for first place.[9] So, for example, if the best score in an agent's neighborhood was obtained by two people following strategy 1, three people following strategy 4, and one person following strategy 5, that agent will adopt strategy 1 with probability $\frac{1}{3}$, strategy 4 with probability $\frac{1}{2}$, and strategy 5 with probability $\frac{1}{6}$.

Imitate with probability proportional to success. Here, as before, each agent compares her score with those of her neighbors, modifying her strategy only if at least one neighbor did strictly better. However, instead of ignoring those players who did better than her but were not the best, this rule assigns to every neighbor who did better a nonzero probability that she will adopt their strategy.

Suppose that b did better than a. The particular probability assigned is proportional to b's relative success, where this is simply the difference between their scores. The greater this value, the more likely it is that a will imitate b. More precisely, suppose that d is the difference between b's score and a's score. Let T be the sum of all of these differences for those members of a's update neighborhood who did better than a. Then the probability that a will adopt b's strategy is d/T.

Imitate best average payoff. This learning rule has players calculate the average payoff of each strategy in their neighborhood and select the one with the highest value. As with imitating the best neighbor, the possibility of ties

---

[9] This seems reasonable since, if several neighbors of an agent A follow σ and receive the highest score in v_a, it would be unwise for A to ignore this information. The simplest way for A to take this information into account is to let the probability of choosing strategy σ be a linear function of the number of people in her neighborhood who follow that strategy. More complicated functions could be used to model risk-averse players who require a certain number of neighbors to follow a maximal strategy before they consider adopting it.

exists, so some kind of tie-breaking rule needs to be given. We use a rule similar to one given previously, the only difference being that instead of randomly choosing a strategy from the set of highest-scoring strategies, we randomly select a strategy from the set of strategies that tie for having the highest average payoff. This learning rule models agents who base their judgment on the general performance of a strategy over the entire group of people who use it. Note, though, that in using this rule agents explicitly ignore the sample size. A high-scoring strategy used by one neighbor will be favored over a very good but not quite as high-scoring strategy used by several neighbors.

Best response. According to this rule, agents adopt the strategy that will confer the highest payoff in the next generation, under the assumption that none of their neighbors change strategies.[10] If there is more than one such strategy, players select a strategy to adopt at random. This rule deviates slightly from the spirit of evolutionary game theory since the persistence of a strategy is not determined by its success in the current generation, but rather by a calculation of the expected payoff a player might reasonably expect to receive in the next generation. However, it is still in the spirit of models of boundedly rational action since agents do not engage in strategic calculations to figure out what strategies their neighbors will use at future times; instead, they blithely proceed on the assumption that the people around them will continue to do what they have done in the past.

One of the benefits of modeling constrained interactions between agents via social networks, as defined above, lies in the generality of the approach. Any possible social relation relevant to determining interaction between individuals can be modeled, so long as the relation is symmetric,[11] reasonably constant over time,[12] and connects the entire population. Yet this generality comes at a cost. The number of different social networks[13] grows very rapidly with the size

---

[10] In the language of Kavka (1986), the agents reason *inductively* rather than *strategically*.

[11] A relation R is symmetric if aRb implies bRa. Equality is a symmetric relation, but the greater-than relation is not.

[12] Relations that are not constant over time require that we use a slightly different conception of a social network. See section 2.2.5 for details.

[13] Determining whether two social networks are "different" can either be very easy or very difficult, depending on how one construes the problem. If the identity of the agents is not taken into account, then determining whether two social networks are different amounts to determining whether two graphs are isomorphic. This is a very difficult problem, although exactly *how* difficult remains unknown. It has not yet been proven to be NP-complete – and, indeed, complexity theorists suspect that it is not – but no one has yet been able to prove exactly what the complexity class of the graph-isomorphism problem is. If the identity of the agents is taken into account, then two social networks can be shown to be different (or identical) by straightforward, and relatively rapid, calculation. See Skiena (1990).

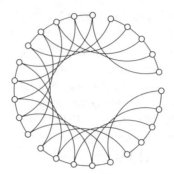

Figure 2.2 A semi-regular social network.

of the population[14] and two randomly chosen social networks may have very different structural properties. For this reason it will prove useful to investigate cultural evolution on social networks by classifying social networks according to their structural properties, checking to see how, if at all, variations in a network's structure affect the long-term evolutionary behavior. That is what we now turn to.

2.2.2 Lattice models

In some cases, the circular-graph representation of a social network is not the most illuminating. Consider the social network shown in figure 2.2. The regularities present in that network suggest that there may be something special about its structure, especially in contrast with a random network like that of figure 2.1(a). Rearranging the nodes, as in figure 2.3, shows that the structure of the network is that of a two-dimensional lattice, a fact hidden by the standard graph representation. Other networks have this property. Figure 2.4 shows a second network, which, upon rearranging the nodes, reveals another regular lattice-like structure, albeit a slightly more complicated one.

What the networks of figures 2.2 and 2.4 have in common is that the regularity in their structure is revealed when we position the nodes on a lattice. A close look at the exact way in which the nodes are connected shows something else: in both figures the nodes are connected according to their relative *spatial* position. In figure 2.3, each node, except for those on the lattice boundary, is

---

[14] If the population size is N, then the number of possible social networks (both connected and unconnected) is $2^{\binom{N}{2}} = 2^{\frac{N(N-1)}{2}}$.

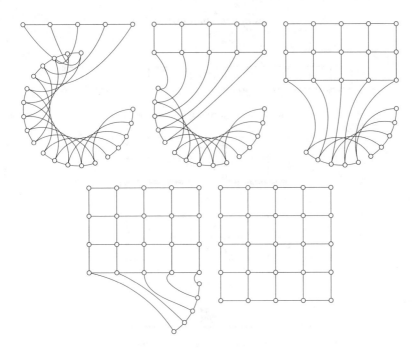

Figure 2.3 Topological transformation of a social network.

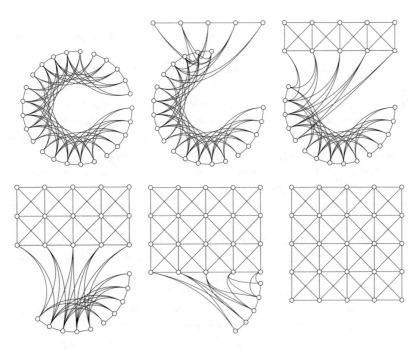

Figure 2.4 Another topological transformation.

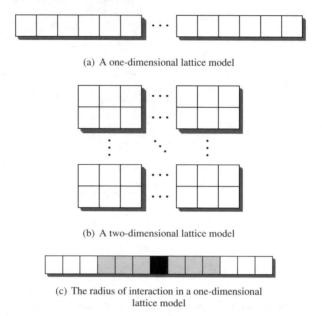

(a) A one-dimensional lattice model

(b) A two-dimensional lattice model

(c) The radius of interaction in a one-dimensional
lattice model

Figure 2.5 Types of lattice models.

connected to neighboring nodes located at the four cardinal compass points: north, south, east, and west. In figure 2.4, each node, except for those on the lattice boundary, is connected to its eight "nearest neighbors."

Lattice models are a special kind of social network in which the connections between agents are defined spatially. Each agent is considered to be located at some cell on an N-dimensional grid, and every cell in the grid is occupied by exactly one agent. In the one-dimensional case, this means that the agents live on a line, as shown in figure 2.5(a). In the two-dimensional case, the agents live on a sheet of graph paper, as in figure 2.5(b). Three-dimensional lattice models take place in a cube-shaped lattice, and so on.

In the one-dimensional case, the neighborhoods are defined by specifying an *interaction radius r*. Every agent located within r cells of the agent a belongs to v_a. Figure 2.5(c) illustrates the neighborhood for the centermost agent, defined by an interaction radius of 3. In the two-dimensional case, one has greater flexibility in the design of a neighborhood. Some common neighbors for the two-dimensional case are shown in figure 2.6. Looking at these neighborhoods reveals that the network of figure 2.3 can thus be thought of as a two-dimensional lattice model using the von Neumann neighborhood (where individuals on the boundary have fewer neighbors than individuals in the interior of the lattice). Similarly, the network of figure 2.4 can be thought of as a two-dimensional lattice model using the Moore (8) neighborhood.

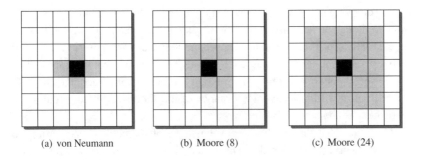

(a) von Neumann   (b) Moore (8)   (c) Moore (24)

Figure 2.6 Three common neighborhoods for two-dimensional lattices.

2.2.3 Small-world networks

The primary virtue of lattice models is that they work well for modeling social networks in which the social relations are correlated, in some fashion, with the spatial positions of the agents. For social systems in which the relevant relations are not correlated with spatial position, other network models need to be developed. The question, then, is that of how to choose an appropriate network model from the large set of possible networks. At this point it proves useful to consider some results from social psychology.

Most people, at some point in their life, have experienced the following phenomenon: at a social event you begin talking with a stranger and, in the course of the conversation, it becomes clear that you both know the same person. This experience, the *small-world phenomenon*, has entered popular culture as the belief that any two people in the world are connected by a short sequence of friends, family, and acquaintances – the so-called "six degrees of separation." This popular story has its roots in experimental social psychology.

In 1967, Stanley Milgram conducted an experiment in which he sent a number of letters to people living in Omaha, Nebraska, with the request that they forward the letter to a named "target" living in Boston. If the person who originally received the letter did not know the named target, the recipient was requested to mail the letter to someone they personally knew whom they judged more likely to know the target. Milgram provided some information about the target, such as his or her job and the general area in which they lived, so that the recipient of the letter had some information on which to decide whom to mail the letter to. The sequence of mailings thus initiated formed a chain connecting the original recipient to the target. What Milgram found was that, of the sixty letters successfully received by the target, the average number of people in the chain was about six.

No one yet knows whether we are all connected by "six degrees of separation," although additional experiments are being conducted. Yet, even if it is not true, strictly speaking, it is at least approximately true for many kinds of social networks. For the sake of argument, suppose that it is true; that is, suppose that, in the social network mapping the relation "is a friend or an acquaintance of" for the entire world, the average distance of the shortest path connecting any two nodes is about six.

Consider what this implies about the shape of the network. According to the 2001 world-population data sheet compiled by the Population Reference Bureau, there were a little more than 6.1 billion people on the planet mid-way through 2001. The total number of possible edges in a social network containing 6.1 billion people is

$$2^{\binom{6\,100\,000\,000}{2}} = 2^{\frac{6\,100\,000\,000 \times 6\,099\,999\,999}{2}} \approx 2^{1.86 \times 10^{19}}.$$

Each person in the world knows only a very small fraction of the 6.1 billion people, and so contributes a very small number of edges to the world's social network. People are generally quite bad at estimating their total number of friends and acquaintances, so it is difficult to determine a person's average number of friends and acquaintances, but let's err on the side of safety and suppose that each person knows 10 000 other people – an overestimate, to be sure. This means that the total number of edges in the network is about 3.05×10^{13} ($6.1 \times 10^{13}/2$, dividing by two was necessary to avoid counting each edge twice), or about 0.000 05 percent of the total number of possible edges. The close connectedness of the network is remarkable in light of its sparsity.

Sparse, clustered networks in which the typical path length between any two nodes is nonetheless low were dubbed "small-world" networks by Watts and Strogatz (1998) (see also Watts, 1999). Figure 2.7 illustrates what a small-world network might look like. Each node in the network belongs to a relatively small, clustered group. In the network displayed, each node connects to at least ten others, five to the "left" and five to the "right"; call these edges *cluster edges*. In addition, some nodes have additional edges, which link them to a randomly chosen node elsewhere in the network; call these edges *bridge edges*.

If the only connections which existed were the cluster edges, the network would not be a "small-world" network. The only path connecting two nodes located on opposites sides of such a network would involve following a chain of connections around the ring to arrive at the other side. The inclusion of bridge edges serves to greatly shorten paths between nodes because they function as "short cuts."

For a concrete example of the importance of bridge edges in collapsing social distance, consider the variant of the "six degrees of separation" story

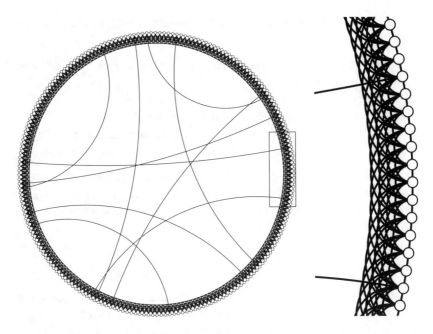

Figure 2.7 A small-world network (the box indicates the zoomed region).

that says everyone is only six handshakes away from anyone else in the world. Now, I grew up in Alaska, I have a number of friends who still live there, and a few acquaintances who have never left. According to the handshake story, all of my friends are only six handshakes away from every head of state. How is this possible? Not long ago, I shook hands with the son of a head of state. Assuming that the son and his father shake hands, that gives me a "handshake distance" of 2 between myself and the leader of that country, and my friends a "handshake distance" of 3. Heads of state often shake hands when they meet during official state functions as a sign of good will, and the social network of current heads of state is fairly well connected. It is likely, then, that my having shook hands with a son of a head of state places me within a handshake distance of 5 of *every* head of state. If so, then all of my friends in Alaska are within a handshake distance of 6 of every head of state – just as the variant of the "six degrees" story requires. In this context, I function as a "bridge edge" between my friends who have never left Alaska and the current heads of state, connecting two otherwise isolated groups.

Watts (1999) provides three different algorithms for producing small-world networks. We will adopt a variant of the algorithm known as the "β-model." In our variant of the β-model, small-world networks are generated in the following way.

1. Begin with a one-dimensional lattice (considered to wrap at the edge) with a fixed interaction radius r.
2. For each edge $e = \{i, j\}$ in the network, do the following.
   (a) Generate a uniform random number s between 0 and 1.
   (b) If $s < \beta$, add another edge to the network connecting one of the vertices incident on e to another randomly chosen node in the network.

For certain values of β, typically between 0.001 and 0.1, the network produced by this algorithm is a small-world network. It is important not to use too large a value of β since then the resulting network will more closely resemble a randomly generated network than a small-world network.

2.2.4 Networks of bounded degree

Another kind of social network, different in kind from lattice models and small-world networks, consists of one in which the number of edges each node is incident on (the *degree* of a node) is constrained between a certain minimum value, denoted k_{min}, and maximum value, denoted k_{max}. Figure 2.8 shows nine such networks, for various values of k_{min} and k_{max}. These networks fill an important area between lattice models, small-world networks, and completely random graphs. Both lattice models and small-world networks share the property that each node has almost the same number of neighbors, where the neighbors of each node occur in a more or less regular pattern.[15] Networks of bounded degree share the property that each node has almost the same number of neighbors (provided that the difference between k_{min} and k_{max} is not too great) but do not require that the wiring pattern of the network display any regularities. Such networks are not "truly random" networks, because of the enforced limits on the degree of each node, but they are as "random as one can get" within those limits.

2.2.5 Dynamic networks

In all of the social networks considered thus far, the presence of an edge between any two agents means that those two agents will interact every generation.

---

[15] The number of neighbors is only "almost" the same because, in lattice models, networks with fixed boundary conditions give nodes on the edge of the lattice fewer neighbors than nodes in the interior of the lattice. Small-world networks, as defined by Watts (1999), hold the degree of each node fixed, rewiring a small subset of edges to turn them into shortcuts.

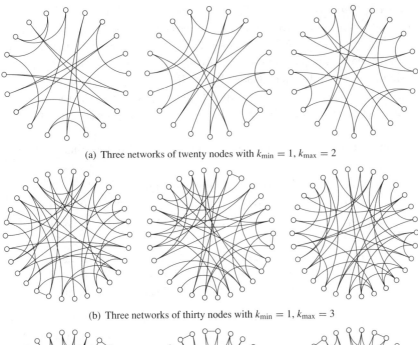

(a) Three networks of twenty nodes with $k_{min} = 1, k_{max} = 2$

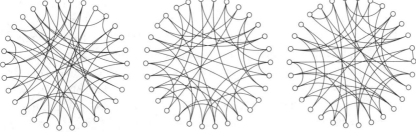

(b) Three networks of thirty nodes with $k_{min} = 1, k_{max} = 3$

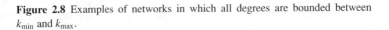

(c) Three networks of thirty nodes with $k_{min} = 2, k_{max} = 3$

Figure 2.8 Examples of networks in which all degrees are bounded between k_{min} and k_{max}.

Although this assumption is plausible for certain kinds of interdependent decision problems, it might also be the case that some pairs of agents are simply *more likely* to interact than others. This scenario cannot be represented in the framework discussed so far. In our current setup, either two agents interact or they don't. We have not discussed mechanisms by which the social network can change; neither have we allowed for the possibility of probabilistic interactions between agents.

A more general conception of a social network addresses these concerns by changing the semantics of the edges in two ways. First, we allow the network to be *directed*. That is, we treat the edge connecting a to b as different from the one connecting b to a. Second, every possible edge is present (except for edges connecting a node to itself), and is assigned a *weight w*. The weight is converted into the interaction probability of the two individuals connected by the edge, using the method described below. It can also be thought of as a measure of the *social distance* between the two individuals. The entire social network is thus a matrix of numbers listing the respective social distance between any two people.

For a population of seven people, one such social distance matrix is the following:

$$
\begin{pmatrix}
0 & 0.101 & 0.264 & 0.125 & 0.182 & 0.212 & 0.117 \\
0.309 & 0 & 0.074 & 0.195 & 0.254 & 0.036 & 0.133 \\
0.453 & 0.242 & 0 & 0.076 & 0.124 & 0.019 & 0.085 \\
0.283 & 0.178 & 0.07 & 0 & 0.009 & 0.261 & 0.199 \\
0.193 & 0.302 & 0.034 & 0.083 & 0 & 0.16 & 0.228 \\
0.407 & 0.068 & 0.036 & 0.192 & 0.154 & 0 & 0.142 \\
0.123 & 0.08 & 0.373 & 0.26 & 0.062 & 0.102 & 0
\end{pmatrix}
$$

According to the above, the probability of agent 1 interacting with agent 5 is 0.182, and the probability of agent 5 interacting with agent 1 is 0.193. One useful visualization of such networks is shown in figure 2.9 for several weighted networks, including the seven-member one displayed above. In these diagrams, the edge representing the probability of a interacting with b is a directed edge pointing from a to b. The actual probability is represented by the darkness of the arrow: a probability of 1 corresponds to a completely black arrow, a probability of 0 corresponds to a completely white arrow, and probabilities in between are mapped onto the appropriate level of gray.[16]

Dynamic networks allow us to model the process of social-network formation. The model described here is taken from the work of Skyrms and Pemantle (2000) on dynamic models of social-network formation. The basic idea is as follows: suppose that, at the beginning, all pairwise interactions are equally likely (note the similarity to the replicator dynamics) and are set to some base value b. For relatively small models, one can take $b = 1/(N - 1)$, where N is the population size.[17]

---

[16] Intuitively, an interaction with a probability of 1 is "always present" and an interaction with a probability of 0 is "never present." Printed on white paper, a completely black arrow is "always present," and a completely white arrow is "never present." Gray arrows are easier to see the darker they are, i.e., the closer to a probability of 1.

[17] This is not a plausible assumption for large models because the probability of two agents interacting converges to zero. In large models, one could initialize the network in a number of

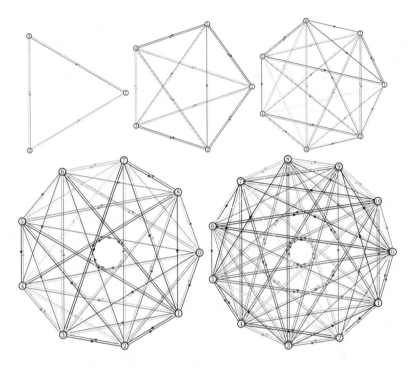

Figure 2.9 Five randomly weighted networks, $N = 3, 5, 7, 9$, and 11.

In the original paper by Skyrms and Pemantle, each generation every agent chooses one neighbor to interact with at random, according to the probabilities specified in the social-distance matrix. Each agent plays the game with those neighbors, and both individuals receive a payoff according to the payoff matrix for the game. (Another variant of this model we shall consider allows each agent to select several neighbors to interact with, according to the probabilities in the social-distance matrix.) At some later time, each agent adjusts her interaction probabilities on the basis of the payoffs she has received so far.

More precisely, suppose that each edge in the lattice has an initial weighting of one. That is, $w_{ij} = 1$ for all $i \neq j$ and let $w_{ii} = 0$ for all i. Let the probability of i interacting with j be

$$\Pr(i \text{ interacts with } j) = \frac{w_{ij}}{\sum_{k \neq i} w_{ik}}. \tag{2.8}$$

ways; one natural one would begin with a basic lattice model, but set the probability of two agents' interaction according to a decreasing function of their distance apart (defined to be the length of the shortest path) in the lattice.

Types of evolutionary models

By setting the initial weightings $w_{ij} = 1$ for $i \neq j$, the beginning probability of i interacting with j is thus $1/(N - 1)$ for all i. Suppose that, in the first round of play, i interacts with agents 1, 4, and 12, receiving payoffs of p_1, p_4, and p_{12}, respectively. If i chooses to adjust her interaction probabilities after this round of interaction, she will adjust the weightings assigned to interacting with agents 1, 4, and 12 as follows:

$$w'_{i1} = w_{i1} + p_1,$$
$$w'_{i4} = w_{i4} + p_4,$$
$$w'_{i12} = w_{i12} + p_{12}.$$

As long as the possible payoffs are nonnegative, the new weightings thus obtained will still yield a probability when normalized according to the rule in equation (2.8). Continuing this evolutionary procedure yields a model in which the social network changes over time.

Once we allow for the possibility of the social network evolving over time, we need to consider the question of the relation between the dynamics governing the evolution of the social network and the dynamics governing the evolution of individual strategies. Do people change their strategies faster or slower than the social network changes? We can parameterize this by introducing a few new global parameters. Let p_e denote the probability that a given agent will adjust her edge weights at the end of any generation, and let p_s denote the probability that a given agent will adjust her strategy at the end of any generation, according to one of rules described in section 2.2.1. If $p_s < p_e$, this means that the structural evolution of the social network occurs faster than the evolution of individual beliefs. Since we will usually consider the case in which the strategic dynamics is slower than the structural dynamics, we may fix $p_e = 1$ and allow p_s to vary between 0 and 1.

3

Cooperation[1]

Clyde Barrow and Bonnie Parker's crime spree ended violently in the early morning of May 23, 1934. After their having evaded the law for almost two years, a posse composed of police officers from Texas and Louisiana intercepted the couple on a highway near Sailes, Louisiana. Ordered to turn themselves over to the law, Bonnie and Clyde instead attempted to flee. The officers opened fire, killing the duo almost instantly. There is no indication that Bonnie and Clyde, even at the very end, ever considered disbanding their criminal cooperative.

Such teamwork is the stuff of legends, but we might wonder what would have happened if the story had ended differently. Suppose that Bonnie and Clyde had met with a less fiery end, an end similar to that of Al Capone: being arrested on charges of tax evasion. To make the story interesting, suppose that, after being arrested, taken to prison, and placed in separate isolation cells, Bonnie and Clyde both receive a visit from the district attorney. The district attorney, speaking to each in private, lays his cards on the table: he knows that Bonnie and Clyde are each guilty of far worse things than tax evasion, but confesses that he can't prove it. However, if one person turns state's evidence against the other, the district attorney promises that he will give the helpful soul a minimal sentence while throwing the book at the other. "Of course," the district attorney admits before leaving the cell, "if you *both* talk, then I can convict you *both*, and neither one of you will get off easy."

The interdependent decision problem Bonnie and Clyde face in this possible world is the well-known *prisoner's dilemma* first introduced by Merrill Flood and Melvin Dresher in 1950. It has the form shown in figure 3.1. The prisoner's dilemma encapsulates the strategic problem of cooperation when individual and collective interests conflict: when choosing the collectively best outcome

---

[1] Portions of this chapter were drawn from Alexander (2003).

	Stay silent	Turn state's evidence
Stay silent	− 7 −7	−2 −50
Turn state's evidence	−50 −2	−30 −30

Figure 3.1 The prisoner's dilemma. Payoffs are listed for (row, column). Values indicate number of years in jail and are negative to reflect the fact that it is time taken away from one's life. It is assumed that less time in jail is better, so both prisoner's favor the option that confers the least amount of time in jail, i.e., the negative number closest to zero.

produces a suboptimal result from the point of view of the individual. The apparent paradox of the prisoner's dilemma is that, if each individual selects what appears to be the best option available, in that it maximizes one's personal payoff no matter what the other person chooses, this leads to a state of affairs *less* desirable than an alternative that could have been obtained had they acted otherwise.

In the story above, Clyde might very well reason as follows: "If I stay silent, I might serve a sentence of only seven years for tax evasion. However, Bonnie could capitalize on this by turning state's evidence, forcing me to go to prison for fifty years. Although I don't like the thought of going to prison for seven years, I prefer it to knowing that Bonnie got off by doing minimal time while I rot in jail. And besides, if *I* turn state's evidence, I could always be lucky and get off with a minimal sentence if Bonnie should be foolish enough to stay silent. Thus I will tell the district attorney whatever he wants to know." Bonnie, pursuing reasoning similar to Clyde's, would arrive at the same decision. The net result lands each person in jail for thirty years. The irony of the situation is that each person, by choosing the option insuring the best possible outcome no matter what the other person does, arrives at a suboptimal state.

It is a long way from Louisiana to the state of nature, but the same problem arises there, too.[2] Hobbes's conception of the natural condition of mankind conceives of life in the state of nature as presenting individuals with essentially a prisoner's dilemma; we need only modify the labels on the strategies. Imagine a situation in which people are essentially equal in strength, no effective civil authority exists to provide protection, resources are in short supply, and all of one's possessions are coveted by others. In such circumstances, people can either choose to "lie low" or "anticipate," where choosing to "lie low" means

---

[2] At least under some interpretations (see Kavka, 1986). However, in his introduction to *Leviathan*, Curley (1994) argues that Hobbes's state of nature is better represented using the Assurance game, or the *Stag Hunt*. We'll consider the Stag Hunt in chapter 4.

that one does not engage in any initial offensive attacks (to take someone else's goods) and choosing to "anticipate" means that one does initiate offensive attacks.[3] Figure 3.2 represents, in a more general form, the problem of strategic choice in the state of nature. Since we do not know the actual payoffs individuals receive from their various actions, variables replace the numerical values inside the matrix.[4] The prisoner's dilemma results whenever an individual's payoffs for the two actions are such that $T > R > P > S$ and $(T + S)/2 < R$.[5] This ranking agrees with the pairing of strategies in the state of nature: the worst outcome arises from choosing to lie low, letting someone else make the first attack; the next worst outcome comes from mutual aggression (both people anticipating); the most peaceful outcome has both parties not initiating attacks; however, as initiating offensive attacks tends to increase one's power (by forcing others to turn their power to one's own end) and thus increases one's ability to satisfy his desires, this is the most individually advantageous outcome.[6]

---

[3] This terminology is due to Kavka (1986).

[4] In all likelihood, individual payoffs for the various actions vary from person to person. Although Hobbes does not allow for absolute pacifists in the state of nature (people who would choose not to anticipate no matter what), working within a Hobbesian framework we can still allow for variability in individual inclinations towards anticipation. Extreme dominators, presumably, would highly value anticipation over lying low, whereas the meek's preference for lying low would be reflected in a greatly reduced preference for anticipation. All we need to insure that pairwise competition among individuals in the state of nature can be formulated as a prisoner's dilemma is that, whatever individual payoffs may be, they all fit the pattern that $T > R > P > S$. However, it should be noted that, because many of the following results depend greatly on the particular values of the payoff matrix, it is not obvious that allowing for individual variation in the payoff matrices will not affect the outcomes of the dynamics. Determining the influence of individual variation in the payoff matrices on the dynamics remains an open question.

[5] The variable names were chosen to assist in remembering this ordering, standing for, respectively, "temptation," "reward," "punishment," and "sucker." We require that $(T + S)/2 < R$ so that repeated alternation of defection and cooperation is less desirable than repeated cooperation. In this chapter, I will at times refer to games in which $T > R > P > S$ but $(T + S)/2 \leq R$ as a prisoner's dilemma as well.

[6] One objection to representing the problem of strategic choice in the state of nature in this way is that it clearly ignores additional complexity introduced by the possibility of *repeated* interaction. Might not players opt for "friendly" behavior (here, lying low) in early stages in order to arrive at a pattern of mutually beneficial cooperation? Although Hobbes does not explicitly consider repeated interaction among individuals in the state of nature, it turns out that doing so would not make any difference. One can argue that defecting behavior dominates in the repeated prisoner's dilemmas just as it does in the one-shot prisoner's dilemma (see Luce and Raiffa, 1957). Suppose that A and B play a prisoner's dilemma repeated N times. When A and B arrive at the final stage of the game, A will recognize that his behavior at this stage cannot possibly influence B's future behavior (since there are no more stages after this one). Thus, the Nth stage of an N-stage prisoner's dilemma poses exactly the same strategic problem as a one-shot prisoner's dilemma. As argued for above, both A and B will choose to defect (here, anticipate). However, since A's and B's behavior in the final stage of the game is known ahead of time, the N-stage prisoner's dilemma reduces to a repeated prisoner's dilemma having $N - 1$ stages. Continuing this backward induction gives the conclusion that the unique dominating strategy in the N-stage repeated prisoner's dilemma has both individuals defecting (anticipating) at each stage. This corresponds nicely to Hobbes's conclusion.

	Lie low (cooperate)	Anticipate (defect)
Lie low (cooperate)	R' R	T' S
Anticipate (defect)	S' T	P' P

Figure 3.2 Individual choice in the state of nature.

Hobbes argued that, in the absence of a strong, centralized, coercive, effective authority capable of imposing sanctions, the state of nature decays into a war of all against all. In such a situation, life is "evil, nasty, brutish, and short." In the absence of any reasonable guarantee that one will enjoy the fruit of one's labor, society cannot flourish because productivity will cease.

Yet one might wonder whether the state of nature would really be as bad as Hobbes envisions. People do often cooperate in situations having the formal structure of a repeated prisoner's dilemma. In the absence of any kind of enforcement mechanism to insure that good behavior will be reciprocated in turn, why should one cooperate? Do self-interested rational actors need society's sword hanging over their heads to make them cooperate?

3.1 The replicator dynamics

Consider the problem of modeling the interactions of boundedly rational agents in the state of nature. Let L denote the strategy of "lying low" and let A denote the strategy of "anticipating" (i.e., of initiating offensive attacks). In a population where a fraction p of the people follow the strategy of lying low and $1 - p$ of the people anticipate, the expected utilities of anticipating and lying low are

$$F(A|\vec{s}) = p \cdot F(A|L) + (1 - p) \cdot F(A|A)$$
$$= p \cdot T + (1 - p) \cdot P$$

and

$$F(L|\vec{s}) = p \cdot F(L|L) + (1 - p) \cdot F(L|A)$$
$$= p \cdot R + (1 - p) \cdot S.$$

Since $T > R$ and $P > S$, the expected utility of anticipating is greater than the expected reward of lying low. From this, it follows that $F(A|\vec{s}) > F(\vec{s}|\vec{s}) >$

Anticipate   Lie low

Figure 3.3 The replicator-dynamics model of the state of nature.

$F(L|\vec{s})$, where $F(\vec{s}|\vec{s})$ is the average fitness of the population. On calculating the rate of change of the frequency of each strategy in the population, we find that

$$\frac{ds_A}{dt} = (1 - p)\big(F(A|\vec{s}) - F(\vec{s}|\vec{s})\big) > 0,$$

$$\frac{ds_L}{dt} = p\big(F(L|\vec{s}) - F(\vec{s}|\vec{s})\big) < 0.$$

Over time, the proportion of the population choosing the non-aggressive strategy of lying low will eventually be driven to extinction. (Provided that there are at least some aggressors initially present.)

Figure 3.3 illustrates the evolution for the replicator-dynamics model of the state of nature. The endpoints of the line segment represent states of the population where everyone anticipates or lies low, respectively. Points on the line segment represent states where some proportion of the population anticipates and the rest lie low – the proportion of the population anticipating/lying low being indicated by how far away the point is from the ends. The point in the middle represents the state where half of the population anticipates and half lies low. The arrows on the line segment point in the direction that evolution moves the population, according to the replicator dynamics. As long as the population contains the smallest fraction of anticipators at the beginning, the evolutionary dynamics carries the population to the state where everyone anticipates – Hobbes's war of all against all. Since the replicator dynamics, in the form we are using, cannot *introduce* new strategies into the population, if the population begins in the state where *absolutely no one* anticipates, it will remain at that state under the evolutionary dynamics. However, the state where absolutely no one anticipates is a very unstable state; the slightest perturbation initiates a sequence of events eventually leading to the war of all against all.

In the Hobbesian state of nature, one may wonder whether the presence of rugged, individualistic cooperators – people willing to anticipate some of the time yet lie low some of the time – might prevent the inevitable slide into the war of all against all. Such tough-minded individuals delay the slide into universal conflict, but we still arrive there all the same – it just takes a little longer. Figure 3.4 illustrates the evolutionary trajectories for a population that includes the strategy "Mix" as well as anticipate and lie low. The strategy "Mix" chooses randomly between anticipating and lying low, adopting either strategy

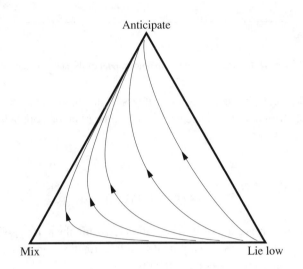

Figure 3.4 A simplex diagram for the three-strategy prisoner's dilemma.

equally often. In a population consisting of three strategies – anticipate, lie low, and randomize between anticipate and lie low with equal probability – the replicator dynamics still carries the population to a final state in which everyone anticipates.

Each point in the interior of the triangle of figure 3.4 uniquely represents a state of the population. Figure 3.5 illustrates how a vector $\langle a, b, c \rangle$, specifying an initial population configuration, can be mapped onto a unique point in the triangle.[7] Imagine an equilateral triangle having an altitude of length k. One can prove that, given a point p somewhere inside or on the edges of the triangle, the sum of the perpendiculars from p to each side of the triangle is equal to k.[8] If we take the triangle to have an altitude of length one, then the lengths a, b, and c in figure 3.5 sum to one. Consequently, we can use p to represent the state vector $\langle a, b, c \rangle$. According to this method of representing population states, each vertex of the triangle corresponds to the state where only one strategy is present in the population, and each side of the triangle represents polymorphic states where only two of the three strategies are present.

Curved paths in figure 3.4 represent evolutionary trajectories followed by the population under the replicator dynamics. Each line has an orientation, or direction, specifying how the path is traversed. The trajectories in figure 3.4

[7] The vector contains strategy frequencies, so a, b, and c are all real numbers between 0 and 1 with the property that $a + b + c = 1$.
[8] This is known as Viviani's Theorem.

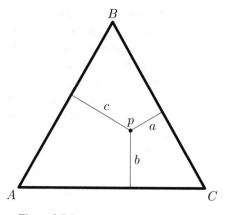

Figure 3.5 Interpreting simplex diagrams.

show the time-evolution of a population from some initial condition or state – the point at the beginning of the trajectory – to some final state.[9] Since all trajectories in the interior of the triangle eventually arrive at the corner labeled "anticipate," this means that any state of the population in which all three strategies are followed by some percentage of people, no matter how small, eventually evolves to the state where everyone anticipates.

The difficulty of evolving cooperative behavior via the replicator dynamics stands in marked contrast with the well-known result of Robert Axelrod. In 1982, Axelrod conducted a computer tournament in which sixty strategies, solicited from a wide range of members of the academic community, were pitted against each other in a "round-robin" competition (Axelrod and Hamilton, 1981; Axelrod, 1982). Each strategy played five "runs" of the repeated prisoner's dilemma against every other strategy. Each "run" consisted of the prisoner's dilemma being repeated a certain number of times, where the number of repeats was fixed in advance, and common among all strategy pairings.

What Axelrod found, both in the original computer tournament and in a second, larger, tournament held later, was that a very simple strategy, one favoring cooperative behavior, won both tournaments. The strategy, known as TIT-FOR-TAT, begins by cooperating and then, in every subsequent round, mimics

---

[9] Strictly speaking, strategies in the replicator dynamics never truly disappear; they just asymptotically approach zero. In figure 3.4, though it may appear as if a certain trajectory reaches a vertex (or side) of the simplex, in actuality no trajectory that begins in the interior of the triangle will reach the boundary in finite time. The path will become arbitrarily close to the equilibrium point, but will not reach it, simply because under the replicator dynamics strategies cannot become extinct.

the play of its opponent in the previous round. If its opponent always cooperates, then TIT-FOR-TAT will always cooperate. If its opponent defects in the nth stage of the game, TIT-FOR-TAT will reciprocate by defecting in the $(n + 1)$st stage of the game; if its opponent should then "apologize" for its nth-stage defection with a cooperative move in the $(n + 1)$st stage, TIT-FOR-TAT will accept the apology by cooperating in the $(n + 2)$nd stage. The simple feedback mechanism employed by TIT-FOR-TAT is, Axelrod found, remarkably successful at rewarding cooperative behavior and punishing defections in certain environments.

The phrase "in certain environments" is crucial to remember. TIT-FOR-TAT's success in Axelrod's tournaments has unfortunately entered popular culture as the belief that TIT-FOR-TAT is, in some sense, the "solution" to, or the optimal strategy to adopt in, the repeated prisoner's dilemma. TIT-FOR-TAT is *not* the optimal strategy – indeed, it can be proven that in the indefinitely repeated prisoner's dilemma no optimal strategy exists.[10] Moreover, Axelrod himself notes that TIT-FOR-TAT would not have won the two computer tournaments if two other "natural" strategies had been submitted. One strategy that would have beaten TIT-FOR-TAT is WIN–STAY, LOSE–SHIFT (also known as "Pavlov"). WIN–STAY, LOSE–SHIFT, like TIT-FOR-TAT, begins by cooperating on the first move, cooperating on future moves if and only if both players adopted the same strategy on the previous move.[11]

TIT-FOR-TAT did very well in Axelrod's computer tournament when paired against strategies selected by game theorists, computer scientists, and many others.[12] Yet how well would TIT-FOR-TAT, or for that matter WIN–STAY, LOSE–SHIFT, perform in an evolutionary environment against a wide range of strategies, some much more sophisticated?[13] We can answer this by constructing a

---

[10] See Axelrod (1984) for a proof of this.

[11] Suppose that player one follows the strategy WIN–STAY, LOSE–SHIFT. If both players cooperate, player one will cooperate on the next move (mutual cooperation is considered to be a "win," and the strategy recommends staying with a win). If both players defect, player one will switch to cooperating on the next move (mutual defection is considered to be a "loss," so player one shifts to the other alternative for the next move, which is in this case cooperation). If player one defects and player two cooperates, player one will continue to defect on the next move (defection against a cooperator is considered to be a "win"). If player one cooperates and player two defects, player one will switch to defection on the next move (cooperating against a defector is a "loss," so player one switches to the other alternative for the next move, which is in this case defection).

[12] Axelrod also included a purely random strategy in the tournament, so that strategy designers could not assume that their opponent was following a rational, or even deterministic, strategy.

[13] Many of the strategies pitted against TIT-FOR-TAT in Axelrod's tournament were certainly worthy of the title "sophisticated." In using the term "sophisticated" here, I am referring only to how many past moves a strategy takes into consideration when determining how to act. TIT-FOR-TAT and WIN–STAY, LOSE–SHIFT both take into account only the prior move of each player. More sophisticated strategies, in my sense of the term, may take into account the two previous moves of each player, or the three previous moves, etc.

replicator-dynamics-like model in which individuals play the repeated prisoner's dilemma using strategies that take into account the past moves of one's opponent.

How might one represent a strategy in the prisoner's dilemma that takes into account an opponent's past moves? Suppose that a strategy has a memory of length M. That strategy must then specify a particular play of the game *conditional* upon every possible way of playing the M previous games. One way this may be done is as follows.[14] In the opening move of the game, there are no previous moves to take into consideration, so the only thing a strategy needs to specify is whether to cooperate or defect. In the second move, though, there are four ways that the opening move might have been played. These are

Opponent's move	My move
Cooperate	Cooperate
Cooperate	Defect
Defect	Cooperate
Defect	Defect

Let us represent "Cooperate" by 0 and "Defect" by 1. If we adopt the convention of writing my opponent's move before my move, as above, these four outcomes can be expressed as 00, 01, 10, and 11; reading these as numerals written in binary, we have just given a mapping from the four possible ways of playing the opening move of the game to the numerals 0, 1, 2, and 3.

Consider a sequence of binary digits of length four, such as 0011. Reading this sequence of digits from left to right, we can interpret this as providing a *conditional* strategy, with a memory of length 1, for the repeated prisoner's dilemma. How? We've just seen how the outcome of a particular play of the two-person prisoner's dilemma can be mapped onto an integer i between 0 and 3. If we start at the leftmost digit of 0011 and move i places to the right, the digit at that place then tells us what to play (0 = Cooperate, 1 = Defect) given that particular prior history of play. So 0011 tells me to cooperate if, in the last move, both I and my opponent cooperated; it tells me to cooperate if my opponent cooperated but I defected; it tells me to defect if my opponent defected and I cooperated; and, lastly, it tells me to defect if my opponent defected and I defected. That is, 0011 represents the conditional response of Tit-for-Tat.

The above scheme does more than provide a mapping for just the opening move of the game. We now have a way to represent an entire *history* of M moves

---

[14] This is neither the only way, nor necessarily the most efficient. For an alternative approach, see Lindgren and Nordahl (1994).

as a nonnegative integer. Suppose that you have played the prisoner's dilemma with your opponent three times, and the outcome of those three previous plays has been Defect–Defect (on the first move), Defect–Cooperate (on the second move), and Cooperate–Defect (on the third move). This game history is mapped to the number 27 under the above scheme. When written in binary, 27 becomes 011011; the first two numerals ("01") represent the Cooperate–Defect outcome of the third move, the second pair of numerals ("10") represents the Defect–Cooperate outcome of the second move, and the last pair of numerals represents the Defect–Defect outcome of the first move.

A strategy with memory M needs to specify what move to play for every possible way of playing the M previous games. We can think of a strategy as broken into $M + 1$ "chunks," the first chunk specifying an opening move, the second chunk specifying a move conditional on the outcome of the first game, the third chunk specifying a move conditional on the outcome of the first and second games, and so on. A strategy of memory 2, then, can be written as follows:

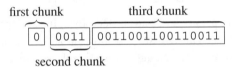

The first chunk indicates that the player will cooperate on the opening move. The second chunk indicates that the player will follow the "tit-for-tat" approach of playing whatever his opponent played in the first game. The third chunk indicates that the player will follow the "anti-tit-for-tat" approach of playing the *opposite* of whatever his opponent played in the second game, except in the cases in which his opponent cooperated both in the first and in the second game (in which case the player cooperates) or defected both in the first and in the second game (in which case the player defects).

Figure 3.6 lists the outcome from one run of the discrete-population replicator dynamics on a model allowing strategies to have a memory of up to five moves.[15] Strategies are represented graphically, using white to indicate

---

[15] This particular model used the discrete replicator dynamics with a fixed population size of 1000 and payoff matrix of figure 3.7. At the beginning of each generation agents were paired at random. After pairing, each agent played five games of the replicator dynamics with his partner, keeping track of the outcome of each game if his memory permitted. (If an agent had a memory length less than five, the oldest outcome was forgotten and the remaining outcomes were shifted down by one, making space for the most recent outcome.) After every agent had played the repeated prisoner's dilemma, there occurred a "reproductive" step in which each agent produced several clones, the number of clones equal to his score. The population size was then normalized by removing agents at random until the fixed size of 1000 was reached. One hundred generations were run for each model.

Strategy 1:

Density: 63, Memory: 5, Play versus self: D, C, C, C, D, C.

Strategy 2:

Density: 244, Memory: 5, Play versus self: D, D, C, D, D, D.

Strategy 3:

Density: 424, Memory: 5, Play versus self: D, C, C, C, D, D.

Strategy 4:

Density: 9, Memory: 5, Play versus self: D, C, C, D, C, C.

Strategy 5:

Density: 260, Memory: 5, Play versus self: D, C, C, C, C, C.

Figure 3.6 Five remaining strategies from a repeated prisoner's dilemma allowing memories of up to five moves.

"cooperate" and black to indicate "defect." The strategy should be read as a single continuous line beginning on the upper left, continuing across and down. Since the length of a strategy does not fit neatly into a rectangle, the end of the strategy is padded with meaningless squares so that it fits into a rectangle. These meaningless squares are colored gray.

The important thing to note about figure 3.6 is that *none* of the surving strategies are TIT-FOR-TAT. Moreover, *none* of the surviving strategies are even "tit-for-tattish," beginning with cooperation and imitating what their opponent did in the first game. All of the strategies listed *begin* with defection, and switch to cooperation later, at least when played against themselves. Moreover, these five "winning" strategies appeared in a model with the deck originally stacked in favor of cooperative strategies: out of 1000 individuals, 250 were originally assigned TIT-FOR-TAT and 250 were originally assigned WIN–STAY,

	C	D
C	2.0	0.0
D	3.0	1.0

Figure 3.7 A payoff matrix for the prisoner's dilemma.

Figure 3.8 The prisoner's dilemma played on a one-dimensional lattice using the payoff matrix of figure 3.7, the learning rule *Imitate-the-Best* and interaction and update radii of 1.

Lose–Shift. The remaining 500 were assigned random strategies with random memory length. Even with the initial bias favoring Tit-for-Tat and Win–Stay, Lose–Shift, these strategies – which did so well in Axelrod's tournament – were driven to extinction. Nevertheless, universal defection did not win out, for *all* of the strategies cooperate with themselves, sometimes to a significant extent. Allowing strategies in the replicator dynamics to have memory mitigates the inevitable slide into the war of all against all.

3.2 Lattice models

Frequent cooperative behavior can arise in models based on the replicator dynamics. How does introducing structure into the interactions affect the emergence of cooperation? Figure 3.8 illustrates one evolutionary trajectory for the prisoner's dilemma played on a one-dimensional lattice with an interaction and update radius of 1, no memory, and the particular payoff matrix of figure 3.7. Cooperators are colored white, defectors black.[16] The initial state of the population is indicated on the top line, with successive generations appearing below. Although a single region of cooperators manages to persist for several generations, by generation 8 the entire population has defected.

Two things stand out from the evolutionary history shown in figure 3.8: the sizeable cooperative region slowly disappears and the collapse of the cooperative region is asymmetric – the left- and right-hand sides do not shrink at the

---

[16] The mnemonic for remembering this is that in the old Westerns the "bad guys" always wore black.

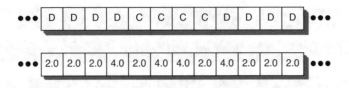

Figure 3.9 Calculation of scores for the cooperative region of figure 3.8.

same rate. This asymmetry, as well as the collapse of the cooperative region, occurs as a result of our choice of the tie-breaking rule. Figure 3.9 illustrates the payoffs received by a region of cooperators surrounded by defectors. Boundary cooperators – those cooperators who have one neighbor defecting and one neighbor cooperating – receive a payoff of 2.0, a score lower than that of each of their neighbors. However, due to the particular choice of payoff matrix, a defector who interacts with one cooperator and one defector receives a score of $3.0 + 1.0 = 4.0$, which equals the payoff received by a cooperator who interacts with two other cooperators, $2.0 + 2.0 = 4.0$. According to our tie-breaking rule, in these circumstances the boundary cooperators select a strategy to adopt at random. If they adopt the strategy used by their cooperating neighbor, the cooperative region will not shrink, even though both boundary cooperators receive an inferior score! However, if either one of the two boundary cooperators adopts the strategy of their neighboring defector, the cooperative region will shrink on that side. Since the best a region of cooperators can do in these circumstances is hold their own, and there is only a 25 percent chance that they will do that in any given generation, eventually the evolutionary pressure drives the cooperative region to extinction. Figure 3.10 illustrates the occurrence of this phenomena in ten randomly initialized worlds.[17]

The cooperative region in these examples *would* be able to resist the defectors if an alternative tie-breaking rule were used. Suppose that the agents employed a more conservative rule: an agent adopts a new strategy if and only if *none* of the highest-scoring agents in his neighborhood employ his current strategy. The idea behind this tie-breaking rule is that agents are somewhat reluctant to change strategies (perhaps due to certain costs imposed by the extra cognition) and will do so only when there is clear evidence that the strategy they have been following is inferior – i.e., when none of the highest-scoring agents in their neighborhood are using it. Under this conservative rule, cooperative regions

---

[17] Universal defection always occurs. In series of 10 000 trials on a one-dimensional lattice of size 200 with $r = 1$, initialized randomly but with both strategies equally likely, 9581 converged to a state in which everyone defects. The remaining trials would have converged to universal defection if the model had run a few generations longer.

Figure 3.10 Ten runs of the one-dimensional prisoner's dilemma, $r = 1$.

are *stable* in one-dimensional lattice models. These cooperative regions are not regions of conditional cooperation as found in the replicator models with memory discussed previously – these are regions of *unconditional* cooperation. Hobbes's war of all against all need not spread without bound; pockets of peace can persist in the center of conflict.

Yet, even if it is true that certain social networks and learning rules facilitate the persistence of cooperative regions in the repeated prisoner's dilemma, the question of how these cooperative regions may form in the first place remains to be answered. The original cooperative region of figure 3.8 was not itself the outcome of an evolutionary process; it appeared in the random initialization of the model. Can cooperative regions evolve in the one-dimensional prisoner's dilemma?

Answering this question requires analyzing the basins of attraction for co-operative regions in the one-dimensional prisoner's dilemma. Analyzing basins of attraction for social-network models in general is a difficult and unresolved problem, but the one-dimensional lattice presents one of the few tractable cases. This good fortune derives entirely from the fact that one-dimensional lattice models are, in many cases, equivalent to one-dimensional cellular automata, and there exist efficient algorithms and analytical techniques for studying cellular automata.

A one-dimensional cellular automaton can be thought of as a sequence of "cells" arranged on a line. Each cell i is assigned a state $s_i \in S$ (the set of possible states is common to all cells) and there is a single transition rule that tells us how the state of every cell changes as a function of its current state and the state of r neighbors on the left and right. The only difference between one-dimensional lattice models, as defined in chapter 2, and one-dimensional cellular automata is that one-dimensional cellular automata have *deterministic* transition rules specifying how the state of each cell changes over time.

One-dimensional lattice models in which agents employ a randomized tie-breaking rule are therefore not cellular automata. However, if agents use a *conservative* tie-breaking rule, like the one described above, and there are only two possible strategies, then the rule specifying how agents adopt new strategies becomes deterministic.[18] In this case, the one-dimensional lattice model is a cellular automaton.

The basic problem with analyzing the basins of attraction for social-network models in general, and cellular automata in particular, is that the dynamical law specifying the evolution of the system is many to one. A single state can have more than one predecessor, and may have many. For example, the state of universal defection has many predecessor states, as figure 3.10 aptly illustrates. Moreover, given any single evolutionary trajectory arriving at universal defection, every single one of the intermediary states may itself have multiple predecessors.[19] The map of the basin of attraction for the state of universal defection will be a richly branching tree.

In 1992, Wuensche and Lesser developed an algorithm for running cellular automata backwards, thus enabling us to map the basin of attraction for any state of any cellular automaton we are interested in.[20] In general, we are not interested in the basin of attraction for an arbitrary state of the population, what

---

[18] Consider what happens when there are only two possible strategies. Either the agent's own strategy belongs to the set of highest-scoring strategies in his neighborhood or it does not. If it does, the agent will not switch strategies. If it does not, then the set of highest-scoring strategies consists of exactly one unique strategy – the one *not* followed by the agent – so the agent will definitely switch to adopt that strategy. The learning rule is thus deterministic. When more than two strategies are possible, then it is possible – even with a conservative learning rule—for there to be more than one strategy in the set of highest-scoring strategies.

[19] This is another important difference between social-network models and the replicator dynamics. Under the replicator dynamics, any state of the population (excepting limit points) may have exactly one predecessor, provided that mutations are not allowed.

[20] Provided that its state space is sufficiently small. In a two-value cellular automaton, the state space grows exponentially with the number of nodes. The state space of a cellular automaton with 300 cells has a size of 2^{300}, which is approximately 2.037×10^{90}. This number is larger than Arthur Eddington's 1924 estimate of the number of protons in the universe (1.574×10^{79}).

we want to know is the basin of attraction for the evolutionarily stable states. In the prisoner's dilemma defined on a one-dimensional lattice with a radius of 1 and the "imitate best neighbor, conservatively" update rule, all convergent states are fixed points: states mapped onto themselves by the evolutionary dynamics.

Figures 3.11, 3.12, 3.13, and 3.14, respectively, catalog the basins of attraction for the prisoner's dilemma played on five-, six-, seven-, and eight-person one-dimensional lattices with $r = 1$.[21] These figures provide maps of the evolutionary trajectories through state space. In these diagrams, the centermost state is the attractor of the basin. States further out from the center are predecessor states. Individual evolutionary trajectories begin at the states furthest from the center and proceed inward. For each individual state, dark squares represent individuals who follow the strategy Defect, and bright squares represent individuals who follow the strategy Cooperate. States that do not have any predecessor states under the evolution dynamics, such as those on the outermost ring, are known as *Garden-of-Eden* states.

For the basin of attraction of "all defect," I have included all states, including ones rotationally equivalent to states already listed.[22] For the other basins of attraction, rotationally equivalent states have been suppressed. As a result the number of states illustrated in each figure does not equal the total number of possible states for the social network.

Although it is true that, in a one-dimensional lattice model with equal interaction and update neighbors of size 1, states containing significant numbers of cooperators can develop and persist, figures 3.11–3.14 reveal that the evolutionary dynamics vastly favors the state of All Defect. Most states with significant numbers of cooperators are Garden-of-Eden states, and stable states under the evolutionary dynamics that contain cooperators are either Garden-of-Eden states or the successor state of a Garden-of-Eden state containing more cooperators than the stable state. In other words, pockets of cooperation may persist over time in a one-dimensional lattice with $r = 1$, unlike in the replicator dynamics, but *they cannot form*. The only way a cluster of cooperators having sufficient size to avoid being eliminated can occur is if the population happens to be initialized in that state.

---

[21] These diagrams of the basins of attraction were produced with Andy Wuensche's Discrete Dynamics Lab, which implements the algorithm described in Wuensche and Lesser (1992), using the representation scheme for social networks from Alexander (2003).

[22] A state S is *rotationally equivalent* to another state S' if S' has the same pattern of cells as S except shifted to the left or right. Since one-dimensional lattices "wrap" at the endpoints, rotationally equivalent states do not qualitatively differ in evolutionary trajectory. Thus, in principle, one can suppress all information about rotationally equivalent states when cataloging basins of attraction because that information is redundant.

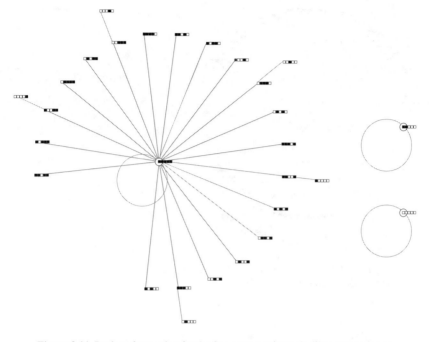

Figure 3.11 Basins of attraction for the five-person prisoner's dilemma played on a one-dimensional lattice, $r = 1$.

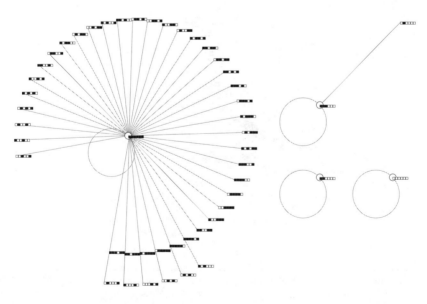

Figure 3.12 Basins of attraction for the six-person prisoner's dilemma played on a one-dimensional lattice, $r = 1$.

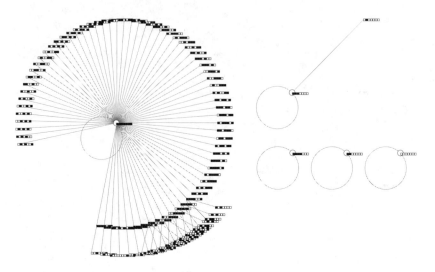

Figure 3.13 Basins of attraction for the seven-person prisoner's dilemma played on a one-dimensional lattice, $r = 1$.

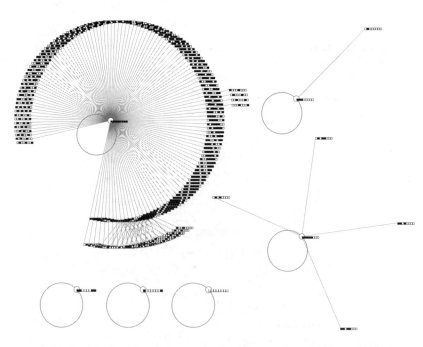

Figure 3.14 Basins of attraction for the eight-person prisoner's dilemma played on a one-dimensional lattice, $r = 1$.

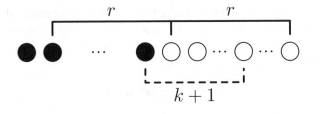

Figure 3.15 Frontier competition in the one-dimensional prisoner's dilemma.

In fact, one can prove that no one-dimensional lattice with interaction and update radii of 1 can have cooperative clusters form. Suppose that we have a cooperator C located on the lattice. If C is isolated, with defectors on both sides, C will be replaced by a defector in the next generation. If C has a cooperator C^* on one side, and a defector D on the other, C will receive a score of $R + S$ and D will receive a score of T plus either T or P (depending on the strategy followed by D's other neighbor). However, since $T + T > T + P > R + S$, it does not really matter what strategy D's other neighbor follows; in either case, D will earn a score greater than C and will therefore not adopt C's strategy.[23] Because C earns a score lower than D, will C switch to adopt D's strategy? It entirely depends on what score C's neighbor C^* earns. Regardless, the "best" C can do from the point of view of encouraging cooperation is to continue to follow the same strategy in the next generation. Cooperation cannot spread from C to his neighboring defector.

If we fix the payoff matrix for the prisoner's dilemma to be that of figure 3.7, the above argument can be generalized for an arbitrary radius. Consider the case in which we have "frontier competition" between a region of cooperators and a region of defectors, as portrayed in figure 3.15. The boundary cooperator cannot persuade the boundary defector to switch strategies because the boundary cooperator has a score of $r(R + S)$, the boundary defector a score of $r(T + P)$, and $r(T + P) > r(R + S)$ because $T + P > R + S$. However, might it be possible for a cooperator in the *interior* of the cooperative region to cause the boundary defector to switch strategies? This possibility doesn't exist when $r = 1$ since no cooperators in the interior of the region can influence the future strategy of the boundary defector. However, when $r > 1$, this possibility exists.

In order for a cooperator in the interior of the cooperative region to cause the boundary defector to switch strategies, a necessary and sufficient condition

---

[23] By similar reasoning applied to D's other neighbor, D will not adopt the strategy Cooperate no matter what.

is that the interior cooperator earn a higher score than the boundary defector.[24] Interior cooperators earn a score of $(r + k)R + (r - k)S$ for some $0 < k < r$, which must exceed the boundary defectors' score of $r(T + P)$. For the payoff matrix of figure 3.7, this requires that

$$(r + k)R + (r - k)S > r(T + P)$$

$$(r + k)2 > 4r$$

$$k > r,$$

which cannot happen, given the bounds on k. Thus it is impossible for a cooperative region to expand into a region of pure defection.

This pessimistic conclusion depends upon our choice of the payoff matrix. The crucial condition which must be satisfied in order for cooperators to expand into regions of defection is that

$$k > r\left(\frac{T + P - R - S}{R - S}\right).$$

Recalling that $0 < k < r$, cooperator expansion can occur only when

$$0 < \frac{(T - R) + (P - S)}{R - S} < 1,$$

that is, when $(T + P)/2 < R$. We can see that the inequality must be strict, for the payoff matrix of figure 3.7 has $(T + P)/2 = R$ and, as we see from the runs in figure 3.10, cooperative regions cannot expand.

Introducing structure into evolutionary games thus transforms the problem of cooperating in the prisoner's dilemma from an impossibility (viz., the replicator dynamics) to a near-certainty, *under certain conditions*. If the payoff matrix satisfies the condition that $(T + P)/2 < R$, the radius of interaction is sufficiently large, and an initial cluster of cooperators exists, cooperation can spread. Figures 3.16(a) and (c) show two models in which cooperators expand to dominate almost the entire world.

If we allow the radius used for the interaction and update neighborhoods to vary, then cooperation can expand to dominate the entire world, as shown in figures 3.16(b) and (d). In local-interaction models, Hobbes's pessimistic conclusion regarding the state of nature need not hold. The war of all against all may be stopped without instituting an all-powerful sovereign. The

---

[24] This condition is also sufficient because the boundary defector, having more cooperating neighbors than any interior defectors, earns a higher score than that of any interior defector. This precludes the possibility of the boundary defector being "supported" by higher-scoring interior defectors, as can happen in the case of boundary cooperators.

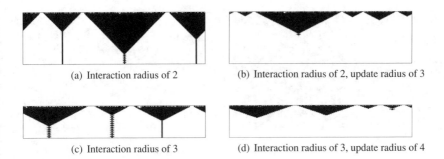

Figure 3.16 Growth of cooperative regions in the one-dimensional prisoner's dilemma: $T = 1.0$, $R = 0.9$, $P = 0.19$, and $S = 0.0$.

self-interested actions of individuals, constrained by the structure of their own interactions, may induce all to cooperate rather than defect.

Moreover, we can give a precise estimate of just how likely it is that cooperation will dominate for a particular payoff matrix. Suppose that the payoff matrix is as follows:

	C	D
C	0.9	0.0
D	1.0	0.1

If $r = 2$, how likely is it that cooperation will dominate? If $r = 2$, cooperation will spread if a cluster of four adjacent cooperators exists, for that gives the interior cooperators scores of 2.7, which exceeds the score of 2.2 earned by boundary defectors. If the two strategies are equally likely, the probability that a group of four adjacent cooperators will appear in the initial state of the population is $\left(\frac{1}{2}\right)^4 = \frac{1}{16}$. By the law of large numbers, as the size of the population increases, the probability that at least one such group will appear converges to unity. This result holds even if the two strategies are *not* equally likely, so long as being a cooperator has positive probability. As the radius of interaction increases, though, it becomes increasingly unlikely that an initial cooperative group of sufficient size will appear – although the limit result still holds.

In the case of two-dimensional lattices, a similar story holds; see Nowak and May (1992, 1993) for details. Cooperative behavior can emerge, although it depends on the original number of cooperators present, as well as on the payoff matrix and neighborhood. Figures 3.17–3.19 illustrate three different evolutionary trajectories depending on the payoff matrix. In figure 3.17, the payoff values are $T = 1.1$, $R = 1$, $P = 0$, and $S = -0.1$. In this case,

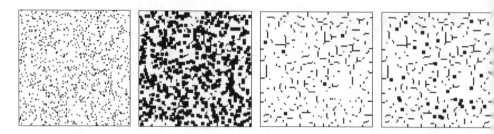

Figure 3.17 A non-war state of nature.

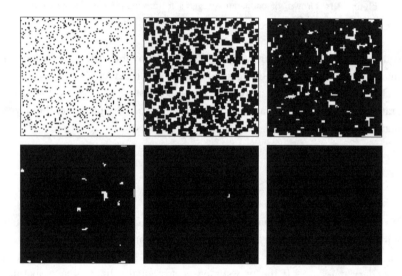

Figure 3.18 The war of all against all.

cooperators and defectors can peacefully coexist. Figure 3.18, using payoff values of $T = 2.7$, $R = 1$, $P = 0$, and $S = -0.1$, shows how "defectors" come to dominate within a relatively short period of time, in agreement with Hobbes's pessimistic assessment of the natural condition of mankind.[25]

Of particular interest is figure 3.19, which uses payoff values of $T = 1.6$, $R = 1$, $P = 0$, and $S = -0.1$. Here, we see a world continually in flux. Cooperative regions can be invaded by regions of defectors, and vice versa. This results in "chaotic" evolutionary behavior, which does not settle down into a

---

[25] Note, though, that these particular payoff values are not a prisoner's dilemma: they violate the requirement that $(T + S)/2 < R$.

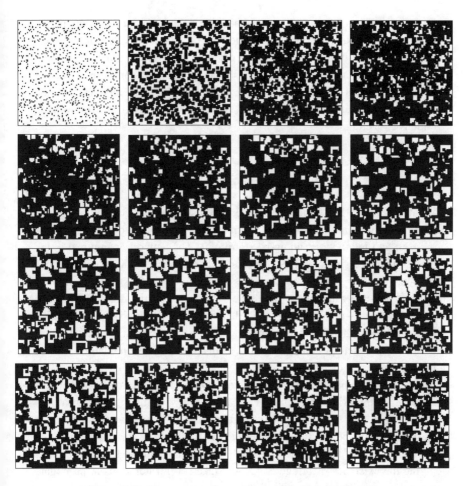

Figure 3.19 Sixteen generations of the spatial prisoner's dilemma.

stable state dominated primarily by cooperators or defectors.[26] Such behavior cannot appear in the one-dimensional case: according to our frontier analysis, if a region of cooperators faces a region of defectors, one of the two regions expands at the expense of the other.

Agent-based lattice models can thus diverge quite far from their replicator-dynamics counterparts. Although the replicator-dynamics model of the

---

[26] This behavior is not chaotic in the traditional sense referred to in nonlinear dynamics. Since there is only a finite number of population states, if the model is run long enough (and no possibility of ties exists), eventually the model must return to a previously encountered state. These models are "chaotic" only in the sense that the period of such a cycle is extremely long (it is not yet known) and there is no apparent pattern to the evolutionary behavior.

prisoner's dilemma suggests that cooperative behavior is unlikely to emerge in the state of nature, the prisoner's dilemma on a lattice reveals that an alternate construal of the dynamics of strategic interaction supports a very different conclusion. The moral of the story is simple. In cases of constrained interaction, if individual payoffs and the topology of the local interactions have the right form, cooperation can flourish in the absence of a central, all-powerful, effective sovereign.

3.3 Small-world networks

What of life off the lattice? Figure 3.20 illustrates four generations of the prisoner's dilemma played on a minimal small-world network using *Imitate the Best* and interaction and update radii of 1. The network is minimal in the sense that only a single bridge edge exists, but that edge, connecting two nodes on opposite sides of the graph, reduces the mean characteristic path length as much as possible with only a single edge. Notice that the introduction of a single bridge edge has – in this case – very little influence. Cooperative regions cannot hold their own when competing against defectors, and within a relatively short period of time defectors dominate, just as in a one-dimensional lattice with an interaction radius of 1.

This makes sense. Regions of the graph far removed from the two vertices incident on the bridge edge have a local topology identical to that of a one-dimensional lattice. The evolutionary trajectories followed by such regions, at least for a short period of time after the model has been initialized, must be identical to that of a one-dimensional lattice. Any anomalous effects introduced by the the existence of bridge edges will take several iterations to propogate through the network before affecting regions far removed from the bridge. Let us call regions whose local interactions are far removed from the influence of bridge edges *provincial* regions.

Although provincial regions evolve according to the same pattern as that followed by a one-dimensional lattice, this shouldn't be taken to mean that small-world networks introduce no new qualitative behavior. Figure 3.21 shows how a single bridge edge allows the survival of two small regions of cooperators that would otherwise be eliminated.[27] Notice, though, that the effect created by the introduction of the bridge edge has relatively little impact beyond that on

---

[27] Removing the bridge edge converts the local topology of the nodes incident on the bridge edge to that of a one-dimensional lattice. The result previously established for one-dimensional lattices with $r = 1$ then applies, and hence the two cooperative regions will be eliminated.

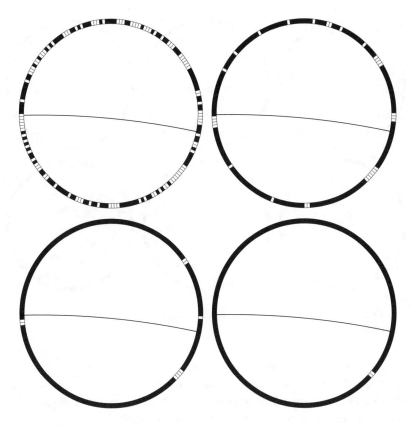

Figure 3.20 The prisoner's dilemma on a minimal small-world network. The next generation is All Defect. The model parameters are $N = 200$, $\beta = 0.003$, $k = 1$, $T = 3.0$, $R = 2.0$, $P = 1.1$, and $S = 0.0$.

the nodes it is incident on: the remainder of the network has rapidly converged to All Defect, just like in the case of the one-dimensional lattice.

This suggests one way to analyze small-world networks. Let us call an agent lying on a bridge edge a *well-connected* agent.[28] Call the immediate region surrounding a well-connected agent a *hub*. If well-connected agents are relatively far apart from each other, the introduction of bridge edges cuts the network into a series of provincial regions – i.e., one-dimensional lattices – connected by hubs. We already know what the evolutionary behavior of the provincial

---

[28] Interpreting the edges in a social network as representative of some social relation, an agent lying on a bridge edge has an extra social relation not shared by his neighbors. Since this social relation spans what would otherwise be a great social distance, the name "well-connected" seems apropos.

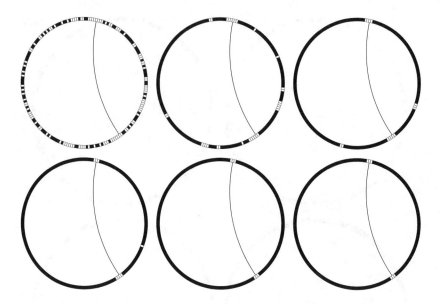

Figure 3.21 A small-world network facilitating the survival of two clusters of cooperators: $N = 200$, $r = 1$, $T = 3.0$, $R = 2.0$, $P = 1.1$, and $S = 0.0$.

regions will be, given the previous results for the prisoner's dilemma on a one-dimensional lattice. Once we understand the evolutionary dynamics around hubs, we can then piece these two together to obtain a complete understanding of the evolutionary dynamics on small-world networks.

In general, the immediate effect of a hub on the evolutionary dynamics will be relatively localized, provided that hubs do not overlap. A well-connected agent will have his score affected due to the extra interaction not shared by his neighbors. As a consequence, a well-connected agent will likely have greater influence over what strategies his neighbors will adopt in future generations. Agents imitate the strategy of their neighbor with the best score, the extra edge increases the probability that a well-connected agent will have the best score, and hence neighboring agents will, in general, imitate the well-connected agent more often than they imitate their other neighbors. In the case illustrated in figure 3.21, the *local* influence of the well-connected agent is profound: the two well-connected agents basically prevent their neighboring cooperators from turning to defection because they earn such a high score. However, once we move away from the hubs into the provincial region of the small-world network, we see the outcome we would expect for that particular payoff matrix and radius in a one-dimensional lattice, namely, defection dominates.

From the point of view of the neighbors of the neighbors of the well-connected agents, the neighbors of the well-connected agents are nothing special; they earn the same score as ordinary agents on a one-dimensional lattice. Consequently the neighbors of the neighbors of well-connected agents evolve according to the rules identified for one-dimensional lattices. This means that the immediate effect of a hub on the evolutionary dynamics when the interaction radius equals 1 ends exactly two spots away from the well-connected agent. With an interaction radius of $r > 1$, the immediate effect of a hub ends as soon as the well-connected agent no longer falls within the neighborhood of an agent, which happens once we move $r + 1$ spots away.

To say that the immediate effect of a hub on the evolutionary dynamics is localized does not mean that hubs cannot *globally* influence the overall outcome of the evolutionary process, though. They can, but they do not always do so. Moreover, the global effect of hubs on the evolutionary dynamics occurs solely through their ability to block the *expansion* of certain regions. To see this, recall that the neighbors of a well-connected agent earn a score equivalent to that of an agent with similar neighbors on a one-dimensional lattice. If, given the particular payoff matrix and radius of interaction, defectors win a frontier competition between cooperators and defectors, a hub cannot reverse this trend. What a hub *can* do, though, is block the expansion of the region of cooperators or defectors. By virtue of having an extra interaction, a well-connected agent may earn a high enough score to prevent his neighbors from switching strategies, *which they would normally do if the well-connected agent had not been present.* If the neighbors of the well-connected agent do not switch strategies, then the expansion of the region encroaching upon the hub is blocked. Since every bridge edge lies on two hubs, this means that an expanding region may be *trapped* between two hubs, and thus prevented from expanding to fill the entire population, as would happen in the case of a one-dimensional lattice. Figure 3.22 illustrates how an expanding region of cooperators can be trapped between two hubs of defectors.

If the payoff matrix and radius of interaction are not of the right form, well-connected agents and hubs may be ineffective at preventing the expansion of certain regions. When agents and hubs are ineffective at preventing expansion, the final convergent state of the network can be very similiar to that of a one-dimensional lattice. Figure 3.23 shows one world in which cooperator expansion continues across hubs without difficulty.

However, even when a well-connected agent is himself ineffective at preventing the expansion of competing regions, the remaining agents belonging to the hub may effectively block expansion. This peculiar effect occurs when the expanding region uses the bridge edge to establish a foothold at another

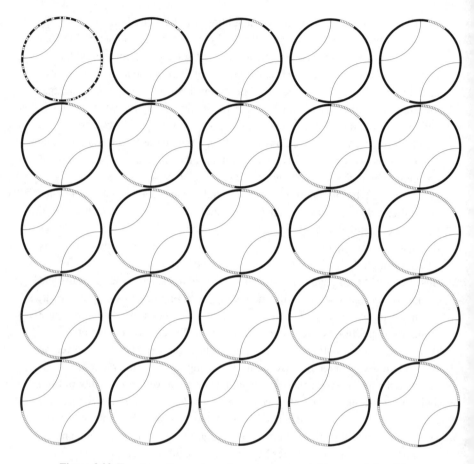

Figure 3.22 Two expanding regions of cooperators trapped between hubs of defectors: $N = 150$, $r = 2$, $T = 1.0$, $R = 0.9$, $P = 0.3$, and $S = 0.0$.

position in the network, and the surrounding members of the hub can exploit the newly introduced strategy. Figure 3.24 shows how expanding cooperative regions, in three instances, successfully take over hubs originally held by defectors. However, in two instances along the northern side of the network, even though cooperators moved in to occupy the key position of the well-connected agent, the remaining defectors in the hub were able to exploit this new cooperator (together with other neighboring cooperators) to protect a small provincial region of defectors that would otherwise have been eliminated.

At this point, we can now characterize the possible convergent states for the prisoner's dilemma played on small-world networks. Each small-world

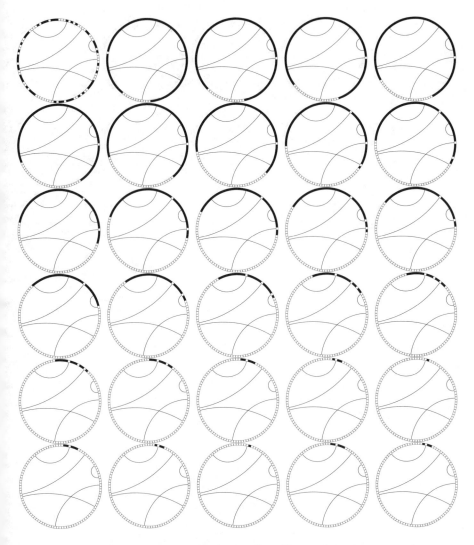

Figure 3.23 Cooperator expansion in a small-world network that is not stopped by well-connected agents or hubs: $N = 101$, $r = 3$, $T = 1.0$, $R = 0.9$, $P = 0.3$, and $S = 0.0$.

network can be decomposed into a set of provincial regions linked by hubs. Each provincial region behaves just like a one-dimensional lattice, and hence will converge under the evolutionary dynamics to one of the possible final states for a one-dimensional lattice. The set of possible final states may include any of All Defect, All Cooperate, and All Cooperate except for few regions of

Figure 3.24 Cooperator expansion in a small-world network that is not stopped by well-connected agents, yet is blocked by hubs: $N = 100, r = 2, T = 1.0, R = 0.9$, $P = 0.3$, and $S = 0.0$.

locally stable defectors.[29] However, the actual set of final states is determined by the payoff matrix and radius of interaction.

---

[29] Recall that one-dimensional lattices states in which almost all agents cooperated still may have had stable pairs of defectors or groups of defectors that would undergo a brief period of expansion followed by collapse.

Given a particular payoff matrix and radius of interaction, the set of possible final states is thus fixed. Whether a particular provincial region evolves to a particular final state depends upon two things: whether hubs are effective at blocking the expansion of regions[30] and what the initial distribution of strategies was in the provincial region. If hubs are effective at blocking the expansion of regions,[31] then the final state followed by a provincial region is determined by its initial distribution of strategies. If hubs are not effective at blocking expansions, the final state of a provincial region depends on its initial distribution of strategies and the initial distribution of strategies of its neighboring provincial regions. If an expanding region (of cooperators or defectors) forms in one of the neighboring provincial regions, and hubs are ineffective at blocking, then that expanding group of cooperators or defectors will spread to neighboring provincial regions.

Figure 3.25 displays the final convergent states for four small-world networks. Inspection shows that all four convergent states conform to the pattern identified. In the first and second models, one may note the existence of groups of defectors in the midst of a region of cooperators, away from any hub. These groups of defectors are stable and form a "blinker" of the type we've seen before. Similar stable groups of defectors can be found in regions of cooperation in one-dimensional lattices.

3.4 Bounded-degree networks

In terms of their effect on the emergence of cooperation, small-world networks provide more of a hindrance than a help. Although small groups of cooperators can survive under conditions that would eliminate them in a one-dimensional lattice (recall figure 3.21), small-world networks can also *prevent* the spread of cooperation via the blocking effect of hubs. Networks with a complicated and irregular structure appear hostile to the emergence of cooperation.

Turning towards networks of bounded degree, this conjecture gains support, as figure 3.26 illustrates. Here, over two thirds of the population originally cooperate, yet within two generations all have switched to defection. The situation portrayed in figure 3.27 is even worse: a single defector manages to overturn a population of cooperators within four generations. Even so, cooperative groups can persist: figure 3.28 shows one population in which eight cooperators remain among twenty-two defectors.

---

[30] Again, this depends on the payoff matrix and radius of interaction.
[31] Either through the scores earned by well-connected agents or by efforts of the rest of the hub, as in figure 3.24.

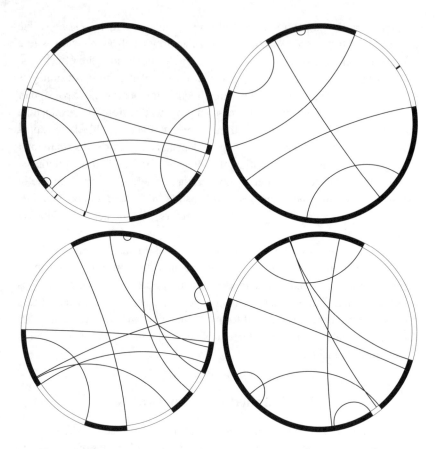

Figure 3.25 Final convergent states of four small-world networks: $N = 1000$, $r = 2$, $\beta = 0.004$, $T = 1.0$, $R = 0.9$, $P = 0.3$, and $S = 0.0$.

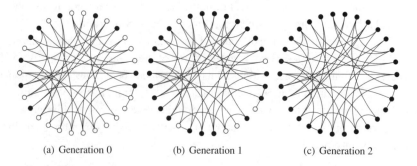

Figure 3.26 Three generations in a bounded-degree network: $N = 30$, $k_{\min} = 1$, $k_{\max} = 3$, and $T = 3$, $R = 2$, $P = 1$, and $S = 0$.

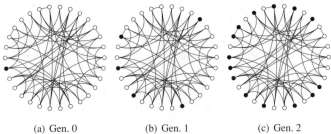

(a) Gen. 0   (b) Gen. 1   (c) Gen. 2

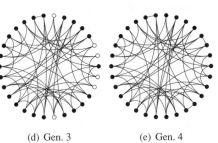

(d) Gen. 3   (e) Gen. 4

Figure 3.27 Four generations in a bounded-degree network: $N = 30$, $k_{min} = 2$, $k_{max} = 4$, and $T = 3$, $R = 2$, $P = 1$, and $S = 0$.

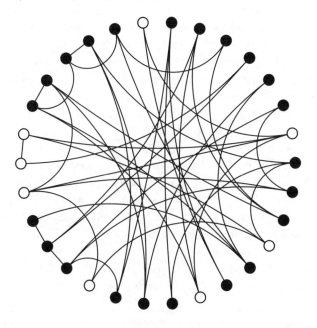

Figure 3.28 A persistent cooperative group in a network of bounded degree, $k_{min} = 2$, $k_{max} = 4$, $T = 1.0$, $R = 0.666$, $P = 0.333$, and $S = 0.0$.

The persistence of cooperation in the network of figure 3.28 can be explained in terms of the network's structure and how cooperators exploit that structure to their benefit. Notice that the maximum number of neighbors for agents in this network is four, and that a single cooperator (located at approximately 3 o'clock) is connected to four other cooperators and no defectors. As a result of these fortuitous connections, this cooperator earns a high enough score to prevent his cooperative neighbors from switching to defection. This provides a base of five cooperators in the population, upon which the persistence of the remaining three cooperators depends.

The cooperative group of figure 3.28 persists, but is dynamically unstable: if the key cooperator located at 3 o'clock is replaced by a defector, the entire cooperative group unravels. Replacing the key cooperator with a defector creates a defector with four cooperating neighbors. In a network where four is the maximum number of neighbors, a defector with four cooperating neighbors earns the highest possible score – one not achievable by any cooperator. Hence, in the next generation, the four neighboring cooperators will switch to defection. One can check that within the next two generations the remaining three cooperators will have switched to defection.

Can cooperative groups form in the prisoner's dilemma played on a network of bounded degree? Strictly speaking, we have already considered this question in previous sections: lattice models and small-world networks are both instances of networks of bounded degree. In the case of lattice models, $k_{min} = k_{max} =$ the number of neighbors. In the case of small-world networks with an interaction radius r, $k_{min} = 2r$ and $k_{max} = 2r + 1$ (assuming that no individual can be on more than one shortcut). Since expansive cooperative groups can form both in lattice models and in small-world networks, they can form in networks of bounded degree.

Nonetheless, both lattice models and small-world networks exhibit a regularity in their wiring patterns that is absent from general networks of bounded degree. The formation and expansion of cooperative groups in the previous two cases depended crucially on their structural regularities. Thus, even if it is *possible* for cooperative groups to form in bounded-degree networks, that doesn't mean that they are *likely* to form.

Table 3.1 shows the results from over one million models, grouped by population size.[32] As the average degree increases, the frequency with which the population goes to a state of All Defect increases as well. The relatively low

---

[32] For each model, an initial probability p was selected and individuals were assigned the strategy Cooperate with probability p (and Defect with probability $1 - p$). The allocation of neighbors was done as follows. For the indicated values of k_{min} and k_{max}, each agent was assigned a degree d with $k_{min} \le d \le k_{max}$ (all values in that range being equally likely). Once each agent had been assigned a degree, the network was randomly wired to satisfy those constraints.

Table 3.1. *Numbers of runs out of 10 000 that converge to All Defect for the indicated k_{min} and k_{max} ($T = 1.0$, $R = 0.666$, $P = 0.333$, and $S = 0.0$)*

| | k_{min} | \multicolumn{9}{c}{k_{max}} | | | | | | | | |
		2	3	4	5	6	7	8	9	10
	1	5185	7111	8062	8433	8686	8752	8720	8760	8692
	2	–	8410	8688	8812	8884	8871	8893	8884	8853
	3	–	–	9244	9192	9112	9093	9007	8963	8954
	4	–	–	–	9370	9354	9215	9199	9169	9114
$N = 15$	5	–	–	–	–	9363	9371	9312	9279	9197
	6	–	–	–	–	–	9369	9350	9329	9339
	7	–	–	–	–	–	–	9346	9396	9345
	8	–	–	–	–	–	–	–	9365	9409
	9	–	–	–	–	–	–	–	–	9420
	1	4091	6003	7438	8455	8937	9199	9227	9262	9287
	2	–	7781	8557	8907	9253	9324	9361	9333	9368
	3	–	–	9442	9423	9496	9484	9475	9412	9448
	4	–	–	–	9627	9660	9581	9545	9502	9492
$N = 30$	5	–	–	–	–	9683	9667	9637	9601	9558
	6	–	–	–	–	–	9693	9686	9688	9642
	7	–	–	–	–	–	–	9673	9668	9671
	8	–	–	–	–	–	–	–	9660	9689
	9	–	–	–	–	–	–	–	–	9689
	1	3076	4858	6441	7798	8790	9228	9482	9520	9621
	2	–	6850	8113	8689	9270	9446	9587	9598	9664
	3	–	–	9412	9319	9547	9617	9646	9702	9708
	4	–	–	–	9760	9788	9777	9781	9751	9745
$N = 60$	5	–	–	–	–	9828	9826	9796	9793	9779
	6	–	–	–	–	–	9851	9836	9831	9835
	7	–	–	–	–	–	–	9806	9827	9831
	8	–	–	–	–	–	–	–	9842	9817
	9	–	–	–	–	–	–	–	–	9858

rate of occurrence of All Defect in networks with $k_{min} = 1$ and $k_{max} = 2$ or 3 occurs because networks in this range are often unconnected and this obviously reduces the extent to which defection can spread. A network consisting of several unconnected components rarely converges to All Defect because, as long as one component initially consists only of cooperators, that component will remain cooperative even if the rest of the network switches to defection. Figure 3.29 displays the initial and final states for one such network, together with their connected components.

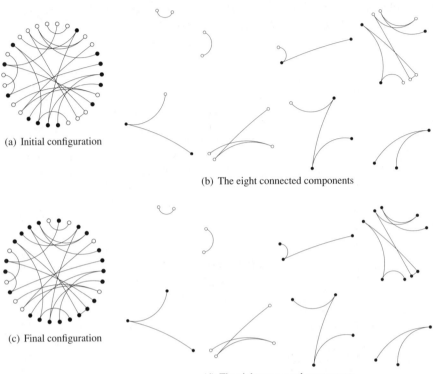

(a) Initial configuration

(b) The eight connected components

(c) Final configuration

(d) The eight connected components

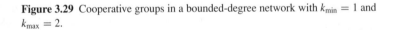

Figure 3.29 Cooperative groups in a bounded-degree network with $k_{min} = 1$ and $k_{max} = 2$.

As k_{min} and k_{max} increase, the probability that a randomly chosen network satisfying those constraints is connected increases as well.[33] Moreover, the evolutionary outcome of the network rapidly converges to that of the prisoner's dilemma played on a completely connected network, namely, All Defect. To see this, suppose that we have a completely connected network consisting of C cooperators and D defectors. Each cooperator is connected to $C - 1$ cooperators and D defectors, and each defector is connected to $D - 1$ defectors and C cooperators. Each cooperator receives a score of $(C - 1) \cdot R + D \cdot S$ and each defector receives a score of $C \cdot T + (D - 1) \cdot P$. Since $(C - 1) \cdot R + D \cdot S < C \cdot T + (D - 1) \cdot P$, each cooperator will switch to defection for the next round.

---

[33] The transition occurs relatively quickly. With $k_{min} = 1$ and $k_{max} = 3$, only about 27.5 percent of the networks are connected. Yet nearly 80 percent of the networks are connected when $k_{min} = 1$ and $k_{max} = 4$, and once $k_{max} = 5$ over 93 percent of the networks are connected.

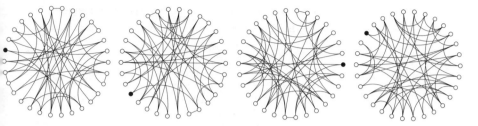

Figure 3.30 Four fixed states in which a single defector exists: $N = 30$, $k_{min} = 2$, $k_{max} = 4$, $T = 1.0$, $R = 0.66$, $P = 0.33$, and $S = 0.0$.

Recall that, both for lattice models and for small-world networks, variations in the payoff matrix made a difference in terms of the likelihood of cooperation emerging. Table 3.2 shows that a similar phenomenon occurs for networks of bounded degree, albeit to a more limited extent. Whereas variations in the payoff matrix for lattice models and small-world networks increased the chance that cooperation would dominate, the irregular, random structure of bounded-degree networks mitigates the evolutionary advantage conferred on cooperators by changes in the payoff matrix. Variations in the payoff matrix *do* affect the frequency with which universal cooperation evolves, but not nearly to the extent found in previous cases.

Universal cooperation does not easily evolve in bounded-degree networks because it is easy for a single defector to be positioned such that he will not be eliminated while, at the same time, not spreading his strategy to his neighbors. Figure 3.30 illustrates four fixed states in which this happens. It is easy to specify conditions under which isolated defectors will not spread. To see this, suppose that D is a defector having the minimum number of neighbors – i.e., two. D then receives a score of $2T$. D's cooperating neighbors earn the maximum possible score when they have the maximum number of neighbors, which is in this case four. When this happens, each cooperating neighbor receives a score of $3 \cdot R + 1 \cdot S = 3R$ (since $S = 0$). As long as $T > \frac{3}{2}R$, D will not switch strategies because he will have earned a higher score than those of his neighbors. The payoff matrix used in figure 3.32 satisfies this condition, so the isolated defector will not be replaced.

Although *isolated* defectors will not be replaced under these conditions, two neighboring defectors who satisfy these conditions will be. If both defectors have only two neighbors, and each defector has the other as a neighbor, both defectors can be replaced. When two defectors neighbor each other, each receives a score of $T + P$. If each defector has as neighbor a cooperator with

Table 3.2. *Numbers of models out of 10 000 that converge to all cooperate*

		k_{max}								
k_{min}	2	3	4	5	6	7	8	9	10
1	312	381	410	441	557	511	582	620	635
2	–	336	313	436	449	477	496	560	572
3	–	–	305	304	374	396	432	514	482
4	–	–	–	353	318	328	374	456	464
5	–	–	–	–	317	325	307	378	401
6	–	–	–	–	–	306	314	309	321
7	–	–	–	–	–	–	327	331	329
8	–	–	–	–	–	–	–	340	311
9	–	–	–	–	–	–	–	–	311

$T = 1.0$
$R = 0.666$
$P = 0.333$
$S = 0.0$

k_{min}	2	3	4	5	6	7	8	9	10
1	338	360	526	695	863	1043	1138	1269	1263
2	–	330	419	599	731	932	959	1088	1239
3	–	–	320	459	574	740	852	1034	1069
4	–	–	–	337	496	648	738	866	997
5	–	–	–	–	334	534	686	749	887
6	–	–	–	–	–	320	464	631	744
7	–	–	–	–	–	–	297	462	643
8	–	–	–	–	–	–	–	313	446
9	–	–	–	–	–	–	–	–	306

$T = 1.0$
$R = 0.9$
$P = 0.3$
$S = 0.0$

k_{min}	2	3	4	5	6	7	8	9	10
1	318	395	492	787	1053	1246	1295	1459	1453
2	–	302	424	618	830	1106	1158	1246	1338
3	–	–	343	494	724	826	998	1090	1170
4	–	–	–	304	556	711	869	934	1047
5	–	–	–	–	378	563	719	821	930
6	–	–	–	–	–	355	583	706	755
7	–	–	–	–	–	–	321	495	650
8	–	–	–	–	–	–	–	292	492
9	–	–	–	–	–	–	–	–	348

$T = 1.0$
$R = 0.9$
$P = 0.225$
$S = 0.0$

k_{min}	2	3	4	5	6	7	8	9	10
1	335	404	517	861	1226	1402	1588	1506	1667
2	–	328	453	651	945	1149	1333	1400	1484
3	–	–	316	487	756	991	1174	1210	1272
4	–	–	–	354	606	811	982	1096	1157
5	–	–	–	–	383	627	798	900	998
6	–	–	–	–	–	364	592	810	829
7	–	–	–	–	–	–	345	577	676
8	–	–	–	–	–	–	–	338	528
9	–	–	–	–	–	–	–	–	331

$T = 1.0$
$R = 0.9$
$P = 0.18$
$S = 0.0$

four neighbors (three of whom cooperate), then each defector will have one neighbor who earns a score of $3R + S = 3R$. Since it is impossible to have a prisoner's dilemma with positive payoffs such that $T + P \geq 3R$, each defector will thus switch to cooperation in the next generation.

The difficulty of eliminating defectors from the population suggests that measuring the tendency for cooperation to emerge by looking at the number of models that converge to All Cooperate misleads by imposing too stringent a requirement. If so, then we need to find an alternative measure. One worth considering looks at the proportion of models in which the total number of cooperators *increases* on going from the initial state to the final state. If we adopt this measure, we find that variations in the payoff matrix can have a notable effect on the emergence of cooperation, as shown in table 3.3.

At the end of the day, though, it does seem that what one should concentrate on is the *total* number of cooperators present when the model arrives at a fixed state. If we view the prisoner's dilemma as a model of the decision problem encountered by people in the natural condition of mankind, we, like Hobbes, are not interested in knowing whether the number of people who lie low has a slight tendency to increase. Rather, the important question concerns the overall disposition of the population. Are people, in the absence of an absolute, centralized, effective, coercive authority more likely to anticipate than to lie low? This question concerns the *total number* of people in the population who follow a particular strategy.

Table 3.4 shows the frequencies with which a randomly initialized population evolves to a state in which at least half of the population cooperates. Although the exact frequency varies as a function of k_{min}, k_{max}, and the particular payoff matrix, note that for certain values of these parameters over 40 percent of the time we arrive at a state in which over half of the population cooperates. It is also not uncommon to arrive at a state in which over half cooperate more than 30 percent of the time. Cooperation can emerge, albeit with difficulty, in bounded-degree networks.

Thus we see that the state of nature, even in a randomly structured environment, need not collapse into a war of all against all. This result is interesting when contrasted with the analysis of the state of nature provided by the replicator dynamics. In a random-mixing environment in which all pairwise interactions are equally likely, universal defection dominates. In a structured environment in which all pairwise interactions are not equally likely – but otherwise determined at random – cooperation can emerge and sometimes dominates. The structure of rational interaction, even when *randomly structured*, can make a difference.

Table 3.3. *Numbers of models out of 10 000 in which the total number of cooperators increases between the initial and final states*

					k_{max}					
	k_{min}	2	3	4	5	6	7	8	9	10
	1	0	110	140	191	240	240	282	326	345
	2	–	0	3	111	159	169	239	266	254
	3	–	–	0	2	79	81	151	205	198
$T = 1.0$	4	–	–	–	0	0	3	63	117	134
$R = 0.666$	5	–	–	–	–	0	0	1	59	74
$P = 0.333$	6	–	–	–	–	–	0	0	0	1
$S = 0.0$	7	–	–	–	–	–	–	0	0	0
	8	–	–	–	–	–	–	–	0	0
	9	–	–	–	–	–	–	–	–	0
	1	0	230	717	1077	1292	1402	1374	1323	1288
	2	–	84	532	850	1035	1207	1164	1189	1241
	3	–	–	274	561	726	944	986	1074	1051
$T = 1.0$	4	–	–	–	204	488	730	833	849	907
$R = 0.9$	5	–	–	–	–	111	479	600	698	790
$P = 0.3$	6	–	–	–	–	–	120	302	483	607
$S = 0.0$	7	–	–	–	–	–	–	53	272	468
	8	–	–	–	–	–	–	–	35	221
	9	–	–	–	–	–	–	–	–	34
	1	0	246	951	1781	1954	1887	1727	1668	1603
	2	–	90	853	1680	1663	1676	1556	1520	1455
	3	–	–	728	1401	1396	1271	1308	1302	1302
$T = 1.0$	4	–	–	–	1156	1022	1011	1081	1102	1169
$R = 0.9$	5	–	–	–	–	585	683	842	897	990
$P = 0.225$	6	–	–	–	–	–	247	557	654	784
$S = 0.0$	7	–	–	–	–	–	–	125	379	538
	8	–	–	–	–	–	–	–	97	336
	9	–	–	–	–	–	–	–	–	79
	1	0	239	939	2168	2431	2267	1986	1811	1820
	2	–	91	888	2055	2188	1955	1865	1731	1640
	3	–	–	727	1931	1979	1848	1669	1515	1461
$T = 1.0$	4	–	–	–	1616	1684	1561	1430	1373	1367
$R = 0.9$	5	–	–	–	–	1368	1140	1139	1110	1155
$P = 0.18$	6	–	–	–	–	–	709	746	926	885
$S = 0.0$	7	–	–	–	–	–	–	269	522	615
	8	–	–	–	–	–	–	–	215	373
	9	–	–	–	–	–	–	–	–	122

Table 3.4. *Numbers of models out of 10 000 that converge to a final state in which at least half of the population cooperates*

	k_{min}	k_{max}								
		2	3	4	5	6	7	8	9	10
	1	1891	1113	958	758	737	643	699	710	699
	2	–	640	637	661	573	588	598	639	625
$T = 1.0$	3	–	–	351	399	428	461	505	574	543
$R = 0.666$	4	–	–	–	353	319	398	446	496	505
$P = 0.333$	5	–	–	–	–	317	327	360	398	440
$S = 0.0$	6	–	–	–	–	–	306	314	310	358
	7	–	–	–	–	–	–	327	331	329
	8	–	–	–	–	–	–	–	340	311
	9	–	–	–	–	–	–	–	–	311
	1	2384	2522	2752	2887	2741	2493	2314	2172	1948
	2	–	2461	2704	2752	2588	2406	2111	1987	1925
$T = 1.0$	3	–	–	2717	2586	2350	2232	2035	1951	1800
$R = 0.9$	4	–	–	–	2337	2127	2030	1911	1770	1689
$P = 0.3$	5	–	–	–	–	1750	1746	1632	1658	1579
$S = 0.0$	6	–	–	–	–	–	1393	1337	1424	1415
	7	–	–	–	–	–	–	999	1117	1210
	8	–	–	–	–	–	–	–	849	900
	9	–	–	–	–	–	–	–	–	694
	1	2292	2535	3056	3396	3332	3038	2633	2461	2255
	2	–	2528	3196	3446	3218	2926	2628	2389	2240
$T = 1.0$	3	–	–	3372	3476	3030	2587	2410	2210	2072
$R = 0.9$	4	–	–	–	3378	2856	2497	2207	2079	1979
$P = 0.225$	5	–	–	–	–	2657	2237	1905	1916	1852
$S = 0.0$	6	–	–	–	–	–	1853	1629	1717	1644
	7	–	–	–	–	–	–	1114	1410	1446
	8	–	–	–	–	–	–	–	1068	1239
	9	–	–	–	–	–	–	–	–	929
	1	2344	2515	3024	3754	3633	3365	2973	2588	2545
	2	–	2568	3236	3945	3640	3313	3021	2627	2432
$T = 1.0$	3	–	–	3420	4060	3597	3261	2824	2437	2343
$R = 0.9$	4	–	–	–	4029	3435	3037	2648	2364	2185
$P = 0.18$	5	–	–	–	–	3354	2811	2403	2110	1999
$S = 0.0$	6	–	–	–	–	–	2526	2131	1957	1750
	7	–	–	–	–	–	–	1764	1575	1566
	8	–	–	–	–	–	–	–	1176	1333
	9	–	–	–	–	–	–	–	–	1016

3.5 Dynamic networks

Social networks clearly influence the state that a population of boundedly rational agents playing the prisoner's dilemma may evolve to. As we have seen, if groups of cooperators can form, it is even possible for cooperative behavior to dominate in the population. Yet is it plausible to think that groups of cooperators may form in an initially unstructured population?

Recall Skyrms and Pemantle's model of social-network formation. Figure 3.31 shows the first five generations of a dynamic social network consisting of seven individuals. In this model, each person chooses another individual to visit according to the interaction probabilities specified in the matrix; at the beginning, all interactions are equally likely (except for self-interactions, which have probability zero).[34] When i visits j, they play one round of the prisoner's dilemma, using the indicated payoff matrix. Unlike in the previous models in which each person received a payoff from participating in the game, here only the person who *initiated* the visit receives a payoff.[35]

After the first few generations, a pattern appears. Cooperators begin to prefer to visit cooperators and to avoid visiting defectors. Given the payoff matrix and the dynamics of network formation, this preferential association is to be expected: when cooperators visit defectors, that interaction is not reinforced because the sucker's payoff S equals zero. When a cooperator visits a cooperator, he receives the reward R for cooperating, which increases the probability that he will visit that cooperator in the future. In the limit, cooperators will solely associate with cooperators and avoid defectors.

In addition, notice that defectors, on the other hand, begin to prefer to visit cooperators and to avoid visiting defectors. This outcome is somewhat surprising because when a defector visits a defector he receives a nonzero payoff, unlike the case when a cooperator visits a defector. Nevertheless, defectors still learn to prefer visiting cooperators because the payoff they receive is higher than that received from visiting defectors. These patterns of preferential association are formed relatively quickly: after five generations the preference of cooperators for cooperators and of defectors for cooperators is clearly visible. Figure 3.32 illustrates the pattern of preferences that has formed after 1000 generations. At this point, the preference patterns are relatively fixed.

---

[34] The probability in row i, column j is the probability of i visiting j on any given day. Each row and column is considered to be numbered from 0 to $N - 1$, where N is the size of the population.

[35] This model implements the network-formation dynamics of Skyrms and Pemantle (2000).

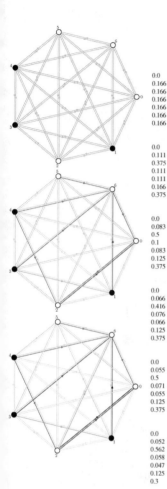

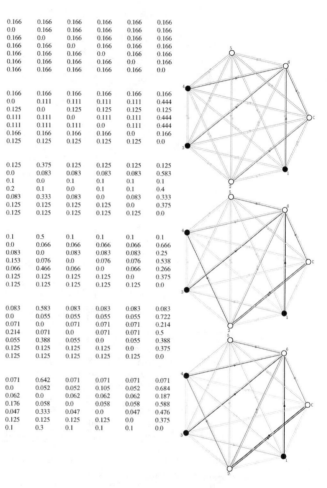

```
0.0     0.166   0.166   0.166   0.166   0.166   0.166
0.166   0.0     0.166   0.166   0.166   0.166   0.166
0.166   0.166   0.0     0.166   0.166   0.166   0.166
0.166   0.166   0.166   0.0     0.166   0.166   0.166
0.166   0.166   0.166   0.166   0.0     0.166   0.166
0.166   0.166   0.166   0.166   0.166   0.0     0.166
0.166   0.166   0.166   0.166   0.166   0.166   0.0


0.0     0.166   0.166   0.166   0.166   0.166   0.166
0.111   0.0     0.111   0.111   0.111   0.111   0.444
0.375   0.125   0.0     0.125   0.125   0.125   0.125
0.111   0.111   0.111   0.0     0.111   0.111   0.444
0.111   0.111   0.111   0.111   0.0     0.111   0.444
0.166   0.166   0.166   0.166   0.166   0.0     0.166
0.375   0.125   0.125   0.125   0.125   0.125   0.0


0.0     0.125   0.375   0.125   0.125   0.125   0.125
0.083   0.0     0.083   0.083   0.083   0.083   0.583
0.5     0.1     0.0     0.1     0.1     0.1     0.1
0.1     0.2     0.1     0.0     0.1     0.1     0.4
0.083   0.083   0.333   0.083   0.0     0.083   0.333
0.125   0.125   0.125   0.125   0.125   0.0     0.375
0.375   0.125   0.125   0.125   0.125   0.125   0.0


0.0     0.1     0.5     0.1     0.1     0.1     0.1
0.066   0.0     0.066   0.066   0.066   0.066   0.666
0.416   0.083   0.0     0.083   0.083   0.083   0.25
0.076   0.153   0.076   0.0     0.076   0.076   0.538
0.066   0.066   0.466   0.066   0.0     0.066   0.266
0.125   0.125   0.125   0.125   0.125   0.0     0.375
0.375   0.125   0.125   0.125   0.125   0.125   0.0


0.0     0.083   0.583   0.083   0.083   0.083   0.083
0.055   0.0     0.055   0.055   0.055   0.055   0.722
0.5     0.071   0.0     0.071   0.071   0.071   0.214
0.071   0.214   0.071   0.0     0.071   0.071   0.5
0.055   0.055   0.388   0.055   0.0     0.055   0.388
0.125   0.125   0.125   0.125   0.125   0.0     0.375
0.375   0.125   0.125   0.125   0.125   0.125   0.0


0.0     0.071   0.642   0.071   0.071   0.071   0.071
0.052   0.0     0.052   0.052   0.052   0.105   0.684
0.562   0.062   0.0     0.062   0.062   0.062   0.187
0.058   0.176   0.058   0.0     0.058   0.058   0.588
0.047   0.047   0.333   0.047   0.0     0.047   0.476
0.125   0.125   0.125   0.125   0.125   0.0     0.375
0.3     0.1     0.3     0.1     0.1     0.1     0.0
```

Figure 3.31 Six generations of a dynamic network. Successive generations are listed from top to bottom, with the graphical representation of the interaction probabilities displayed on alternating sides to conserve space: $T = 3$, $R = 2$, $P = 1$, and $S = 0$.

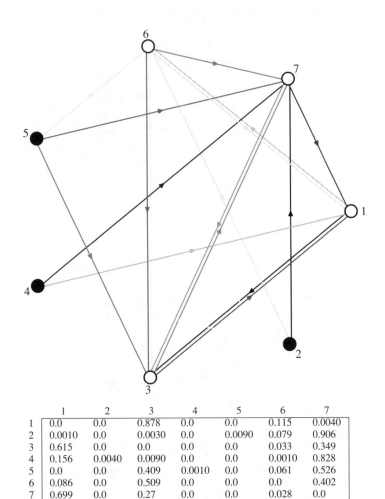

	1	2	3	4	5	6	7
1	0.0	0.0	0.878	0.0	0.0	0.115	0.0040
2	0.0010	0.0	0.0030	0.0	0.0090	0.079	0.906
3	0.615	0.0	0.0	0.0	0.0	0.033	0.349
4	0.156	0.0040	0.0090	0.0	0.0	0.0010	0.828
5	0.0	0.0	0.409	0.0010	0.0	0.061	0.526
6	0.086	0.0	0.509	0.0	0.0	0.0	0.402
7	0.699	0.0	0.27	0.0	0.0	0.028	0.0

Figure 3.32 Interaction probabilities for the dynamic social network of figure 3.31 after 1000 interactions (with no strategic dynamics): $T = 3$, $R = 2$, $P = 1$, and $S = 0$.

After 1000 generations, the probability that a cooperator will interact with a defector has nearly vanished.[36] Is this convergence merely an artifact of the payoff matrix? The preference pattern formed by defectors suggests not, but

---

[36] The interaction probabilities listed in figure 3.32 have been rounded to five significant figures. A nonzero probability of each node interacting with every other node (except itself) still remains. Although the interaction probabilities may converge to zero in the limit, it is not possible, given the dynamics of the model, for the interaction probabilities to reach zero in finite time.

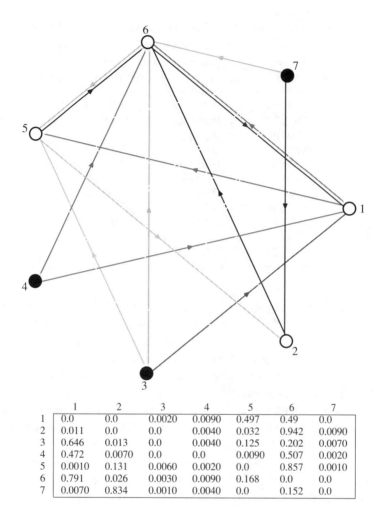

	1	2	3	4	5	6	7
1	0.0	0.0	0.0020	0.0090	0.497	0.49	0.0
2	0.011	0.0	0.0	0.0040	0.032	0.942	0.0090
3	0.646	0.013	0.0	0.0040	0.125	0.202	0.0070
4	0.472	0.0070	0.0	0.0	0.0090	0.507	0.0020
5	0.0010	0.131	0.0060	0.0020	0.0	0.857	0.0010
6	0.791	0.026	0.0030	0.0090	0.168	0.0	0.0
7	0.0070	0.834	0.0010	0.0040	0.0	0.152	0.0

Figure 3.33 Interaction probabilities for a dynamic social network after 1000 interactions (with no strategic dynamics): $T = 4$, $R = 3$, $P = 2$, and $S = 1$.

we can check this by choosing a payoff matrix that assigns a nonzero value to the sucker's payoff. Figure 3.33 shows that raising the sucker's payoff to a nonzero amount by shifting all payoffs up one unit makes very little difference. Even with the elevated payoff matrix, the greatest probability of a cooperator visiting a defector is only 0.9 percent after 1000 generations.

Table 3.5 lists the typical conditional interaction probabilities resulting after 50 000 generations for the prisoner's dilemma with payoff matrix $T = 1.0$, $R = 0.66$, $P = 0.33$, and $S = 0.0$. Let $\Pr(\sim C|C)$ denote the probability of

Table 3.5. *Mean conditional interaction probabilities after 50 000 generations
with just one interaction per agent, per round, allowed*

	$\Pr(\sim C\|C)$	$\Pr(\sim D\|C)$	$\Pr(\sim C\|D)$	$\Pr(\sim D\|D)$
$N = 3$	0.501 5	0.388	0.768 11	0.111 01
$N = 4$	0.672 3	0.251 75	0.864 82	0.075 93
$N = 5$	0.804 08	0.166	0.937 52	0.029 88
$N = 6$	0.885 89	0.095	0.965 95	0.019 06
$N = 7$	0.935 64	0.058 76	0.984 75	0.004 91
$N = 8$	0.965 46	0.028 83	0.988 99	0.004 37
$N = 9$	0.987 18	0.011	0.995 68	0.000 36
$N = 10$	0.986 96	0.010 99	0.994 48	0.000 25
$N = 11$	0.992 71	0.004	0.995 23	0.001 18
$N = 12$	0.993 43	0.003 96	0.995 81	0.000 3
$N = 13$	0.996 21	0.001	0.995 7	0.000 14

a cooperator interacting with a cooperator[37] and let $\Pr(\sim D|C)$ denote the
probability of a cooperator interacting with a defector. The remaining two
columns denote similar values for defectors. Each conditional probability listed
was obtained by averaging the results of 1000 models. Although we know that
cooperators will always, in the limit, associate only with cooperators, a similar
result appears to hold for defectors.

The structural dynamics considered thus far assumes that people do not
change strategy over time. Allowing individuals to change strategies creates a
separate layer of strategic dynamics running alongside of the structural dynamics. When strategic dynamics are included, each agent has a certain probability
p of updating his strategy after a round of visits. If an agent chooses to update his strategy, he selects one (or more) individuals at random according to
his interaction probabilities, and then uses those people as his neighbors for
imitate-the-best dynamics.

The fact that both defectors and cooperators always develop preferences for
associating solely with cooperators, as well as tending to form clusters, becomes
important when strategic dynamics are included. Assuming that cooperators and
defectors tend to aggregate into clusters, the interaction probabilities converge
to zero and unity as suggested in table 3.5, more than one interaction is allowed,
and one other modest condition (stated below), it seems that *cooperation will*

---

[37] This notation is slightly unusual, admittedly; "$\Pr(\sim C|C)$" should be read as "the probability of
interacting with a cooperator, given that I cooperate." The notation "$\sim C$" is meant to denote
interacting with a cooperator.

always dominate in the limit as the probability of an agent updating his strategy shrinks to zero. If more than one interaction is not allowed, the theorem does not hold.

The modest condition concerns the size of the clusters which form. If the payoff matrix for the prisoner's dilemma is T, R, P, and S, cooperation always dominates when the cluster size exceeds T/R. If the cluster size does not exceed this value, than cooperation cannot dominate.

The argument is short and intuitive. As the frequency of strategic updating shrinks to zero, so does the chance that the first strategic update occurs before the structural dynamics lock individuals into clusters of cooperator–cooperator and defector–cooperator pairings. Once these clusters have formed, cooperators are essentially prevented from switching to defection. In order for a cooperator to become a defector, the cooperator would need to include a defector in the set of people from among whom he selects which one to imitate. Since the probability of a cooperator interacting with a defector is virtually zero, it is extremely unlikely that this will happen.

Similarly, the clusters effectively encourage defectors to become cooperators. When a defector decides to update his strategy, he examines several randomly selected individuals to see whether they did better than he himself did and, if so, he adopts a new strategy according to the imitate-the-best rule. However, each defector's interaction probabilities make it highly likely that only cooperators are included in the set of people he examines. Thus, if a defector switches strategies at all, he will switch to become a cooperator.

Given that clusters form, there is a nonzero probability that each defector will switch to Cooperate when multiple interactions are allowed. If one of the cooperators the defector observes interacts with every cooperator in his cluster, that cooperator earns a score of $C \cdot R$ where C denotes the size of the cluster. If the defector interacts only with one cooperator, he earns a score of T. Since $C \cdot R > T$, that defector's score is strictly less than that of one of the cooperators he observes, so the defector will become a cooperator. In the long run, the chance of this situation occurring for each defector occurs with probability unity.

Lastly, note that, when only one interaction is allowed, cooperation will not dominate in the limit. Once the structural dynamics has essentially driven the cooperator–cooperator and defector–cooperator interaction probabilities to fixation, the chance that a defector will earn a score lower than that of any cooperator is virtually zero. Defectors interact only with cooperators, receiving that maximal payoff T, and cooperators interact only with cooperators, receiving the second-highest payoff R. Even when a defector chooses to update his strategy, he will find that he earned the higher score and will not switch.

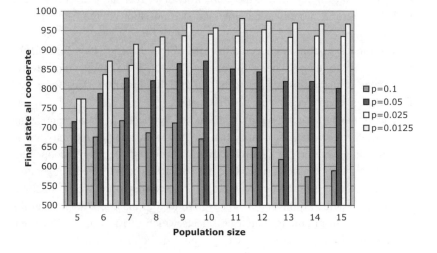

Figure 3.34 Numbers of models out of 1000 that converge to All Cooperate under the coevolution of structure and strategy when multiple interactions are allowed.

Figure 3.34 charts the convergence behavior for the prisoner's dilemma played on a dynamic network with both structural and strategic dynamics. The probability p that an individual will update his strategy at the end of the current generation was assigned one of four possible values: 0.1, 0.05, 0.025, and 0.0125. One can see how, as p approaches zero, the probability of the world arriving at a state of universal cooperation sharply increases. For $p = 0.0125$, universal cooperation occured over 95 percent of the time.

Hobbes's pessimistic conclusion regarding the natural condition of mankind need not hold – even if the strategic problem faced by people in the state of nature has the form of the prisoner's dilemma. Self-interested agents who act solely to maximize their individual expected utility may cooperate with each other in the absence of a strong, effective, centralized, coercive authority. The structure of society may prevent the war of all against all as effectively as the sword.

4

Trust[1]

It is difficult to imagine life without the Internet. It has made available affordable, real-time video conferencing; a plethora of information (some of which is even true); an unbelievable variety of downloadable entertainment (some of which is even legal); the chance to find your true love among a large pool of candidates (some of whom are even of the gender they claim to be); and, of course, the ability to hunt online.

In January 2005, John Lockwood and Howard Giles became the first people to hunt collaboratively even though they were separated by a distance of 45 miles. From the comfort of his home, using a rifle connected to a mechanism that allowed it to be aimed and fired via the Internet, Giles shot and severely wounded a wild hog eating from a feed box on Lockwood's ranch in Texas. Unfortunately, since the hog was only wounded by Giles's bullet, Lockwood had to deliver the final two shots in person.[2] This nonstandard method of hunting generated a substantial amount of debate, with bills banning Internet hunting being introduced in a number of states shortly thereafter.

Although times have changed since Rousseau analyzed the problem of collaborative hunting in *A Discourse on Inequality* (1775), the basic problem remains the same. As Lockwood and Giles found out, two people need to collaborate in order to ensure that the hunt is successful. If one person chooses to hunt and the other does not, the hunt may be unsuccessful, and the person who chooses to hunt winds up achieving nothing more than a waste of effort. The person who chooses not to hunt doesn't waste his effort, though, and so isn't as badly off as the person who wound up hunting solo.

---

[1] Portions of this chapter are drawn from Vanderschraaf and Alexander (2005).
[2] http://www.hsus.org/wildlife/wildlife_news/pay_per_view_slaughter.html.

Table 4.1. *The Stag Hunt (or the Assurance game), where* $x > y \geq z > 0$

	Hunt Stag	Hunt Hare
Hunt Stag	(x, x)	$(0, y)$
Hunt Hare	$(y, 0)$	(z, z)

Because talk of the Hog Hunt sounds a bit silly, and also because Rousseau considered the problem in terms of hunting stag, let's switch to the language of Rousseau. The game known as the Stag Hunt has two strategies: Hunt Stag and Hunt Hare. The attraction of hunting stag is that, if the hunt is successful, the payoff to each stag hunter is large. The attraction of hunting hare is that it's much easier, and virtually guaranteed to succeed, although it confers a lower payoff. The optimal outcome, both individually and collectively, occurs when both individuals choose Hunt Stag. The worst outcome from any hunter's point of view occurs when he chooses to hunt stag and his partner defaults on the collaborative hunt, going off to pursue a hare. It makes little difference to the hare hunter what choice his companion makes.

Table 4.1 summarizes the symmetric, two-player Stag Hunt.[3] The Stag Hunt plays an important role in moral and political philosophy. Philosophers use the Stag Hunt to represent collective-action problems ranging from cooperation in the Hobbesian state of nature to pollution control and political revolutions. The Stag Hunt also illustrates some of the challenges of accounting for equilibrium selection in games. In this game, All Hunt Stag as well as All Hunt Hare are *coordination equilibria* (Lewis, 1969) with the property that neither player's payoff is improved if one of them deviates from hunting stag or hunting hare. The All Hunt Stag equilibrium is collectively optimal and yields to each player his highest possible payoff.[4] However, each player is certain to obtain a positive payoff only if he chooses Hunt Hare. Should rational players contribute to an optimal outcome or play it safe?

The Stag Hunt provides a model of the formation of trust, since the answer as to what a rational player should do depends upon her degree of belief as to

---

[3] The Stag Hunt may also be called the Assurance game. If one chooses to differentiate between Stag Hunts and Assurance games, the dividing line concerns whether $y = z$ or $y > z$. Stag Hunts, in the narrow sense, have the form $y = z$, whereas Assurance games have the form $y > z$. I will adopt the broader sense of the Stag Hunt used by Skyrms (2003, pp. 3–4), throughout this chapter (see also Sen, 1967).

[4] Which is an important difference between the Stag Hunt and the prisoner's dilemma.

what the other player (or players) will do. It depends, in a word, on how much you *trust* your fellow companion to Hunt Stag.

The classical game theory of von Neumann and Morgenstern (1944) and Nash (1950a, 1951a, 1951b) provides no determinate answer to this question. Harsanyi and Selten (1988) tried to answer it by introducing a refinement of the Nash equilibrium concept called *risk dominance*. A strategy s is a player's best response to a strategy profile of the other players (or a probability distribution over these profiles) when s maximizes the player's payoff given this profile (or distribution). If the players in a symmetric 2×2 game each assign a uniform probability distribution over the other's pure strategies and s^* is the unique best response to both, then (s^*, s^*) is the risk-dominant equilibrium. In the Stag Hunt, Hunt Stag is risk-dominant if $x > y + z$, but Hunt Hare is risk-dominant if $y + z > x$.[5]

Harsanyi and Selten argue that a player should follow her part of a risk-dominant equilibrium since this strategy is the best response over the larger share of possible probabilities with which the other player follows his pure strategies (Harsanyi and Selten, 1988, pp. 82–83). Risk dominance is an important concept in game theory, but it raises obvious questions: why *shouldn't* a player's probabilities over her opponent's strategies lie outside the range that makes her end of the risk-dominant equilibrium her best response? Why shouldn't a player optimistically assign a high probability to her counterpart choosing Hunt Stag, even if All Hunt Hare is risk-dominant? Or, similarly, why shouldn't a player pessimistically assign a high probability to her counterpart choosing Hunt Hare, even if All Hunt Stag is risk-dominant? In the end, there really is no determinate solution to the Stag Hunt. Given appropriate probabilities reflecting a player's beliefs about what the other player will do, either pure strategy can be a best response. Rational players might fail to follow an equilibrium at all, even if they have common knowledge of their rationality.[6]

---

[5] The way to think of risk dominance is as follows. Suppose that you know nothing at all about what strategy your opponent will play. Because of this, you assume that they will select a strategy at random by flipping a fair coin (or n-sided die if there are more than two strategies). The strategy which maximizes your payoff under these circumstances is risk dominant. For the Stag Hunt, your expected payoff if you hunt stag and your opponent follows a mixed strategy assigning equal probability to both strategies is $\frac{1}{2}x + \frac{1}{2} \cdot 0$; your expected payoff if you hunt hare in the same situation is $\frac{1}{2}y + \frac{1}{2}z$. Thus, the strategy Hunt Stag is risk dominant if and only if $\frac{1}{2}x + \frac{1}{2} \cdot 0 > \frac{1}{2}y + \frac{1}{2}z$.

[6] Lewis (1969, pp. 56–57) presented the first analysis of common knowledge. A proposition A is Lewis-common knowledge among a group of agents if each agent knows that all know A and knows that all can infer the consequences of this mutual knowledge. Lewis-common knowledge implies the following better-known analysis of common knowledge: A is common knowledge for a group of agents if each agent knows A, each agent knows that each agent knows A, and so on, throughout all finite levels.

Trust and cooperation are not separable concepts, and interesting connections exist between the Stag Hunt and the prisoner's dilemma as well. Let us return, briefly, to Axelrod's analysis of the prisoner's dilemma found in *The Evolution of Cooperation*. Recall that Axelrod was interested in the relatively remarkable success displayed by the strategy TIT-FOR-TAT, which begins with cooperation on the first round of play, and then mimics the strategy played by its opponent during the previous round.

TIT-FOR-TAT, as a strategy governing behavior, is used by a variety of organisms, ranging from stickleback fish (Milinski, 1987) to soldiers involved in trench warfare during World War I (Axelrod, 1984). Axelrod claims that the essential property of TIT-FOR-TAT which makes it such an advantageous strategy to use is that it is "collectively stable." By this he meant that, if everyone in the population follows it, no alternative strategy can invade (Axelrod, 1984, p. 56).[7] Axelrod states that TIT-FOR-TAT is collectively stable in the following proposition:

> *Proposition 2*. TIT-FOR-TAT is collectively stable if and only if w is large enough. This critical value of w is a function of the four payoff parameters T, R, P, and S.

The argument given in support of this claim (see Axelrod, 1984, pp. 207–208) proceeds by showing that, in the infinitely iterated prisoner's dilemma, TIT-FOR-TAT cannot be invaded by ALL DEFECT or the strategy alternating Defection and Cooperation. Instead of conceiving of this as a question concerning the evolutionary stability of TIT-FOR-TAT, let's think of it as a problem of strategy adoption in indefinitely iterated games. Suppose that you are told that you will play the indefinitely iterated prisoner's dilemma, and may adopt either the strategy of TIT-FOR-TAT or ALL DEFECT. Which should you choose?

Consider what happens in the case in which TIT-FOR-TAT plays against ALL DEFECT with a shadow of the future of w.[8] When TIT-FOR-TAT plays against TIT-FOR-TAT, it always cooperates, so the payoffs received for the indefinitely iterated game in this case are simply

$$F(\text{TIT-FOR-TAT}|\text{TIT-FOR-TAT}) = R + Rw + Rw^2 + Rw^3 + \cdots$$

$$= \sum_{t=0}^{\infty} Rw^t = \frac{R}{1-w}.$$

---

[7] It must be noted that whether an alternative strategy can invade depends critically on the set of strategies available. When strategies with memory greater than one prior move are permitted, TIT-FOR-TAT can be invaded and replaced by other strategies. See Lindgren and Nordahl (1994).

[8] The phrase "shadow of the future" refers to the rate at which expected future payoffs are discounted. Discount rates are drawn from the interval [0, 1), which insures that the infinite series below converge.

	C	D			Tit-for-Tat	All Defect
C	(2, 2)	(0, 3)	$\xrightarrow{w=\frac{3}{4}}$	Tit-for-Tat	(8, 8)	(3, 6)
D	(3, 0)	(1, 1)		All Defect	(6, 3)	(4, 4)

Figure 4.1 Payoffs for the infinitely iterated prisoner's dilemma between Tit-for-Tat and All Defect with a shadow of the future of $\frac{3}{4}$.

Payoffs for the other cases are easily calculated as well:

$$F(\text{Tit-for-Tat}|\text{All Defect}) = S + Pw + Pw^2 + Pw^3 + \cdots$$

$$= S + \sum_{t=1}^{\infty} Pw^t = S + \frac{Pw}{1 - w},$$

$$F(\text{All Defect}|\text{All Defect}) = P + Pw + Pw^2 + Pw^3 + \cdots$$

$$= \sum_{t=0}^{\infty} Pw^t = \frac{P}{1 - w},$$

and

$$F(\text{All Defect}|\text{Tit-for-Tat}) = T + Pw + Pw^2 + Pw^3 + \cdots$$

$$= T + \sum_{t=1}^{\infty} Pw^t = T + \frac{Pw}{1 - w}.$$

If the payoffs for the one-shot prisoner's dilemma are $T = 3$, $R = 2$, $P = 1$, and $S = 0$, with a shadow of the future of $\frac{3}{4}$, we obtain the matrix in figure 4.1. Notice that the resulting *strategic* problem of choosing between Tit-for-Tat and All Defect has the form of a Stag Hunt – and one in which Tit-for-Tat (the label corresponding to "Hunt Stag") is risk-dominant.

What about the second part of the argument – where the choice of strategies for the infinitely iterated game is between Tit-for-Tat and simply alternating between Defect and Cooperate? The remaining three payoffs are easily calculated as well:

$$F(\text{Tit-for-Tat}|\text{DCDC}) = S + Tw + Sw^2 + Tw^3 + \cdots$$

$$= \sum_{t=0}^{\infty} (Sw^{2t} + Tw^{2t+1}) = \frac{S + Tw}{1 - w^2},$$

$$F(\text{DCDC}|\text{Tit-for-Tat}) = T + Sw + Tw^2 + Sw^3 + \cdots$$

$$= \sum_{t=0}^{\infty} (Tw^{2t} + Sw^{2t+1}) = \frac{T + Sw}{1 - w^2},$$

	C	D		Tit-for-Tat	DCDC
C	(2, 2)	(0, 3)	Tit-for-Tat	(8, 8)	(5.14, 6.86)
D	(3, 0)	(1, 1)	DCDC	(6.86, 5.14)	(5.71, 5.71)

Above the arrow between the matrices: $w = \frac{3}{4}$, with arrow $\longrightarrow$.

Figure 4.2 Payoffs for the infinitely iterated prisoner's dilemma between Tit-for-Tat and the strategy which alternates between Defect and Cooperate, with a shadow of the future of $\frac{3}{4}$.

and

$$F(\text{DCDC}|\text{DCDC}) = P + Rw + Pw^2 + Rw^3 + \cdots$$

$$= \sum_{t=0}^{\infty}(Pw^{2t} + Rw^{2t+1}) = \frac{P + Rw}{1 - w^2}.$$

As figure 4.2 shows, with payoffs of $T = 3$, $R = 2$, $P = 1$, and $S = 0$, with $w = \frac{3}{4}$, the strategic problem of choosing between Tit-for-Tat and Defect–Cooperate in the infinitely iterated prisoner's dilemma *also* has the strategic form of a Stag Hunt! This means that the collective stability of Tit-for-Tat has less to do with particularly nice properties of Tit-for-Tat[9] and much more to do with the fact that the real underlying game being analysed by Axelrod was a Stag Hunt, and one in which the strategy of Hunt Stag was risk-dominant. In such a case, straightforward maximization of expected utility recommends choosing Hunt Stag – or, as we've been calling it, Tit-for-Tat. As for why Tit-for-Tat is capable of driving out "invaders," we will see later that, under a wide range of evolution dynamics, small perturbations away from All Hunt Stag are inexorably hauled back to the All Hunt Stag equilibrium.

One connection between cooperation and trust, then, is that indefinitely iterated problems of cooperation are, effectively, problems of trust. What about the other direction? What are indefinitely iterated problems of trust? Consider, as a special case, the indefinitely iterated Stag Hunt, in which players have a choice of using either Tit-for-Tat or All Defect.[10] It turns out, in this case, that the payoffs for the indefinitely iterated game *remain* a Stag Hunt, regardless of the size of the shadow of the future! So iterated problems of cooperation become problems of trust, but iterated problems of trust remain problems of trust.

To see this, consider the convergent payoffs of the indefinitely iterated game, as shown in figure 4.3. Let $X = x/(1 - w)$, $Y = y + zw/(1 - w)$,

---

[9] Namely, the fact it is "not envious," nor the "first to defect," that it "[reciprocates] both co-operation and defection," and is "not too clever" (Axelrod, 1984, p. 110).

[10] In this case, the strategy All Defect refers to always hunting hare.

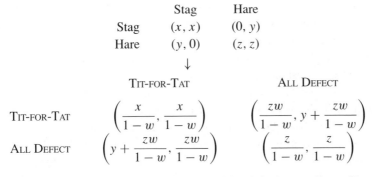

Figure 4.3 The indefinitely iterated Stag Hunt with a choice between Tit-for-Tat and All Defect, with a shadow of the future of w.

$Z = z/(1 - w)$, and $Q = zw/(1 - w)$. What we need to show is that $X > Y \geq Z > Q$. Let's work through this from left to right.

$X > Y$. Notice that we may write $x/(1 - w)$ as $x + xw/(1 - w)$. In the original Stag Hunt, $x > y \geq z$, so $xw/(1 - w) > zw/(1 - w)$ and hence $X > Y$.

$Y \geq Z$. Using the same trick as before, expand $z/(1 - w)$ to $z + zw/(1 - w)$. The fact that $Y \geq Z$ then follows from the fact that, in the original Stag Hunt, $y \geq z$.

$Z > Q$. Since w is between 0 and 1, and all the payoffs in the original Stag Hunt are positive, it follows that $z/(1 - w) > zw/(1 - w)$.

This shows that the payoffs in figure 4.3 stand in the right relation to each other to be a Stag Hunt.

One may wonder what happens if individuals approach the indefinitely iterated Stag Hunt as slightly more sophisticated strategic thinkers. It is well known that, although Tit-for-Tat does reasonably well in a variety of different environments, other strategies of roughly equal complexity can outperform it. For example, Axelrod (1984, p. 39) notes how Tit-for-Tat would have lost in his first computer tournament had an alternative strategy, Tit-for-Two-Tats, been submitted. Similarily, Nowak and Sigmund (1993) show how Win–Stay, Lose–Shift also outperforms Tit-for-Tat in certain situations.

A player employing Tit-for-Two-Tats begins by cooperating (or hunting stag) for the first two generations, and then chooses to cooperate (hunt stag) anytime his partner has cooperated (hunted stag) at least once in the past two plays. Win–Stay, Lose–Shift begins by defecting (hunting rabbit) in the first generation and then flips between cooperating and defecting (hunting stag and hunting rabbit) whenever he earns a payoff below some critical threshold.

WIN–STAY, LOSE–SHIFT thus corresponds to a strategy that a boundedly rational agent would use, namely, one who seeks to "satisfice" rather than maximize. What threshold do individuals following WIN–STAY, LOSE–SHIFT use? For simplicity, and since the games we are considering have four payoff values, let's take the threshold to lie between the top two and bottom two values. A player following WIN–STAY, LOSE–SHIFT in the repeated prisoner's dilemma will flip behavior whenever he receives a payoff of P or S, whereas a player following WIN–STAY, LOSE–SHIFT in the Stag Hunt will flip behavior whenever he receives a payoff of z or 0. (Although the definition of the Stag Hunt which I'm using allows for the possibility of $y = z$, assume that $y > z$ for the rest of this argument.)

Calculating the payoffs for the four combinations of TIT-FOR-TWO-TATS versus WIN–STAY, LOSE–SHIFT in indefinitely iterated games is straightforward, although slightly more complicated that what we've seen so far. Let's now consider the four possibilities in detail. In the following, I use the symbol "S" to indicate a play of Hunt Stag, and "H" to indicate a play of Hunt Hare.

TFTT versus TFTT. The game play proceeds as follows:

	round					
	0	1	2	3	4	$\cdots$
TFTT	S	S	S	S	S	$\cdots$
TFTT	S	S	S	S	S	$\cdots$

The expected payoff is then

$$F(\text{TFTT}|\text{TFTT}) = \sum_{t=0}^{\infty} x w^t = \frac{x}{1-w}.$$

TFTT versus WSLS. The game play proceeds as follows:

	round							
	0	1	2	3	4	5	6	7	$\cdots$
TFTT	S(0)	S(0)	H(z)	H(y)	S(0)	S(0)	H(z)	H(y)	$\cdots$
WSLS	H(y)	H(y)	H(z)	S(0)	H(y)	H(y)	H(z)	S(0)	$\cdots$

In the table above, the strategy played in round i is followed in parentheses by the payoff earned. Note that the pattern repeats every four generations. The payoffs are then

$$F(\text{TFTT}|\text{WSLS}) = \sum_{t=0}^{\infty}(0w^{4t} + 0w^{4t+1} + zw^{4t+2} + yw^{4t+3})$$

$$= \sum_{t=0}^{\infty}(zw^{4t+2} + yw^{4t+3}) = \frac{w^2(wy + z)}{1 - w^4}.$$

WSLS versus TFTT. Using the above sequence of play, we calculate

$$F(\text{WSLS}|\text{TFTT}) = \sum_{t=0}^{\infty}(yw^{4t} + yw^{4t+1} + zw^{4t+2} + 0w^{4t+3})$$

$$= \frac{y + wy + w^2z}{1 - w^4}.$$

WSLS versus WSLS. The game play looks like the following:

	generation			
	0	1	2	$\cdots$
WSLS	H(z)	S(x)	S(x)	$\cdots$
WSLS	H(z)	S(x)	S(x)	$\cdots$

After generation 1, both players will continue to hunt stag. The payoffs are then

$$F(\text{WSLS}|\text{WSLS}) = z + \sum_{t=1}^{\infty} xw^t = z + \frac{xw}{1 - w}.$$

Given these calculations, the payoff matrix for the infinitely iterated Stag Hunt between TIT-FOR-TWO-TATS and WIN–STAY, LOSE–SHIFT with a common discount rate w is

	TFTT	WSLS
TFTT	$\left(\dfrac{x}{1 - w}, \dfrac{x}{1 - w}\right)$	$\left(\dfrac{w^2(wy + z)}{1 - w^4}, \dfrac{y + wy + w^2z}{1 - w^4}\right)$
WSLS	$\left(\dfrac{y + wy + w^2z}{1 - w^4}, \dfrac{w^2(wy + z)}{1 - w^4}\right)$	$\left(z + \dfrac{xw}{1 - w}, z + \dfrac{xw}{1 - w}\right)$

Because TIT-FOR-TWO-TATS and WIN–STAY, LOSE–SHIFT embody such different spirits in terms of how one can approach an indefinitely iterated game (one is forgiving, the other crafty and opportunistic), it makes sense to allow the shadow of the future to vary across these two different strategies. If TIT-FOR-TWO-TATS has a discount rate of w_1 and WIN–STAY, LOSE–SHIFT a discount rate of w_2, the payoff matrix for the indefinitely iterated game is

$$
\begin{array}{ccc}
 & \text{TFTT} & \text{WSLS} \\
\text{TFTT} & \left(\dfrac{x}{1 - w_1}, \dfrac{x}{1 - w_1} \right) & \left(\dfrac{w_1^2(w_1 y + z)}{1 - w_1^4}, \dfrac{y + w_2 y + w_2^2 z}{1 - w_2^4} \right) \\
\text{WSLS} & \left(\dfrac{y + w_2 y + w_2^2 z}{1 - w_2^4}, \dfrac{w_1^2(w_1 y + z)}{1 - w_1^4} \right) & \left(z + \dfrac{x w_2}{1 - w_2}, z + \dfrac{x w_2}{1 - w_2} \right)
\end{array}
$$

The indefinitely iterated Stag Hunt with choice between TIT-FOR-TWO-TATS and WIN–STAY, LOSE–SHIFT has a more complicated structure than the indefinitely iterated Stag Hunt with choice between TIT-FOR-TAT and ALL DEFECT. It also has the following curious property: let $x = \frac{9}{8}$, $y = \frac{17}{16}$, $z = 1$, $w_1 = \frac{3}{16}$, and $w_2 = \frac{1}{4}$. These values satisfy all of the requirements for a Stag Hunt, yet, when we plug them into the payoff matrix for the indefinitely iterated Stag Hunt, we obtain

	TFTT	WSLS
TFTT	(1.384, 1.384)	(0.042, 1.396)
WSLS	(1.396, 0.042)	(1.375, 1.375)

which may look more familiar if we replace the numbers by variables:

	TFTT	WSLS
TFTT	(R, R)	(S, T)
WSLS	(T, S)	(P, P)

When we allow for slightly more complex strategies, and differing discount rates, the indefinitely iterated Stag Hunt becomes a prisoner's dilemma! Iterated problems of cooperation can become problems of trust, and iterated problems of trust can become problems of cooperation.

There are several morals to the story. First, the prisoner's dilemma and the Stag Hunt are intimately related; depending on the approach one takes to the indefinitely iterated game, each can be transformed into the other. This makes sense. Although cooperation and trust are different concepts, the two notions are related.

The second moral is philosophical in nature. The Stag Hunt and the prisoner's dilemma have both been used by political philosophers to model the state of nature. The fact that the indefinitely iterated Stag Hunt can become a prisoner's dilemma, and vice versa, means that, at the end of the day, there really isn't a right answer to the question of which better represents the state of nature. We have no choice but to examine both games if we want to understand the state of nature.

There is, however, yet another moral to the story, which returns us to a theme introduced at the end of chapter 1. If one wants to leave the state of nature, it helps if one is not too smart. By "too smart," I mean too much given to strategic thinking. The Stag Hunt does not converge to a prisoner's dilemma until we consider the more structurally complex strategies of TIT-FOR-TWO-TATS and WIN–STAY, LOSE–SHIFT. As long as persons adopt simpler approaches to the iterated game, the Stag Hunt remains the Stag Hunt, and the strategy of Hunt Stag becomes risk-dominant. Under these conditions, the entire population could spontaneously, without communicating, and without being threatened by the Hobbesian sovereign, choose to hunt stag and move to the socially optimal equilibrium.

We may speculate all we like about how this may happen. What we really need to do, now, is inspect a number of evolutionary models to see whether boundedly rational individuals really will converge upon the socially optimal equilibrium of Hunt Stag.

4.1 The replicator dynamics

Let S denote the strategy Hunt Stag, and H the strategy Hunt Hare. If p stands for the proportion of the population which follows the strategy Hunt Stag, then the average fitness of an individual choosing to hunt stag is

$$F(S|\vec{s}) = p \cdot F(S|S) + (1 - p) \cdot F(S|H)$$
$$= xp + (1 - p) \cdot 0 = xp.$$

Similarily, the average fitness of an individual choosing to hunt hare is

$$F(H|\vec{s}) = p \cdot F(H|S) + (1 - p) \cdot F(H|H)$$
$$= yp + (1 - p) \cdot z.$$

The average fitness of the population, $F(\vec{s}|\vec{s})$, equals the weighted sum of these two terms:

$$F(\vec{s}|\vec{s}) = p \cdot F(S|\vec{s}) + (1 - p) \cdot F(H|\vec{s})$$
$$= xp^2 + (1 - p) \cdot (yp + (1 - p)z).$$

Under the replicator dynamics, the rate of change of the strategy Hunt Stag is simply

$$\frac{ds_S}{dt} = p(F(S|\vec{s}) - F(\vec{s}|\vec{s})) = p(xp - F(\vec{s}|\vec{s}))$$

and the rate of change of the strategy Hunt Hare is

$$\frac{ds_H}{dt} = (1 - p)(F(H|\vec{s}) - F(\vec{s}|\vec{s})) = (1 - p)(yp + (1 - p)z - F(\vec{s}|\vec{s})).$$

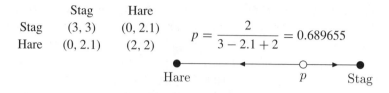

Figure 4.4 The Stag Hunt modeled using the replicator dynamics.

The number of stag hunters in the population increases exactly when $xp - F(\vec{s}|\vec{s}) > 0$. This relation can be nicely expressed in terms of the payoffs as follows:

$$xp > xp^2 + (1 - p)(yp + (1 - p)z),$$
$$0 > -xp(1 - p) + (1 - p)(yp + (1 - p)z),$$
$$0 > -xp + yp + (1 - p)z,$$
$$p > \frac{z}{x - y + z}.$$

Figure 4.4 illustrates what happens when we model the Stag Hunt using the replicator dynamics. The points on the left and right of the diagram correspond to the states All Hunt Hare and All Hunt Stag, respectively. Points in the middle of the diagram represent mixed states of the population.[11] An unstable equilibrium exists at the point where the proportion of stag hunters equals $z/(x - y + z)$. However, once the proportion of stag hunters exceeds this, evolution under the replicator dynamics carries the population inexorably towards the state in which everyone hunts stag. Likewise, once the population of stag hunters has dropped below this critical value, the population converges to All Hunt Hare.

Consider our earlier question regarding equilibrium selection in the Stag Hunt. Under the replicator dynamics, this question is entirely determined by the initial state of the population. Whether a social contract will form depends only on whether the number of people inclined to form a social contract exceeds the critical threshold of $z/(x - y + z)$.

However, there is another, more disturbing, implication for social-contract formation; according to the replicator dynamics, it is impossible for individuals in the state of nature to leave the state of nature by gradual means. Consider this: in the state of nature, no one trusts anyone else, so everyone hunts hare. Suppose,

[11] The point directly in the middle of the line corresponds to the state in which half of the population follows Hunt Stag and half follows Hunt Hare. From this midpoint, the proportion of hare hunters increases linearly as one moves to the left (until you eventually arrive at the state of All Hunt Hare) and the proportion of stag hunters increases linearly as one moves to the right (until you eventually arrive at the state of All Hunt Stag).

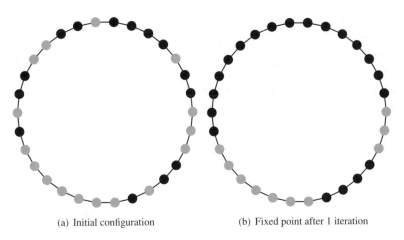

(a) Initial configuration   (b) Fixed point after 1 iteration

Figure 4.5 The Stag Hunt played on a ring.

though, that one clever person realizes that everyone would be much better off if they trusted each other (only a little bit!) and acted collaboratively. If this person manages to persuade a few other individuals to work with him, what has effectively happened is that a few Stag Hunters have appeared in the population. In terms of the diagram of figure 4.5, the new state of the population – the one containing a few Stag Hunters – has moved off the leftmost point of the diagram to a point slightly to the right, in the interior.

Yet, this new point still lies within the basin of attraction for All Hunt Hare. If people act as boundedly rational agents, as modeled by the replicator dynamics, the brilliant insight of the clever person will be lost. The few Stag Hunters will either be driven to extinction, or decide – after a few rounds of poor payoffs – to switch back to their original untrusting behavior.[12] The only way a social contract can form is through a sudden, and radical, shift in the population. But we know that collaborative efforts towards a jointly optimal outcome can arise gradually, and can slowly spread throughout a population. It is time to consider alternative models of cultural evolution.

4.2 Lattice models

Consider the Stag Hunt played on a ring of 100 individuals, with each player interacting with his immediate neighbors on the right and left. Assume also that everyone uses *Imitate-the-Best* as the learning rule, choosing a new strategy

---

[12] Whether the Stag Hunters are driven to extinction or decide to switch strategies depends on whether you interpret the replicator dynamics as a model of biological or cultural evolution. See the discussion in chapter 2.

from their immediate neighbors on the left and right. When we consider such a model, with payoffs of $x = 3$ and $y = z = 2$, we find that it always rapidly converges to a fixed state consisting of some mix of stag hunters and hare hunters after one generation. Figure 4.5 illustrates one such model in its initial and final configurations. Light gray represents the strategy Hunt Stag, and black represents Hunt Hare.

This is easily explained. An isolated stag hunter surrounded by two hare hunters receives a payoff of 0, and hence will switch to hunting hare (since his neighboring hare hunters always receive a payoff of 4). Each member of a cluster of two stag hunters, side-by-side, earns a payoff of 3 – better than before! – but will still switch to hunting hare, because each stag hunter sees a hare hunter who did better than themselves. However, clusters of three or more stag hunters are stable; each stag hunter on the boundary receives an inferior payoff of 3, but does not switch to Hunt Hare because their update neighborhood includes a stag hunter who receives the optimal payoff of 6.

Notice also that, in this case, a given hare hunter h will never switch to hunting stag. Regardless of whether h has one or two stag hunters as his neighbors, h always receives a payoff of 4. His neighboring stag hunters (suppose that there are two, s_1 and s_2) cannot receive a payoff of more than 3, because every agent in this model has exactly two neighbors, and we already know that s_1 and s_2 have one hare hunter as a neighbor – namely, h! So h continues to hunt hare, and s_1 and s_2 will switch to hunting hare unless they belong to a cluster of three or more stag hunters.

This proves, for the payoff matrix $x = 3$ and $y = z = 2$, that, regardless of the initial distribution of strategies, the Stag Hunt played on a ring with *Imitate-the-Best* reaches a fixed point in the dynamics after exactly one generation; and that fixed point cannot contain more stag hunters than were initially present in the population. Under these conditions, the social contract cannot form. The social contract is a Garden-of-Eden state, accessible only if the random coin flips that assign strategies to persons happen to make everyone stag hunters at the outset.

What if we allow for experimentation? Under these conditions, it does not make much of a difference. Figure 4.6 displays the Stag Hunt run on a cycle of length 400 with a mutation rate of 20 percent. Each time a mutant appears, he adopts the strategy Hunt Stag or Hunt Hare with equal frequency. Mutant stag hunters who pop up amid a cluster of hare hunters will disappear in the next generation (as argued above).[13] If a group of three or more stag hunters appears

---

[13] The reason why single stag hunters appear at all in the figure has to do with when the image was taken in the order of events. The order of events is as follows: take a snapshot, interact, update, then mutate. Each row displays the state of the population at the *beginning* of that

Figure 4.6 A Stag Hunt on a cycle of length 400, with a mutation rate of 20 percent; 200 generations are displayed.

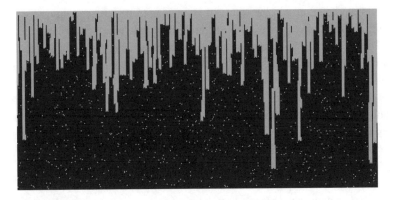

Figure 4.7 Displacing the social contract. The stag hunt ($x = 3$, $y = z = 2$) with a mutation rate of $\mu = 0.025$.

at once, it will persist until eroded away by mutant hare hunters. As figure 4.6 shows, even when mutations are present, the population contains more hare hunters than stag hunters, and spends its time closer to the state All Hunt Hare than to All Hunt Stag.

Although mutations are incapable of *moving* the population into a social contract, will a social contract at least be stable if ever reached? Unfortunately not. Figure 4.7 shows how easily even a small amount of mutation can cause a

generation, and hence contains the mutants who were introduced at the *end* of the previous generation. A sharp eye will notice that, on occasion, an isolated stag hunter appears to persist for more than one generation. Why does this happen? With a mutation rate of 20 percent, there is a 10 percent chance that an individual who had mutated into a stag hunter at the end of the previous generation will again mutate into a stag hunter at the end of the current generation. This gives the appearance of isolated stag hunters persisting for more than one generation.

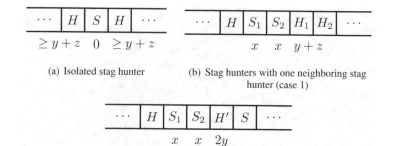

(a) Isolated stag hunter

(b) Stag hunters with one neighboring stag hunter (case 1)

(c) Stag hunters with one neighboring stag hunter (case 2)

Figure 4.8 The key arrangements of stag and hare hunters for a local-interaction model with an interaction and update radius of 1.

population beginning in the state All Hunt Stag to be replaced, in a relatively short period of time, by the state in which most individuals hunt hare.

The differences between this simple local-interaction model and the replicator dynamics are striking. Under the replicator dynamics, the state All Hunt Stag is evolutionarily stable; mutant hare hunters are driven to extinction. In this local-interaction model, the state All Hunt Stag is no longer evolutionarily stable because mutant hare hunters gradually accumulate in the population until they finally push the stag hunters out. This happens even though Hunt Stag is an evolutionarily stable strategy in the sense of Maynard Smith and Price.[14]

The above analysis fixed a specific payoff matrix, but the argument easily generalizes. Let the payoffs $x > y \geq z > 0$ be given. Figure 4.8 displays the key arrangements of stag and hare hunters that we need to consider. A stag hunter with no neighboring stag hunters still receives a payoff of zero, and will switch to hunting hare in the next generation. The case in which a stag hunter has exactly one neighbor who hunts stag is more interesting. If Hunt Hare is risk-dominant, both stag hunters will switch to hunting hare: each stag hunter receives a payoff of x, and each of their hare-hunting neighbors receives a payoff of *at least* $y + z$.[15]

However, if Hunt Stag is risk-dominant, we need to consider just *how much* it is risk-dominant. If Hunt Stag is risk-dominant, we know that $x > y + z$, but no constraints are placed on where $2y$ fits into that ordering. It may be the case

---

[14] Recall the definition: a strategy σ is said to be evolutionarily stable if and only if, for any mutant μ, either (a) σ does better playing against σ than μ does against σ, or (b) μ does just as well playing against σ as σ, but σ does better playing against μ. Let σ denote the strategy Hunt Stag, and μ the strategy Hunt Hare. Then $\Delta F(\sigma, \sigma) > \Delta F(\mu, \sigma)$ because $3 > 2$, so Hunt Stag is evolutionarily stable.

[15] The payoff could be greater, as case 2 illustrates.

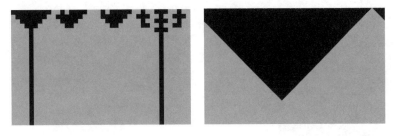

(a) Hunt Stag risk-dominant, $2y > x$ (b) Hunt Stag risk-dominant, $x > 2y$

Figure 4.9 The spread of risk-dominant Hunt Stag under two different conditions.

that $x > 2y > y + z$ or that $2y > x > y + z$. If $x > 2y > y + z$, then, both in case 1 and in case 2, the hare hunter adjacent to S_2 will switch to hunting stag in the next generation. This initiates a contagion effect, so that the entire population will end up hunting stag if at least two adjacent hare hunters are present in the initial population.

However, if $2y > x$, the strategy of Hunt Hare will be adopted by stag hunters even if they have one other stag hunter as a neighbor (i.e., in case 2 of figure 4.8). Figure 4.9 illustrates this effect of the weak and strong senses of risk dominance.[16] In figure 4.9(a), single hare hunters will not be eliminated from the population. Moreover, in the upper right-hand corner of figure 4.9(a), we see how an initial distribution of strategies that conforms to the pattern ...SSHSSHHHSSHSS... will fall into a cycle of length 2. In the world of figure 4.9(b), though, Hunt Stag is contagious and eventually drives the hare hunters out.

When Hunt Stag is only weakly risk-dominant, mutations have a much greater effect, as shown in figure 4.10. There, both models were initialized using random initial conditions (both strategies equally likely) and a common mutation rate of 10 percent. In figure 4.10(a), mutations introduce hare hunters into the population, who persist either until they mutate back into stag hunters, or until Hunt Stag manages to drive them out.[17] In figure 4.10(b), isolated hare hunters are immediately driven out of the population. This minor difference in

---

[16] A strategy S is *weakly risk-dominant* if S is risk-dominant, in the normal sense defined earlier, but yet S fails to prevent competing strategies from replacing it, or initiating contagion effects. A strategy S is *strongly risk-dominant* if it is risk-dominant and also prevents competing strategies from replacing it, or initiating contagion effects. Since the existence of contagion effects depends upon the underlying structure of society, it is entirely possibly for a strategy to be weakly risk-dominant for some social structures but not others. I leave this context-dependence implicit, since it will be clear from the discussion which social structures I have in mind.

[17] Although an isolated hare hunter will persist indefinitely, because $2y > x$, two adjacent hare hunters may switch to hunting stag, because $x > y + z$, as inspection of figure 4.9(a) shows.

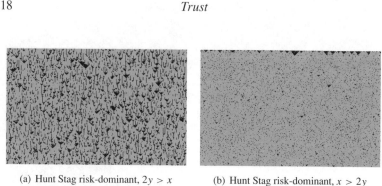

(a) Hunt Stag risk-dominant, $2y > x$ (b) Hunt Stag risk-dominant, $x > 2y$

Figure 4.10 Two types of risk dominance, with mutation.

(a) Interaction radius of 1, update radius of 2

(b) Interaction radius of 2, update radius of 3

Figure 4.11 Trust is contagious in the Stag Hunt ($x = 3$, $y = z = 2$).

the dynamics has a relatively large effect on the typical distribution of strategies: in figure 4.10(a), individuals hunt hare approximately 20 percent of the time, whereas they hunt hare only 6 percent of the time in figure 4.10(b). Although the social contract is not easily displaced when Hunt Stag is weakly risk-dominant, its hold upon society is more tenuous.

In the previous chapter, we saw that allowing for the interaction and up-date neighborhoods to differ in size enabled cooperative behavior in the pris-oner's dilemma to spread. Does the same effect occur in the Stag Hunt? As figure 4.11 shows, when the update neighborhood is larger than the interaction neighborhood, trust is contagious, even when Hunt Hare is the risk-dominant

Figure 4.12 The emergence of a social contract, with payoffs of $x = 3$ and $y = z = 2$, an interaction radius of 1 and an update radius of 2.

strategy. A social contract can form locally and then spread to the entire population.

We can say a bit more about the conditions under which this happens. Suppose that the interaction neighborhood has a radius of n, and that the update neighborhood has a radius of k. Let us also consider the special case in which $y = z$. Each hare hunter receives a constant payoff of $2ny$, no matter whom he interacts with. A contagion effect occurs whenever a stag hunter, say s^*, who falls within the update neighborhood of the outermost hare hunter, receives a payoff greater than $2ny$. This occurs whenever the number of stag hunters within s^*'s interaction neighborhood equals or exceeds $c > 2n(y/x)$.

For the typical payoff matrix we've been considering, with $x = 3$ and $y = z = 2$, if the interaction neighborhood has radius 1, every person in the interaction neighborhood of a stag hunter has to hunt stag in order to start a contagion.[18] Larger interaction radii, though, only require a sizable subset of a stag hunter's interaction neighborhood to hunt stag in order to start a contagion.

One important consequence of unequal neighborhoods is that it makes it possible for a social contract to emerge gradually from the state of nature. Figure 4.11 showed how, from an initial state containing *both* stag hunters and hare hunters, the population can evolve to a state in which all hunt stag. Figure 4.12 goes further and shows the emergence of a social contract from a

---

[18] In this case, the critical number of stag hunters must exceed $\frac{4}{3}$, so there must be at least two stag hunters present.

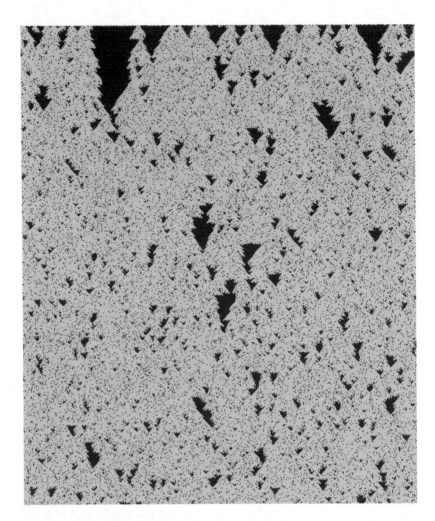

Figure 4.13 The Stag Hunt ($x = 3$, $y = z = 2$) played on a ring, with an interaction radius of 1 and an update radius of 2, with stag hunters mutating into hare
hunters 10 percent of the time.

world containing *only* hare hunters. With a mutation rate of 5 percent, eventually
a group of stag hunters exceeding the critical size appears. This group of
stag hunters spreads throughout the population, eventually transforming the
population to the state in which all hunt stag (save for the occasional mutant).

Not only do unequal neighborhoods make it possible for social contracts
to form, but also they make social contracts very resilient. Compare the result
of figure 4.13 with that of figure 4.7. Even if the only mutations which occur

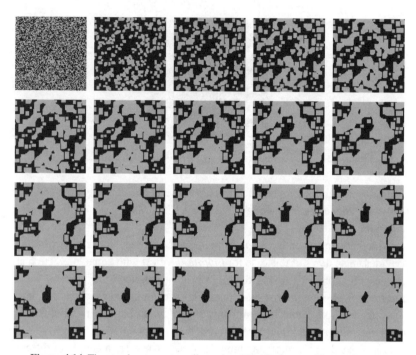

Figure 4.14 The stag hunt on a two-dimensional lattice, for equal interaction and update neighborhoods (Moore (8)), with $x = 3$ and $y = z = 2$.

transform stag hunters into hare hunters – a form of mutation that is biased against the social contract, and maximally effective at overturning the social order – we see that stag hunters successfully drive out hare-hunter rebellions. Even when hare hunters manage to take over a nontrivial amount of the population, stag hunters manage to reestablish the social contract within a short period of time.

So much for *Imitate-the-Best* play on a ring. What happens when individuals use the *Best Response* learning rule? Ellison (1993) examined this case at length. He found[19] that the long-run behavior of local interactions with *Best Response* is generally determined by which strategy is risk-dominant. That is, with a small amount of mutation, the population spends the majority of its time in the state in which everyone follows the risk-dominant strategy.

Imitation, then, succeeds in establishing the social contract under conditions where elementary strategic reasoning fails. Both imitation and best-response behavior lead the population to All Hunt Stag under conditions where stag

---

[19] See also the discussion in Skyrms (2003).

$8y$	$8y$	$8y$	$8y$	$8y$
$8y$	$3x$	$5x$	$3x$	$8y$
$8y$	$5x$	$8x$	$5x$	$8y$
$8y$	$3x$	$5x$	$3x$	$8y$
$8y$	$8y$	$8y$	$8y$	$8y$

Figure 4.15 A square region of stag hunters, with payoffs indicated for all.

hunting is risk-dominant, but only imitation succeeds in leading the population to the socially optimal outcome All Hunt Stag when hare hunting is risk-dominant.

What happens when we move from one to two dimensions? Skyrms (2003) provides an analysis of this case for *Imitate-the-Best* with equal interaction and update neighborhoods (using the eight nearest neighbors). Figure 4.14 illustrates a typical outcome for such a model. From an initial random assignment of strategies (both Hunt Stag and Hunt Hare equally likely), initial clusters of stag hunters form, and then spread throughout the population.

How does the spread of stag hunting occur? There are a couple of different mechanisms at work.[20] To begin, assume that we have a simple Stag Hunt, rather than an Assurance game (so that $y = z$) and consider what happens when we have a square region of stag hunters surrounded by hare hunters, as shown in figure 4.15.

If Hunt Stag is risk-dominant, $\frac{1}{2}x > y$, so $4x > 8y$. The twelve hare hunters on the edges of the box, each of whom receives a payoff of $8y$, will switch to hunting stag in the next round of play because they have a stag hunter earning $5y$ in their update neighborhood. The new stag-hunting region forms a cross and, from here on, continually advances by one until the entire population has been converted to hunting stag, as shown below.

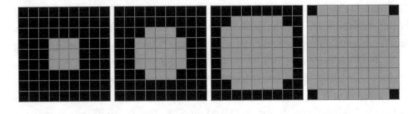

---

[20] In order to keep the analysis short, I won't go into details about what happens in two dimensions when one allows the interaction and update neighborhoods to differ in size.

$7x$	$6x$	$5x$	$6x$	$7x$
$6x$	$8y$	$8y$	$8y$	$6x$
$5x$	$8y$	$8y$	$8y$	$5x$
$6x$	$8y$	$8y$	$8y$	$6x$
$7x$	$6x$	$5x$	$6x$	$7x$

Figure 4.16 A square region of hare hunters, with payoffs indicated for all.

If Hunt Hare is risk-dominant, this means that $\frac{1}{2}x < y$. Notice, though, that this does not suffice to determine whether $8y < 5x$ or $5x < 8y$. If the former holds, Hunt Hare is only weakly risk-dominant, and hunt stag will still succeed in spreading throughout the population, although the pattern is slightly different from that in the previous case, as shown below.

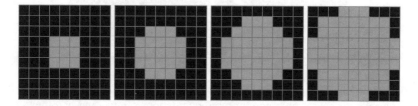

However, if Hunt Hare is strongly risk-dominant, then the square region of stag hunters of figure 4.15 (and, indeed, any rectangular region of stag hunters with x and y dimensions exceeding 3) is static. The surrounding hare hunters earn payoffs greater than that of any adjacent stag hunters, and so will not switch to hunting stag in the next round. However, the eight stag hunters on the edges of the square are prevented from adopting Hunt Hare in the next generation by the lone stag hunter receiving a payoff of $8x$ in the interior of the square. We have an evolutionary stalemate.

How is it, then, that Hunt Stag manages to drive all competing hare hunters to extinction in figure 4.14? With a payoff matrix of $x = 3$ and $y = z = 2$, Hunt Hare is strongly risk-dominant, and hence prevents the expansion of rectangular regions of stag hunters. What's going on?

As Skyrms (2003) notes, the key to explaining this requires consideration of what happens when a region of hare hunters is surrounded by stag hunters. Figure 4.16 shows the necessary positioning of strategies, with payoffs. When $x = 3$ and $y = 2$, the *corners* of the hunt-hare region succumb to attack by stag hunters, since $6x > 8y$. Whenever a region of hare hunters has a corner

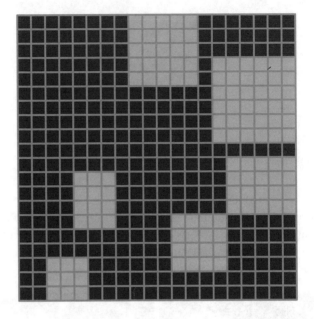

Figure 4.17 A stag hunt ($x = 3, y = z = 2$) in a dynamically stable configuration, using the Moore (8) interaction and update neighborhoods.

surrounded by stag hunters, that corner will be replaced by stag hunters. It is possible to have stable polymorphic populations of stag and hare hunters, though, as figure 4.17 shows.

How often does All Hunt Stag emerge on a two-dimensional lattice? Skyrms (2003, p. 37) notes that

> Simulations show that if we start out with 50 percent or more stag hunters, we almost always end up with a population of all stag hunters. If we start with 10 percent hare hunters, we almost always end up with a population of all hare hunters. Both these states are stable. A mutant hare hunter immediately converts to stag hunting in a population of stag hunters, just as a mutant stag hunter converts to hare hunting in a population of hare hunters.

It is important to realize that this claim holds only for certain cases of the Stag Hunt, such as the one in which $x = 3$ and $y = z = 2$. Variant forms of the Stag Hunt, even when Hunt Hare is risk-dominant, have very different tendencies.

To see why, recall the key feature which enabled stag hunters to be able to invade regions of hare hunters: the corners were susceptible. The version of the Stag Hunt studied by Skyrms had Hunt Hare as the risk-dominant strategy, but it also had the property that $6x > 8y$. Notice that, if we take $x = 9$ and

$y = z = 8$, we obtain a Stag Hunt with Hunt Hare risk-dominant, yet it is also the case that $8y > 7x$. The corners are no longer susceptible! Moreover, an isolated Hare Hunter receives a payoff of 64, and her surrounding stag-hunting neighbors receive payoffs of only 63. In this case, a single mutant hare hunter in a population of stag hunters will not convert to hunting stag. Skewing the payoffs this way has served to alter radically the basins of attraction for the All Hunt Stag equilibrium.[21]

Thus, whether Hunt Stag or Hunt Hare dominates in two-dimensional lattice models thus depends on a variety of factors. It depends on the payoff matrix, and it depends on the relationship between the payoff matrix and the shape of the interaction and update neighborhoods. However, little has been said above about learning rules other than *Imitate-the-Best*. What happens if we consider individuals to be slightly more strategically sophisticated, updating using the *Best Response* learning rule?

Over the past decade or so, several authors (Young, 1993, 1998; Kandori *et al.*, 1993; Ellison, 1993, 2000; Morris, 2000) have proved a set of results that establish important connections between risk-dominant equilibria in a wide class of games and the stochastically stable equilibria (Foster and Young, 1990) of a variety of adaptive dynamics. Informally, an equilibrium is *stochastically stable* if it is robust against a low but steady bombardment of stochastically independent random mutations in the dynamics. If a game has a stochastically stable equilibrium, then, over an infinite sequence of plays, individuals who update according to the underlying adaptive dynamics perturbed with independent random mutations will gravitate to this equilibrium a nonnegligible part of the time. If the game has a unique stochastically stable equilibrium, then, over infinitely many plays, the players gravitate to this equilibrium for all but a negligible amount of time.

According to the *Best Response* dynamic, a player follows a strategy that yields the highest payoff against the strategies her neighbors have just followed.[22] This dynamic explicitly assumes that players react myopically to their situation.[23] It has been shown (Ellison, 1993; Young, 1998) that, if the players in a local-interaction model play a game with a risk-dominant equilibrium, the strategy of this equilibrium characterizes the unique stochastically stable

---

[21] Although, if interaction and update neighborhoods can differ in size, then this result no longer holds. The reason, of course, is that having the larger update neighborhood allows mutant hare hunters to peek inside regions of stag hunting, seeing stag hunters who receive the maximum possible payoff in the game.

[22] It is thus a kind of "naïve" best response, that involves minimal strategic deliberation.

[23] That is, they do not look "too far" into the future.

equilibrium of the system under the best-response learning rule with independent random mutation.

The relationship between risk dominance, a static concept from rational-choice game theory, and stochastic stability, a dynamic concept, is of fundamental theoretical importance. Nevertheless, it is not clear how far stochastic-stability results go towards explaining how players in the real world might interact more successfully. Consider the following: suppose that we have a population of individuals positioned on a lattice, and that each agent plays the Stag Hunt with his Moore (8) neighbors. Let us choose the payoff matrix $x = 6$, $y = 3$, and $z = 2$, so that the risk-dominant strategy is Hunt Stag. If players in this system update according to the *Best Response* learning rule, with independent random mutations, then the stochastically stable equilibrium of this system is All Hunt Stag. Moreover, All Hunt Stag is the unique stable attractor of the *Best Response* learning rule for *any* positive rate of mutation, no matter how small (Young, 1998). In particular, if the system starts in the *suboptimal* All Hunt Hare equilibrium, use of *Best Response* with random mutations should eventually move the entire population to the optimal All Hunt Stag equilibrium.

Yet how long does it take for this movement to occur? We can test this by initializing a model in the All Hunt Hare state, introducing a small number of mutants at the end of each generation, and then running the model to see what happens. Figure 4.18 displays the state of the model after 100 000 000 generations, with a 5 percent mutation rate. Whenever a mutant appeared, he chose the strategy Hunt Stag or Hunt Hare with equal probability.[24] The relatively high mutation rate was selected deliberately so as to bias the dynamics against the initial All Hunt Hare equilibrium.

Although All Hunt Hare is not stochastically stable, it proves surprisingly robust in the face of independent random mutations. After a *hundred million* generations, the population is still effectively in All Hunt Hare, with a sprinkling of mutational noise on top. The inability of the population to move away from this state means that the Hunt Stag mutants were consistently overwhelmed and were unable to establish a permanent foothold and, hence, incapable of overthrowing the incumbent Hunt Hare equilibrium. Indeed, one might say that, in this simulation, the suboptimal All Hunt Hare equilibrium gave the appearance of being stochastically stable!

It might be objected that the test of the attracting power of All Hunt Stag in this example is too severe. Perhaps rational agents would seldom, if ever,

---

[24] If we halve the mutation rate, this corresponds to a process of mutation whereby a mutant, *with certainty*, adopts the strategy opposite to the one he held previously.

Figure 4.18 The state of the model after 100 000 000 iterations. Black players follow Hunt Hare; light players follow Hunt Stag.

all begin by following Hunt Hare. It turns out that relaxing this a little doesn't make much of a difference. Even if the population begins with as many as 20 percent of the players following Hunt Stag, the *Best Response* learning rule can converge to, and never leave, All Hunt Hare.

Starting the population at All Hunt Hare is not so farfetched. Social dilemmas occur when individuals are reluctant to contribute towards a common good, even when they realize that all are better off if all contribute. A local-interaction Stag Hunt models a social dilemma whereby a player contributes to the common good by following Hunt Stag and withholds his contribution by following Hunt Hare. Suppose initially that the benefits of the common good are small compared with the security of not contributing, so that all tend to follow Hunt Hare so as to avoid the costs of contribution. Then conditions change, making the relative benefit of the common good significantly greater. The model of figure 4.18 corresponds to such a situation, since All Hunt Stag, in this case, is both optimal and risk-dominant. However, it is also the case that at least *half* of a player's interaction neighbors must change from Hunt Hare to Hunt Stag before Hunt Stag becomes the player's best response. What we see is that players who respond best to their neighbor's previous strategies can have great difficulty making the transition from consistently following Hunt Hare to consistently following Hunt Stag, even in the presence of continual mutations to help them over the initial hurdle, and *even* when it is clear that All Hunt Stag is the individually and collectively optimal outcome. The initial All Hunt Hare state models a social system ripe for reform, but the dynamics reveal that the road to social reform can be a long one.

Theory tells us that random mutations will lead players to converge to stochastically stable equilibria almost surely in the long run. Yet we have just seen that independent random mutations can fail to reach the stochastically stable equilibrium in anything approaching a reasonable time span. This fact casts doubts upon the explanatory power of stochastic-stability theorems applied to local interactions between humans. Most, if not all, social networks change and even dissolve long before the people in the network approach a 100 millionth consecutive round of interactions, yet a network of players who mutate independently can fail to approach its long-run limit over 100 million rounds. If stochastic-stability theorems require extraordinarily long waiting times – as we have seen they do – how can such theorems be relevant for explaining why actual people behave the way they do? No person changes his belief 100 million times in the course of his life, much less within a single repeated game. While it is, no doubt, true that 100 million rounds of interaction constitutes a short period of time from the point of view of the ergodic theory underlying stochastic-stability theorems, one must appreciate a crucial difference between physical and social systems. Ergodic theory provides useful analyses of physical phenomena simply because, according to the time scale of many physical events, each elementary component (i.e., atom, molecule, etc.) can be involved in an extraordinarily large number of interactions during a relatively short period of time. The same is not true for social systems. Social and physical systems fail to be analogous precisely where it would be required if ergodic theory were to be explanatorily relevant.

What, though, if mutations in the dynamics can be *correlated*? Peter Vanderschraaf proposed a model[25] of correlated mutations in the Stag Hunt along the following lines: suppose, as before, that we have players arranged on a 100×100 lattice (which wraps at the edges) who play the Stag Hunt with their eight nearest neighbors. Also, as before, suppose that each player updates his strategy using the *Best Response* learning rule. However, whereas before mutations appeared independently, now suppose that mutations are correlated according to the following process. If a given player i spontaneously mutates at the end of generation t, then every one of i's Moore (24) neighbors imitates

---

[25] See Vanderschraaf and Alexander (2005).

i's strategy at the end of generation t with probability $\lambda_i(t)$.[26] Members of a certain subset of these 24 players thus have their strategies at the end of generation t correlated with i's mutant strategy. The particular value of $\lambda_i(t)$ is simply chosen, in generation t, at random from the uniform distribution over $[0, 1]$.[27] When this happens, player i is said to be a "Leader." Vanderschraaf considered the occurrence of leaders to be relatively unlikely, and proposed that the probability of Leaders appearing was only 0.0001, so that on average one Leader appeared in the model each generation. A Leader mutates to Hunt Stag with probability $\frac{1}{2}$ and to Hunt Hare with probability $\frac{1}{2}$.[28]

What happens when we start the population at the suboptimal All Hunt Hare state, but allow Leaders to exercise influence over individuals? Surprisingly we find that, in every simulation, within 800 generations stag hunters come to dominate the entire population, except for occasional areas of hare hunters that emerge due to the effect of correlated mutation.[29] However, when this happens, these clusters of hare hunters are quickly overwhelmed, and soon revert to hunting stag. Figure 4.19 depicts the population state in the 100th, 300th, 500th, and 700th generations of one simulation.

Note that the system converged rapidly to the All Hunt Stag equilibrium even though at any given stage the overall mutation rate was bounded from above by $25 \cdot \frac{1}{10\,000} = 0.0025$, the overall expected mutation rate if *all* of a "leader" player's Moore (24) neighbors imitated the "leader's" strategy. In

---

[26] Why use the Moore (24) neighborhood rather than just the Moore (8) neighborhood? Quite often one's social influence spreads beyond one's immediate neighbors or acquaintances. It is not uncommon for the following situation to occur: A knows B, B knows C, and A does not know C. Nevertheless, A exerts influence upon C through B, because B tells C that A believes something or did something. The Moore (24) neighborhood is a crude first approximation at capturing this phenomenon, since the Moore (24) neighborhood equals the twice-iterated Moore (8) neighborhood. Clearly other influence neighborhoods are worthy of examination, but this shall be left a topic for further study.

[27] One might consider the use of randomly chosen probabilities as an extreme case. However, this is not an entirely implausible assumption. For example, I may have an extremely skeptical neighbor, yet *he* may have a neighbor who is capable of being easily influenced. In such a case, I may have little influence over my immediate neighbor, yet have considerable influence over my neighbor's neighbor. Lifting the assumption of randomly chosen probabilities requires making further assumptions about the way influence is exercised and implemented in the social system, which would require an argument unto itself.

[28] One could also allow independent random mutations to appear alongside the mutations correlated with the Leaders. However, in the simulations developed in Vanderschraaf and Alexander (2005), the independent mutation rate was set to 0 so that the Leaders received no additional help in attempting to persuade their Moore (24) neighbors to adopt their new strategy.

[29] Similar results were obtained when the model was perturbed in various ways, such as setting $\lambda_i(t)$ to be constant over the Moore (24) neighborhood, or varying the sizes of the neighborhoods of correlated mutation.

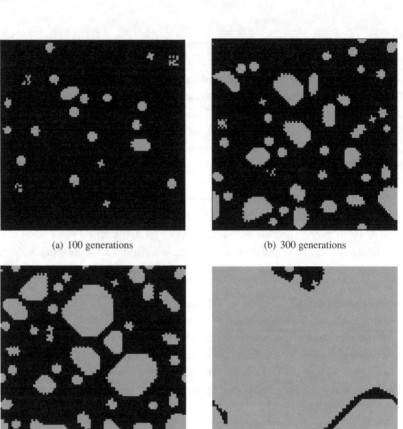

(a) 100 generations   (b) 300 generations

(c) 500 generations   (d) 700 generations

Figure 4.19 The spread of Hunt Stag via influence neighborhoods. Black players follow Hunt Hare; light players follow Hunt Stag.

Vanderschraaf's model, the total amount of mutation is much less important than the simple fact that mutations are correlated.

The correlation described in this case is a correlation over a Leader's influence neighborhood. A natural way to justify this sort of correlation in strategies is to allow for the possibility of costless communication, or what game theorists call "cheap talk." If players can communicate, then they can correlate their strategies with the leader players whose messages they receive.[30] The correlated mutation of influence neighborhoods moves the network game from

---

[30] For a nice discussion of how cheap talk can create new evolutionarily stable equilibria, and transform the size of the basins of attraction of preexisting equilibria, see Skyrms (2003).

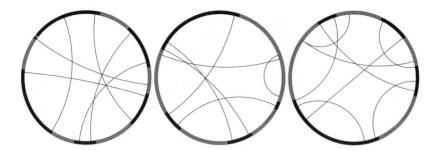

Figure 4.20 Three fixed states for the Stag Hunt ($x = 3$, $y = z = 2$) on small-world networks, with an interaction radius of 1 and an update radius of 2, and the learning rule *Imitate-the-Best*.

the suboptimal to the optimal equilibrium, even though the influence neighborhoods rarely appear. The road to reform can be shortened considerably by the introduction of influence neighborhoods.

4.3 Small-world networks

In chapter 3, we saw how the final state of local-interaction models of the prisoner's dilemma, played on a particular type of small-world network, can be predicted if we know the convergence patterns of the prisoner's dilemma on one-dimensional lattices. Can we do the same for local-interaction models of the Stag Hunt? As figure 4.20 suggests, yes, we can.

We know that, when the interaction and update neighborhoods differ in size (with the update neighborhood being larger), hunting stag is contagious. Once a cluster of stag hunters of sufficient size appears, eventually everyone in the population (if the structure of local interaction is that of a ring) will hunt stag. The only thing we need to determine is the effect of hubs in small-world networks – those individuals who receive slightly higher payoffs due to the presence of an additional edge.

Consider an arrangement of players as illustrated in figure 4.21, where the hubs are occupied by hare hunters. Assume, for the sake of argument, that the network continues to the left of S_1 and to the right of S_4 with continuous regions of stag hunters. Lastly, let's concentrate on the case in which individuals update strategies using *Imitate-the-Best*. If the interaction and update neighborhoods are the same (and are as indicated), then the hare-hunting region is stable unless the benefit of hunting stag is very great indeed (i.e., $x > y + 2_z$); the higher payoffs awarded to H_1 and H_6 insure that none of the interior players will switch strategies.

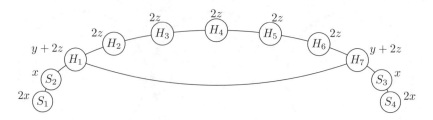

Figure 4.21 A simplified portion of a small-world network, with payoffs.

Suppose, though, that the update neighborhood consists of all players one or two steps away from a given individual. In this case, S_1 falls within the update neighborhood of H_1 and, likewise, S_4 falls within the update neighborhood of H_7. Is Hunt Stag contagious?

It depends on the payoffs. Suppose that Hunt Hare is risk-dominant, so that $y + z > x$. Using the canonical Stag Hunt studied by Skyrms (2003), with $x = 3$ and $y = z = 2$, the presence of hubs prevents the normal contagion effect of Hunt Stag from spilling into the region of hare hunters. Both H_1 and H_7 receive scores of 6, which exceeds the score earned by any stag hunter visible to individuals in the region between H_1 and H_7. However, with payoffs of $x = 4$, $y = 3$, and $z = 2$, even though Hunt Hare is risk-dominant, it is also the case that $2z < y + 2z < 2x$. So H_1 and H_7 will switch to hunting stag in the next generation, and Hunt Stag will spread to take over the region of hare hunters.

What happens if people update using *Imitate Best Average Payoff*? Suppose that the interaction and update neighborhoods are the same. Then H_1 sees that hare hunters have an average payoff of $\frac{1}{2}(y + 4z)$ and stag hunters have an average payoff of x.[31] If the payoffs are $x = 8$, $y = 7$, and $z = 2$, Hunt Hare is risk-dominant. At the same time, $\frac{1}{2}(y + 4z) < x$, so H_1 and H_7 would switch to hunting stag in the next generation, if the learning rule doesn't require that a player be explicitly dissatisfied with his strategy before revising it. In the following generation, the two hub players (each of whom now hunts stag) will receive a payoff of $2x$. When H_2 and H_6 go to update strategies, they will see that hare hunters receive an average payoff of $2z$ and stag hunters receive an average payoff of $2x$. Both H_2 and H_6 will switch to hunting stag.

What if the update neighborhood consists of all players one or two steps removed from a given player? In this case, H_1 sees that hare hunters receive an average payoff of $\frac{1}{4}(y + 8z)$ and stag hunters an average payoff of $4x/3$. If

---

[31] Recall that the averages are calculated as follows: the total score received by all individuals following a certain strategy in your update neighborhood is divided by the number of people following that strategy in your update neighborhood.

$x = 3$ and $y = z = 2$, then Hunt Hare is risk-dominant and $\frac{1}{4}(y + 8z) > 4x/3$, so H_1 and H_7 will not switch to stag hunting. However, if $x = 4$, $y = 3$, and $z = 2$, then Hunt Hare is risk-dominant but $\frac{1}{4}(y + 8z) < 4x/3$ *and* $2x > y + z$. This means that the H_1 and H_7 will switch to hunting stag and initiate a contagion effect.

Lastly, what happens if individuals use *Best Response*? This case is easily analysed, since we do not need to consider differences between interaction and update neighborhoods. If H_1 hunts hare, he will receive a payoff of $y + 2z$, whereas he would receive a payoff of x for hunting stag. If Hunt Hare is risk-dominant, he clearly won't switch strategies. The region of hare hunters is safe from invasion in this case. But what if Hunt Stag is risk-dominant? Would H_1 switch to hunting stag? As we've seen, it's possible for Hunt Stag to be risk-dominant and yet have $y + 2z > x$. When this happens, both H_1 and H_7 will not switch to hunting stag, and hence this situation will prevent the contagion effect of Hunt Stag from spreading into the region of hare hunters bounded by H_1 and H_7. If Hunt Stag is sufficiently risk-dominant, though, a contagion effect will exist even if there are very few stag hunters present initially, as figure 4.22 shows.

There are other types of small-world network besides the ones considered so far. Consider a hierarchical social ordering whereby each person has two individuals who work beneath them. If we draw a social network representing this ordering, it will be a binary tree with N vertices. If we add a new edge to the tree, linking two individuals who are otherwise quite far apart in the graph, we have started to transform the graph into a small-world network. Figure 4.23 shows what one such social network would look like for 1023 individuals, in two different representations.

Suppose that individuals play the Stag Hunt with their neighbors, using a payoff matrix of $x = 3$ and $y = z = 2$. Also assume that the update neighborhood consists of all individuals connected by a path of length one or two. If people use *Imitate-the-Best*, how often does Hunt Stag emerge in this hierarchical environment? Simulations show that, from completely random initial conditions, stag hunting dominates approximately 86 percent of the time. This makes the story sound a bit worse than it really is, because many of those random initial conditions contain very few stag hunters. If stag hunters constitute approximately 20 percent of the population under the initial conditions, then the population arrives at the All Hunt Stag state roughly 95 percent of the time.

Given the ease with which Hunt Stag spreads through the heirarchy, can the presence of a bridge edge block its propogation, like in the other small-world networks we've considered? Consider a smaller tree with a single bridge edge,

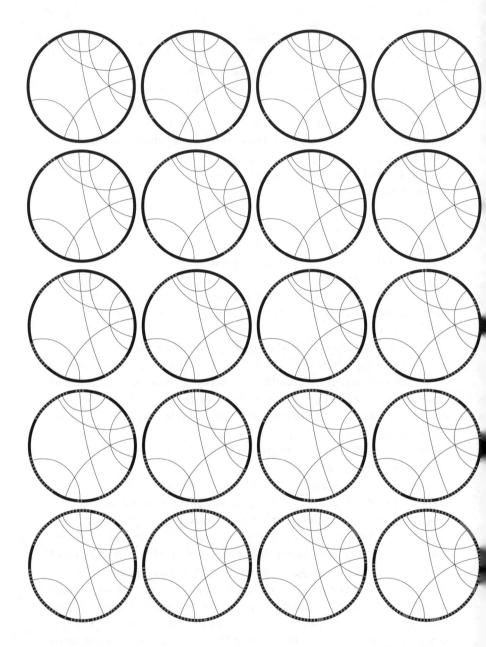

Figure 4.22 Hunting stag can be contagious under *Best Response* ($x = \frac{5}{2}$, $y = \frac{3}{2}$, and $z = \frac{1}{4}$).

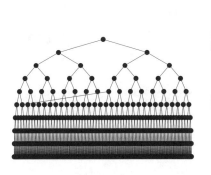

(a) A standard embedding of a complete binary tree on 1023 vertices

(b) A radial embedding of a complete binary tree on 1023 vertices

Figure 4.23 Two forms of a hierarchical social network.

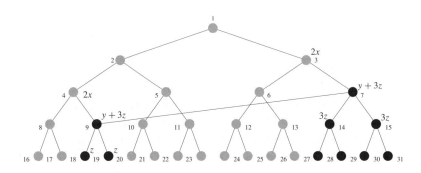

Figure 4.24 A binary tree with a single bridge edge.

as shown in figure 4.24. For the sake of argument, I assume that Hunt Stag has spread throughout the network except for the subtrees rooted at players 7 and 9. Payoffs for all of the relevant players are indicated as well.

If players switch strategies using *Imitate-the-Best*, what will happen if the interaction and update neighborhoods are of equal size and are as indicated? If Hunt Stag is risk-dominant, then $2x > y + 3z$ (which follows immediately from the definition of risk dominance combined with the definition of the Stag Hunt), so all of the hare hunters will be driven to extinction over the next few generations. If Hunt Hare is risk-dominant, then the outcome depends upon the payoff matrix. For example, with payoffs of $x = 3$ and $y = z = 2$, players 7 and 9 both earn a payoff of 8, and the stag hunter adjacent to them earns

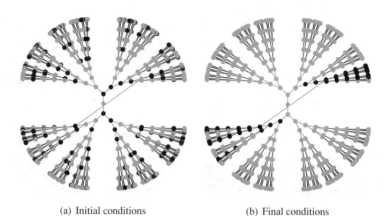

(a) Initial conditions   (b) Final conditions

Figure 4.25 The effectiveness of bridge edges at blocking the spread of Hunt Stag, for the learning rule *Imitate-the-Best*, payoffs $x = 5$ and $y = z = 4$, and unequal sizes of interaction and update neighborhoods.

a payoff of only 6.[32] In this case, the regions of hare hunters are stable and will not be driven out. However, if $x = 6$, $y = 5$, and $z = 2$, then $y + 3z < 2x$, even though $y + z > x$, so players 7 and 9 will switch to hunting stag in the next generation. The bridge edge was, in this case, unsuccessful at blocking the spread of Hunt Stag.

What happens if everyone's update neighborhood consists of all players one or two steps away? In this case, whether players 7 and 9 switch from hunting hare to hunting stag depends on how their payoffs compare with the payoffs of players 6 and 2, respectively. Players 6 and 2 both receive payoffs of $3x$. Will this provide sufficient incentive for 7 and 9 to switch? If Hunt Stag is risk-dominant, then, yes, players 7 and 9 will switch to hunting stag, and we have a contagion effect again. If Hunt Hare is risk-dominant, then, again, it depends. The canonical payoff matrix of $x = 3$ and $y = z = 2$ satisfies $y + 3z < 3x$, so the contagion effect happens in *this* case, but with payoffs of $x = 5$, $y = z = 4$, we have $y + 3z > 3x$, so the bridge edge prevents the spread of Hunt Stag. Figure 4.25 shows the outcome of one simulation in which this happened.

4.4 Bounded-degree networks

We have seen how trust can emerge in a variety of social settings with more (or less) difficulty, depending on the social structure. However, some social

---

[32] Will the *stag hunter* switch to hunting hare in the next generation? No. Player 3 has player 6 in his update neighborhood, and player 6 receives a payoff of 9. Player 4 likewise has player 2 in his update neighborhood, who also receives a payoff of 9.

Table 4.2. *Convergence results for the Stag Hunt played on 10 000 randomly generated bounded-degree networks ($k_{min} = 2$, $k_{max} = 4$) with equal interaction and update neighborhoods, using Imitate-the-Best*

Proportion of stag hunters	Number of models
$p = 1$	1517
$0.9 \leq p < 1$	909
$0.8 \leq p < 0.9$	554
$0.7 \leq p < 0.8$	426
$0.6 \leq p < 0.7$	389
$0.5 \leq p < 0.6$	351
$0.4 \leq p < 0.5$	418
$0.3 \leq p < 0.4$	456
$0.2 \leq p < 0.3$	571
$0.1 \leq p < 0.2$	851
$0.0 < p < 0.1$	76
$p = 0$	3482

networks are effectively *random*. How likely is it that trust will emerge in a randomly wired environment?

Consider a bounded-degree network of forty nodes, in which each node has at least two and no more than four edges. Assume that individuals update using *Imitate-the-Best*, that the interaction and update neighborhoods are equal, and that the payoff matrix is our canonical Hunt Hare risk-dominant case, with $x = 3$ and $y = z = 2$.

If we run 10 000 simulations, starting from random initial conditions[33] and a randomly chosen bounded-degree network, what happens? Table 4.2 summarizes the results for one series of simulations. Most often, the population arrives at the state All Hunt Hare; less often, it ends up at All Hunt Stag. The rest of the time the population arrives at a polymorphic state consisting of some stag hunters and some hare hunters.

In previous sections, we've seen how allowing the interaction and update neighborhoods to differ in size had a huge influence on the ability of Hunt Stag to dominate the population. Does the same effect occur here? Table 4.3 shows the outcome of another set of 10 000 simulations, for which the sizes of the interaction and update neighborhoods were unequal. In this case, the update neighborhood consisted, as before, of all players connected to an individual by a path of length one or two.

---

[33] Strategies are selected according to a randomly chosen distribution, in addition to being randomly assigned to individuals.

Table 4.3. *Convergence results for the Stag Hunt played on 10 000 randomly generated bounded-degree networks ($k_{\min} = 2$, $k_{\max} = 4$) with unequal interaction and update neighborhoods, using Imitate-the-Best. The update neighborhood consisted of all individuals within a path of length 2.*

Proportion of stag hunters	Number of models
$p = 1$	5818
$0.9 \leq p < 1$	138
$0.8 \leq p < 0.9$	91
$0.7 \leq p < 0.8$	66
$0.6 \leq p < 0.7$	70
$0.5 \leq p < 0.6$	40
$0.4 \leq p < 0.5$	50
$0.3 \leq p < 0.4$	35
$0.2 \leq p < 0.3$	59
$0.1 \leq p < 0.2$	40
$0.0 < p < 0.1$	7
$p = 0$	3586

Unequal sizes of neighborhoods *do* cause the population to arrive at All Hunt Stag much more frequently, yet this happens because the likelihood that we will arrive at a stable polymorphic state has radically declined. The number of cases in which we arrive at the All Hunt Hare equilibrium has actually *increased* from 3482 to 3586.

What happens if individuals use *Best Response*? Consider a Stag Hunt for which $x = 9$ and $y = z = 5$. In this game, the risk-dominant strategy is Hunt Hare, so All Hunt Hare is the unique stochastically stable equilibrium of the evolutionary dynamics. Simulations verify this claim. In bounded-degree networks, we find that, under *Best Response* with a small amount of mutation, models converge to All Hunt Hare even if we start at the All Hunt Stag equilibrium. Moreover, these random mutations never generated a permanent foothold of stag hunters, even when the system was bombarded with a mutation rate of 10 percent for 100 000 periods. These results are not surprising, given that only All Hunt Hare is stochastically stable.

However, the All Hunt Hare equilibrium does not retain its high attracting power when we look at correlated mutations using Vanderschraaf's notion of an influence neighborhood. Of course, since we are no longer working with the regular structure of a two-dimensional lattice, we cannot simply take the influence neighborhood to be the Moore (24) neighborhood of a given player. But there is a natural analogue: the set of all individuals connected to a player

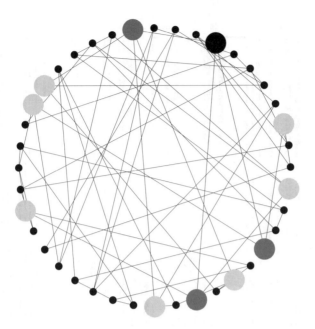

Figure 4.26 An influence neighborhood for a bounded-degree network. The "Leader" vertex is colored black, vertices one step away are colored dark gray, and vertices two steps away are colored light gray.

within two steps. Figure 4.26 shows what one such influence neighborhood would look like.

Figure 4.27 displays the outcome of one simulation of the Stag Hunt played on a thirty-player bounded-degree network ($k_{min} = 4$ and $k_{max} = 8$) with influence neighborhoods. In this model, Leader mutants occurred with probability 0.001. Each time a Leader appeared, he adopted the strategy Hunt Stag or Hunt Hare at random, each strategy being equally likely. All individuals within two steps of the Leader adopted his selected strategy with probability $\lambda_i(t)$, as before. After 5000 generations, the pattern is clear: although Hunt Hare is the risk-dominant strategy, neither All Hunt Hare nor All Hunt Stag is stochastically stable. The population bounces back and forth between the two states, spending relatively little time in polymorphic population configurations.

It is a bit strange, though, for Leaders to be as likely to be hare hunters as they are to be stag hunters. Being a Leader means that you have considerable influence over others. If you have considerable influence over others, they must *trust* you to be right more often than not. But hare hunters are not inclined to trust their fellow players.

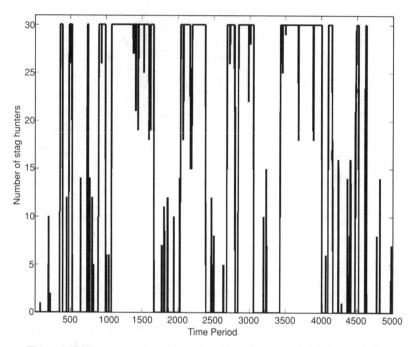

Figure 4.27 The number of stag hunters in a thirty-player bounded-degree network obtained using the *Best Response* learning rule, with influence neighborhoods.

What happens if influence neighborhoods may appear at different rates and in different sizes across the pure strategies? Consider the following modified implementation of influence neighborhoods: at each time step, independent Hunt Hare mutants appear with probability 0.1, and Hunt Stag mutants appear with probability 0.001. When a stag hunter appears, everyone within two steps of the mutant stag hunter adopts the strategy Hunt Stag with probability $\lambda_i(t)$ chosen at random from [0, 1]. In this variation, only stag hunters – being inclined to trust their fellows – have neighborhoods of influence.

As figure 4.28 illustrates, this dynamic *always* converged to the optimal All Hunt Stag equilibrium, even though All Hunt Hare is stochastically stable. Moreover, this convergence occurred and persisted even though, on average, 10 percent of the players spontaneously mutated to Hunt Hare. In this case, All Hunt Stag is the unique stable attractor of *Best Response* with influence neighborhoods, even though Hunt Hare is the risk-dominant strategy! What makes this result especially striking is that hare hunters appear 100 times as often as Leader Hunt Stag mutants appear. Moreover, even when a Hunt Stag-following Leader appears, the influence of that *particular* Leader might be

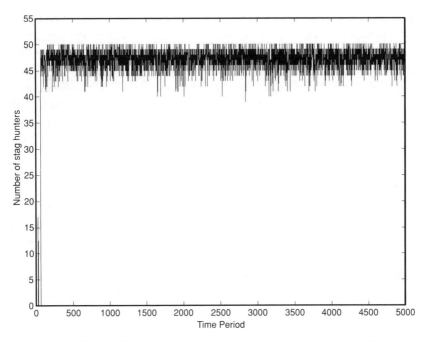

Figure 4.28 The effective convergence of a bounded-degree network to All Hunt Stag under *Best Response*, via influence neighborhoods, even though Hunt Hare is the risk-dominant strategy.

weak, depending on the value of $\lambda_i(t)$, which is randomly selected each time a Leader appears. Even so, the high influx of untrusting Hunt Hare mutants cannot prevent the overthrow of the state of nature, because efforts to establish a social contract are correlated. Although trusting, influential Leaders appear seldom in the social network, the coordinated play across their influence neighborhoods enables advocates of the social contract to push the population out of the state of nature, and to suppress the deviant Hunt Hare mutants who rebel against the social contract.

Influence neighborhoods, even when they appear at random, can drive a population out of the state of nature and into the optimal equilibrium. This transition can be robust against a high rate of independent mutation, even when the suboptimal equilibrium of the Stag Hunt game is risk-dominant. The *stability* of the optimal equilibrium, here, depends upon the fact that the trusting stag hunters have managed to correlate their efforts, while the untrusting hare hunters have not.

How might one explain this ability of stag hunters to correlate their activity? One could allow differences in the ability to communicate between types of individuals. That is, stag hunters may have access to some communication channel that they can use to send messages to those in their influence neighborhoods, whereas hare hunters may have no such reliable means of communicating. This is not as farfetched as it sounds. Stag hunters are – by virtue of their willingness to hunt stag – more inclined towards activities requiring trust than are their fellow hare hunters, and certain forms of communication require significant levels of trust in order to be effective. Consider Osama bin Laden's transferring of messages throughout the al-Qaida network via couriers. Such a communication method, albeit slow, is highly secure and effective, provided that the couriers are not only trusted, but also trustworthy.

If differences in communication ability occur in this way, then, even though stag-hunting Leaders appear seldom in the network, their ability to signal their plans to others enables those over whom they have influence to coordinate more effectively. On the other hand, even though hare-hunting mutants appear at a much higher rate, they are unable to communicate effectively and, hence, cannot coordinate their activity. So stag hunters can overthrow the hare-hunting equilibrium, establish a social contract, and even manage to fight off a continual high influx of new hare hunters.

4.5 Dynamic social networks

Social structure makes a difference for the emergence of trust, but where does the structure come from? Can individuals belonging to an unstructured population in the state of nature form social ties? If they engage in strategic learning at the same time as they form social ties, will the population wind up at All Hunt Stag, All Hunt Hare, or some polymorphic mix of the two strategies?

Let's start with the simplest question for dynamic social networks.[34] If people don't revise their strategies, but do revise their interaction probabilities, what kind of social structure emerges when members of a mixed population of stag and hare hunters interact? Figure 4.29 illustrates the initial and final states for a dynamic social network of ten individuals. In this diagram, we can see that stag hunters learn to interact only with stag hunters, and hare hunters learn to interact only with other hare hunters. This happens because stag hunters don't receive any payoff when they interact with hare hunters, so those pairings aren't reinforced, and *that* means that stag hunters learn to

---

[34] See also Skyrms (2003), which contains a more extensive discussion of dynamic social networks for the Stag Hunt, including combination games (the Stag Hunt together with a resource allocation problem) that I won't consider here.

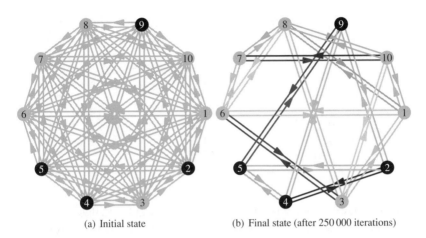

(a) Initial state   (b) Final state (after 250 000 iterations)

Figure 4.29 The Stag Hunt on a dynamic network. Payoffs are $x = 3$ and $y = z = 2$, with interaction probabilities updated after each round of interaction. No strategic updating is permitted, and no discounting of the past occurs.

avoid interacting with hare hunters. Although hare hunters receive payoffs no matter whom they interact with, the fact that stag hunters avoid interacting with them means that Hare–Hare interactions are reinforced twice as often as Stag–Hare interactions. Eventually, this uneven reinforcement causes hare hunters to associate only with each other. This always happens.

If the structural dynamics always leads to the formation of exclusive Stag–Stag and Hare–Hare interactions, one might think that nothing interesting can happen when we add strategic dynamics. After all, regardless of whether individuals update using *Imitate-the-Best* or *Best Response*, won't the population always remain as it started? If people revise strategies using *Imitate-the-Best*, stag hunters will imitate only stag hunters, and hare hunters will imitate only hare hunters. Likewise, if people revise strategies using *Best Response*, no change occurs because the best response to a group of players who exclusively hunt hare is to hunt hare, and the best response to a group of players who exclusively hunt stag is to hunt stag.

This neglects an important point: people can update strategy at a different rate from that at which they update their interaction probabilities. Strategic dynamics won't make a significant difference (at least in the short and medium run) if people revise their strategies too infrequently.[35] However, if people

---

[35] Why would it make a difference in the long run? Recall that the interaction probabilities converge to 0 and 1 only in the limit. This means that there is always a nonzero chance that a stag hunter will choose to interact with a hare hunter (although this is very unlikely). When this happens, if the stag hunter also elects to revise his strategy, he may end up adopting Hunt Hare.

Table 4.4. *The Stag Hunt on a ten-person dynamic social network*

Update probability	All Hunt Stag	All Hunt Hare
$p = 0.5$	5102	4898
$p = 0.25$	6097	3899
$p = 0.1$	6837	3132
$p = 0.05$	7166	2744
$p = 0.025$	7172	2566
$p = 0.01$	6755	2472

revise strategy at rates not too different from the rate at which they update their interaction probabilities, then strategy revision can occur before players lock in to (nearly) exclusive Stag–Stag and Hare–Hare preferences.

Table 4.4 shows the results from a series of simulations. A ten-person dynamic social network was initialized with a randomly chosen set of strategies. The interaction probability was set to 1, so each person engaged in at least one interaction every round (some people participated in more than one interaction, if they were visited by another). The probability of strategic updating was varied between 0.5 and 0.01, as indicated in the table. Whenever an individual elected to update his strategy, he did so using *Imitate-the-Best*.

Notice that, as the update probability decreases from 0.5 to 0.01, the probability of convergence to All Hunt Stag increases to nearly 72 percent, then begins to decrease. The decrease occurs because, when individuals update their strategy on the average of every 100 interactions, the structural dynamics tend to lock in to exclusive Stag–Stag and Hare–Hare visits before the strategic dynamics can begin to reshape the population. Once exclusive visitation preferences[36] form, strategic dynamics won't change the population at all, for the reasons discussed earlier; and it doesn't take too long for the probabilities to converge "for all practical purposes." Figure 4.30 illustrates the interaction probabilities after 100 generations for a ten-person network. Notice that, while some hare hunters still visit stag hunters (namely, players 3, 7, and 10), none of the stag hunters visit hare hunters with anything approaching a significant probability.

One thing not taken into consideration is the fact that people tend to assign greater weight to more recent experiences than to past experiences. What are

---

[36] Or nearly exclusive preferences, since probabilities won't converge to 0 short of the limit.

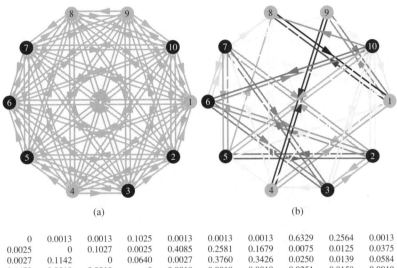

0	0.0013	0.0013	0.1025	0.0013	0.0013	0.0013	0.6329	0.2564	0.0013
0.0025	0	0.1027	0.0025	0.4085	0.2581	0.1679	0.0075	0.0125	0.0375
0.0027	0.1142	0	0.0640	0.0027	0.3760	0.3426	0.0250	0.0139	0.0584
0.1472	0.0019	0.0019	0	0.0019	0.0019	0.0019	0.0251	0.8158	0.0019
0.0510	0.4894	0.0030	0.0390	0	0.0090	0.1771	0.1111	0.0090	0.1111
0.0111	0.2293	0.3006	0.0022	0.0066	0	0.1269	0.0155	0.0244	0.2828
0.0185	0.1777	0.3262	0.0503	0.1564	0.1511	0	0.0822	0.0291	0.0079
0.9591	0.0020	0.0020	0.0265	0.0020	0.0020	0.0020	0	0.0020	0.0020
0.3074	0.0016	0.0016	0.6812	0.0016	0.0016	0.0016	0.0016	0	0.0016
0.0716	0.0467	0.0654	0.0155	0.1152	0.3956	0.0093	0.2523	0.0280	0

Figure 4.30 Interaction probabilities after 100 interactions.

reasonable values to pick for discounting the past? Experiments conducted by Bereby-Meyer and Erev (1998) suggest that the discount rate which best matched people's behavior was 0.997; other data, cited by Skyrms (2003), suggest that reasonable rates fall in the range 0.9 to 0.999. If people discount the past at a rate of 0.925 and play a Stag Hunt with $x = 4$, $y = 3$, and $z = 2$, we find that Hunt Stag acquires the upper hand. With a discount rate of 0.925, as the frequency of strategic updating *decreases*, the probability that we will arrive at the All Hunt Stag population state *increases*, as seen in table 4.5.

Note that, when only one stag hunter is initially present, the population must arrive at the state All Hunt Hare. The stag hunter will never receive a positive payoff and, hence, whenever he elects to update his strategy, he will imitate the first hare hunter he can. However, once the number of stag hunters initially present has increased to two, under the structural dynamics, the two stag hunters will tend to pair up with each other. This pairing results in each stag hunter receiving a payoff of 8, and tends to move the entire population

Table 4.5. *The emergence of trust in a ten-person dynamic social network with a discount rate of 0.925 and a rate of strategy updating of p; 10 000 simulations were performed for each choice of p, and the payoff matrix had x = 4, y = 3, and z = 2*

p	All Hunt Stag	Pr(All Hunt Stag|Initial number of Stag Hunters)									
		1	2	3	4	5	6	7	8	9	10
0.5	5876	0	0.088	0.279	0.535	0.749	0.871	0.955	0.985	0.999	1
0.25	6799	0	0.211	0.552	0.759	0.909	0.980	0.994	0.997	1	1
0.1	7446	0	0.510	0.807	0.945	0.978	0.995	0.998	1	1	1
0.05	7716	0	0.639	0.902	0.984	1	1	1	1	1	1
0.025	7984	0	0.791	0.956	0.989	0.999	1	1	1	1	1
0.01	8029	0	0.874	0.983	0.998	0.998	1	1	1	1	1

to All Hunt Stag over 87 percent of the time (as indicated in the last row of the table). When there are three or more stag hunters, convergence to All Hunt Stag is virtually certain. Trust and social structure can grow together.

Thus we see how social structure exercises a powerful influence on the emergence of trust in a variety of social structures: lattices, small-world networks, and bounded-degree networks. All of these structures exhibit a general tendency to promote trusting over untrusting behavior. Yet this tendency is not universal. Trust does not *always* emerge, but trust does occur more often than one might initially suspect, especially in cases in which the untrusting behavior is risk-dominant. Given the connections between the prisoner's dilemma and the Stag Hunt, and the results from chapter 3, there are many roads out of the state of nature.

5

Fairness[1]

How do we understand justice? Thrasymachus argued in the *Republic* that it was merely the interest of the stronger party, whereas Glaucon argued that justice derived from mutually beneficial mutual agreement. These two answers barely touch the question, of course, for the answer depends greatly upon what sense of "justice" we speak of, among many other things. Of the two main types of justice – distributive and corrective – in this chapter I concentrate on the former, in a very general sense. The discussion will turn to issues of corrective justice in the following chapter, again understood in a very broad sense. In both chapters, I argue that justice emerges out of the self-interested actions of rational agents as a mutual agreement of a very special kind.

The common element to both, a mutual agreement of a special kind, suggests that justice arises as an outcome of a process of rational deliberation, in which several parties meet to negotiate a settlement. Negotiating a settlement is a complex process, with many strategic considerations having to be made by each party. Such considerations include whether one should state up-front everything one wants at the beginning of negotiations or hold off from stating these wants until later. The best course of action for each person would seem to depend upon what everyone else does. Seeking to ground our notion of justice and fairness upon the outcome of a mutual agreement among persons places us squarely within the realm of game theory.

In its most general form, the distribution problem consists of a set of goods to be distributed among the members of a population subject to two constraints.

1. No good is assigned to two members of the population.
2. Each good is assigned to some member of the population.

---

[1] Portions of this chapter are drawn from Alexander and Skyrms (1999) and Alexander (2000).

148

A *solution* to the distribution problem is an assignment of a set of goods to each member of the population subject to the above constraints.[2]

A principle of distributive justice provides a criterion for identifying a solution to a distribution problem as "just" or "unjust." A theory of distributive justice is a set of consistent principles of distributive justice, where two principles are consistent if they do not disagree in their classification of a solution to a distribution problem. If a solution to a distribution problem satisfies a principle of distributive justice, then the solution is considered just, relative to that principle; otherwise the solution is unjust, also relative to that principle. Although a theory of distributive justice may identify several different solutions to the distribution problem as just, if we require that all theories of distributive justice worthy of consideration be consistent, it follows that no theory identifies the same solution as both just and unjust.

Consider the following scenario. Two people, Sid and Nancy, face a distribution problem: they have happened across some resource, say a cake, which they are to divide amongst themselves. How are they to agree on how to share it? We may envision the following approach: both Sid and Nancy write down, on a slip of paper, how much of the cake they want, expressed as a single numeric quantity,[3] and hand them to a referee. If the sum of their individual requests does not exceed the amount of cake available, the referee awards both Sid and Nancy what they asked for; if the sum of their individual requests exceeds the amount of cake, neither Sid nor Nancy gets anything. (Perhaps the referee reveals each person's request and absconds with the cake while they argue.)

This common way of framing the distribution problem typically meets with some common objections, so let's handle them right away. Many people object

---

[2] One might object that the formulation of a distribution problem offered here cannot be the most general form because, according to the first clause, no goods are to be shared among members of the population, and we all know that many goods are shared. To handle the case of goods that can be shared (like cricket bats and roads) we simply modify our description of the good to be distributed. Instead of conceiving of the good (the bat) as a single item to be assigned to one and only one agent, we do not assign the bat itself but time-shares of the bat, one time-share to each person who is to share it. This allows us to make the simplifying assumption that no good can be assigned to two members of the population without loss of generality, at the cost of a very slight increase in complexity in how we treat shared goods.

Regarding the second clause, it also might be objected that requiring each good to be assigned to some person means that we cannot treat cases in which some goods remain unassigned. We may wish to leave some goods unassigned if we think that assigning goods to individuals confers some right of possession, and hence some authority to determine how the good will be used or consumed. If the goods in question include natural resources, one might object to this framework: we might very well want to leave some goods unassigned so that no one may use them, thereby leaving those goods unexploited or unconsumed for later generations to enjoy. This situation may be easily handled in our framework by enlarging the population to include "non-actors," who, when assigned goods, simply leave them untouched.

[3] This excludes the possibility of each person asking for "As much as possible."

to the inclusion of the referee because the referee's interests and preferences do not factor into the story at all. Although this is true, the objection fails to understand the function of the referee. The referee serves merely as a hook upon which we hang the rules of the game. In this game, if the two players' requests – obtained in private, without communication – are not compatible, neither player receives anything. Criticisms about the role played by the referee, then, translate into criticisms about the rules of the game.[4] Why do players receive nothing if they do not separately (and privately) choose compatible requests?

The flippant answer is that those simply are the rules of the game and, were that not the case, Sid and Nancy would be playing a different game. The non-flippant answer is that this game captures bargaining problems in which failure to agree on how to split the good causes the good to be lost. Think of the bargaining problem faced by the music industry and various retailers offering to construct an online service for selling music. The "cake" in this case is the amount of (possible) profit that the two parties can earn. The two parties have to reach agreement before the profit can be earned (and shared) because, without the music industry agreeing to participate, the online music retailers have nothing to sell and, without the online retailers, the music industry will continue their current practice. Hence, failure to reach agreement leaves each party in the status quo, with no new profit whatsoever.[5] Another problem having this kind of structure is wage negotiations between a firm and its workers. These negotiations often result in disputes over how the extra capital generated by the workers and the firm ought to be distributed (see Binmore, 1998, p. 69): if no agreement between the management and the workers can be reached, a strike often ensues, possibly resulting in the depletion of extra capital to divide between the workers and the firm. Treating the extra capital to be divided as the cake, this situation roughly approximates that of the game under discussion.

What of the claim that the decision regarding which strategy to adopt must be made without communication occurring between the two parties? If both players are well-informed and know everything there is to know about the other party[6] then there is nothing to be gained by pre-play communication. If I already know everything there is to know about you, nothing you tell me in pre-play communication will help me make a better judgement about what strategy to adopt. By assumption, I know what offers and threats you are likely

---

[4] In chapter 7, I introduce and examine an N-player version of divide-the-cake. This version enables us to include the referee as another player. It turns out that this makes some difference, but not as much as one might think.

[5] Ignoring negotiation costs, etc.

[6] Admittedly, there are problems with this assumption. To begin with, we never know everything there is to know about the other party.

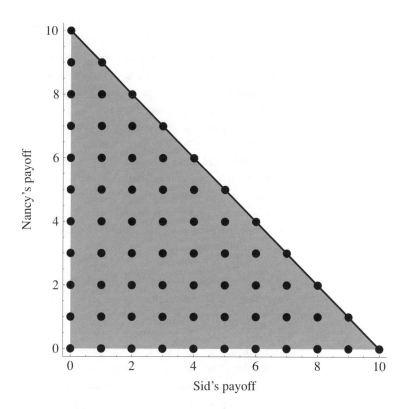

Figure 5.1 Divide-the-cake played with a cake size of 10.

to make, and whether you actually will carry out a threat if I do not play the way you want me to. Such pre-play communication serves as mere "cheap talk" since it cannot alter the course of gameplay.[7]

Let us add a few more conditions to the game: we further suppose that neither Sid nor Nancy has any prior claim to the cake and that neither of them has any special needs. With respect to the particular task of dividing the cake, the two are perfectly symmetric in every relevant sense. Adding these assumptions transforms this game into the simplest version of the bargaining problem due to Nash (1950b). The game is generally known as the Nash bargaining game, or divide-the-cake. If the cake is sliced into ten equal pieces, the payoffs for this game correspond to the points of figure 5.1 (all other combinations of strategies award 0 to both players).

---

[7] However, among boundedly rational individuals, cheap talk can make an important difference in terms of what outcomes occur. See, for example, Skyrms (2003).

In this game, a player's strategy is the number of slices of cake she requests. With a cake of size C, there are $C + 1$ possible strategies to choose from and $C^2 + 2C + 1$ possible pairings of strategies. Many of these possible pairings of strategies are suboptimal in that they do not result in a distribution of the entire cake – some of it is wasted – and other combinations of strategies are suboptimal in the sense that they overshoot the total amount of cake available, in which case neither Sid nor Nancy will receive anything. In principle, nothing prevents the two players from adopting strategy pairs that are suboptimal in either sense. In some cases it might even make sense for the two players to adopt strategies that lead to a suboptimal outcome: if Sid believes that Nancy will ask for more than half of the cake, and Sid wants to ensure that he receives at least *some* cake, then he should choose his strategy taking this belief into account. If both Sid and Nancy seek to maximize the amount of cake they receive, though, we would expect them to coordinate their choices on Pareto-efficient strategy pairs.[8]

In divide-the-cake, strategy pairs that exhaust the whole cake have an important property: neither player benefits by changing his or her strategy if the other player does not change as well. Suppose that Sid and Nancy have settled upon the following distribution: Sid receives three quarters of the cake and Nancy receives one quarter. Although Nancy may view this distribution as unfair, she cannot improve her situation by changing strategies; increasing her demand to anything greater causes the sum of demands to exceed the amount of cake available, leaving both with nothing. Decreasing her demand to something less moves Nancy to a outcome point that confers even less cake, so she will not favor this outcome, either. All of the Pareto-efficient pairs of divide-the-cake have this property, which is to say that they are all Nash equilibria.[9]

When two rational individuals play a game, it makes sense to assume that they will eventually settle upon a pair of strategies that constitutes a Nash equilibrium, provided that both players understand the rules of the game and the payoffs of the game accurately reflect each player's personal preferences. In divide-the-cake, we would be surprised if two players in symmetric circumstances arrived at any outcome other than the 50–50 split. In perfectly symmetric circumstances, the 50–50 split strikes us as the only *fair* outcome.

---

[8] A pair of strategies (σ_1, σ_2) is said to be *Pareto-efficient* if it is not possible to improve one player's payoff without decreasing the payoff to the other player. In divide-the-cake, all Pareto-efficient strategies have the property that the payoffs exhaust the amount of cake available.

[9] Moreover, all of the Pareto-efficient pairs which assign at least some cake to both players are *strict* Nash equilibria. The pair assigning all of the cake to, say, Sid is not a strict Nash equilibrium because Nancy's payoff does not decrease if she switches strategies.

Identifying the 50–50 split as the only fair outcome means that if someone attempted to distribute the cake in a way other than 50–50, in conditions of perfect symmetry and absence of prior claim to the cake, we would think the proposed distribution unjust and that person's behavior subject to sanction. The severity and type of sanctions imposed generally depend upon a host of contextual factors. Often the mere threat of sanctions, combined with the general knowledge that those sanctions are sufficiently likely to be imposed, motivates individuals to act accordingly, i.e., to share the cake equally. The sanctions imposed by the moral norm for failing to share the cake equally thus solve the equilibrium selection problem by changing the agent's expected payoffs for a proposed distribution. Whereas perfectly rational agents in perfectly symmetric situations have no reason, in the absence of the norm, for preferring the 50–50 split over the 60–40 split (since both are strict Nash equilibria), the existence of the moral norm gives them a clear reason for coordinating on one Nash equilibrium out of the many possible.

This explanation as to why we identify the 50–50 split as "fair" makes our conception of fairness, in this case, ultimately instrumental. We adopt the 50–50 split because deviation from that generally accepted outcome makes us subject to sanctions by others. We identify certain outcomes as "fair" because labeling those outcomes, and not others, as "fair" proves useful in resolving interdependent decision problems having multiple equilibria. That is, outcomes identified as "fair" are solutions to the equilibrium selection problem. Yet, even if one is willing to entertain this as a possible explanation for why we consider the 50–50 split "fair," an important question remains to be answered. Why the 50–50 split instead of the 60–40 split?

One might suspect that the 50–50 split gives a greater amount of cake to each player, over the long run, than the 60–40 split. Depending on what one means by play "over the long run," it isn't difficult to construct cases in which this claim is false. In an indefinitely repeated game of divide-the-cake, any division of cake that exhausts the total amount of cake available and randomly assigns cake to individuals by the toss of a fair coin is equally good. Simply note that, with a cake of size C, divided into two portions k and $C - k$, the expected payoff for each player over the long run is $\frac{1}{2} \cdot k + \frac{1}{2}(C - k) = C/2$. In the long run, any division is as good as the equal split if shares are assigned at random using a fair coin.

If appealing to maximization of long-run expected utility doesn't suffice, perhaps we need to take the appeal to norms more seriously.[10] The problem

---

[10] For a discussion of social norms, what they are, and how they influence individual action, see Bicchieri (2006).

with this account is that it merely serves to push the explanatory burden back one step, for any behavior can be explained by postulating the existence of a sufficiently strong norm (moral or otherwise) that serves to regulate behavior. Norms impose costs upon deviant individuals and, with a large enough cost, compliance with virtually any behavior can be secured (recall the Hobbesian sovereign). Explaining a general tendency to favor the 50–50 split by appealing to the action of a social norm simply replaces one question by another. Where did that norm come from? In the absence of a satisfactory response to the etiological question of the social norm, we haven't really explained anything. Why does that norm exist rather than some other one? Although it is presumably true that there is a social norm invoked in circumstances like divide-the-cake[11] – in effect saying that if you ask for more than half of the cake you will be seen as "greedy" and this is a bad thing – we need to say more.

Perhaps an evolutionary explanation exists. It is certainly true that, in a population where everyone demands half of the cake, no alternate strategy (greedy or modest) can invade. Any mutant requesting more than half of the cake would receive nothing and would eventually be driven to extinction.[12]

---

[11] In 1974, Nydegger and Owen conducted a series of experiments in which they had people play two games of divide-the-cake in the laboratory. In the first game, subjects played divide-the-cake using a dollar as the cake. In the second game, play was restricted by the additional constraint that player 1 could not receive more than 60 cents. (According to Nash's analysis of the bargaining problem, since this additional rule applies only to points away from the unconstrained solution point, it should not affect the solution. However, according to the bargaining theory of Kalai and Smorodinsky (1975), this constraint *should* influence the solution point. Behavior in the second game reflects tendencies on the subjects' behalf to prefer one bargaining solution over another.) In both experiments, all pairs of subjects choose in a matter consistent with Nash's solution, opting for the 50–50 split.

Some doubt over the generality and significance of the results may be warranted given the small sample size. Nydegger and Owen used only ten pairs of subjects, all male undergraduates from the same university. Even so, the claim that "[t]he outcome of this study is quite impressive if for no other reason than the consistency of its results" (Nydegger and Owen, 1974, p. 244) seems correct. Ken Binmore has also confirmed, in private communication, that people *always* opt for the 50–50 split in experiments under conditions of perfect symmetry (provided that they haven't been trained by earlier experiments to do something different).

[12] In some replicator-dynamics models, although fitness is assumed to be proportional to the amount of cake received, it need not be true that receiving no cake confers zero fitness upon an individual. (In the biological interpretation, this means that the payoffs correspond to changes in the Darwinian fitness of individuals. In the cultural interpretation, this means that all strategies that are present in the population have a certain base chance of being imitated by others.) If so, then even mutant strategies receiving no cake need not become extinct. Nonetheless, it will be true that individuals receiving some cake have a higher fitness than those receiving no cake, so even if mutants who receive no cake do not have a fitness of zero, they will produce fewer offspring than will those who follow competing strategies. Over time the *proportion* of individuals following a mutant strategy conferring zero fitness may asymptotically approach 0, although the absolute number of individuals following that strategy continues to increase. It is in this sense – relative frequency approaching zero – that talk of "extinction" is to be understood.

Mutants requesting less than half of the cake would always receive the amount of cake they asked for, but because such mutants have a lower fitness (measured in terms of the amount of cake received) than do those asking for half of the cake, even these "modest" mutants would be driven out of the population.

Asking for half of the cake is an evolutionarily stable strategy: in a population where everyone asks for half of the cake, no mutant can invade. This shows that, in a population where everyone seeks to maximize the amount of cake they receive, the state in which everyone opts for the 50–50 split, once arrived at, will persist over time. Yet how likely is it that the population will arrive at the state in which everyone follows the 50–50 split? This is the crucial question to which we now turn.

5.1 The replicator dynamics

In *Evolution of the Social Contract*, Brian Skyrms (1996, pp. 9–10) suggested the following evolutionary model to explain the existence of the equal split:

> Individuals, paired at random from a large population, play our bargaining game. The cake represents a quantity of Darwinian fitness—expected number of offspring—that can be divided and transferred. Individuals reproduce, on average, according to their fitness and pass along their strategies to their offspring. In this simple model, individuals have their strategies programmed in, and the strategies replicate themselves in accord with the evolutionary fitness that they receive in the bargaining interactions.

Skyrms has the replicator dynamics in mind here and, even though he speaks of biological evolution, we need not take this literally. As shown in chapter 2, the replicator dynamics admits both cultural and biological interpretations.

How likely is it that a randomly chosen initial configuration of the population will evolve, under the replicator dynamics, to a state in which everyone follows the strategy of fair division? Let us assume that the cake is sliced into ten equally sized pieces. Figure 5.2(a) illustrates the evolutionary trajectories for a population consisting solely of people who ask for four, five, and six slices of cake, respectively.

Because the replicator dynamics is deterministic, the evolutionary trajectories cannot cross. The point in the interior of figure 5.2(a) at which it looks as if several paths cross is really an illusion. If we magnify the region indicated by the black rectangle, shown in figure 5.2(b), we see that four paths come very close to each other, but veer off at the last minute.

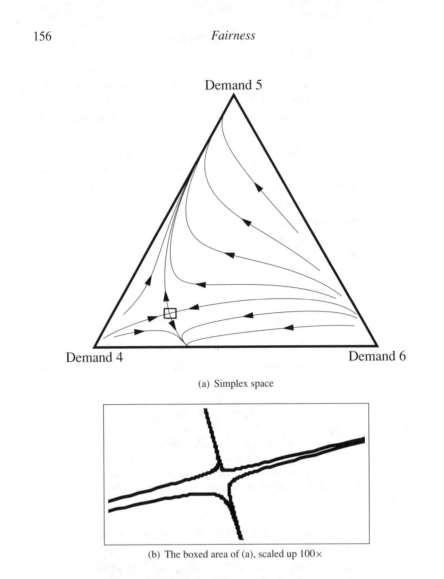

(a) Simplex space

(b) The boxed area of (a), scaled up 100×

Figure 5.2 Divide-the-dollar restricted to three strategies.

Notice also that, although the state in which everyone asks for half of the cake is evolutionarily stable,[13] it is not the only one. As figure 5.2(a) shows, there is another stable state in which both of the strategies Demand 4 and

---

[13] Which can be seen from figure 5.2(a) in that all of the paths in the vicinity of the Demand 5 equilibrium converge to that point. Any mutant trying to invade a pure population of fair dividers corresponds to a displacement of the population from the apex of the triangle to a new point in the nearby vicinity. Since all points in the nearby vicinity lie on trajectories returning to the pure Demand 5 equilibrium, this means that the new mutants will eventually be driven to extinction.

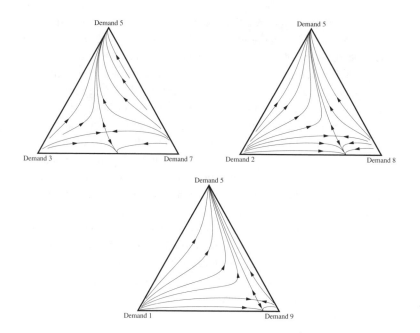

Figure 5.3 Simplex-space plots for the game of divide-the-cake restricted to three strategies.

Demand 6 are present. Moreover, this equilibrium point has a significant basin of attraction.[14] Since the Demand 4–Demand 6 polymorphism conforms neither with the actual behavior of individuals in divide-the-cake, nor with any moral norms that we take to apply in this or similar circumstances, these greedy–modest polymorphisms create what Skyrms calls a "polymorphic pitfall" on the "evolutionary road to justice."

Demand 4–Demand 6 is not the only polymorphic pitfall that appears in the replicator-dynamics model of the Nash game. Figure 5.3 illustrates three other polymorphic pitfalls. Notice that also the Demand 3–Demand 7 polymorphism is an evolutionarily stable state, and that its basin of attraction is rather large as well. In general, *all* of the strict Nash equilibria are polymorphic pitfalls. The only Nash equilibrium which lacks a sizable basin of attraction (and hence isn't a polymorphic pitfall) is the 0–10 equilibrium.[15]

---

[14] In these diagrams, the size of the basin of attraction for an equilibrium corresponds to the area inside the triangle in which the trajectories converge to that equilibrium.

[15] The 0–10 equilibrium does not have a sizable basin for the following reason: the Demand 0 strategy, which must be present in order for Demand 10 to receive a nonzero payoff, always earns 0, the lowest possible payoff of any strategy in the game. If any other strategy exists in

The polymorphic pitfalls are the evolutionary analogue of the equilibrium selection problem from traditional game theory. In the nonevolutionary case, we face the problem of choosing between competing Nash equilibria with no compelling reason in principle for selecting any particular equilibrium. In the evolutionary case, we face the problem that there can be more than one evolutionarily stable state, and which stable state the population arrives at may purely be a coincidence arising from its initial state; some initial states lead to everyone electing to ask for half of the cake, whereas other initial states lead to outcomes in which some ask for more than half of the cake and others ask for less than half. *Both* of these present a problem for giving a rational justification for why one ought to ask for half in the game of divide-the-cake, but for different reasons. The first problem centers on the fact that, in the absence of further information about what strategy my opponent is going to play, there is no knockdown argument for preferring the 50–50 split over any other option, even when the game is iterated. The second problem is that, even when players do not try to reason strategically about the situation, instead using simple imitative rules to choose their future strategies, the 50–50 split is only one possible outcome among many.

Skyrms recognizes the explanatory problem raised by the presence of unfair polymorphisms and suggests one possible resolution. As previously noted, the replicator dynamics assumes all pairwise encounters among individuals to be equally likely. What if the interactions between individuals are *correlated*, so that each strategy type has an increased chance of interacting with members of its own kind? Let us denote the amount of correlation by ε, where $\varepsilon = 0$ means absolutely no correlation between strategies (i.e., purely random pairwise encounters) and $\varepsilon = 1$ means perfectly correlated interactions (i.e., no one interacts with anyone of a different kind). The probability of the strategy σ_i interacting with itself, which normally is s_i in the uncorrelated replicator dynamics, increases to $s_i + \varepsilon(1 - s_i)$. The probability of σ_i interacting with some other strategy σ_j, where $j \neq i$, correspondingly decreases to $s_j - \varepsilon \cdot s_j$. Figure 5.4 illustrates the effect of correlation when $\varepsilon = 0.1$ and $\varepsilon = 0.2$.

Introducing correlation into the replicator-dynamics model has noticeable consequences on the basins of attraction for fair division. In figure 5.4(a),

---

the population, Demand 0 will do worse than the population average, so the proportion of individuals following Demand 0 will shrink in the next generation. One consequence of this is that the number of individuals who follow Demand 0 never increases and, in fact, always decreases as long as another strategy exists. An initial 0–10 polymorphism thus converges (quite rapidly) to the state in which everyone demands 10. This point is highly unstable, and any mutation will cause the population to converge to some other equilbrium point. Polymorphic pitfalls must be evolutionarily stable states, and the 0–10 equilibrium is not evolutionary stable.

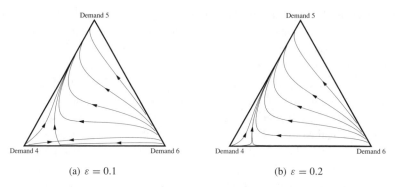

Figure 5.4 The simplex space for the 4–5–6 Nash game with correlation.

the basin of attraction for the unfair Demand 4–Demand 6 polymorphism has shrunk to a fraction of its former size. By the time the correlation coefficient reaches 0.2, the unfair polymorphisms have virtually disappeared.[16] Since pairwise interactions between individuals are likely to be not perfectly random, but somewhat correlated, the fact that incorporating correlation into the replicator-dynamics model increases the size of the basin of attraction for fair division strengthens the evolutionary explanation for why the norm of fair division is so widely held.

Summarizing these results, Skyrms (1996) states that

> In a finite population, in a finite time, where there is some random element in evolution, some reasonable amount of divisibility of the good and some correlation, we can say that it is likely that something close to share and share alike should evolve in dividing-the-cake situations. This is, perhaps, a beginning of an evolutionary account of the origin of our concept of justice.

Perhaps this is so, but it is worth concentrating on two crucial assumptions underlying the replicator-dynamics model. First, Skyrms explicitly refers to the population under study as *finite*. This assumption seems inappropriate given that an important assumption of the replicator dynamics is that the population must be large enough to justify identifying the expected fitness of an individual following a strategy with the expected fitness of that strategy. In small, finite

---

[16] For example, one of the trials displayed in figure 5.4(b) was begun at the initial point (0.992 87, 0.000 13, 0.007) (the frequencies of Demand 4, Demand 5, and Demand 6, respectively), which still converged to fair division even though less than 0.1 percent of the population initially followed fair division. The initial state (0.01, 0.002 96, 0.987 04) converged to fair division as well. However, if the initial frequency of fair division were lowered further, we would still arrive at an unfair 4–6 polymorphism. The primary point, though, is that it does not take much correlation to eliminate, for all practical purposes, the basin of attraction for the 4–6 polymorphism.

populations, this assumption need not be true. Second, the replicator dynamics converges to fair division in the majority of cases only when there is a certain amount of positive correlation in the population. Where does this correlation come from, and why is it only positive?

Positive correlation means that strategies are more likely to interact with themselves than with other strategies. Positive correlation tips the tables in favor of fair division since the 50–50 split is the highest-scoring strategy that plays well against itself. In the 60–40 polymorphism, the strategy which asks for 60 percent of the cake does not play well against itself: two players who ask for 60 percent both receive nothing according to the rules of the game. Hence positive correlation introduces selection pressure against the strategy of asking for 60 percent. Although players who ask for 40 percent *do* play well against themselves, they don't receive as high a payoff as people following the 50–50 split, so there is selective pressure against the strategy which asks for 40 percent. With enough positive correlation, the success of the 50–50 split is assured.[17]

The above objection to Skyrms's replicator dynamics is due to D'Arms, Batterman, and Górny (1998), who developed a finite-population model incorporating both positive and negative correlation. Negative correlation, here, means just that individuals tend to avoid interacting with members of their own kind, preferring to interact with individuals following different strategies. Negative correlation works in favor of strategies that ask for more than half of the cake, and doesn't significantly harm strategies that ask for significantly less than half of the cake. D'Arms *et al.* (1998) note that allowing both positive and negative correlation *reintroduces* the polymorphic pitfalls. The moral of the story, then, is that widespread evolution of distributive justice in the replicator dynamics depends crucially upon the assumption of positive correlation.

5.2 Lattice models

As we've seen for the prisoner's dilemma and the Stag Hunt, local interaction models give rise to results very different from that of the replicator dynamics. The game of divide-the-cake proves no different. To begin, consider the evolution of distributive justice on a lattice, where spatial position generates

---

[17] Consider the limiting case with perfect correlation. Here, people asking for 60 percent of the cake always receive nothing; people asking for 40 percent of the cake always get what they ask for, as do people who ask for 50 percent. However, those asking for 50 percent do better both than those asking for 60 percent (who earn nothing) and than those asking for 40 percent (who earn only 40 percent), so the strategies of asking for 40 and 60 percent become extinct.

Strategy	Color	Strategy	Color	Strategy	Color
Demand 0	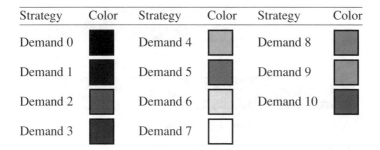	Demand 4		Demand 8	
Demand 1		Demand 5		Demand 9	
Demand 2		Demand 6		Demand 10	
Demand 3		Demand 7			

Figure 5.5 Color representation of strategies in the Nash bargaining game.

(a) The evolution of fair division from uniform initial conditions with an interaction radius of 1

(b) The evolution of fair division from a 4–5–6 polymorphism with initial distribution ⟨0.4, 0.2, 0.4⟩ with an interaction radius of 1

Figure 5.6 Divide the dollar played on a one-dimensional lattice.

correlation between strategies in a natural way. Figure 5.5 lists the correspondence between colors and strategies for the Nash bargaining game used in subsequent diagrams.

Figure 5.6 illustrates the evolution of fair division on a one-dimensional lattice consisting of 200 individuals from two different initial conditions. The interaction and update neighborhoods are equal and involve only each person's immediate left and right neighbor. Players adopt new strategies using *Imitate-the-Best*. In figure 5.6(a), all eleven strategies from Demand 0 to Demand 10 are equally likely to appear. In figure 5.6(b), the only strategies initially present

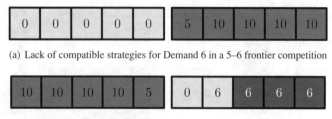

(a) Lack of compatible strategies for Demand 6 in a 5–6 frontier competition

(b) The strategy Demand 3 supporting Demand 6

Figure 5.7 Frontier competition between fair division and Demand 6. Colors represent individual strategies and numbers are individual scores calculated using an interaction radius of 1.

are Demand 4, Demand 5, and Demand 6, which are assigned to individuals randomly using the distribution $\langle 0.4, 0.2, 0.4 \rangle$, which gives a small advantage to the 4–6 polymorphism. The first generation appears on the topmost line with successive generations listed beneath. Aside from the obvious success with which fair division dominates, examination of the figures reveals two features that need explanation. First, on the left-hand side of figure 5.6(a) we see fair division successfully invading a region occupied by the strategy of Demand 6, yet towards the center we find a vertical line that represents a group of individuals following Demand 6 who resist invasion by fair dividers. What is it about that arrangement of Demand 6 near the center that allows them, unlike their fellow cohorts on the left, to resist invasion? Second, if one inspects figure 5.6(b) carefully, one will notice that the relentless advance of fair division occasionally pauses, proceeding to continue the advance in the next generation. Why?

Fair division successfully invades the region of Demand 6 on the left of figure 5.6(a) because, there, the strategy of Demand 6 is isolated: no compatible strategies exist in the nearby vicinity. Consequently, the Demand 6 individual on the frontier between Demand 6 and Demand 5 finds himself at a significant disadvantage: his right-hand neighbor demands 5 and his left-hand neighbor demands 6, so in both interactions the Demand 6 frontier competitor earns a score of zero. However, the frontier competitor who demands 5 earns a score of 5 because *his* right-hand neighbor follows a compatible strategy. Moreover, because all of the Demand 6 neighbors of the Demand 6 frontier competitor *also* earn scores of zero (they, too, have no compatible strategies surrounding them), the only viable strategy for the Demand 6 frontier competitor to imitate, from his point of view, is that of fair division. Consequently, the Demand 6 individual on the frontier switches to fair division for the next generation. Figure 5.7(a) illustrates this scenario.

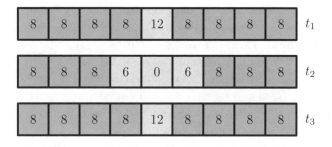

Figure 5.8 The existence of "blinkers" in a 4–6 polymorphism.

However, as the standoff between Demand 6 and fair division in the center of figure 5.6(a) reveals, fair division does not always succeed in displacing Demand 6 in a frontier competition. If the Demand 6 strategy on the frontier is supported by compatible strategies in the interior, a stalemate can ensue. The reason for the stalemate occuring near the center of figure 5.6 is shown in figure 5.7(b). There we see how the frontier Demand 6 persists even though it receives a score of zero because the neighboring Demand 6 on his right earns the best score in his neighborhood. In this configuration, none of the individuals participating in the frontier competition will switch strategies in the next generation, producing an evolutionary stalemate. This is the same phenomenon as we saw in chapter 3 in the case of the prisoner's dilemma: strategies on the frontier can avoid being replaced when they are supported from the interior.

The sequence of events shown in figure 5.6(b) indicates how fair division can successfully invade regions occupied by a 4–6 polymorphism. In local-interaction models with imitative strategies, strategy polymorphisms often result in the existence of so-called "blinkers": stable local structures of period 2 in which certain individuals oscillate between following one strategy and following another. With an interaction and update radius of 1, a 4–6 polymorphism settles into such "blinkers" consisting of an expanding and collapsing group of individuals whose strategy is Demand 6. (Figure 5.8 shows why blinkers form by calculating the scores for individuals following Demand 4 and Demand 6 in the vicinity of the blinker.) When the blinker is in its collapsed state, the 4–6 polymorphism is vulnerable to invasion. Consider the scores which result when a fair divider is next to the lone individual following Demand 6: the individual whose strategy is Demand 6 earns 6, the fair divider 5, and the individual following Demand 4 on the other side of the one following Demand 6 earns 8. The fair divider does not switch strategies, because he is supported by his adjacent neighbor who also holds the strategy of Demand 5 yet earns a score of 10. However, the frontier individual following Demand 6 has no other high-scoring individuals following Demand 6 to support him; hence, the individual following Demand 6 switches to the strategy of Demand 4 in the next generation. This elimination of the sole individual following Demand 6 results in a frontier competition between Demand 5 and Demand 4, which is easily proved to lead to the elimination of Demand 4. It is also easy to show that, if a region of fair division is adjacent to the blinker in its expanded state, fair division will be able to invade as well.

The arguments we've developed can be generalized, and doing so allows us to see why fair division almost always dominates for the game of divide-the-cake played on a one-dimensional lattice. The first task at hand is to identify what happens in frontier competitions between competing strategies. Once we have determined the behavior in frontier competitions, we can use this to determine which pairs of frontiers are "stable" when paired against each other – that is, the frontiers result in a stalemate in which neither side advances – and which are "unstable," meaning that one side advances at the expense of the other.

Suppose that the cake is divided into C pieces and let the common interaction and update radius be r. There are a few easy cases to consider.

Frontier competition between s_1 and s_2, when $s_1 + s_2 \leq C$, $s_1 \leq C/2$, and $s_2 \leq C/2$. We can assume without loss of generality that $s_1 < s_2$. Since the two strategies s_1 and s_2 are compatible, and each strategy is compatible with itself, each player receives the number of slices of cake he asks for no matter whom he plays. With an interaction radius of r, each player following s_1 receives $2rs_1$ slices of cake, and each player following s_2 receives $2rs_2$ slices of cake. Since $s_1 < s_2$, the region following s_2 wins the frontier competition and successfully invades the region held by s_1. This is the situation of figure 5.6 for the frontier competition between Demand 4 and Demand 5.

Frontier competition between s_1 and s_2, when $s_1 + s_2 \leq C$, $s_1 > C/2$, and $s_2 \leq C/2$. In this situation, s_1 and s_2 are compatible, s_2 is self-compatible, but s_1 is not self-compatible.[18] This would be, for example, the situation occurring when a region of Demand 6 faces a region of Demand 4. Since s_1 is not self-compatible, the individual on the boundary of the s_1-region earns a score of rs_1, and the individual on the boundary of the s_2-region earns a score of $2rs_2$ (as do all members of the s_2-region). If $s_1 > 2s_2$, the s_1-region will win the

---

[18] By symmetry of notation, the following argument also covers the case when $s_1 \leq C/2$ and $s_2 > C/2$.

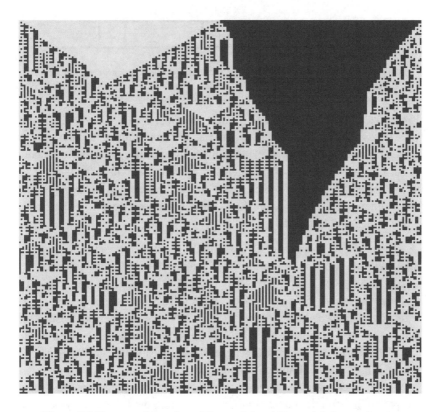

Figure 5.9 The mutual invasion of Demand 6 and Demand 3 from a frontier competition when $r = 2$.

frontier competition, invading the s_2-region; if $s_1 < 2s_2$, the s_2-region wins the frontier competition, invading the s_1-region. If $s_1 = 2s_2$, a stalemate ensues when $r = 1$. If $r > 1$, individuals within r units of the boundary will earn scores less than rs_1 and will also have some chance of switching to the strategy s_2, since their update neighborhood overlaps the s_2-region. In this case, the frontier competition will disappear through a process of "mutual invasion," as illustrated in figure 5.9. Notice, though, that in this process of mutual invasion neither strategy is entirely eliminated from the population.

Frontier competition between s_1 and s_2, when $s_1 + s_2 > C$, $s_1 \leq C/2$, and $s_2 > C/2$. In this case, s_1 is self-compatible but s_2 is not, and the strategies s_1 and s_2 are not compatible. Given this, s_2 will never earn a nonzero score and s_1 always will, so the s_1-region will invade the s_2-region. An example of this is the frontier competition between Demand 4 and Demand 7 with a cake size of 10.

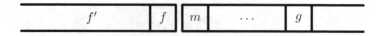

Figure 5.10 Frontier competition between fair division and a greedy–modest polymorphism.

Frontier competition between s_1 and s_2, when $s_1 + s_2 > C$, $s_1 > C/2$, and $s_2 > C/2$. Since the strategies s_1 and s_2 are not compatible, and neither strategy is compatible with itself, all individuals in both regions receive a score of zero. However, no one will switch strategies because no individual with a nonzero score exists. This produces a stalemate between the two regions, and is the situation existing in figure 5.6 in the competition between the strategies of Demand 7 and Demand 9.

The above four cases cover all possibilities when we have a frontier competition between two regions occupied by a single strategy. Let us call a strategy asking for more than half of the cake a "greedy" strategy and one asking for less than half of the cake a "modest" strategy. The first case proves that, in a region consisting solely of modest strategies, where at least one person asks for half of the cake, eventually all will adopt the strategy of asking for half of the cake. The third case proves that, whenever fair division faces a purely greedy region, fair division will ultimately dominate.

What happens when a region of fair division faces a greedy–modest polymorphism in a frontier competition? Suppose that, on the boundary between the two regions, a fair divider faces a modest individual, with all fair dividers on the left and the greedy–modest polymorphism on the right. The situation envisioned is that of figure 5.10. Let's consider this in stages.

Can the fair divider be replaced by a modest individual? Not given the situation illustrated. Located $r - 1$ spaces to the left of the fair divider f on the frontier is a fair divider f' who interacts with $2r - 1$ fair dividers and one modest individual. Hence f' earns a score of $2r \cdot C/2$, which is greater than any possible score obtainable by a modest individual. Since f' falls within the update neighborhood of f, the frontier fair divider will never adopt the modest strategy in the next generation. Furthermore, since f' falls within the update neighborhood of the $r - 2$ fair dividers between f and f', none of these fair dividers will switch to a modest strategy, either.

Can the fair divider be replaced by a greedy individual? It *is* possible for this to happen, but it ultimately harms the greedy–modest polymorphism in the long run. To see this, suppose that somewhere within r spaces of f on the right there is a greedy individual g. Because f' earns a score of rC, in order for a greedy individual to replace f, the greedy individual g must earn a score

Figure 5.11 Invasion of a minimal 3–7 polymorphism by fair division in a frontier competition.

strictly greater than rC. Let M be the number of modest individuals in the neighborhood of g. In order for the score of g to exceed rC, it must be the case that M is at least $r + 1$ since g cannot ask for more than C pieces of cake.

If we suppose, then, that g has enough modest individuals in his neighborhood to earn a score higher than f, what happens? The boundary fair divider f (perhaps with some other fair dividers), will switch to g, but so will *all* modest individuals within g's neighborhood. Since M is at least $r + 1$, this creates a frontier competition between a region of fair dividers and greedy individuals, on one side, and greedy individuals and the rest of the greedy–modest polymorphism on the other. Since we have already proved that fair division can invade a pure region occupied by greedy strategies, fair division will be able to invade and recoup the lost territory in the next generation. In most cases, the fair dividers will win more territory than they lost, resulting in a net gain for fair division. Figure 5.11 illustrates this for a simple frontier competition between fair division and a minimal 3–7 polymorphism. By applying this argument again to the new frontier competition with the shifted boundary, we can see that fair division – even if occasionally pushed back by an unusually successful greedy strategy – will ultimately expand, driving out the entire greedy–modest polymorphism. In short, whenever there is a small cluster of fair dividers present in a population that follows the strategy of *Imitate-the-Best*, the spread of fair division is inevitable.

What happens in two dimensions? Figure 5.12 illustrates a typical evolutionary trajectory for a randomly initialized world on a two-dimensional lattice in which all strategies are equally likely, with the Moore (8) neighborhood used both for interaction and for updating. The upper-left image shows the original state of the world. Successive generations are presented left to right by rows so that the leftmost image of row $n + 1$ is the successor to the rightmost image of row n. As we see, by the end of the ninth generation the majority of the population has adopted the strategy Demand 5.[19]

---

[19] Except for two small regions of Demand 4 and Demand 6 in the center and bottom center of the world. By the eleventh generation, all agents followed the strategy of fair division. These images were suppressed because the trajectory is obvious.

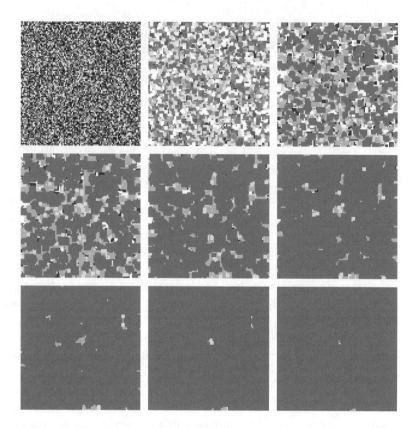

Figure 5.12 The emergence of fair division from a randomly initialized world, with all strategies equally likely, under the Moore (8) neighborhood.

Close inspection of figure 5.12 shows that fair division begins to gain the upper hand after the first generation, and establishes an appreciable presence by the end of the second. One might wonder whether this rapid increase in the number of fair dividers occurs primarily because of the initial success fair division has under the initial conditions, namely, when strategies are more or less uniformly distributed. Such situations will typically hold only in relatively few cases and, even then, the approximately uniform distribution of strategies will not persist much beyond the first generation; after that, players change strategies in ways that will certainly move the frequencies of strategies in the population away from uniformity. However, if the first few generations provide fair division with an advantage not shared by other strategies, this small initial advantage might allow fair division to expand to occupy regions of sufficient size that other strategies cannot displace it.

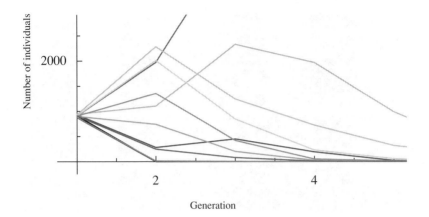

Generation

Figure 5.13 Proportions of the population following each strategy for the first four generations of figure 5.12.

Let s_i denote the probability that a given player interacts with an individual following strategy i. The expected payoff for all strategies in divide-the-cake, where strategies are randomly distributed on the lattice, is

$$E(\text{Demand } i) = n_i \sum_{0 \le j \le 10-i} i s_j,$$

where n_i is the number of neighbors in the interaction neighborhood of each player. Since this value is common to all players, it can be ignored. It is easy to calculate the expected fitness for all strategies for any vector $\langle s_0, \ldots, s_{10} \rangle$ of strategy frequencies. In the case we are considering $s_i = s_j$ for all i and j, so we can factor out this common value of $\frac{1}{11}$ from the sum. The expected payoff of strategy i under uniform conditions is $\frac{1}{11} i (10 - i + 1)$, which means that Demand 5 and Demand 6 tie, with expected values under uniform initial conditions of $\frac{30}{11}$. The success of fair division thus cannot be explained by it having an advantage under uniform circumstances that is not shared by other strategies. Figure 5.13 shows this to be true: the two strategies exhibiting the most extreme growth in the first two generations are Demand 5 and Demand 6. In fact, the rate of growth of Demand 6, due to random fluctuations in the positioning of strategies on the lattice, actually exceeds that of Demand 5.

A closer look at figure 5.12, especially the regions temporarily occupied by unfair polymorphisms, suggests that fair division's success in frontier competitions in two dimensions proceeds along lines similar to that in one dimension. Figure 5.14 illustrates a frontier competition between fair division and the 4–6 polymorphism. (In order to preserve the frontier, the lattice does not wrap at the boundary.) Over time, we see that fair division slowly invades the region

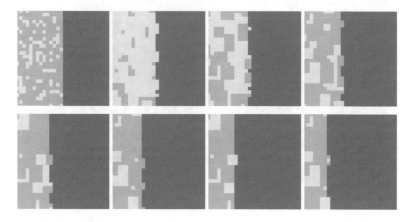

Figure 5.14 A frontier competition between fair division and the 4–6 polymorphism in two dimensions.

originally occupied by the unfair polymorphism. Within eight generations, fair division has made significant progress towards eliminating the unfair population. (This rapid elimination of unfair strategies occurs because of the relatively small dimensions of the lattice. On a 100 × 100 lattice, fair division completely dominates typically within sixty generations.) If the lattice is allowed to wrap at the edges, fair division dominates twice as fast because the unfair polymorphism is eaten away from both sides at once.

The type of neighborhood used both for interaction and for updating has little effect on the convergent state of the population, although it does influence the path followed to reach that state. Figure 5.15 illustrates the different evolutionary trajectory followed by a population begun in an initial state similar to that of figure 5.12, but using the von Neumann neighborhood for interaction and updating instead. Although fair division still wins out in the end, it takes longer due to the reduced size of the imitation neighborhood. Figure 5.16 again considers a world having similar initial conditions to those of the previous two, but using the Moore (24) neighborhood. On account of the greater radius of interaction of the Moore (24) neighborhood, fair division moves to fixation considerably faster than in any of the previous models. The larger neighborhood also allows the unfair polymorphisms (in this series, the unfair polymorphism is the familiar Demand 4–Demand 6 polymorphism) to establish their strongest presence yet (measured in terms of the average area occupied by a region of unfair polymorphisms) before being overrun.

Table 5.1 summarizes the final convergent state of the world for several different combinations of neighborhoods and dynamics. The neighborhoods

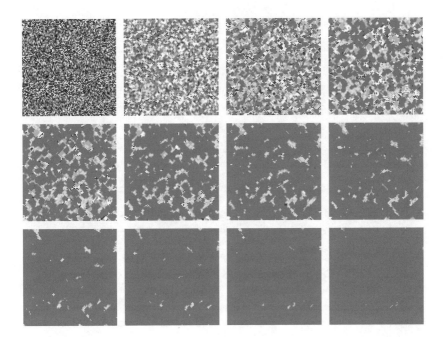

Figure 5.15 The emergence of fair division from a randomly initialized world, with all strategies equally likely, under the von Neumann neighborhood.

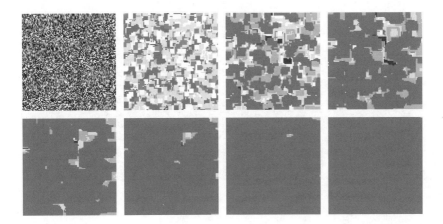

Figure 5.16 The emergence of fair division from a randomly initialized world, with all strategies equally likely, under the Moore (24) neighborhood.

Table 5.1. *Convergence results based on neighborhood and dynamic*

Neighborhood	Dynamics	Polymorphism						
		0–10	1–9	2–8	3–7	4–6	5	Other
Von Neumann	Imitate with probability relative to success	0	0	0	0	29	9970	1
	Mimic best neighbor	0	0	0	0	26	9966	8
	Imitate best average strategy	0	0	0	0	13	9984	3
Moore (8)	Imitate with probability relative to success	0	0	0	0	26	9973	1
	Imitate best neighbor	0	0	0	0	26	9908	66
	Imitate best average strategy	0	0	0	0	24	9970	6
Moore (24)	Imitate with probability relative to success	0	0	0	8	110	9879	3
	Imitate best neighbor	0	0	0	21	220	9721	38
	Imitate best average strategy	0	0	0	0	62	9934	4
Type 1	Imitate with probability relative to success	0	0	0	3	47	9949	1
	Imitate best neighbor	0	0	0	3	62	9933	2
	Imitate best average strategy	0	0	0	0	29	9962	9
Type 2	Imitate with probability relative to success	0	0	0	0	32	9899	69
	Imitate best neighbor	0	0	0	0	43	9868	89
	Imitate best average strategy	0	0	0	0	28	9924	48
Type 3	Imitate with probability relative to success	0	0	0	3	42	9950	5
	Imitate best neighbor	0	0	0	3	62	9933	5
	Imitate best average strategy	0	0	0	0	32	9965	3

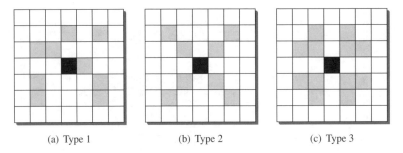

(a) Type 1   (b) Type 2   (c) Type 3

Figure 5.17 Three nonstandard neighborhoods used in table 5.1.

examined include the von Neumann, Moore (8), and Moore (24), as well as three nonstandard types indicated in figure 5.17. The type-1 nonstandard neighborhood was randomly constructed by choosing a subset of the Moore (24) neighborhood by a series of coin tosses. The important point to note is that, in general, mean times to convergence are quite rapid. Models using the Moore (8) neighborhood usually converged to fair division within sixteen generations. This is a considerable improvement over the results of Skyrms (1996) and Kandori *et al.* (1993), whose stochastically stable equilibrium selects only the equilibrium of fair division in the limit. The larger Moore (24) neighborhood leads to faster convergence because the radius of influence of any given single player is greater (table 5.2).

Does the evolution of fair division at all depend on the amount of cake individuals attempt to split? In *Evolution of the Social Contract*, Skyrms (1996) reported an interesting relationship between granularity of the good and the distribution of the resulting polymorphism. If we assume that players divide a cake consisting of ten slices, we find that under the replicator dynamics fair division takes over the population roughly 62 percent of the time with some percentage of the population falling into one of the 1–9 or 2–8 polymorphic traps. However, increasing the total number of pieces the cake is sliced into leads to an increase in the total number of populations that will evolve into something "near" fair division. In particular, Skyrms found that a cake divided into 200 pieces went to fair division ±3 pieces approximately 94.1 percent of the time; all trials went to fair division ±11 pieces (table 5.2).

Since most populations evolving on the lattice arrive at a pure state of fair division already, one natural question inverts the one considered by Skyrms: how *coarsely* can we slice the cake while still attaining fair division? Table 5.3 lists the results as the cake size varies from ten to two pieces, for each of the three dynamics considered, under the Moore (8) neighborhood. Lattice-based models exhibit a strong tendency for the strategy most akin to fair division to

Table 5.2. *Mean convergence times*

Neighborhood	Dynamics	Population composition					
		0–10	1–9	2–8	3–7	4–6	Fair
Von Neumann	Imitate with probability relative to success	—	—	—	—	25.4	23.9
	Imitate best neighbor	—	—	—	—	22.7	26.3
	Imitate best average strategy	—	—	—	—	32.2	23.9
Moore (8)	Imitate with probability relative to success	—	—	—	—	17.9	16.4
	Imitate best neighbor	—	—	—	—	28.0	15.4
	Imitate best average strategy	—	—	—	—	17.2	14.6
Moore (24)	Imitate with probability relative to success	—	—	—	13.9	17.2	14.9
	Imitate best neighbor	—	—	—	32.3	22.8	12.8
	Imitate best average strategy	—	—	—	—	18.7	10.6
Type 1	Imitate with probability relative to success	—	—	—	22.0	21.8	15.2
	Imitate best neighbor	—	—	—	24.0	10.7	12.69
	Imitate best average strategy	—	—	—	—	11.2	11.4
Type 2	Imitate with probability relative to success	—	—	—	—	22.4	15.6
	Imitate best neighbor	—	—	—	—	16.3	15.3
	Imitate best average strategy	—	—	—	—	16.6	13.7
Type 3	Imitate with probability relative to success	—	—	—	17.7	20.7	14.4
	Imitate best neighbor	—	—	—	24.0	10.7	12.7
	Imitate best average strategy	—	—	—	—	11.5	12.0

become fixated in the population. When the size of the cake is even, admitting a perfect 50–50 split, in the vast majority of cases the model converges to a state in which the appropriate strategy dominates (i.e., Demand 4 when the cake is divided into eighths). When the number of pieces into which the cake is divided is odd, so that no even split is possible,[20] the population tends to become "as close as possible" to the 50–50 split. (In chapter 7, the multiplayer version of divide-the-cake shows a similar tendency, converging as closely as possible to the egalitarian distribution across N persons.) In these cases, "as close as possible" means a polymorphic state in which, for an N-piece cake, one strategy demands $\lfloor N/2 \rfloor$ and the other demands $\lfloor N/2 \rfloor + 1$.

Randomly initialized populations almost always converge to fair division. Nonetheless, as the statistical results above indicate, in some small fraction of the cases unfair polymorphisms persist. Fair division typically fails to dominate when too few people initially follow that strategy. When isolated and paired against incompatible strategies, fair division may be driven to extinction by the end of the first generation. Once fair division has been eliminated, the population then evolves to some other polymorphic state.

The persistence of polymorphic pitfalls in the cases discussed so far stems from the fact that no mechanism exists for reintroducing a strategy into the population once it has been eliminated. If we allow individuals to experiment with novel strategies – the cultural evolutionary analogue of mutations – we obtain a virtual guarantee that a population will converge to fair division within a reasonable amount of time, no matter what the initial state of the population was. I say a "virtual guarantee" because random mutations introduce an inescapable stochastic element into the model, which prevents us from being able to say, with certainty, what population state the model will have reached at some future time.[21]

For example, consider a world in which no one initially follows the strategy of fair division, but where, in each generation, each player has a 10 percent

---

[20] Recall that agent strategies are restricted to integer values, so that the natural strategy of asking for 4.5 slices of the cake when the total cake size equals 9 slices cannot be employed.

[21] This qualification does not prove to be that important in practice – at least for the game of divide-the-cake. The extreme tendency of populations to converge to fair division means that, even if a substantial proportion of the population spontaneously mutated into members of another polymorphism, they would be readily driven out. The only way this could be prevented from happening is if *all* of the members of the population mutated at once to another polymorphism. The low probability of such an event means that this possibility exists in a sense that matters only to philosophers. For example, if every individual in the population mutates (this is equivalent to assuming the probability of mutation equals 1) the probability that each mutant on a 100×100 lattice converts to strategies in a compatible polymorphic pair, such as 4–6 or 3–7, is $(\frac{2}{11})^{10\,000} \approx 2.361 \times 10^{-7404}$. This probability becomes significantly lower if we assume a more realistic mutation rate of, say, $\mu = 0.001$. In this case, the probability plummets from 2.361×10^{-7404} to $2.361 \times 10^{-37\,404}$.

Table 5.3. Convergence results for a shrinking cake

Cake size	Dynamics	Polymorphism						
		0–10	1–9	2–8	3–7	4–6	5	Other
10	Mimic best neighbor	0	0	0	0	2	998	0
	Imitate best average strategy	0	0	0	0	2	998	0
	Imitate using relative success	0	0	0	0	3	997	0
9	Mimic best neighbor	0	0	0	0	5[10]	0	995[11]
	Imitate best average strategy	0	0	0	0	1*	0	999[12]
	Imitate using relative success	0	0	0	0	17*	0	983[13]
8	Mimic best neighbor	0	0	0	0	999[1]	0	1[1]
	Imitate best average strategy	0	0	0	0	998*	0	2[3]
	Imitate using relative success	0	0	0	0	1000*	0	0
7	Mimic best neighbor	0	0	0	3	0	0	997[14]
	Imitate best average strategy	0	0	0	3	0	0	997[15]
	Imitate using relative success	0	0	0	4	0	0	996[16]
6	Mimic best neighbor	0	0	0	998*	0	0	2[4]
	Imitate best average strategy	0	0	0	1000*	0	0	0
	Imitate using relative success	0	0	0	995*	0	0	5[5]
5	Mimic best neighbor	0	0	1	0	0	0	999[17]
	Imitate best average strategy	0	0	1	0	0	0	999[18]
	Imitate using relative success	0	0	2	0	0	0	998[19]

4	Mimic best neighbor	0	0	0	1000*	0	0	0
	Imitate best average strategy	0	0	0	999*	0	0	1[6]
	Imitate using relative success	0	0	0	997*	0	0	3[7]
3	Mimic best neighbor	1	0	0	0	0	0	999[20]
	Imitate best average strategy	0	0	0	0	0	0	1000[21]
	Imitate using relative success	0	0	0	0	0	0	1000[22]
2	Mimic best neighbor	997*	0	0	0	0	0	3[8]
	Imitate best average strategy	1000*	0	0	0	0	0	0
	Imitate using relative success	998*	0	0	0	0	0	2[9]

Note: [1]Of these, 973 were pure states of Demand 4. [2]A 3–5 polymorphism (3609, 6391). [3]Two 3–5 polymorphisms: (3736, 6264), (3813, 6187). [4]Two 2–4 polymorphisms: (5112, 4888), (5196, 4804). [5]Five 2–4 polymorphisms: (3273, 6727), (3484, 6516), (3380, 6620), (3476, 6524), (3589, 6411). [6]A 1–3 polymorphism (2563, 7437). [7]Three 1–3 polymorphisms: (2147, 7853), (2233, 7767), (2135, 7865). [8]In all three worlds, the strategy of Demand 1 became extinct early on, leaving the population in an unstable equilibrium of (1, 0, 9728, 34, 34, 36, 1, 90, 28, 0, 48), (22, 0, 5682, 129, 571, 884, 556, 430, 960, 128, 638), and (69, 0, 5771, 1646, 321, 86, 187, 626, 844, 115, 335). [9]Both worlds contain unstable equilibria in which all strategies are present: (4, 7, 5241, 212, 90, 195, 280, 495, 2387, 572, 517) and (2, 11, 2440, 523, 646, 988, 702, 1831, 105, 1040, 1712). [10]Four of these states contained only Demand 4. [11]One 3–6 polymorphism and one 3–5 polymorphism, with the rest being 4–5 polymorphisms. [12]Three 3–6 polymorphisms, the rest 4–5 polymorphisms. [13]Three 3–6 polymorphisms, the rest 4–5 polymorphisms. [14]One 2–5 polymorphism and one 2–4–5 polymorphism, the rest 3–4 polymorphisms. [15]Five 2–5 polymorphisms, the rest 3–4 polymorphisms. [16]Two 2–5 polymorphisms, the rest 3–4 polymorphisms. [17]Two 1–3–4 polymorphisms, the rest 2–3 polymorphisms. [18]One 1–3–4 polymorphism, the rest 2–3 polymorphisms. [19]All 2–3 polymorphisms. [20]One world containing the unstable equilibrium (0, 0, 1074, 1070, 1011, 1111, 1125, 1083, 1110, 1175, 1241), the rest 1–2 polymorphisms. [21]One world containing the unstable equilibrium (15, 3, 108, 4220, 254, 146, 525, 855, 2335, 1520, 19), the rest 1–2 polymorphisms. [22]Three unstable equilibria of the following form: (6, 0, 8764, 9, 10, 806, 60, 95, 116, 53, 81), (86, 0, 2958, 1357, 648, 2611, 263, 1159, 618, 81, 219), and (10, 10, 129, 1650, 4478, 4, 289, 253, 964, 1080, 1133), the rest 1–2 polymorphisms. * All states contain only the strategy making the lowest demand of the pair.

chance of mutating (a relatively high mutation rate). For all practical purposes, in a population of any significant size within one or two generations a mutation will introduce the strategy of fair division into the population.[22] There remains a small chance that no mutation will introduce the strategy of fair division into the population within t generations, for any t. Admittedly, this chance goes to zero as $t \to \infty$ (and does so rather quickly), giving us the "virtual guarantee" that the population will eventually converge to fair division spoken of earlier. Of course, when we speak of a population "converging to a state of fair division," we must adapt the definition of "converge" accordingly so that it makes sense to talk of a population having converged to a state of fair division even when a small fraction of the players follows other strategies, since this will most typically be the case in the presence of mutations. We also must specify which learning rule we speak of, for mutation does not always produce fair dividers in the long run, regardless of the learning rule. Figure 5.21 below shows how mutation can produce a suboptimal outcome when agents use a naïve best-response rule.

Figure 5.18 illustrates how even a small mutation rate suffices to overturn an unfair population within a few generations. The images in this particular series were not sampled at constant intervals, so one should not take apparent differences in the diffusion rate of the Demand 5 strategy to be significant. The total number of generations required for fair division to achieve complete domination was exactly thirty.

The amount of time required to move a population from a polymorphic pitfall to a state in which almost everyone[23] follows fair division depends on the frequency of mutations μ. Inspection of figure 5.18 reveals that the key step in the emergence of fair division is the introduction of the Demand 5 strategy into a site surrounded by sufficiently many compatible ones (in this case, the only compatible strategy is Demand 4). Figure 5.19 shows a close-up of the first few generations after such a critical mutation has occurred. If μ is small (or if there are not many sites with compatible strategies), obviously one will have to wait longer. In comparison with the time required for the model of Kandori *et al.* (1993) to return to fair division if it becomes trapped in a polymorphic pitfall, the wait in this case seems hardly significant: the run portrayed in figure 5.18, which had $\mu = 0.0005$, had the critical mutation occurring in the second generation.

---

[22] This assumes that when a mutation occurs there is a reasonable chance that any other strategy will result. (The probability distribution determining the frequency with which mutant strategies arise, though, need not be uniform.)

[23] We must qualify this because a nonzero mutation rate typically results in a small amount of mutational "noise" appearing each generation.

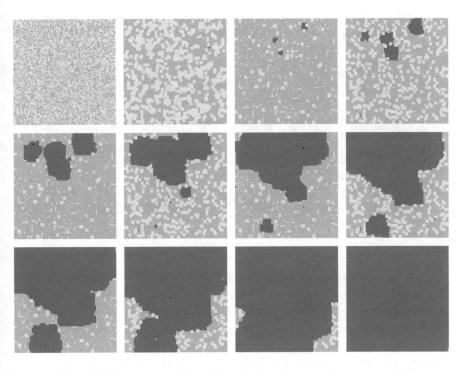

Figure 5.18 Emergence of fair division out of a 4–6 polymorphism as a result of mutation.

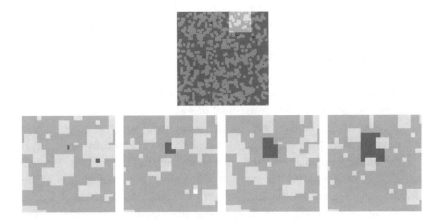

Figure 5.19 A close-up of the critical mutation in figure 5.18.

Fairness

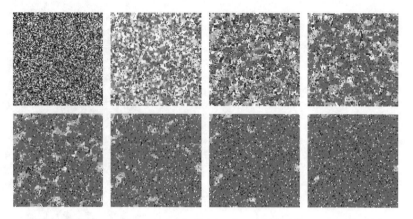

Figure 5.20 The persistence of fair division in a world with an unusually high mutation rate ($\mu = 0.1$).

Mutations may move a population trapped in an unfair polymorphism to a state in which almost everyone follows the strategy of Demand 5, but can the opposite happen as well? Can mutations cause a population to leave a state in which (almost) everyone opts for the equal split for a state in which almost everyone follows one strategy of an unfair polymorphism? For *Imitate-the-Best* the answer is a qualified no. It is possible, albeit very unlikely, for every agent in the population to mutate into an agent following one strategy of an unfair polymorphic pair in the same generation. Mutations may, in principle, cause the population to jump from a state of fair division into any other state, but the chance of this happening is extremely low. If the mutation rate is μ, then the probability of n mutations occurring, none of which transforms an agent's strategy to that of fair division, equals $\left(\frac{10}{11}\mu\right)^{n}$.[24] Although a population *may* be tranformed out of a state in which fair division dominates by mutation, one would expect to wait an extraordinarily long time for this to occur, even with a relatively high mutation rate. If $\mu = 0.05$, then the probability of such mutations occurring for 200 agents (much less a population of several thousand) is 3.2769×10^{-269}. Furthermore, given the ease with which mutations move a population away from an unfair polymorphism towards fair division, even if such an unlikely population shift did occur, it would not last for long. Brought together, all of this means that states in which most follow the strategy of fair division have remarkable stability properties, even in the presence of a large amount of mutation. Figure 5.20 illustrates the robustness properties of fair division in an extreme case.

---

[24] Assuming that the probability of any strategy produced via mutation is equally likely, with a cake size of 10.

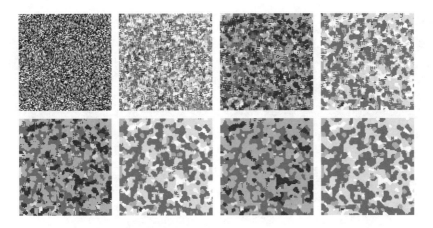

Figure 5.21 The disadvantageous state resulting when all players employ the best-response update rule.

Thus far we have seen how boundedly rational agents who act to maximize individual gain using *Imitate-the-Best* may successfully arrive at uniform agreement on behavior corresponding to our norms of share-and-share-alike. What happens when agents follow a more sophisticated learning rule, like *Best Response*? Will they arrive at the same outcome more rapidly? Interestingly, this turns out to be not true in general, as figure 5.21 illustrates. In that figure all agents use *Best Response*, explicitly adopting that strategy calculated to yield the best expected payoff under the assumption that neighboring agents will not change their strategies in the next generation. We find that the best-response update rule leads to an extremely suboptimal outcome, measured from the point of view of an individual agent's utility. In the regions alternating between the strategies of Demand 4 and Demand 6, each agent receives on average only two slices of cake, in notable contrast with the five slices received each turn by their fair-playing brothers.[25]

Do mutations prevent the *Best Response* from coordinating on the suboptimal equilibrium? It turns out that introducing mutants into the population can make the situation much worse. Figure 5.22 shows a population that began under uniform initial conditions with a mutation rate of 0.1. (Using a high mutation rate approximates running the model at a lower mutation rate for a longer time, provided that any two mutants that appear are not so close that

---

[25] The average payoff for agents in the "blinker" region equals 2 because, when an agent and all of his neighbors follow Demand 6, no one receives anything. In such a situation, the best-response strategy for a given agent (assuming that none of his neighbors change their strategies) would be to follow Demand 4. Thus, in the next generation, all agent requests can be satisfied; each agent receives cake according to the pattern 0, 4, 0, 4, 0 . . ., giving an average payoff of two.

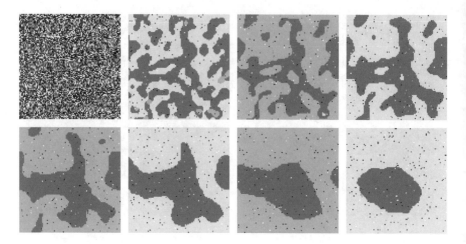

Figure 5.22 The disadvantageous state resulting when all players employ the best-response update rule (with mutations).

both of them can affect the interactions or payoffs of any other single player.) In the absence of mutation, as seen in figure 5.21, stable local regions of fair division or 4–6 polymorphisms form. In the presence of mutation, gradual consolidation of regions occurs until, after more than 22 000 generations, the entire population (save for the mutants) has converged to the terribly suboptimal 4–6 polymorphism! The lesson to take away is that, in strategic environments it is, on occasion, to a player's benefit not to be too clever when updating strategies.

5.3 Small-world networks

As argued in previous chapters, the final states to which small-world networks converge can be analyzed by considering the small-world network to be a series of one-dimensional lattices connected by hubs. Figure 5.23 illustrates the final convergent state of the game of divide-the-cake played on five small-world networks with an interaction radius of 1. Fair division dominates in two of the five worlds, occupies approximately half of the population in two others, and does not appear at all in one.

With an interaction and update radius of 1, hubs can block the expansion of fair division if the hubs surrounding the region of fair division are suitably populated by individuals following other strategies. For example, consider a region of Demand 5 surrounded on both sides by hubs occupied by the strategy

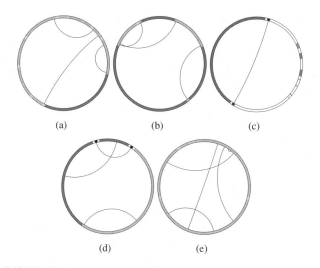

Figure 5.23 The final convergent states of divide-the-cake played on five small-world networks, $r = 1$.

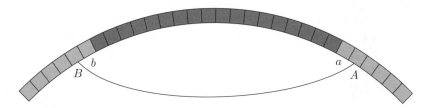

Figure 5.24 A region of fair division trapped between two hubs occupied by Demand 4.

Demand 4, as illustrated in figure 5.24. If the bridge edge did not exist, players a and b would adopt the strategy Demand 5 in the next generation. However, because the bridge edge exists, players A and B each earn a score of 12 since they both have three neighbors rather than just two. This success of A and B prevents a and b from adopting the strategy of fair division even though a and b receive a lower score than do their fair-playing neighbors. The important feature here is that the higher score earned by A and B "supports" the poor-performing boundary players and effectively blocks the expansion of fair division.

Divide-the-cake played on a small-world network enables us to say something useful about the medium- and long-run dynamics. In the absence of mutation, the possible long-run convergence patterns for a small-world network can be predicted as follows. Consider the set of basins of attraction for the game of divide-the-cake played on lines of various length (the relevant lengths are determined by the bridge edges, which effectively cut the ring into segments). Weight each of these basins of attraction by the proportion of state space it occupies. Then the set of possible long-run convergence patterns for the small-world network is obtained by simply piecing these smaller segments together, with the probability of any given outcome occuring being the product of weightings assigned to each individual section. In the absence of mutation, it is not meaningful to distinguish between the outcomes of the evolutionary dynamics in the medium and long run – once the population has settled into a stable state, it will remain there indefinitely.

However, if mutations *are* allowed, but at a sufficiently low level, then it becomes possible to differentiate between the outcomes of the dynamics over the medium and long run. With a low mutation rate, the population will first converge to one of the possible patterns described above – this is the medium-run outcome. As mutants are slowly introduced, though, eventually a fair divider will appear in one of the regions occupied by another polymorphism. In most cases,[26] this Demand 5 mutant will expand in the next generation and begin a frontier competition between the unfair polymorphism and a local region of fair dividers. As we've seen earlier, such frontier competitions always end in favor of fair division. Over the long run, the population will eventually settle into a state in which almost everyone follows the strategy of fair division.[27]

5.4 Bounded-degree networks

Consider the interactive situation represented in figure 5.25. There we have fifteen individuals playing divide-the-dollar on a bounded-degree network with $k_{min} = 2$ and $k_{max} = 3$. One noteworthy feature of this kind of network is that it features a particularly small population, especially compared with the local-interaction models considered so far in this chapter. In a small population, any initial assignment of strategies done according to a randomly chosen vector

---

[26] This qualification is necessary because it is possible for the polymorphic region to contain a number of blinkers. If the random mutation event happens to place the fair divider right in the middle of a blinker (or between two adjacent blinkers), the fair divider may not interact with any compatible strategies, thus earning a score of 0 and being eliminated at the end of the round.

[27] This qualification is needed for two reasons. First, because of the standard reason that having a nonzero mutation rate means that there is always some chance (albeit small) of having unfair dividers appear. The second reason is that, as some of the previous figures have illustrated, the extra payoff conferred to players incident on a bridge edge can lead to the preservation of small islands of strategies other than Demand 5. When such islands appear, the only way to displace them is via mutation, which may take a very long time.

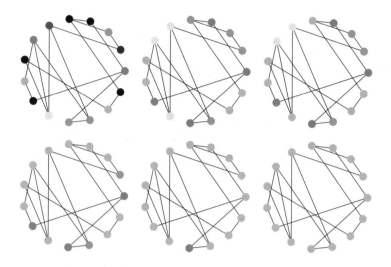

Figure 5.25 Divide-the-dollar played on a bounded-degree network, with $k_{min} = 2$, $k_{max} = 3$, $N = 15$.

from the strategy simplex[28] might not include representatives of all possible strategies. As figure 5.25 shows, there are only six of eleven possible strategies included. In this case, the population converged to Demand 4 in six generations.

For a *fixed* topology, how likely is it that fair division will emerge? Taking the topology of figure 5.25 as a benchmark, let us draw 10 000 random vectors from the strategy simplex and use these to generate 10 000 initial assignments of strategies (one assignment of strategies for each random vector) to the fifteen individuals.[29] Using the above network both for interaction and for updating, and the learning rule of *Imitate-the-Best*, what are the convergence results?[30]

---

[28] For the game of divide-the-dollar with a cake size of C, the strategy simplex is the set of vectors $\vec{v} = \langle v_0, v_1, \ldots, v_C \rangle$ such that $v_i \geq 0$ for $0 \leq i \leq C$ and $\sum_{i=0}^{C} v_i = 1$. If $\vec{v}$ is a vector from the strategy simplex and $P = \{1, \ldots, N\}$ is the population of agents, an initial assignment of strategies to P done according to $\vec{v}$ is a set of strategies $\{\sigma_1, \ldots, \sigma_N\}$ chosen randomly using the distribution $\vec{v}$. Since we consider only pure strategies, this means that $\sigma_i = j$ with probability v_j. For small N, strategies might not be present in the original assignment even if $\vec{v}$ places positive probability on that strategy.

[29] The same vector can give rise to many different initial assignments of strategies, due to sampling. For example, using *Mathematica* to select fifteen strategies according to the distribution $\langle 0.158, 0.0809, 0.2158, 0.0428, 0.0189, 0.2066, 0.0504, 0.0576, 0.0485, 0.09, 0.03 \rangle$, two different evaluations of the same command returned $\{6, 10, 5, 3, 1, 9, 1, 4, 8, 6, 8, 3, 10, 7, 1\}$ and $\{3, 6, 10, 6, 8, 7, 3, 9, 6, 1, 5, 3, 3, 10, 6\}$. I ignore this fact in the following.

[30] What does "convergence" mean in cases in which the model may land in a cycle of period 2 or longer? The definition of convergence used here is the following: run the model forward for ten generations (so that any initial transient noise dies out). If, at generation t, where $t > 10$,

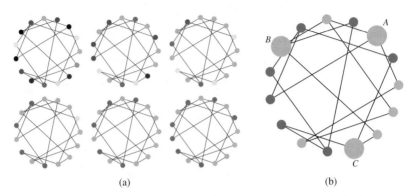

Figure 5.26 A bounded-degree network that converges to a nonstandard polymorphic state.

In such a model, we find convergence to fair division 3038 times. The 4–6 polymorphism occurs 2195 times, and the 3–7 polymorphism occurs 598 times. The remaining possibilities occur much less frequently. We find the 2–8 polymorphism in only 74 of the 10 000 simulations, and the 1–9 polymorphism occurs only 10 times. (As one might expect, the 0–10 polymorphism never occurs.) However, if you add up these values, it seems that nearly half of the simulation runs have gone missing. Only 5915 of the 10 000 runs converged to a polymorphism. What happened?

Figure 5.26(a) reveals what happened. Bounded-degree networks, as we've seen before, can behave quite differently from lattice models and small-world networks. Whereas no lattice model can have a stable polymorphic population

the state of the model at t equals the state of the model at some time $t' < t$, then the model has "converged." The *state* of the model at time t is the assignment of strategies $\langle \sigma_1, \ldots, \sigma_N \rangle$ to all N players. Two states $s_t = \langle \sigma_1^t, \ldots, \sigma_N^t \rangle$ and $s_{t'} = \langle \sigma_1^{t'}, \ldots, \sigma_N^{t'} \rangle$ are equal if $\sigma_i^t = \sigma_i^{t'}$ for $i \in \{1, \ldots, N\}$. This somewhat awkward definition of convergence is required in order to catch cases in which the model falls into cycles of period 2 or longer. It is also necessary because there exist basins of attraction in bounded-degree networks that have no exact period. For example, polymorphisms of Demand 4 and Demand 6 can have ties occurring among the highest scorers in an individual's update neighborhood (both Demand 4 and Demand 6 can earn scores of 12), which means that the tie-breaking rule may be invoked. For certain configurations, this can produce nonperiodic behavior, although it "clusters" around a basin of attraction. For example, one bounded-degree network of twenty individuals with $k_{\min} = 2$ and $k_{\max} = 4$ converged to a 4–6 polymorphism that exhibited such nonperiodicity. The numbers of individuals following Demand 4 and Demand 6 for sixty generations after "convergence" were, respectively, {14, 19, 15, 15, 14, 19, 15, 15, 14, 18, 15, 15, 14, 19, 15, 15, 14, 18, 15, 15, 14, 19, 15, 15, 14, 19, 15, 15, 14, 19, 15, 15, 14, 18, 15, 15, 14, 18, 15, 15, 14, 18, 15, 15, 14, 18, 15, 15, 14, 18, 15, 15, 14, 19, 15, 15} and {6, 1, 5, 5, 6, 1, 5, 5, 6, 2, 5, 5, 6, 1, 5, 5, 6, 2, 5, 5, 6, 1, 5, 5, 6, 1, 5, 5, 6, 1, 5, 5, 6, 2, 5, 5, 6, 2, 5, 5, 6, 2, 5, 5, 6, 2, 5, 5, 6, 2, 5, 5, 6, 1, 5, 5}.

Table 5.4. *The nonstandard mixed states for divide-the-dollar played on a bounded-degree network*

Mixed states	Total
4, 5, 6	1428
3, ..., 7	1141
2, ..., 8	488
1, ..., 9	446
Other	582

consisting of Demand 5 and Demand 4 (with a cake size of 10), such stable states exist in bounded-degree networks.

To see how such nonstandard polymorphic states can be stable, consider figure 5.26(b). Of all the individuals following Demand 4 in the population, only A, B, and C interact with individuals following Demand 5. Both A and B interact with exactly one such person, and C interacts with two. However, A, B, and C all have interaction neighborhoods of size 3, giving them a total score of 12. The Demand 5 individuals with whom A, B, and C interact have interaction neighborhoods of size 2, so these individuals following Demand 5 earn a score of only 10. Thus, A, B, and C receive a higher payoff than anyone they interact with and, so, under *Imitate-the-Best*, neither A, B, nor C will switch strategies, leaving a stable polymorphism. The three players serve to shield the rest of the Demand 4 group from the rest of the population.

Table 5.4 lists the nonstandard mixed states that were previously omitted. One word about how these states were counted: although the 1428 mixed states labeled "4, 5, 6" are guaranteed to have all three strategies present,[31] all remaining mixed states guarantee only that at least one individual followed a strategy between the endpoints and that no one followed a strategy lying beyond the endpoints. For example, the "3, ..., 7" mixed state could have twelve individuals following Demand 3, two individuals following Demand 7, and only one person following Demand 6; however, no "3, ..., 7" mixed state will ever include an individual following Demand 2 or Demand 10.

The results we have been discussing so far were obtained using 10 000 different initial conditions on the same underlying topology. What difference does varying the underlying network make? Table 5.5 lists the results from

---

[31] If no individuals following Demand 5 were present, this "mixed state" would collapse into a standard 4–6 polymorphism.

Table 5.5. *Convergence results for divide-the-cake played on* 10 000
bounded-degree networks where $N = 15$, $k_{min} = 2$, *and* $k_{max} = 3$

Polymorphism	Total	Mixed state	Total
Fair division	3486	4, 5, 6	811
4–6	2361	3, ..., 7	924
3–7	659	2, ..., 8	512
2–8	85	1, ..., 9	511
1–9	11	1, ..., 10	639
0–10	1		

a second run of 10 000 models in which the ith model used the same initial conditions as for the ith model of the run reported earlier and in table 5.4, but with a different, randomly chosen, bounded-degree network.[32] Comparing the results of the two, we see that random variation of the underlying topology does make a difference in the convergence behavior, but primarily involving the presence of mixed population states. Fair division still dominates most frequently – 3486 times out of 10 000 when the topology is varied, compared with 3038 times out of 10 000 when the topology is held fixed – but mixed states consisting of Demand 4, 5, and 6 appear only 811 times out of 10 000 compared with 1428 times out of 10 000 with a fixed topology where $k_{min} = 2$ and $k_{max} = 3$. This makes sense: networks with low values of k_{max} tend to have more than one connected component, and, when there is more than one connected component, separate groups of fair dividers and other polymorphisms can form independently.

The above suggests that fair division does reasonably well when played on bounded-degree networks – in the sense that it becomes the predominant strategy quite often – yet it does so with significantly less frequency than on the lattice. This change is due to the irregular structure of the interaction and update neighborhoods. On the lattice, everyone has the same number of

---

[32] Each bounded-degree network was randomly chosen as follows. Let N denote the number of vertices in the network. A random-degree vector $\vec{v}$ of length N was constructed, where v_i specified the desired degree of the ith vertex. (The particular distribution of degrees was constructed using a random probability distribution over the finite set $\{k_{min}, ..., k_{max}\}$.) Given such a vector $\vec{v}$, the graph used both for the interaction neighborhood and for the update neighborhood was made using the *Combinatorica* command `RealizeDegreeSequence`, if possible. Since not all degree sequences are realizable, if a randomly generated degree sequence turned out to be not realizable, a different random-degree vector was generated. (*Combinatorica* is a standard package included with *Mathematica*, and was written by Steven Skiena and Sriram Pemmaraju.)

neighbors (ignoring edge effects) and my neighbors and yours overlap to a great extent. In a bounded-degree network, the social structure is less uniform. Even if you and I are spatially adjacent on the circle, not only may we not interact with each other, but also we may share no common neighbors. The irregularity of the graph structure – variable number of neighbors plus the lack of overlap of the neighborhood structures – allows irregular polymorphisms, like the 5–4 polymorphism, to survive, and makes it more difficult for fair division to dominate.

Introducing mutations alters the situation. Figure 5.27 illustrates the medium-run behavior for four bounded-degree networks with a mutation rate of 10 percent. Each network contains twenty individuals with $k_{min} = 1$ and k_{max} of 2, 4, 6, and 8, respectively. The initial state of each network appears on the left and a plot of time-series data for 500 generations is shown on the right. In all cases, fair division becomes dominant within a relatively short period of time. In addition, note that, once fair division has become dominant, mutations are rarely able to knock fair division from its privileged position of being followed by the majority of the population. In cases in which this does happen, such as the second plot with $k_{max} = 4$, the reintroduction of the Demand 5 strategy by mutations soon restores the population to a state in which the majority follows fair division. Note also that, the more the edge density increases (that is, as the average number of social interactions increases), the harder it is to displace fair division by mutation. The more friends you play with, the more likely it is that you will play fair, and the less likely you are to stop playing fair once you start.

Table 5.6 and 5.7 show convergence data for a number of bounded-degree networks when mutations are permitted. Networks with fifteen individuals had a mutation rate of 10 percent, networks with thirty individuals a mutation rate of 5 percent, and networks with sixty individuals a mutation rate of 2.5 percent. Two facts immediately leap out from the page. The first is that, with the exception of the networks with low k_{min} and k_{max}, all networks converge to fair division; the second is that, again excepting networks with low k_{min} and k_{max}, convergence does not take long at all.

Why don't networks with low k_{min} and k_{max} tend to converge as readily to fair division? It all has to do with connectivity. Consider the networks consisting of fifteen individuals. Of these, *all* that failed to converge to fair division within 1000 generations were disconnected graphs. This does not mean, though, that only connected graphs converge to fair division: for networks with $k_{min} = 1$ and $k_{max} = 2$, only 127 of the 567 which converged to fair division were connected. What happens is that connectivity greatly speeds up the rate at which convergence to fair division occurs: the 127 connected graphs had a mean

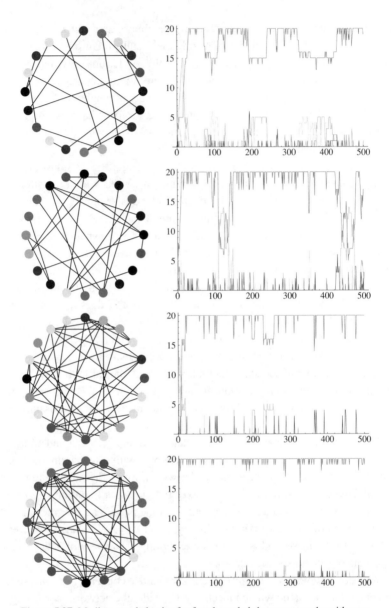

Figure 5.27 Medium-run behavior for four bounded-degree networks with a mutation rate of 10 percent. The *x*-axis indicates the generation, and the *y*-axis the number of individuals who follow a particular strategy.

Table 5.6. *Numbers of runs out of* 1000 *that converge to Demand half for the indicated* k_{min} *and* k_{max} *within* 1000 *generations*

	k_{min}	k_{max}								
		2	3	4	5	6	7	8	9	10
	1	567	852	954	980	992	997	999	1000	1000
	2	–	1000	1000	1000	1000	1000	1000	1000	1000
	3	–	–	1000	1000	1000	1000	1000	1000	1000
	4	–	–	–	1000	1000	1000	1000	1000	1000
$N = 15$	5	–	–	–	–	1000	1000	1000	1000	1000
	6	–	–	–	–	–	1000	1000	1000	1000
	7	–	–	–	–	–	–	1000	1000	1000
	8	–	–	–	–	–	–	–	1000	1000
	9	–	–	–	–	–	–	–	–	1000
	1	359	699	887	960	987	996	999	998	1000
	2	–	1000	1000	999	1000	1000	1000	1000	1000
	3	–	–	1000	1000	1000	1000	1000	1000	1000
	4	–	–	–	1000	1000	1000	1000	1000	1000
$N = 30$	5	–	–	–	–	1000	1000	1000	1000	1000
	6	–	–	–	–	–	1000	1000	1000	1000
	7	–	–	–	–	–	–	1000	1000	1000
	8	–	–	–	–	–	–	–	1000	1000
	9	–	–	–	–	–	–	–	–	1000
	1	223	544	777	911	971	989	993	999	999
	2	–	1000	1000	1000	1000	1000	1000	1000	1000
	3	–	–	1000	1000	1000	1000	1000	1000	1000
	4	–	–	–	1000	1000	1000	1000	1000	1000
$N = 60$	5	–	–	–	–	1000	1000	1000	1000	1000
	6	–	–	–	–	–	1000	1000	1000	1000
	7	–	–	–	–	–	–	1000	1000	1000
	8	–	–	–	–	–	–	–	1000	1000
	9	–	–	–	–	–	–	–	–	1000

convergence time of 18 generations, whereas the 440 which were disconnected had a mean convergence time of 180.5 generations, slightly over a tenfold increase! In addition, the number of connected components matters. Those disconnected graphs that managed to converge to fair division had, on average, only 2.7 connected components, whereas the disconnected graphs that failed to converge to fair division (within 1000 generations) had, on average, 5.6 connected components. Lastly, the *size* of each connected component matters:

Table 5.7. *Average numbers of generations taken to converge to Demand half*

	k_{min}	k_{max}								
		2	3	4	5	6	7	8	9	10
	1	144.1	92.6	56.8	39.7	33.4	32.4	34.9	34.3	33.1
	2	–	27.9	32.5	28.5	28.2	29.6	33.0	30.5	31.9
	3	–	–	27.6	26.1	25.3	27.3	31.6	32.7	31.0
	4	–	–	–	26.0	23.4	26.6	27.1	27.1	28.2
$N = 15$	5	–	–	–	–	18.9	24.4	27.1	25.4	28.5
	6	–	–	–	–	–	24.2	24.2	26.6	24.3
	7	–	–	–	–	–	–	22.7	22.1	24.6
	8	–	–	–	–	–	–	–	20.2	20.3
	9	–	–	–	–	–	–	–	–	19.0
	1	193.6	133.0	94.7	63.9	43.8	41.8	44.1	46.4	46.1
	2	–	39.2	51.2	40.2	33.4	38.0	41.7	42.1	50.3
	3	–	–	32.9	30.5	27.9	32.9	38.9	37.6	45.7
	4	–	–	–	27.9	21.9	32.0	40.9	42.6	47.5
$N = 30$	5	–	–	–	–	20.2	32.5	39.3	38.6	48.1
	6	–	–	–	–	–	29.5	39.1	45.0	46.0
	7	–	–	–	–	–	–	37.4	40.7	45.8
	8	–	–	–	–	–	–	–	36.9	43.9
	9	–	–	–	–	–	–	–	–	36.2
	1	252.7	149.0	142.4	98.6	79.6	64.0	54.0	58.6	59.4
	2	–	29.4	29.2	24.6	19.9	17.0	16.5	17.6	20.1
	3	–	–	15.3	15.4	14.3	14.6	16.2	16.8	19.9
	4	–	–	–	11.9	10.7	11.7	14.8	16.1	20.1
$N = 60$	5	–	–	–	–	8.1	10.7	14.1	15.8	18.7
	6	–	–	–	–	–	10.9	14.7	16.5	19.6
	7	–	–	–	–	–	–	14.2	15.2	18.4
	8	–	–	–	–	–	–	–	14.5	16.7
	9	–	–	–	–	–	–	–	–	15.1

the disconnected graphs which converged to fair division had connected components with 5.54 agents per component, on average, whereas disconnected graphs failing to converge to fair division had connected components with only 2.67 agents per component, on average.

This all makes sense, on reflection. Disconnected graphs effectively model isolated populations that never come into contact. The only way such a model can converge to everyone following fair division is if separate acts of mutation move each isolated subpopulation to a state following fair division. If there

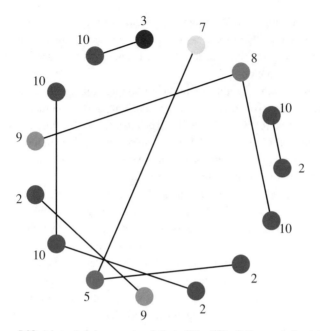

Figure 5.28 A bounded-degree network that will be difficult to move to the state in which everyone asks for half of the cake through mutation. Vertex labels indicate the player's strategy.

are many connected components, separate acts of mutation need to move each connected component to a state of fair division. When the connected components are of small size, there is a lower probability that one person inside the connected component will mutate in a way that serves to move the connected component to a state in which all share equally. These factors alone would slow down the rate of convergence, but there are other factors at work.

Recall that, to avoid sampling bias, we are drawing initial population states using randomly chosen *distributions*. That is, we first select a random probability distribution over all eleven strategies and then, using this probability distribution, randomly assign strategies to individuals in the population. Many initial strategy assignments to individuals belonging to disconnected social networks will make convergence to fair division more difficult because not only do mutations need to introduce the strategy of fair division into *each* separate connected component, but also mutations will need to target *specific* individuals.

Consider figure 5.28, which illustrates one network that will be difficult to move to the state in which everyone asks for half of the cake via mutation. Of the six connected components, only one has the strategy Demand 5 initially present. According to the learning rule of *Imitate-the-Best*, that entire connected component will switch to asking for half of the cake in the next round.[33] All other connected components, though, will remain as they are because every player earns a score of zero.

Now suppose that the players in the remaining components begin to experiment with alternative strategies. Notice that four of these components feature strategies compatible with Demand 5. The *easiest* way for fair division to take over would be for individuals adjacent to these compatible strategies to mutate into fair dividers. If that happened, imitative learning would cause the rest of the component to switch to fair division within two iterations. Of course, since we are placing no constraints on the kinds of novel strategies that may be introduced into the population, it is possible for the agents following strategies compatible with fair division to adopt strategies incompatible with fair division. If that happens, we have a case like the last connected component in figure 5.28 (look for the cluster of three players following Demand 9, Demand 8, and Demand 10). In that component, it isn't enough for just a *single* player to adopt the strategy of fair division: a new fair divider will still receive a score of 0. (At least in this case the new mutant fair divider won't be persuaded to stop asking for half of the cake since all of his neighbors also earn a score of 0.) Here, multiple mutations are required in order to convert the component to fair division: one to introduce a fair divider, and a second to introduce a strategy compatible with it.

In short, the more connected components there are, the harder it is to move the entire population to fair division because – although fair division is likely to be imitated – imitation works only within a single component. The smaller a connected component is, the harder it is to get that connected component to follow fair division because contagion effects are less likely to help with the transition. In the limiting case of a single vertex not connected to any other vertex, the only way to move to fair division is via mutation. In the next-simplest case, that of two vertices connected by a single edge, nearly a fifth of all possible initial conditions will require two independent mutations in order to arrive at a state of fair division. When there are eleven possible strategies, ranging from Demand 0 to Demand 10, five of the eleven are incompatible

---

[33] The individual following Demand 5 will earn a score of 5 due to his one neighbor following the compatible strategy of Demand 2. The individual following Demand 7 will receive a score of 0 because his only neighbor follows the incompatible strategy of Demand 5, and the individual following Demand 2 will earn a score of 2. The highest-scoring individual in the update neighborhood of both the Demand 2 and the Demand 7 players is the Demand 5 player, so they will adopt the strategy Demand 5 for the next round. The Demand 5 player will not switch strategies because none of his update neighbors received a higher score.

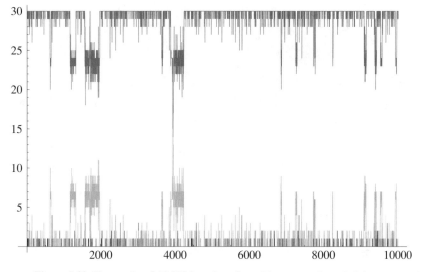

Figure 5.29 The results of 10 000 iterations for a thirty-person bounded-degree network, with $k_{min} = 2$, $k_{max} = 4$, and $\mu = 0.05$.

with fair division. Of the 121 possible assignments of strategies to two vertices, $\frac{25}{121} \approx 20.66$ percent have strategies incompatible with Demand 5 assigned to both vertices, necessitating two independent mutations in order to have that component move to a state of fair division.

Once a bounded degree network has settled into a state of fair division, can mutations move it to an unfair state? This is not possible on the lattice and, for all practical purposes, is not possible on bounded-degree networks, either. Figure 5.29 plots the distribution of strategies for a thirty-person bounded degree network over 10 000 generations, with a mutation rate of 5 percent. Fair division generally dominates, and only once (for a very brief period of time, around generation 4000) is surpassed in frequency by the strategy Demand 4.

5.5 Dynamic networks

Fairness emerges with considerable frequency on a variety of social networks. Yet all of these simulations assume that the underlying social network has been specified ahead of time. If we allow the social structure to be generated over time, is it still the case that fairness emerges as readily as before?

Figure 5.30 illustrates the beginning and end states of a dynamic network consisting of fifteen individuals. The dynamics considered here is the basic one-person interactions discussed in section 2.2.5; that is, each person selects

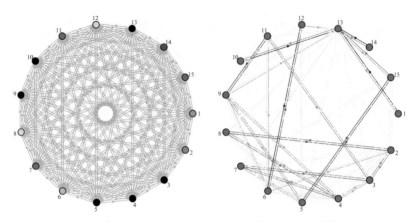

(a) Initial state   (b) State after 1000 iterations

$$
\begin{pmatrix}
0 & 0 & 0.001 & 0.021 & 0 & 0 & 0 & 0 & 0.001 & 0.024 & 0 & 0 & 0.943 & 0.008 & 0 \\
0 & 0 & 0.257 & 0.087 & 0.041 & 0.095 & 0.045 & 0.398 & 0.009 & 0.002 & 0 & 0.001 & 0.031 & 0 & 0.032 \\
0.001 & 0.238 & 0 & 0.136 & 0.004 & 0.014 & 0.347 & 0 & 0.001 & 0.007 & 0.205 & 0.003 & 0.039 & 0.001 & 0.004 \\
0.006 & 0.065 & 0.12 & 0 & 0.026 & 0.059 & 0.256 & 0.256 & 0.14 & 0 & 0.021 & 0.006 & 0.035 & 0.01 & 0 \\
0 & 0.039 & 0.004 & 0.03 & 0 & 0 & 0.106 & 0.068 & 0.182 & 0.002 & 0.002 & 0.035 & 0.041 & 0 & 0.49 \\
0 & 0.131 & 0.022 & 0.1 & 0 & 0 & 0.023 & 0.001 & 0.124 & 0.007 & 0.11 & 0.448 & 0.026 & 0 & 0.008 \\
0 & 0.05 & 0.375 & 0.314 & 0.117 & 0.017 & 0 & 0 & 0 & 0.004 & 0.007 & 0 & 0.077 & 0 & 0.039 \\
0 & 0.484 & 0 & 0.363 & 0.092 & 0.002 & 0 & 0 & 0 & 0.002 & 0 & 0 & 0.055 & 0 & 0 \\
0.001 & 0.008 & 0.001 & 0.159 & 0.183 & 0.082 & 0 & 0 & 0 & 0.006 & 0.432 & 0 & 0.125 & 0.001 & 0.002 \\
0.014 & 0.001 & 0.007 & 0 & 0.001 & 0.005 & 0.004 & 0.001 & 0.008 & 0 & 0.02 & 0.023 & 0.899 & 0.014 & 0.003 \\
0 & 0 & 0.244 & 0.03 & 0.002 & 0.094 & 0.008 & 0 & 0 & 0.528 & 0.023 & 0 & 0.069 & 0.001 & 0.001 \\
0 & 0.003 & 0.008 & 0.016 & 0.088 & 0.734 & 0 & 0 & 0 & 0.045 & 0 & 0 & 0.106 & 0 & 0 \\
0.166 & 0.01 & 0.018 & 0.015 & 0.015 & 0.005 & 0.029 & 0.013 & 0.059 & 0.234 & 0.026 & 0.016 & 0 & 0.25 & 0.144 \\
0.006 & 0 & 0.001 & 0.026 & 0 & 0 & 0 & 0 & 0.001 & 0.022 & 0.001 & 0 & 0.941 & 0 & 0.003 \\
0 & 0.038 & 0.004 & 0 & 0.551 & 0.006 & 0.041 & 0 & 0.002 & 0.005 & 0.001 & 0 & 0.350 & 0.002 & 0
\end{pmatrix}
$$

(c) Interaction probabilities

Figure 5.30 A fifteen-person dynamic network playing divide-the-dollar.

one individual at random (using his personal probability vector) with whom to play divide-the-dollar. Each player receives the appropriate payoff for their choice of strategy and, at the end of each round of interaction, each player updates his personal probability vector. In addition, the simulation shown in figure 5.30 gives each person a 50 percent chance of revising his strategy using *Imitate-the-Best* at the end of each round of play. If a player chooses to revise his strategy, he selects another person from the population at random (again using his personal probability vector), and compares his payoff with that of the randomly selected individual.

What we see is that, after 1000 iterations, all individuals follow the strategy of fair division. Figure 5.31 shows a time-series plot of the distribution of strategies for each of the 1000 iterations. Within 200 iterations, fair division obtains the upper hand in the population and eventually drives all competing strategies to extinction shortly after 800 iterations.

This particular success of fair division depended on a number of factors. The most obvious and important one is that fair division was initially represented in the population. (Since we didn't allow individuals to experiment with adopting

Table 5.8. *Convergence patterns for a dynamic social network playing divide the dollar (N = 15, updating of interaction probabilities occurred every round, and the probability of strategic updating was $\frac{1}{2}$). The total number of simulations run was 10 000. Each simulation was run for 1000 iterations.*

All Demand	Total	All Demand	Total
1	3	6	325
2	22	7	1242
3	565	8	561
4	2517	9	146
5	3624	10	5

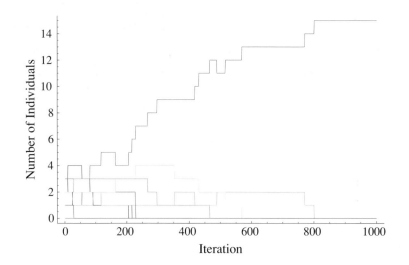

Figure 5.31 A time-series plot of the number of individuals following each strategy, for a basic fifteen-member dynamic network.

novel strategies, there would have been no way for fair division to dominate had it not initially been represented.) But the most crucial nontrivial factor is that the few fair dividers initially present were able to pair up with compatible strategies early on. Had the fair dividers been unable to do so, they would have switched to another strategy capable of generating positive payoffs.

In the absence of experimentation, it's not uncommon for fair division to be driven to extinction. As table 5.8 shows, in 10 000 simulations (each beginning from a randomly selected distribution), fair division drove all other strategies to extinction only 36 percent of the time.[34] However, since each model was initialized using a randomly selected set of strategies,[35] in many cases the strategy of fair division wasn't present in the initial population. If we look at only those cases in which fair division was initially present, we find that, of the 5979 simulations which contained fair division among the original strategies, 3624 of them converged to the state in which everyone asks for half of the cake, more than 60 percent of the time.

---

[34] There were another fifty-one simulations in which fair division was present, but these cases are highly anomalous insofar as they had only a single fair divider present when the simulation was terminated. In these cases, the final population state consists entirely of strategies asking for more than half of the cake, so no individual receives a payoff greater than 0. The reason why such odd states evolved is that the initial distribution of strategies typically consisted of a very small number of non-greedy strategies. The average number of individuals asking for less than half of the cake was 3.5 and, of these, the most commonly followed strategy was to ask for nothing! Consequently, the non-greedy individuals would very quickly be replaced by greedy individuals, leaving the population frozen in a state in which everyone was squabbling over cake and no one received anything.

[35] A "stick-breaking" algorithm was used to choose an initial set of strategies for the population: ten random numbers between 0 and 1 were selected and sorted into increasing numerical order. This partitions the interval [0, 1] into eleven segments. If segments are numbered from 0 to 10, beginning with the segment whose left endpoint is 0, the length of the ith segment can be viewed as the probability of strategy i being present in the initial population. This algorithm gives unbiased sampling from the space of all possible initial states of the population.

6

Retribution

Symmetries are important in bargaining games. Symmetric games represent situations in which every person at the negotiating table is essentially equal, in the sense that each faces the same set of possible gains or losses. In other words, the payoff I receive if I follow s and you follow s' is the same as the payoff you would receive if I followed s' and you followed s.

Important as symmetric games are, many games played in real life are asymmetric. On the African savannah, competition between impala and leopards provides a striking example of a naturally occurring asymmetric game. Leopards are carnivores, capable of running at speeds exceeding 60 miles an hour. Impala, a type of African antelope, are herbivores and possess great leaping abilities: long jumps exceeding 11 meters have been recorded, as well as jumps of more than 3 meters in height. These differences in natural endowments between the two species give rise to key asymmetries in the strategy sets available to members of each species during an interaction. Leopards try to kill and eat impala, but impala do not try to kill and eat leopards. The differences in the individual strategy sets are reflected in the possible payoffs to each player: impala face death if they choose the wrong strategy in an encounter, whereas leopards merely face going hungry for a bit longer.

In the social world, many types of interaction are asymmetric. Our conception of property rights creates an asymmetry between buyers and sellers. The strategy sets between the two players are not equal, and, if buyers and sellers cannot agree on the final price of a good, our mutual belief in these property rights dictates that, at the disagreement point, the seller keeps the good offered for sale.

The best-known, and most widely studied, example of an asymmetric bargaining game is the ultimatum game.[1] In the ultimatum game, one player is

---

[1] The related "dictator game" being a close second.

assigned the role of ultimatum "proposer" and the second player the role of ultimatum "receiver." The proposer has an initial endowment of some good and must offer a certain amount of the good to the receiver (this is the "ultimatum"). The receiver may then either accept or reject the offer. If the offer is accepted, the receiver gets the amount offered and the proposer gets the amount remaining. If the offer is rejected, neither player receives anything. In the following, I will often say that the proposer issues a "demand" to the ultimatum receiver. Thinking of the interaction in terms of issuing a demand ("You must agree to this amount, or no deal!") fits in better with the name of the game. According to this terminology, the demand is just the amount of the good that the ultimatum proposer insists upon keeping for himself, and hence equals the original amount of the good minus the proposed offer.

The situation modeled by the ultimatum game differs considerably from that of divide-the-cake, as do the strategic considerations involved during deliberation. For sake of discussion, assume that player 1 received one dollar and that offers are restricted to increments of one dime. The extended-form representation of this game is shown in figure 6.1. In that diagram, the circles represent choice points. The root node represents player 1's choice and is the start node for the game. Payoffs to each player are listed at the terminal nodes of the tree, the first element in the ordered pair being the payoff to player 1, the second the payoff to player 2. As the game tree indicates, a strategy for the ultimatum game must consist of two parts: (1) a specification of what offers a player will make when in the role of proposer and (2) a specification of what offers a player will accept when in the role of receiver.

Many Nash equilibria exist in the ultimatum game. Any strategy pair in which the ultimatum proposer offers i pieces to the other player and the receiver accepts offers of $n - i$ pieces is a Nash equilibrium. However, in some forms of the ultimatum game no strict Nash equilibria exist. To see this, note that the structure of the game allows inessential changes to be made to a strategy in ways that are not called into play. Consider the case in which the cake divides into n pieces and we forbid purely altruistic behavior whereby a player demands nothing and purely greedy behavior whereby a player demands everything; in this case, the game has $2^{n-1} \cdot (n - 1)$ possible strategies.[2] Any Nash equilibrium will consist of strategies that issue ultimatums of m pieces and accept offers of m pieces. However, there are 2^{n-2} strategies that issue ultimatums of m pieces and accept offers of m pieces, all of which are indistinguishable in

---

[2] There are $n - 1$ possible offers one may make as an ultimatum proposer. Considering the set of the $n - 1$ possible offers, as the ultimatum receiver one can accept any subset of these offers (including the empty set). Thus there are 2^{n-1} acceptance strategies.

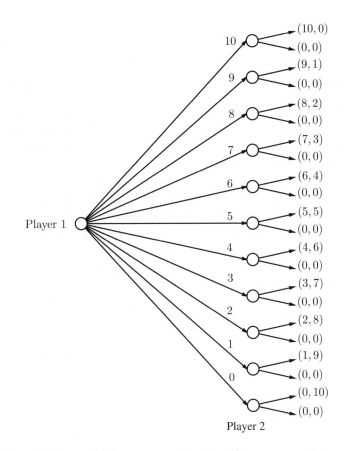

Figure 6.1 An extended-form representation of the ultimatum game with player 1 in the role of ultimatum proposer.

terms of their expected payoff in a population issuing ultimatums of m pieces; a player may freely switch among any of these strategies without doing any worse, which means that there are no strict Nash equilibria.[3]

Given that so many Nash equilibria exist for the ultimatum game, some have suggested that perhaps the concept of a Nash equilibrium is not the right solution concept for this game. Suppose that player 2 decides at the start that she will accept only offers of 50¢ or more, rejecting all other offers out of dislike of the unfair division (although she does not mind an unfair division

---

[3] There are 2^{n-2} such strategies because, although they all accept offers of m pieces, they may accept any combination of offers of $1, \ldots, m-1, m+1, \ldots, n-1$ pieces, and there are 2^{n-2} such combinations.

if it favors her). Now suppose that player 1 offers her only 30¢. According to player 2's original strategy, she ought to reject this offer outright; however, doing so will leave her *worse* off than she will be if she accepts the offer, even though she may be unhappy over the division. The strategy which accepts only offers of 50¢ does well when played against itself, but it requires one to commit oneself to a course of action that, when the time comes to act on it, is not in the best interest of the individual. Some strategies in the ultimatum game require individuals to commit themselves to courses of action that would require them to go against their explicit self-interest.

Attempts at providing appropriate refinements of the concept of a Nash equilibrium have spawned a veritable cottage industry. Some have argued that the appropriate solution concept for the ultimatum game is subgame perfection, in which an equilibrium is *subgame perfect* if the strategies present in that equilibrium are also in equilibrium when restricted to any subgame. Consider the strategy which makes only fair offers (half of the cake) and accepts only fair offers. Call this strategy "Fairman." Although Fairman is in a Nash equilibrium when paired with itself (no player can do better by changing her strategy), it is not subgame perfect: if a Fairman's hand trembles when slicing the cake, causing him to offer slightly less than half of the cake to the other player, the recipient will reject the offer, leaving both with a payoff of zero. It would have been better for the recipient Fairman to accept the offer, even though it is less than half of the cake, because then at least both would walk away from the encounter with some payoff.

More generally, in a mixed population containing players of all strategies, Fairman does not do as well as the strategy which makes a fair offer but accepts any offer. (Call this strategy "Easy Rider.") If one thinks a credible equilibrium of a game must be subgame perfect, the number of credible equilibria is fewer than the number of Nash equilibria. If players act to maximize expected utility, proposers should demand the entire cake minus a very small amount (if the cake is infinitely divisible), or should demand $N - 1$ pieces, if the cake has N pieces. Receivers, on the other hand, should accept any nonzero offer.

The ultimatum game first began to receive serious attention in 1982 when Güth, Schmittberger, and Schwarze found in a seminal experiment that, in many cases, people failed to play subgame-perfect strategies. In the experiment by Güth *et al.*, graduate students in economics from the University of Cologne were divided into two groups of equal size, with all players in the first subgroup assigned the role of ultimatum proposer and all players in the second subgroup assigned the role of ultimatum receiver. Subjects from the first group were paired randomly with subjects from the second group and informed of the random pairing, so no ultimatum proposer would have reason to believe he knew the identity of his particular receiver.

Ultimatum proposers were instructed to write their demands on a slip of paper, which was then given to the receiver. After examining the ultimatum, the receiver then wrote their response as to whether the offer was accepted. Güth *et al.* found that demanding half was the most popular strategy, used one third of the time with an acceptance rate of 100 percent. Greedy strategies demanding more than 75 percent occurred only 24 percent of the time and had an acceptance rate of 75 percent.

When the same subjects were brought back one week later for a repeat of the experiment, ultimatum proposers tended to move closer to the subgame-perfect strategy, with 43 percent making greedy demands. However, although proposers tended to move towards subgame-perfection in their behavior, more receivers tended to move away from subgame-perfection, choosing to reject greedy offers. Overall, the total acceptance rate dropped to 56 percent. Summarizing their results, Güth *et al.* concluded that "[S]ubjects often rely on what they consider a fair or justified result . . . subjects do not hesitate to punish if their opponent asks for 'too much' " (Güth *et al.*, 1982, p. 384).

This requires qualification, since a separate consistency check discovered that subjects were generally willing to let their opponents "get away with" more than they were willing to ask for (or so subjects claimed). After the two trials, Güth *et al.* ran an experiment in which all subjects participated both as ultimatum proposer and as ultimatum receiver. Subjects were first given forms on which they indicated what their demand would be as ultimatum proposer. Afterwards, a second form was distributed on which subjects wrote what offer(s) they would accept as ultimatum receivers. Responses to the first question were randomly paired with answers to the second question (allowing for the possibility that a subject might play the ultimatum game with himself or herself), and the ultimatum proposer paid the appropriate amount.

Although most subjects gave responses as ultimatum receivers consistent with their demands as proposers, this did not hold in general. Five of the thirty-seven subjects (13.5 percent) gave inconsistent responses.[4] More surprising, though, was the fact that nearly half (seventeen of thirty-seven) of the subjects were willing to accept demands from another player that were greater than their own. On average, such players would accept demands which were 1.20DM *more* than what they themselves requested. The modal "leniency" for this set of seventeen players was 0.50DM, but four players were willing to accept demands that gave the proposer 2DM above what they requested. (One should note that the total payoff to both players was 7DM, so some players were

---

[4] A subject's response when in the role of ultimatum receiver is said to be *inconsistent* with that subject's demand made as an ultimatum proposer if the subject would reject the demand he makes. In table 6.1, the strategies S2, S3, S6, and S8 are inconsistent in this sense.

quite lenient regarding the "greedy" demands they would accept from their opponent.) Although players do reject proposals that they judge to give "too much" to their opponent, some players have high thresholds for what they consider to be "too much."

The results of Güth *et al.* surprised many because players generally failed to play the game-theoretic solution. If game theory did not capture the behavior of individuals in the simple situation modeled by the ultimatum game, what reason was there for thinking game-theoretic analyses of more-complex situations would be of any predictive value? With the predictive role of game theory at stake, many subsequent experiments were performed in the attempt to determine the relevant factors which influenced people's behavior.

The story is too complicated to retell in detail here; see Thaler (1988), Roth (1995), and Güth and Tietz (1990) for more comprehensive surveys. In short, though, it turns out that there are many different ways in which societies have learned to play the ultimatum game. In some, people tend to make and accept moderately fair offers, as reported by Güth, Schmittberger, and Schwarze. In others, people tend to make hyperfair offers (i.e., giving away more than half of the cake) and these offers are subsequently *rejected*.[5] If we just concentrate on the behavior noted by Güth *et al.* in the original series of experiments – a general tendency to make and accept fair offers – is it possible to provide an evolutionary explanation?

Since many possible strategies in the ultimatum game have an odd structure (for example, the strategy in which a person demands seven pieces of the cake and accepts only offers of one, two, and five), we need to restrict our discussion to a subset of the total set of possible strategies. One restricted version considers the set of strategies listed in table 6.1. This version, which I will call the *ultimatum subgame* to distinguish it from the case in which all possible strategies are present, considers a select set of eight strategies. The four named strategies are the most interesting, since only these have the coherence expected of a rational agent.[6] We include the other four strategies primarily to allow all possible acceptance types into the population.

---

[5] See Henrich *et al.* (2004). The proposed explanation for this behavior is that, in these societies, the large offer would be interpreted as a gift and, by accepting the offer, the ultimatum receiver would incur an obligation to return a similar gift in the future.

[6] Imagine populations consisting of each of the eight possible strategies in table 6.1. The four unnamed strategies have the irrational property that they do not accept their own demands, meaning that in a world containing only that strategy all agents receive no utility during any interaction. On the other hand, the four named strategies accept their own offers, so a world consisting purely of those strategies will be one in which agents receive a certain amount of utility after each interaction. Pure populations of the four strategies are Pareto-optimal since no cake goes to waste during any interaction.

Table 6.1. *Common strategies for the ultimatum subgame*

	Role	
	Proposer	Receiver
S1 (Gamesman)	Demand 9	Accept all
S2	Demand 9	Reject all
S3	Demand 9	Accept 5, Reject 9
S4 (Mad Dog)	Demand 9	Accept 9, Reject 5
S5 (Easy Rider)	Demand 5	Accept all
S6	Demand 5	Reject all
S7 (Fairman)	Demand 5	Accept 5, Reject 9
S8	Demand 5	Accept 9, Reject 5

There are several ways to model this bargaining situation in an evolutionary context. One could divide the population into two different groups, the Proposers and Receivers, such that agents belonging to the Proposer population always assume the role of ultimatum proposer, and agents belonging to the Receiver population always assume the role of ultimatum receiver. Another alternative keeps the population as a single group, assuming instead that all individuals are equally likely to be the ultimatum proposer or receiver, leaving it to chance to decide who has what role. One can think of fate flipping a fair coin to decide who has initial possession of the cake.

In what follows, I assume that the role a particular agent holds in an interaction with another agent is determined randomly each time they interact. Thus, a single agent may both propose and receive ultimatums in a single generation and may give an ultimatum to a neighboring agent one generation while receiving an ultimatum from the same neighbor later. This means that both components of an individual's strategy (i.e., what they shall demand when in the role of ultimatum giver and what they will accept when in the role of receiver) will typically be exercised each generation.

6.1 The replicator dynamics

In *Evolution of the Social Contract*, Brian Skyrms does not use the ultimatum game to tell a story about the origin of norms of fairness, generosity, or retribution. Instead, he emphasizes that evolution need not respect modular rationality. A strategy exhibits modular rationality if it specifies a rational choice (given the agent's underlying preferences) at each possible choice point. In the ultimatum game, if we assume that people want more cake rather than less, the strategies of Fairman and Mad Dog are not modularly rational since they require the agent to perform an action that gives her no cake when an alternative action, giving her some cake, is also available.

In principle, there is no reason why we cannot interpret his replicator-dynamics model of the ultimatum game along the same lines as we did the replicator-dynamics model of the Nash bargaining game in the previous chapter. Skyrms certainly thinks nothing prevents us from doing so, for he writes "Why have norms of fairness not been eliminated by the process of evolution? . . . How then could norms of fairness, of the kind observed in the ultimatum game, have evolved?" (Skyrms, 1996). Is it possible for norms of fairness to evolve under the replicator dynamics?

In the ultimatum subgame, there are eight possible strategies players might follow. In a world where all strategies are equally likely, Fairmen become extinct and a polymorphism containing roughly 87 percent Gamesmen and 13 percent Mad Dogs results (Skyrms, 1996, p. 31). However, not every mixed population leads to the extinction of Fairmen; in particular, a mixed state consisting of 30 percent Fairman and equal proportions of the remaining strategies evolves to a state in which Gamesman, Mad Dog, and all other strategies except for Easy Rider and Fairman are extinct. There are other plausible initial conditions that converge to states in which norms of fairness dominate, such as the initial condition given by the state vector $\langle 0.32, 0.02, 0.10, 0.02, 0.10, 0.02, 0.40, 0.02 \rangle$.

Although Skyrms does not broach the question of whether polymorphic pitfalls exist for the ultimatum game, it is easy to see that they do, just as in the Nash bargaining game. Figure 6.2 illustrates the simplex for the ultimatum game when we restrict the possible strategies to Gamesman, Mad Dog, and Fairman. The basin of attraction for a pure Fairman state fills only one quarter of the phase space. Not only does the problem of polymorphic pitfalls exist for the ultimatum game, but also it is *worse* than the problem encountered in the Nash bargaining game.[7]

---

[7] Some may think that the problem of polymorphic pitfalls is mitigated somewhat in the case of the ultimatum game due to the fact that the outcome is efficient. In the Nash bargaining game, the outcome is inefficient because, in a population containing a mix of Demand 4 and Demand 6, there are times when two people following Demand 4 get paired to play the game, which causes two pieces of cake to be wasted. In the cases considered here for the ultimatum game, all of the resource gets distributed in the polymorphic pitfalls, so there is no waste. Although this is so, there is still an *explanatory* problem in that the polymorphic pitfalls do not represent the behavior we find in human populations. Fair division in the ultimatum game is the modal offer, at least according to the results of Güth *et al.* (1982), but, in these replicator-dynamics models, that outcome occurs too infrequently.

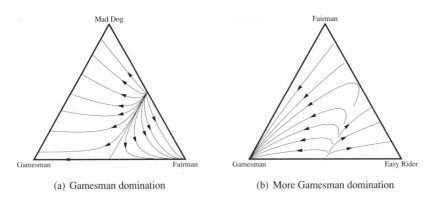

(a) Gamesman domination   (b) More Gamesman domination

Figure 6.2 Simplex diagrams for the ultimatum game.

If we run simulations in which the initial conditions are selected at random, how often does the norm of fairness emerge? Out of 10 000 trials, a norm of fairness emerged in only 15 percent of the cases. All other cases converged to a state consisting solely of Gamesmen and Mad Dogs.[8]

Introducing correlation into the model will not eliminate the polymorphisms, unlike in the Nash bargaining game. On account of the structure of the ultimatum game, the expected payoff for Gamesman interacting with Gamesman (or Mad Dog) equals the expected payoff for Fairman interacting with Fairman (or Easy Rider). Introducing correlation in the ultimatum game merely serves to change the rate at which the population traverses an orbit in phase space. In the limiting case of perfect correlation, when the correlation coefficient ε equals 1.0, there will be some initial fluctuation in the frequencies as the self-incompatible strategies S2, S3, S6, and S8 are eliminated. Once they are absent, though, the strategy frequencies will remain frozen at their current values. Under perfect correlation, the expected payoffs for Gamesman, Mad Dog, Fairman, and Easy Rider are equal. If we want to tell an evolutionary story for how norms of fairness emerged in the ultimatum game, we will have to look beyond the correlated replicator dynamics.

---

[8] The simulations were done with *Mathematica* using the continuous replicator dynamics. Since the continuous replicator dynamics never causes a strategy to become extinct in a finite amount of time, if it originally has a presence in the population, the following rule was used for determining when a simulation "converged" to a particular outcome: a solution to the set of differential equations, given the initial conditions, was calculated numerically for the time interval [0, 10 000]. If, at $t = 10\,000$, a strategy's representation in the population was less than 10^{-10}, it was considered to be extinct.

	Strategy	Color
Gamesman	Demand 9, accept all	
S2	Demand 9, accept nothing	
S3	Demand 9, accept 5	
Mad Dog	Demand 9, accept 9	
Easy Rider	Demand 5, accept all	
S6	Demand 5, accept nothing	
Fairman	Demand 5, accept 5	
S8	Demand 5, accept 9	

Figure 6.3 Color representation of strategies in the ultimatum game.

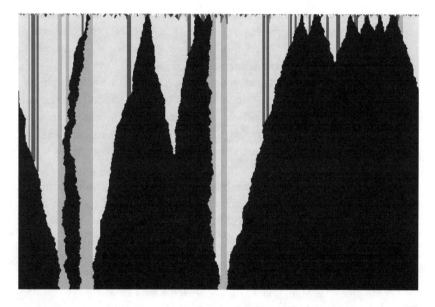

Figure 6.4 The ultimatum game played on a 200-person ring with *Imitate-the-Best*.

6.2 Lattice models

To begin, consider the ultimatum game played on a 200-person cycle, where each agent interacts and learns from his immediate neighbors (one on the left and one on the right) using *Imitate-the-Best*. Figure 6.4 illustrates the evolutionary trajectory for one randomly initialized world, using the color scheme indicated in figure 6.3.

Regions occupied both by Easy Rider and by Fairman are perfectly static. This makes sense, because, in the absence of strategies that make unfair offers, both Easy Rider and Fairman are payoff-equivalent and so there is no reason for the imitative dynamics to favor one over the other. However, it is also the case that frontier competitions between Mad Dog and Fairman are static as well. This seems peculiar, because Mad Dog rejects fair offers. Why does this arrangement prove to be locally stable?

Consider what happens in the interaction between players at the boundary. The scenario envisioned is the following:

$$\boxed{\cdots \mid f_2 \mid f_1 \mid m_1 \mid m_2 \mid \cdots}$$

where f_1 and f_2 follow the strategy Fairman and m_1 and m_2 follow the strategy Mad Dog. (Also assume that all unlisted players to the left follow Fairman, and all unlisted players to the right follow Mad Dog.) In the interaction between f_1 and m_1, it doesn't really matter who is assigned the role of ultimatum proposer. If it is f_1, he makes a fair offer to m_1, who rejects it. If it is m_1, he makes an unfair offer to f_1, who rejects it. In either case, neither player receives anything from the interaction. Consequently, the only payoff f_1 receives is from his interaction with f_2 (and it does not matter who is assigned the role of proposer, here), so f_1's total score will be 5. Likewise, the only nonzero payoff m_1 will receive is from his interaction with m_2.

Suppose that m_1 is assigned the role of ultimatum proposer in his interaction with m_2. In this case, m_1 makes an unfair offer to m_2, which is accepted, and hence m_1 receives a payoff of 9. Why doesn't f_1 adopt the strategy Mad Dog? He won't switch to Mad Dog because f_2, who appears in f_1's update neighborhood, receives a total score of 10 since f_2 is surrounded by two Fairmen. This high-scoring Fairman in the interior thus prevents the region of Mad Dog from advancing, even though the Mad Dog player on the boundary earned a higher score than did the Fairman on the boundary.

Now suppose, though, that m_1 is assigned the role of ultimatum *receiver* in his interaction with m_2. In this case, m_1 accepts the unfair offer from m_2 and receives a paltry payoff of 1. Yet the region of Fairmen does not manage to invade because, even though m_1 earned a lower score than f_1, the interior Mad Dog player m_2 received a payoff of 9 from his interaction with m_1. In this case, it is the high-scoring Mad Dog in the interior which prevents the boundary from moving to the right.

If interaction and update neighborhoods are unequal, say with agents learning from their two nearest neighbors on the right and left, the story changes. Whereas the maximum possible score for a Fairman who interacts with two

Figure 6.5 Unequal interaction and update neighborhoods (interaction radius of 1, update radius of 2) destabilize the frontier competition between Fairman and Mad Dog.

people is 10, the maximum possible score for a Mad Dog who interacts with two people is 18.[9] If the update neighborhood extends further than the interaction neighborhood, Fairmen on or close to the boundary may see interior Mad Dogs receiving payoffs greater than 10, and switch strategies. Figure 6.5 illustrates this process.

Another point of interest concerns regions occupied both by Gamesman and by Mad Dog. Although these two strategies are behaviorally indistinguishable in the absence of other strategies,[10] chance plays a big role in determining how well any particular player does. If a Gamesman or Mad Dog is lucky and assigned the role of proposer in the majority of his interactions, he can earn a high enough score to cause others to imitate his strategy. This explains the randomly shifting boundary between Gamesman and Mad Dog in figure 6.5. Whether Gamesman or Mad Dog comes to dominate a region is entirely a matter of chance.

Lastly, note that frontier competitions between regions of Fairmen and Gamesmen lead to the eventual elimination of the strategy of Fairman. We've seen that frontier competitions between Fairmen and Mad Dogs are stable. Although Gamesmen are more lenient (they are willing to accept any offer made), when a Gamesman accepts a fair offer this serves only to increase *both* players' scores by the same amount. How does this translate into an advantage for Gamesman?

---

[9] The Mad Dog may be assigned the role of ultimatum proposer in both interactions. If the unfair offers are accepted, then the Mad Dog receives a payoff of 9 from each interaction.
[10] Both make and accept unfair offers.

Table 6.2. *Random assignment of roles to players favors Gamesman in a frontier competition against Fairman*

	f_2	f_1		g_1		g_2		g_3
1.	10	5	$\rightarrow$	$0+1$	$\rightarrow$	$9+1$	$\rightarrow$	?
2.	10	5	$\rightarrow$	$0+1$	$\rightarrow$	$9+9$	$\leftarrow$	?
3.	10	5	$\rightarrow$	$0+9$	$\leftarrow$	$1+1$	$\rightarrow$	?
4.	10	5	$\rightarrow$	$0+9$	$\leftarrow$	$1+9$	$\leftarrow$	?
5.	10	10	$\leftarrow$	$5+1$	$\rightarrow$	$9+1$	$\rightarrow$	?
6.	10	10	$\leftarrow$	$5+1$	$\rightarrow$	$9+9$	$\leftarrow$	?
7.	10	10	$\leftarrow$	$5+9$	$\leftarrow$	$1+1$	$\rightarrow$	?
8.	10	10	$\leftarrow$	$5+9$	$\leftarrow$	$1+9$	$\leftarrow$	?

Consider table 6.2. The top of the table lists the names of five players, two following Fairman and three following Gamesman. Although chance determines who issues the ultimatum in the interaction between f_1 and f_2, this makes no difference to the outcome: both players receive a payoff of 5 from the interaction. This is not the case for the interactions between f_1 and g_1, g_1 and g_2, and g_2 and g_3. The eight rows of the table list all of the possible ways in which the assignment of roles to these players may take place. For each relevant pairwise interaction, an arrow points to the ultimatum proposer. Payoffs listed for a player on a given row are written in the form $l + r$, where l denotes the payoff received from the left interaction, and r the payoff received from the right interaction. (The total payoff received, then, is simply the sum.)

The boundary Fairman, f_1, will switch to becoming a Gamesman only when g_1 earns a payoff strictly greater than 10.[11] This happens in rows 7 and 8, where g_1 earns a score of 14. So f_1 will switch to Gamesman 25 percent of the time.

Why does g_1 rarely switch to Fairman? (Take a close look at figure 6.4, it does happen.) Rows 1, 2, 5, and 6 are the only cases in which g_1 earns a lower score than that of f_1. In rows 1, 2, and 6, although g_1 earns a lower score than that of f_1, g_2 earns a *strictly higher* score than that of f_1. When g_1 goes to imitate the best, he thus continues to employ the Gamesman strategy. Moreover, in the one remaining case – row 5 – player g_2 earns a score *equal* to that of f_1, so, half of the time that the assignment of roles conforms to this

---

[11] According to the rule of *Imitate-the-Best*, there would also be a chance of f_1 switching to Gamesman if f_1 earned a score less than 10 and g_1 earned a score of 10. When there occurs a tie between maximally scoring players in an agent's update neighborhood, a coin is flipped to determine who is imitated. It just so happens that this cannot happen in this case.

pattern, g_1 will continue to employ the Gamesman strategy. In short, g_1 will switch to Fairman only $\frac{1}{16}$th of the time.

How often does a norm of fairness, or retribution, emerge? Let us take a "norm of fairness" to mean that the majority population follows the strategy of Easy Rider or Fairman. Likewise, take a "norm of retribution" to mean that the majority follows the strategy of Fairman. The emergence of an unfair norm corresponds to the majority of the population following the strategy of Gamesman or Mad Dog.

With these definitions, figure 6.6 illustrates three problems for determining the emergence of norms of fairness. First, we need to make precise what we mean by "the majority" of the population following a certain strategy or combination of strategies. Do we mean a simple majority, or some supermajority? Second, once we've made precise the definition of convergence to a norm, it need not happen within a short period of time. The model of figure 6.6 ran for 1000 generations, keeping a mix of Gamesman, Mad Dog, Easy Rider, and Fairman the entire time.[12] Finally, given the role that chance plays, the population might not ever converge to a norm, although the chance that this will not happen if we run the model a very long time is small.

Yet, even so, one thing seems clear: interaction on the ring virtually precludes the emergence of norms of fairness or retribution. This becomes evident from looking at the results of frontier competitions: a frontier competition between Fairman and Mad Dog leads to a stalemate; A frontier competition between Easy Rider and Mad Dog leads to the extinction of Easy Rider; a frontier competition between Fairman and Gamesman almost always leads to the extinction of Fairman; and one between Easy Rider and Gamesman almost always leads to the extinction of Easy Rider.

Once a population falls into the state consisting only of the four named strategies, the outcome is clear: the elimination of norms of fairness. How likely is it that a randomly initialized model falls into a state conducive to the elimination of fairness? Out of a series of 10 000 simulations, each started at a random initial condition, not one *failed* to evolve to a state in which only the four named strategies were present.

Does mutation help the emergence of a norm of fairness, as in the case of divide-the-cake? As figure 6.7 shows, the answer is no. Although small groups of Fairmen or Easy Riders can be inserted into the population, and may persist

---

[12] Many people would consider 1000 generations to be an extremely short period of time. However, if these are truly supposed to be interpreted as models of cultural evolution, then 1000 iterations of a strategy-revision process is rather a lot. How many times do you revise your strategies in the course of a day, a week, or a month?

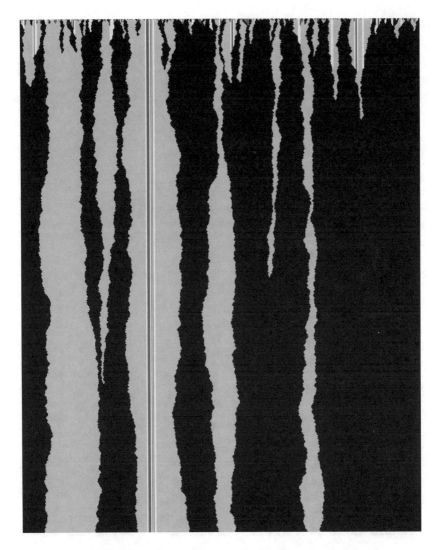

Figure 6.6 The failure of a norm to emerge in the ultimatum game played on a cycle (interaction radius and update radius of 1).

for a short period of time, they are eventually driven out. The only strategies which persist in the long run are Gamesman and Mad Dog.

In two dimensions, the story is much the same. Figure 6.8 illustrates a typical evolutionary trajectory for a randomly initialized world where people play the ultimatum game with their neighbors, using the Moore (8) neighborhood both for interaction and for updating. As before, within the first few generations the

Figure 6.7 Mutations do not assist the emergence of fairness in the ultimatum game (mutation rate of 1 percent, equal sizes of interaction and update neighborhoods).

majority of the population has become Gamesman or Mad Dog, and, within twelve generations, Fairman has become extinct.

In all of the lattice models considered so far, the initial assignment of strategies has been selected from a random distribution over all eight strategies. Assuming that a sizable number of agents will follow the strategies S2, S6,

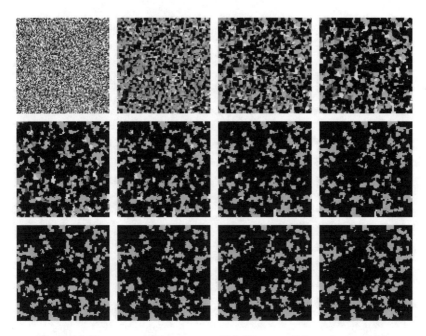

Figure 6.8 The success of Gamesman and Mad Dog over Fairman in a randomly initialized world, with all strategies equally likely, under the Moore (8) neighborhood.

S3, or S8 may strike one as implausible. The strategies S2 and S6 do not accept any offers whatsoever, so agents following those strategies must prefer receiving no cake to receiving any cake, at least when someone else issues the ultimatum. One could tell a story to rationalize such behavior, but, by and large, this sort of behavior would probably not occur very frequently. Similarly, one would expect to find few agents following S3 or S8, since these *refuse* to accept the very offers they make. What happens if we initialize the model in a state in which strategies are distributed according to Skyrms' "plausible initial state" vector $\langle 0.32, 0.02, 0.1, 0.02, 0.1, 0.02, 0.4, 0.02 \rangle$? (Recall that, under the replicator dynamics, this state leads to a final population containing 56.5 percent Fairmen and 43.5 percent Easy Riders.) As figure 6.9 shows, this initial state, too, ultimately converges to Gamesman and Mad Dog.

As in the one-dimensional case, allowing mutations to occur does not significantly change the short-term behavior of the model. For low mutation rates, $\mu < 0.01$, the population settles into the standard Gamesman–Mad Dog polymorphism about as rapidly as if no mutations were allowed. For higher mutation rates, i.e., $\mu \geq 0.01$, this standard convergence pattern becomes increasingly hidden behind mutational noise as μ increases. For $\mu = 0.1$, one can clearly

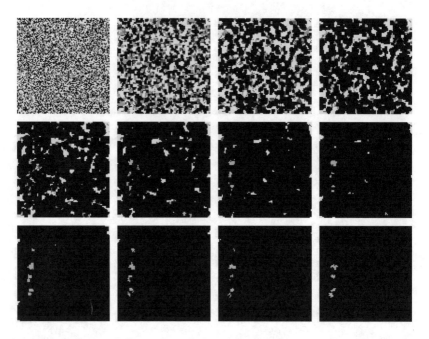

Figure 6.9 Domination by Gamesman in a world initialized from the plausible
initial state vector $\langle 0.32, 0.02, 0.1, 0.02, 0.1, 0.02, 0.4, 0.02 \rangle$.

see the population converging to the standard polymorphism behind the speckle
of mutations, but, by the time $\mu = 0.5$, mutational noise completely obscures
the convergence pattern in the background.

One surprising fact about the ultimatum game, which runs counter to the
behavior of divide-the-cake, is that the state consisting purely of Fairmen (or
of Fairmen and Easy Riders) is extremely *unstable* in the presence of mutation.
The replicator dynamics allows stable Fairman–Easy Rider polymorphisms,[13]
provided that the amount of mutation allowed is sufficiently small. However,
on the lattice, the presence of any mutation whatsoever causes the system to
converge eventually to a Gamesman–Mad Dog polymorphism.

Figure 6.10 illustrates a typical evolutionary trajectory for a two-dimensional
lattice beginning in a state in which all follow the Fairman strategy. In a mixed
population containing only Fairmen and Easy Riders, the two strategies are
indistinguishable; hence, any Fairman who mutates into an Easy Rider will
remain since his score will be identical to that of his Fairman neighbors. Over
time, the number of Easy Riders steadily increases. Ultimately, a Fairman

---

[13] See Skyrms (1996).

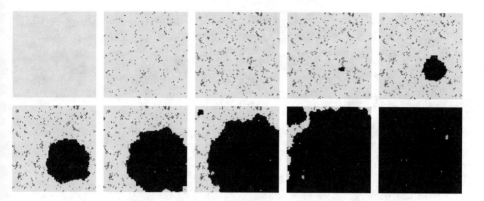

Figure 6.10 The extinction of Fairman through the process of mutation.

who mutates into a Gamesman uses the presence of Easy Riders to establish a foothold in the population and then proceed to drive all other strategies to extinction. The particular run portrayed had a mutation rate of 0.001. Similar behavior occurs for any reasonable value of μ, except that it takes much longer for the critical mutation to occur if μ is small, and much less time if μ is large.

Intuitions about the evolution of populations playing the ultimatum game shaped by the replicator dynamics would lead one to expect Gamesmen to be able to infiltrate a population successfully only after a certain percentage have become Easy Riders. After all, such must be the case (at least for the replicator dynamics) if Fairman–Easy Rider polymorphisms are stable for certain mutation rates. Yet such intuitions turn out to be misleading, as figure 6.11 shows. In these four images, we see just how little the growth of a Gamesman cluster in a Fairman population depends upon the presence of Easy Riders: only one Easy Rider exists in the neighborhood of the Gamesman mutant whose strategy spreads to his entire interaction neighborhood. Contrary to our expectations, the most substantial growth occurs in regions consisting purely of *Fairman*.[14]

We have seen the phenomenon of Gamesman advancing into regions occupied by Fairmen in the one-dimensional case. Figure 6.12 shows that the same can happen in the two-dimensional case. If we initialize a world containing only Fairmen, with a small cluster of Gamesmen positioned anywhere in the world, then the Gamesman cluster may nevertheless spread to overtake the

---

[14] Careful examination reveals that, in the fourth slide of figure 6.11, the upper-right "Gamesman" seems to appear in a location inaccessible from the previous generation. First, the "Gamesman" in question is not, in fact, a Gamesman, but an S2 agent (the limited color palette available creates this confusion). Second, this S2 agent appeared by mutation, as did several other transitory strategies in the other slides, so there is no problem with the model.

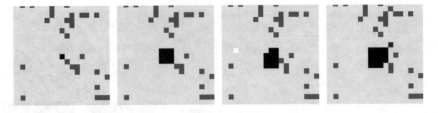

Figure 6.11 Close inspection of Gamesman mutation.

Figure 6.12 A successful Gamesman invasion in a world containing no Easy Riders (using the von Neumann neighborhood).

entire world. So Gamesman domination does not critically depend upon having a minimal level of Easy Riders present. This raises the following question: "What role does Easy Rider have in aiding Gamesman domination?"

In short, the answer is "a relatively minor one, less important than you might think, but still essential." The role played by Easy Rider in Gamesman expansion is essential because an isolated Gamesman has probability 0 of surviving indefinitely in a pure population of Fairmen. To see this, suppose that a player G from an initially pure population of Fairmen mutates into a Gamesman. Let m be the number of neighbors of G for whom he is assigned the role of ultimatum proposer, and let $N(G)$ denote the neighbors of G, with $|N(G)|$ standing for the number of neighbors of G.

Suppose, for the time being, that $0 < m$. In this case, G's score equals $5 \cdot (|N(G)| - m)$. If $m < |N(G)|$, there exists a neighbor of G who did not receive an ultimatum from G. Call this player F^*. Then F^*'s score is $5 \cdot |N(F^*)|$, which, on the lattice, is greater than the score of G, so G will replace his strategy by the Fairman strategy for the next generation. If $m = |N(G)|$, then G receives a score of 0 since all offers he makes will be rejected. In this case, G will replace his strategy in the next round by the Fairman strategy, since none of his neighbors will have a score of 0. The only stable state arises when $m = 0$, since in this case G issues no ultimatums and accepts all offers made to him, so G's score will equal $5 \cdot |N(G)|$. Only in this last case will G follow the Gamesman strategy for more than one generation. Yet two points deserve notice. First, in the last case G's score equals that of his neighbors, so G does not replace his Gamesman strategy at the end of the current generation, but he does not spread his Gamesman strategy to surrounding cells, either. Second, the probability of this last case occurring is $1/2^{|N(G)|}$, so the probability that G will continue to follow the Gamesman strategy for n generations is $1/(2^{|N(G)|})^n$, which converges to 0 as $n \to \infty$.

Now consider what happens when the population has a few Easy Riders sprinkled throughout. If an isolated cell mutates into a Gamesman, nothing will have changed from the above; but if a player G adjacent to an Easy Rider mutates into a Gamesman, the story changes entirely. If G issues an ultimatum to the Easy Rider and receives ultimatums from all his other neighbors, G's score equals $5 \cdot (|N(G)| - 1) + 9$, which exceeds the score of all of his neighbors. This means that all of G's neighbors will adopt the Gamesman strategy in the subsequent round, resulting in the rapid expansion seen between the first two generations of figure 6.11. With no Easy Riders present, the best a Gamesman mutant can do is hold her own, but the presence of even a single Easy Rider makes it possible for a Gamesman to establish a significant presence within a single generation.

Any Gamesman adjacent to a single Easy Rider has only a $1/2^{|N(G)|}$ chance of obtaining such a score because the assignment of roles must occur in exactly the right way; but when the number and distribution of Easy Riders is such that a single Gamesman mutant may be adjacent to several at once, the odds of obtaining a score sufficient to spread the Gamesman strategy increase markedly. For example, consider the situation in which the Gamesman mutant has two Easy Rider neighbors. A sufficient condition for G to expand to occupy all of $N(G)$ is that G receives a score of $5 \cdot |N(G)| + 1$ or more (exceeding the maximum Fairman–Easy Rider score of $5 \cdot |N(G)|$). There are exactly $|N(G)| + 1$ ways in which this may happen: G may issue an ultimatum to exactly one Easy Rider while receiving ultimatums from the Fairmen and the remaining Easy Rider (two ways, each producing a score of $5(|N(G)| - 1) + 9$); G may issue ultimatums to both Easy Riders while receiving ultimatums from the Fairmen (one way, with a score of $5(|N(G) - 2| + 18$); or G may issue ultimatums to both Easy Riders and one Fairman while receiving ultimatums from the remaining Fairmen ($|N(G)| - 2$ ways, with a score of $5(|N(G)| - 3) + 18$). Any other possibility lowers G's score below the critical amount needed to spread the Gamesman strategy.

An isolated single Gamesman in a mixed population of Fairmen and Easy Riders has only three possibilities – die out immediately, remain confined to a single site, or expand to take over all of $N(G)$. Since expansion occurs only when the Gamesman earns a score greater than $5|N(G)|$, we can use this to calculate the probability that an isolated Gamesman will expand as a function of the number of Easy Riders in $N(G)$.

Let e and f be the numbers of Easy Riders and Fairmen in $N(G)$, respectively, let $N = |N(G)|$, and assume that G is isolated in a neighborhood containing only Easy Riders and Fairmen. Trivially, $e + f = N$. Let n be the number of Easy Riders to which G issued ultimatums and m be the number of Fairmen to which G issued ultimatums. Then G's score is $5(N - (n + m)) + 9n$. If G is to expand, he must have a score exceeding $5N$, so we have an upper bound on the size of m:

$$5(N - (n + m)) + 9n > 5N$$
$$9n > 5(n + m)$$
$$\frac{4}{5}n > m.$$

We know that n must be as least 1 in order for G to expand (since m is an integer, possibly zero). Thus, the values of m that allow G to expand to fill $N(G)$ are all integers m such that $0 \le m$ and $m < \frac{4}{5}n$.

Let $\lfloor\!\lfloor k \rfloor\!\rfloor$ denote the greatest integer less than k. Then the number of ways in which the ultimatum game may be played between G and her neighbors such that G expands to fill $N(G)$ for the next generation is precisely

$$\sum_{i=1}^{e} \sum_{j=0}^{\lfloor\!\lfloor \frac{4}{5}i \rfloor\!\rfloor} \binom{e}{i}\binom{f}{j}.$$

To see this, fix $1 \le i \le e$ as the number of Easy Riders in $N(G)$ to which G issued ultimatums. Now, G may issue ultimatums to i Easy Riders and no Fairmen in $\binom{e}{i}$ ways. Additionally, G may issue ultimatums to i Easy Riders and one Fairman in $\binom{e}{i}\binom{f}{1}$ ways. In general, G may issue ultimatums to i Easy Riders and j Fairmen in $\binom{e}{i}\binom{f}{j}$ ways. The total number of ways in which G may issue ultimatums to i Easy Riders while receiving a score greater than $5N$ is given by the sum

$$\binom{e}{i}\binom{f}{0} + \binom{e}{i}\binom{f}{1} + \cdots + \binom{e}{i}\binom{f}{j}$$

for the appropriate j. By previous argument, the appropriate value of j is $\lfloor\!\lfloor \frac{4}{5}i \rfloor\!\rfloor$. Thus, G may issue ultimatums to i Easy Riders while receiving a score greater than $5N$ in exactly

$$\sum_{j=0}^{\lfloor\!\lfloor \frac{4}{5}i \rfloor\!\rfloor} \binom{e}{i}\binom{f}{j}$$

ways. Summing over i gives the claim.

With only one Easy Rider in $N(G)$, the ultimatum game permits the expansion of G in exactly one way:

$$\sum_{i=1}^{1} \sum_{j=0}^{\lfloor\!\lfloor \frac{4}{5}i \rfloor\!\rfloor} \binom{e}{i}\binom{f}{j} = \binom{1}{1}\binom{f}{0} = 1.$$

Thus, the probability that an isolated mutant Gamesman adjacent to a single Easy Rider will expand is $1/2^{|N(G)|}$, or $\frac{1}{256}$ for the Moore (8) neighborhood. However, with two Easy Riders, the number of ways in which the game may be played favoring G markedly increases:

$$\sum_{i=1}^{2} \sum_{j=0}^{\lfloor\!\lfloor \frac{4}{5}i \rfloor\!\rfloor} \binom{e}{i}\binom{f}{j} = \binom{2}{1}\binom{f}{0} + \binom{2}{2}\binom{f}{0} + \binom{2}{2}\binom{f}{1} = 2 + 1 + f.$$

For the Moore (8) neighborhood, the ultimatum game favors G nine times, raising the probability of G expanding to $\frac{9}{256}$, nearly a tenfold increase. Table 6.3 lists the probabilities that G will expand to fill all of $N(G)$ for various parameters.

Under the Moore (8) neighborhood, an isolated Gamesman surrounded by three Easy Riders has a 14.45 percent chance of taking over all of $N(G)$ in the next round. Although this is a relatively low probability, when mutations occur the population will soon collect enough Easy Riders to increase significantly the frequency of Easy Rider–Gamesman interactions. If one or two such interactions take place every generation, it will not be long before the Gamesman takeover begins.

Once a block of Gamesman has appeared in a polymorphic Fairman–Easy Rider population, it rapidly spreads to take over the entire population, as previously noted. We now turn to the question of why the resident Fairman–Easy Rider population seems virtually incapable of stopping the spread of the greedy strategy once it has obtained a foothold in the population. We've already analyzed this on the ring; it is more complicated in two dimensions.

Table 6.3. *The probability a Gamesman will expand as a function of e*

von Neumann		Moore (8)		Moore (24)			
e	$\Pr(G)$	e	$\Pr(G)$	e	$\Pr(G)$	e	$\Pr(G)$
1	$\frac{1}{16}$	1	$\frac{1}{256}$	1	5.96×10^{-8}	13	0.42
2	$\frac{5}{16}$	2	$\frac{9}{256}$	2	1.49×10^{-6}	14	0.59
3	$\frac{11}{16}$	3	$\frac{37}{256}$	3	1.79×10^{-5}	15	0.74
4	$\frac{15}{16}$	4	$\frac{93}{256}$	4	1.39×10^{-4}	16	0.85
		5	$\frac{163}{256}$	5	5.41×10^{-4}	17	0.93
		6	$\frac{219}{256}$	6	1.70×10^{-3}	18	0.97
		7	$\frac{247}{256}$	7	5.03×10^{-3}	19	0.991
		8	$\frac{255}{256}$	8	0.014	20	0.998
				9	0.036	21	0.999
				10	0.081	22	≈ 1
				11	0.16	23	≈ 1
				12	0.28	24	≈ 1

This phenomenon depends on two factors: the stochastic element present in the ultimatum game (i.e., the assignment of roles to individuals) and the constrained interactions between individuals. One concept we need to introduce is the idea of the *support* of a player P. Define the *support* of a player P to be all the players in his neighborhood who follow the same strategy. These players "support" P in the sense that their presence reduces the chance that P will change her strategy to a different one during the update phase. For example, consider the extreme case in which the support of P equals P's entire neighborhood. If P "changes" her strategy at all, she can adopt only a strategy followed by one of her neighbors; but if her neighbors all follow exactly the same strategy, P can only "change" her strategy to the one she currently follows, which does not alter the state of the world.[15]

We can explain why Gamesmen dominates so readily if the following two claims hold in a typical frontier competition between Gamesmen and Fairmen.

---

[15] If this sounds like an implausible example, realize that this happens all the time inside a pure population of Gamesmen. Individuals who, through unlucky coin flips, were assigned the role of ultimatum receiver in all their interactions, will earn a score lower than those of all of their opponents. Thus, in keeping with the imitate-the-best-neighbor update rule, these unlucky souls will seek to change their strategy at the end of the current generation to one that did better. Unfortunately, the only strategy they can choose is the Gamesman strategy.

1. Whenever a boundary Gamesman G earns a lower score than some Fairman F in his update neighborhood, a member of G's support usually earns a higher score than F.
2. It is relatively likely that a boundary Gamesman earns a score greater than that of any member of a boundary Fairman's support.

Indeed, this was what we saw in the one-dimensional case. We thus face a problem of calculating the probabilities that an agent will switch strategies at the end of the current generation.

To begin, notice that there are three possible interpretations of what we mean when we say "calculate the probability that an agent will switch strategies at the end of the current generation." If we just want the probability that an agent will update her strategy using *Imitate-the-Best*, we merely need to determine the probability that she earns a score lower than that of at least one of her neighbors. However, we may want to know not just the probability that an agent will update her strategy, but the probability that she adopts a strategy *different* from the one she currently follows. This requires a different analysis: we must calculate the probability that the agent in question earns a score strictly less than all neighbors not belonging to her support. Finally, we may want to know how likely it is that the agent *may* adopt a strategy different from the one currently followed. This case requires that we determine the probability that an agent earns a score less than that of at least one agent following a different strategy. To make matters tricky, none of these three probabilities need be the same, although, to be sure, we can state qualitative relationships among them.

Let us now consider the first question: "How likely is it that a Fairman, in a frontier competition, will earn a lower score than that of his immediate Gamesman neighbor?" Answering this requires us to examine only the interactions occurring between the Fairman and his immediate neighbors, and the Gamesman and his immediate neighbors. If agents use the von Neumann neighborhood for interacting and updating, the relevant interactions are those shown in figure 6.13(a). (Figure 6.13(b) shows the interactions needed for analyzing the Moore (8) neighborhood.) In both diagrams, agent G follows the Gamesman strategy and agent F follows the Fairman strategy. The strategies of neighboring agents are indicated by the label "g" or "f," depending on whether they are Gamesmen or Fairmen. Dashed lines indicate interactions for which the assignment of the role of ultimatum proposer does not really matter, because it will not affect the payoff to the players involved. Edges are numbered for later reference.

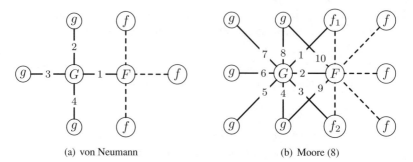

(a) von Neumann   (b) Moore (8)

Figure 6.13 Relevant interactions for determining probabilities for a two-person subset of the spatialized ultimatum game.

For the von Neumann neighborhood, G may issue ultimatums to none, some, or all of his Gamesman neighbors; at the same time, he might issue an ultimatum to F. Although one does not know in advance whether G will or will not be an ultimatum giver or receiver for any particular interaction in any particular generation, if one is given an assignment of roles for each pairwise interaction, one can calculate the scores that G and F would receive.[16]

First, some notation. Let $\vec{r} = \langle r_1, \ldots, r_m \rangle$ be a vector specifying role assignments, using either 0 or 1. (It will often prove useful to vary the interpretation of the 0 or 1 depending on which interaction we are talking about.) If n is an integer, we will write $n\vec{r}$ to mean the vector $\langle nr_1, \ldots, nr_m \rangle$, multiplying each component by n. For a vector $\vec{v} = \langle v_1, \ldots, v_m \rangle$, we define $\vec{v} + n$, for an integer n, to mean $\langle v_1 + n, \ldots, v_m + n \rangle$. Finally, let $|\vec{v}| = \sum_i v_i$, the sum of all the components of $\vec{v}$.

For the von Neumann neighborhood, there are only four role assignments we need to concern ourselves with. These are the edges labeled with a number in figure 6.13(a). Given a role vector $\vec{r} = \langle r_1, r_2, r_3, r_4 \rangle$, we then know the scores both for G and for F. Let us interpret $r_1 = 1$ as meaning that F is the ultimatum proposer for that interaction (with $r_1 = 0$ meaning that G is the proposer). For all other r_i, we interpret $r_i = 1$ as meaning that G is the ultimatum proposer.

Given these conventions, the score of G equals $5r_1 + |8\langle r_2, r_3, r_4 \rangle + 1|$. The score for F equals $5r_1 + 15$. Since there are only sixteen possible assignments

---

[16] Notice that, for this case, we do not need explicitly to keep track of the roles held by F. Interactions between Fairmen yield the same score to each regardless of who issued the ultimatum, so we do not need to keep track of whether F issued or received ultimatums from her three Fairman neighbors. The only interaction F has with someone who is not a Fairman is with G. Thus, if we explicitly keep track of the roles G has, we implicitly know F's score.

of roles, we can straightforwardly enumerate all of the possibilities:

$\vec{r}$	G	F	$\vec{r}$	G	F
$\langle 0, 0, 0, 0 \rangle$	3	15	$\langle 0, 1, 0, 0 \rangle$	11	15
$\langle 0, 0, 0, 1 \rangle$	11	15	$\langle 0, 1, 0, 1 \rangle$	19	15
$\langle 0, 0, 1, 0 \rangle$	11	15	$\langle 0, 1, 1, 0 \rangle$	19	15
$\langle 0, 0, 1, 1 \rangle$	19	15	$\langle 0, 1, 1, 1 \rangle$	27	15

$\vec{r}$	G	F	$\vec{r}$	G	F
$\langle 1, 0, 0, 0 \rangle$	8	20	$\langle 1, 1, 0, 0 \rangle$	16	20
$\langle 1, 0, 0, 1 \rangle$	16	20	$\langle 1, 1, 0, 1 \rangle$	24	20
$\langle 1, 0, 1, 0 \rangle$	16	20	$\langle 1, 1, 1, 0 \rangle$	24	20
$\langle 1, 0, 1, 1 \rangle$	24	20	$\langle 1, 1, 1, 1 \rangle$	32	20

Notice that G earns a lower score than F eight times, and F earns a lower score than G eight times as well. If this were all there was to the story, each strategy would be equally likely to replace the other. Explaining the advance of Gamesman under the von Neumann neighborhood, as seen in figure 6.12, thus requires that we consider the scores earned by the members of the update neighborhood of G and F, as well.

The same type of analysis can be performed for the Moore (8) neighborhood. Here, though, the role vector $\vec{r}$ has ten components. Let us adopt the convention that a 1 for r_2, r_9, and r_{10} means that F was the proposer, a 1 for r_1 means that f_1 was the proposer, and a 1 for r_3 means that f_2 was the proposer. For all other components, a 1 indicates that G was the proposer. Given these conventions, the score for G is $|5\langle r_1, r_2, r_3 \rangle| + |8\langle r_4, r_5, r_6, r_7, r_8 \rangle + 1|$, and the score for F is $|5\langle r_2, r_9, r_{10} \rangle| + 25$.

As before, one can go through and enumerate all of the possible assignments of roles to players. Since there are $2^{10} = 1024$ possibilities, they cannot be listed here like we did for the von Neumann case. However, it is easy to determine computationally what the scores both for G and for F would be. It turns out that G earns a lower score than F in exactly 512 of the 1024 cases, and F earns a lower score than G in the remaining 512 cases.

Thus, explaining why Gamesmen are so successful in spreading into Fairman territory requires that we consider scores earned by the update neighbors, as well. A Gamesman in a frontier competition will be replaced by a Fairman only if every neighbor in the Gamesman's support has a lower score than that of some Fairman in the Gamesman's neighborhood (and that Fairman earned a higher score than did the Gamesman). This raises the complexity of the situation considerably, for the sample space increases exponentially with the number of pairwise interactions.[17] As the number of pairwise interactions increases, not only does the number of possible score distributions grow, but so also does

---

[17] Each pairwise interaction between agents A and B can proceed in two ways: A can issue the ultimatum to B, or vice versa. For n independent pairwise interactions, the size of the sample space is 2^n.

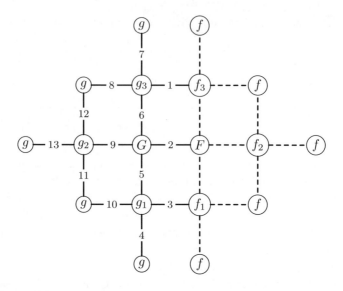

Figure 6.14 A complete interaction map for players in a frontier competition between Gamesman and Fairman, using the von Neumann neighborhood.

the number of ways in which any one particular score distribution may be obtained.

Consider the complete interaction map for a boundary Gamesman in a frontier competition with Fairmen as indicated in figure 6.14. (It is the "complete" interaction map because it lists all of the interactions both for a boundary Gamesman and for all of his immediate neighbors.) There are thirteen edges for which the assignment of roles matters for determining whether G will change strategies. The number of possible assignments that need to be considered is $2^{13} = 8192$. It is straightforward to set interpretative conventions on the components of a role vector, as above, for calculating scores. On performing the same kind of analysis as earlier, but over a slightly larger space, we find the following.

- Out of the 8192 possible assignments, 7779 lead to outcomes in which *either* G has a higher score than F *or* at least one of g_1, g_2, and g_3 has a higher score than F. This prevents G from switching to Fairman.
- There are only 264 possible assignments of roles that *may* lead to G adopting the strategy of Fairman. This happens when a tie between g_2 and F occurs. This happens when both g_2 and F earn a score of 20, and G earns a score of 8 or 16.

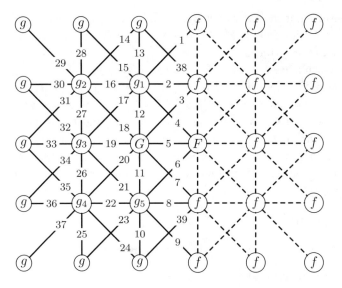

Figure 6.15 A complete interaction map for players in a frontier competition between Gamesman and Fairman, using the Moore (8) neighborhood.

- There are only 149 possible assignments of roles that lead to G adopting the Fairman strategy, with certainty.
- There are 2560 different assignments that give G a score greater than 20, thereby causing F to switch to the Gamesman strategy, with certainty, in the following round.

To summarize, G has approximately a 1.8 percent chance of becoming a Fairman the following round, but F has a 31.25 percent chance of becoming a Gamesman.

Thus we see how, for the von Neumann neighborhood, eventual Gamesman domination of a population of Fairmen can be explained entirely in terms of the support of each strategy. A boundary Gamesman seldom switches strategies to become a Fairman because, typically, at least one of his Gamesman neighbors earns a score greater than those of all of his Fairman neighbors, thus insuring that he will continue to use the Gamesman strategy for the next round of play. On the other hand, a boundary Fairman tends to switch strategies to become a Gamesman because frequently (roughly a third of the time) her Fairman neighbors do not earn scores high enough to beat out her Gamesman neighbor.

In principle, nothing prevents us from analyzing the case for the Moore (8) neighborhood using the same method as for the von Neumann neighborhood. (Figure 6.15 illustrates the complete interaction map for the Moore (8) neighborhood.) In practice, though, because the number of edges that need to be considered increases from thirteen to thirty-nine, the size of the role space becomes prohibitively large. Whereas a space of size 2^{13} can be exhaustively searched in mere fractions of a second on a computer, one of size 2^{39} takes much, much longer.

Instead, we can use random sampling to estimate the probabilities of G switching to become a Fairman and of F switching to become a Gamesman. Out of $100\,000\,000$ randomly selected role assignments for the thirty-nine edges, it turns out that F switches to become a Gamesmen 52.5 percent of the time. In contrast, G switches to become a Fairman about 1.9 percent of the time. The structure of social interactions on the lattice thus greatly favors the spread of Gamesman.

6.3 Small-world networks

Consider a small-world network where the default underlying structure is that of a simple cycle. Each player interacts with, and learns from, his fellow players on the immediate left and right. Let p_i and p_j be two players connected by a bridge edge, and suppose that no other bridge edge is incident on the players $p_{i+1}, \ldots, p_{j-1}$. How does this affect the evolutionary dynamics under *Imitate-the-Best*?

Consider the network shown in figure 6.16. Suppose that p_{11} through p_{19} follow the Fairman strategy and that all other players follow Mad Dog. Players p_{11} and p_{19} each interact with two Fairmen, receiving payoffs of 10, and one Mad Dog, receiving payoffs of zero. The Mad Dog does not receive anything from his reaction with his Fairman neighbor, and will receive either 1 or 9 from the interaction with his Mad Dog neighbor, depending on the outcome of the coin toss.

Let's fix the discussion on p_{10}. If he *wins* the coin toss and issues a proposal to p_9, it turns out that p_{10} is more likely to become a Fairman than would be the case if he lost the coin toss to p_9. When p_{10} issues the ultimatum, he receives a payoff of 9, and p_9 receives a payoff of 1. Because p_{10}'s score of 9 is less than that of his neighboring Fairman p_{11}, whether he switches depends entirely on how well p_9, his Mad Dog neighbor, does. If p_9 loses the coin toss with p_8, then p_9 earns a total score of 2, and consequently p_{10} will become a Fairman with certainty. This happens half the time. However, if p_9 wins the coin toss with p_8, then p_9's score is 10. This score equals that of p_{11}, so when p_{10} updates strategies he picks a strategy at random by tossing a fair coin. This happens half the time that p_9 wins the coin toss with p_8. Thus, the total probability that p_{10} becomes a Fairman is $\frac{3}{4}$.

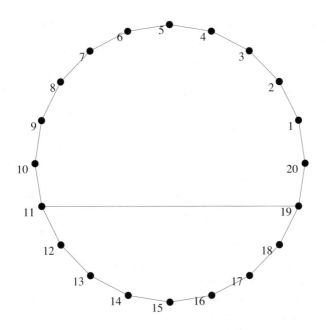

Figure 6.16 A minimal small-world network.

However, if p_{10} *loses* the coin toss with p_9, this means that p_9 receives a payoff of 9 from the interaction. When p_9 interacts with p_8, half the time he earns a score of 18 (when he wins the coin toss) and half the time he earns a score of 10, tying with p_{11}. The only time p_{10} switches to become a Fairman, when he loses the coin toss with p_9, is when p_9 *also* loses his coin toss with p_8, *and then* p_{10} chooses to imitate p_{11} instead of p_9. Thus, the total probability that p_{10} becomes a Fairman is $\frac{1}{4}$.

At some point, though, p_{10} will become a Fairman. Once this happens, he will never switch back to Mad Dog. Then p_{11} will have three neighbors following Fairman and receive a total payoff of 15. This exceeds any possible payoff that p_9 might receive when interacting with one Mad Dog and one Fairman. Hence, p_{10} will never switch back to Mad Dog. Yet this is the furthest that Fairman will advance, for from this point on the local dynamics follows the pattern identified for a one-dimensional lattice.

What happens if $p_{11}, \ldots, p_{19}$ are Fairmen but everyone else is a Gamesman? If p_{11} issues an ultimatum to p_{10}, the offer is accepted and both receive 5 from the interaction. However, p_{10}'s maximum score is 14, which occurs when p_{10} issues an ultimatum to p_9. This, though, is less than the score of 15 that p_{11}

receives (recall that p_{12} and p_{19} are both Fairmen), so the region of Fairmen is protected from the advance of Gamesmen.

If p_{10} issues an ultimatum to p_{11}, the offer is rejected and both receive nothing. The maximum score for p_{10}, in this case, is 9, which occurs when he issues an ultimatum to p_9. However, because p_{11} has two other Fairmen neighbors, p_{11} receives a total score of 10 and thus will not switch strategies.

Suppose, though, that in the original scenario we change p_{11} from following the strategy of Fairman to Easy Rider. If p_{11} issues an ultimatum to p_{10}, nothing changes from the previously examined case when p_{11} was a Fairman. However, if p_{10} issues an ultimatum to p_{11}, the outcome changes significantly. The unfair offer is accepted, giving p_{11} a payoff of 1 and p_{10} a payoff of 9. Now, p_{11}'s total score will be 11 (because p_{12} and p_{19} are both Fairmen) and the maximum score of all of p_{11}'s Fairmen neighbors is 15 (which is earned when p_{19} issues an ultimatum to p_{20}). This makes the region susceptible to invasion: if p_{10} issues an ultimatum to p_9, he earns a total score of 18. In this case, p_{11} will switch to become a Gamesman.

Now that the hub is occupied by a Gamesman, what happens next? There are several possible outcomes, depending on the outcomes of coin flips that assign roles to players. Rather than enumerate them all, let us just consider a couple of cases.

First, it is possible for p_{11} to switch to being a Fairman. Suppose that p_{11} issues ultimatums to everyone he interacts with. Then his total score is 9, since p_{10} accepts the unfair offer but all other players reject the offer. Also suppose that p_{19} issues an ultimatum to p_{20}, a Gamesman. Because p_{19} has another Fairman neighbor, he will earn a total score of 10. Finally, suppose that p_{10} receives an ultimatum from p_9. Then p_{11} earns a score less than p_{19}, and p_{19} also happens to earn a score greater than the scores of every other player in p_{11}'s update neighborhood – so p_{11} will switch to being a Fairman. If this happens, the region of Fairmen demarcated by the bridge edge will be protected from invasion.

Second, it is also possible for p_{11} to switch to being a Fairman while the other player incident on the bridge edge, p_{19}, switches to become a Gamesman. What needs to happen for this to occur is the following: first, p_{20} must issue an ultimatum to p_1 and receive an ultimatum from p_{19}. This gives p_{20} a total score of 14. Second, p_{11} needs to issue an ultimatum to p_{19}, which is rejected. (Remember that we are assuming that players $p_{12}, \ldots, p_{19}$ are Fairmen.) This suffices for getting p_{19} to imitate p_{20}'s strategy during the update phase.

Finally, given the right combination of chance assignments of roles to players, it is possible for p_{11} to spread his Gamesman strategy to the other two players he is connected to, taking control of both nodes connected by the bridge edge. This occurs when he receives ultimatums from his two Fairman neighbors, and issues an ultimatum to his one Gamesman neighbor. His resulting score is 19, which exceeds the score of 12 earned by p_{12} and the maximum possible score of 15 for p_{19}. The spread of Gamesman to such an extent removes all protection to the Fairman region conferred by the bridge edge, and eventually results in its elimination.

A small-world network built on top of a cycle thus provides greater protection for the survival of fair behavior than occurs on the lattice – if fair behavior manages to obtain control of a region protected by a bridge edge. However, if individuals can experiment with novel strategies, or make mistakes, then ultimately we will see the population arrive at a state in which a polymorphic mix of Gamesman and Mad Dog dominates. It may take considerably longer for such a state to occur, compared with what occurs on the lattice, because the spread of Gamesman into regions of Fairmen requires the advantageous positioning of an Easy Rider at one end of a bridge edge.[18] Social structure provides some protection for fairness, in this case, but still not enough.

6.4 Bounded-degree networks

Table 6.4(a) tabulates the results for a series of simulations in which the ultimatum game was played on bounded-degree networks. The underlying network contained fifty individuals, each of whom updated strategies using *Imitate-the-Best*. For each simulation, a completely random assignment of strategies was initially used, as well as a randomly generated network conforming to the indicated parameters. One thousand simulations were run for each of the specified values of k_{min} and k_{max}.

As on the lattice and for small-world networks, strategies that both make and accept fair offers have a rough time of it. The greedy Gamesman–Mad Dog polymorphism comes to dominate the population more than 70 percent of the time in almost all cases (the few exceptions occur in bounded-degree networks with relatively few edges). Polymorphisms of Fairman and Easy Rider dominate much less frequently, with the range typically being between 10 and 20 percent of the time. Even so, the random structure proves more conducive to the evolution of fair offers than is the case on one- and two-dimensional lattices. On one-dimensional lattices, fair offers were, at best, confined to relatively

---

[18] In contrast to the normal one- and two-dimensional lattices, which simply required the creation of a cluster of Gamesmen somewhere in the population.

Table 6.4. Convergence results for the ultimatum game played on a variety of bounded-degree networks. Entries are of the form (g, f), where g indicates the number of simulations which converged to a Gamesman–Mad Dog polymorphism, and f the number of simulations which converged to a Fairman–Easy Rider polymorphism.

	k_{max}							
k_{min}	3	4	5	6	7	8	9	10
2	(525, 64)	(605, 107)	(711, 140)	(734, 163)	(734, 183)	(721, 216)	(715, 215)	(708, 228)
3	—	(767, 131)	(772, 148)	(765, 150)	(736, 197)	(755, 192)	(731, 211)	(725, 225)
4	—	—	(829, 118)	(796, 163)	(778, 162)	(752, 191)	(762, 190)	(737, 197)
5	—	—	—	(797, 143)	(777, 168)	(770, 178)	(773, 171)	(751, 180)
6	—	—	—	—	(795, 134)	(773, 155)	(776, 166)	(728, 196)
7	—	—	—	—	—	(793, 153)	(796, 145)	(770, 152)
8	—	—	—	—	—	—	(791, 123)	(775, 140)
9	—	—	—	—	—	—	—	(764, 144)

(a) Convergence results without mutation.

	k_{max}							
k_{min}	3	4	5	6	7	8	9	10
2	(695, 1)	(743, 4)	(769, 16)	(780, 20)	(828, 31)	(818, 35)	(833, 34)	(854, 42)
3	—	(819, 3)	(859, 8)	(820, 16)	(835, 25)	(840, 41)	(845, 43)	(855, 36)
4	—	—	(868, 4)	(844, 23)	(856, 15)	(854, 25)	(876, 31)	(857, 41)
5	—	—	—	(882, 8)	(888, 13)	(885, 14)	(864, 21)	(873, 26)
6	—	—	—	—	(882, 4)	(885, 14)	(876, 16)	(891, 16)
7	—	—	—	—	—	(904, 5)	(906, 9)	(907, 10)
8	—	—	—	—	—	—	(908, 4)	(912, 12)
9	—	—	—	—	—	—	—	(914, 7)

(b) Convergence results with a mutation rate of 2%.

small regions of the lattice. In two dimensions, strategies making fair offers never came to dominate the population.

What if people experiment with new strategies? As table 6.4(b) illustrates, this only makes matters worse. With an experimentation rate of 2 percent, meaning that a single mutant appears every generation, on average, the frequency with which the Gamesman–Mad Dog polymorphism comes to dominate increases significantly, ranging from a minimum of 69 percent (when $k_{min} = 2$ and $k_{max} = 3$) to a maximum of 91 percent (when $k_{min} = 9$ and $k_{max} = 10$). The behavior of making fair offers evolves more frequently than it does on the lattice, but still not often enough to explain the widespread tendency to make fair offers found by Güth, Schmittberger, and Schwarze.

6.5 Dynamic social networks

Let us begin by considering a population of fifteen individuals using a very simple type of dynamic social network: each player updates his vector of interaction probabilities at the end of each generation, no strategic revision ever takes place, and the past is discounted at a rate of 1 percent. In this framework, populations initialized containing a random mix of Gamesman, Mad Dog, Fairman, and Easy Rider evolve to develop the kind of social structure one would expect: Fairmen learn to interact only with other Fairmen and Easy Riders. Gamesmen learn to interact with Gamesmen, Mad Dogs, or Easy Riders. Easy Riders learn to interact with Fairmen, Easy Riders, or Gamesmen. Mad Dogs associate exclusively with Gamesmen or other Mad Dogs. This makes sense: these pairings are the only ones among the four named strategies which confer nonzero payoffs. Figure 6.17 illustrates the state of one population after 30 000 iterations.

Now suppose that we add strategic updating to the mix. In particular, suppose that each player revises his strategy 1 percent of the time using *Imitate-the-Best*. We keep the discount rate at 1 percent, and assign the initial state of the population using a random distribution over all eight strategies. Out of a series of 1000 simulations, in which each simulation was run for 20 000 generations, we find convergence to the Gamesman–Mad Dog polymorphism in 266 cases, and convergence to the Fairman–Easy Rider polymorphism in 346 cases!

Nonstandard polymorphisms containing a mix of the named fair and unfair strategies occur as well. (The remaining 388 cases are of this type.) Of these 388 cases, Fairman and Easy Rider are followed by seven or more individuals more than 62 percent of the time. In these mixed polymorphisms, the other players follow either Gamesman or Mad Dog; the strategies S2, S3, S6, and S8 do not appear at all.

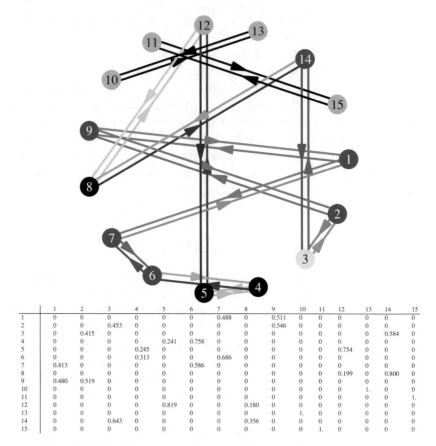

	1	2	3	4	5	6	7	8	9	10	11	12	13	14	15
1	0	0	0	0	0	0	0.488	0	0.511	0	0	0	0	0	0
2	0	0	0.453	0	0	0	0	0	0.546	0	0	0	0	0	0
3	0	0.415	0	0	0	0	0	0	0	0	0	0	0	0.584	0
4	0	0	0	0	0.241	0.758	0	0	0	0	0	0	0	0	0
5	0	0	0	0.245	0	0	0	0	0	0	0	0.754	0	0	0
6	0	0	0	0.313	0	0	0.686	0	0	0	0	0	0	0	0
7	0.413	0	0	0	0	0.586	0	0	0	0	0	0	0	0	0
8	0	0	0	0	0	0	0	0	0	0	0	0.199	0	0.800	0
9	0.480	0.519	0	0	0	0	0	0	0	0	0	0	0	0	0
10	0	0	0	0	0	0	0	0	0	0	0	0	1.	0	0
11	0	0	0	0	0	0	0	0	0	0	0	0	0	0	1.
12	0	0	0	0	0.819	0	0	0.180	0	0	0	0	0	0	0
13	0	0	0	0	0	0	0	0	0	1.	0	0	0	0	0
14	0	0	0.643	0	0	0	0	0.356	0	0	0	0	0	0	0
15	0	0	0	0	0	0	0	0	0	0	1.	0	0	0	0

Figure 6.17 The ultimatum game played on a dynamic social network after 30 000 iterations. The discount rate was 1 percent, and no strategic updating was performed. (The interaction probabilities were truncated at three decimal places, which explains any cases that fail to sum to 1.)

Since none of the final states contain any strategy other than Gamesman, Mad Dog, Fairman, or Easy Rider, what happens if the population *starts* in a state containing some mix of these four? Out of 1000 simulations, 175 converged to the Gamesman–Mad Dog polymorphism and 320 converged to the Fairman–Easy Rider polymorphism. Populations favoring fair offers, then, evolve considerably more often than do populations favoring unfair offers when beginning from initial conditions containing only the named strategies.

Moreover, of the 175 which converged to the Gamesman–Mad Dog outcome, most started out with relatively few individuals making fair offers. In these cases, the mean number of Fairmen or Easy Riders initially present was only 3.2.

Of the 825 simulations which did not converge to an unfair polymorphism, in 542 the total number of individuals following Fairmen or Easy Rider increased over the time the simulation was run. Only in 79 simulations did the total number of Fairmen or Easy Riders decrease without convergence to a complete Gamesman–Mad Dog polymorphism.

Recall our explanatory target: the first significant experimental work on the ultimatum game found that the modal offer for the ultimatum game was half of the cake, which was used approximately a third of the time. "Greedy" offers, by which I mean offers that attempted to keep more than 75 percent of the cake for the ultimatum proposer, were used approximately 25 percent of the time. Do the evolutionary models considered provide a possible explanation of this phenomenon? Unlike the results obtained in previous chapters, where local interaction models tended to favor the emergence of cooperation, trust, and fairness in a relatively straightforward way, here the answer is more complex.

Certain social structures prove extremely hostile towards the evolution of fair offers. The clearest examples of such hostile structures that we've considered are one- and two-dimensional lattices. Here, strategies that make unfair offers (yet play well with themselves) flourish at the expense of those strategies which offer half the cake. If the underlying social structure is that of bounded-degree networks, though, these structures tend to be more conducive to the evolution of fair offers. Nevertheless, even bounded-degree networks result in strategies that make fair offers dominating the population less frequently than was reported by Güth *et al.* (1982) for their experiment.

The story improves somewhat when we turn our attention to dynamic social networks. With a modest discount rate, infrequent imitative learning, and beginning from states containing a random distribution of all eight strategies, those which offer half of the cake came to dominate the population roughly a third of the time. Unfair polymorphisms came to dominate the population roughly 27 percent of the time. This, at least, places us within the right ballpark.

Nevertheless, several caveats should be attached to this possible explanation. First, some would argue that the Güth *et al.* (1982) data are not the right object to try to explain. Binmore *et al.* (1985, 1988) argued that the reported preference for "fair" offers appears as an artifact of Güth's experimental structure. If people have sufficient opportunity to play the game, and come to appreciate its strategic structure, then, claimed Binmore *et al.*, they will eventually move towards the subgame-perfect solution. Indeed, Güth's data provide some support for this, since people did tend to behave more like Gamesmen when they returned to play the ultimatum game a second time after a break.

If the Güth data are not the right explanatory target, though, neither is the subgame-perfect solution. Experimental work has shown (see Henrich *et al.*, 2004) that the types of behavior which exist in the ultimatum game are much more variegated than always making fair offers or always making greedy offers. Since the task of providing evolutionary explanations has to start somewhere, why not start with the Güth data? Since we have some signs of being able to tell an evolutionary story for that data using dynamic social networks, we have some reason to believe that it may be possible to explain the other data using an evolutionary model. An important question for future work is that of how far the explanatory project sketched in this chapter can be extended to account for other varieties of behavior in the ultimatum game.

A second caveat concerns the definition of "convergence." In section 6.5, when I say that a particular strategy or polymorphic pair of strategies has "come to dominate" the population, what I mean is that the entire population has evolved to follow that strategy or pair of strategies. For one type of dynamic social network, this definition stands in pretty good agreement with the frequency of use of fair or unfair offers in the Güth experiments.

However, there are other ways of measuring convergence. For example, we might, instead, use how frequently a particular strategy appears in the final state of the simulation, aggregated over all conducted trials. Each of the 1000 simulations conducted, for a given set of parameters, produced a particular set of strategies used by the fifteen players in the last generation. We can then tabulate the proportion of people following Gamesman or Mad Dog (or Fairman or Easy Rider) out of the 15 000 final strategies. Evaluating convergence in this way, we find that simulation 2, with a discount rate of 1 percent, a rate of strategy updating of 1 percent, and initial conditions randomly selected from all eight possible strategies, had the following convergence patterns: Gamesman was used 27 percent of the time, Mad Dog 16 percent of the time, Easy Rider 35 percent of the time, and Fairman 19 percent of the time.[19] When we evaluate convergence in this way, the simulation results don't look quite so good.

Finally, a third caveat depends on the fact that the evolutionary outcomes reported here for the ultimatum game depend crucially on the formal model used. Page, Nowak, and Sigmund (2000) developed a rather different evolutionary model and found that, on the two-dimensional lattice, "evolution leads to strategies which show some degree of fairness." In their model, strategies consist of an offer amount, p, and an *acceptance threshold*, q. An ultimatum receiver will accept any offer that leaves him with more than his acceptance

---

[19] Failure to sum to 1 due to rounding.

threshold. A second point of difference lies in the propagation of strategies. Strategies spread on the basis of probabilities derived from how successful they were.[20] Fair, or modestly fair, strategies do better on the lattice under this formalization of the ultimatum game than they do if we formalize the bargaining problem using the ultimatum subgame.

Accounting for the variety of behaviors found in the ultimatum game will, I suspect, ultimately require the use of formal models of greater complexity than those I've discussed here. Nevertheless, it is notable how well the simulation data for dynamic social networks accord with the results found by Güth *et al.* (1982). More work obviously needs to be done, but the preliminary results found here should make one hopeful of ultimately being able to provide an evolutionary explanation.

---

[20] This is not quite the same as *Imitate with Probability Proportional to Success.* In the Page *et al.* model, each site in the lattice is considered to generate a certain number of offspring. These offspring then compete with their neighbors to occupy a particular site. The probability that a site s will be occupied by a strategy of type t is equal to the number of offspring of type t at s and its neighboring sites (the Moore (8) neighborhood), divided by the total number of offspring produced by s and its neighboring sites.

7

Multiplayer games

Hume motivates his account of the emergence of conventions with a famous example."Two men," he writes, "who pull at the oars of a boat, do it by an agreement or convention, tho' they have never given promises to each other."[1] Hume's problem can be modeled as a simple two-player game in which each person has a choice of two strategies: Pull or Slack. One can then examine how likely it is that the mutually beneficial outcome of Both Pull emerges. Hume doesn't provide us with specific values for Pulling or Slacking, so, if we want to model this problem using game theory, we have to go beyond what Hume tells us and supplement his account with particular payoff values.

It seems clear that Both Pull is the best outcome for each player. The worst outcome occurs when I Pull and you Slack, because then the boat doesn't move and my effort is wasted. Unless we are both sadists who receive pleasure by forcing the other individual to work hard for no reason, there's no reason why the payoff I receive by Slacking when you Pull should be any different from the payoff I receive when we Both Slack, and vice versa. In this case, the ordinal values for the payoff matrix would be

		You	
		Pull	Slack
Me	Pull	(1, 1)	(3, 2)
	Slack	(2, 3)	(2, 2)

The problem faced by Hume's boatmen is a Stag Hunt, which we examined at length in chapter 4.

Hume may have been content to consider the problem of cooperation in a two-man boat, but Erik the Red would have had no truck with such a simple

---

[1] *A Treatise of Human Nature*, Book III, Part II, Section II, p. 490.

problem. The typical Viking drakkar, or longship, had between twenty and thirty oarsmen, and the largest known drakkar required sixty. The strategic difference between these two situations is noteworthy. In the two-person case, my participation is a *necessary* condition for the boat moving. If I don't row, we won't move. However, in the many-person case, my participation ceases to be a necessary condition of the boat moving, provided that not everyone need row in order to move the boat. Given this, how likely is it that all the oarsmen will settle upon All Pull (or Enough Pull) in the absence of an explicit agreement?

The strategic difference between the boatmen problems faced by Hume and Erik the Red generalizes. We have seen how interaction in structured environments can, in many cases, promote the emergence of cooperative, trusting, and fair behavior. Yet all the games considered thus far are simple two-player games like the one considered by Hume. What happens when we consider multiplayer variants of the prisoner's dilemma, the Stag Hunt, and divide-the-cake in structured environments? What complications does moving from the two-player case to the many-player case pose for the emergence of moral behavior?

7.1 Multiplayer local-interaction models

One complexity arising in the move from two-player games to multiplayer games is the question of how to formulate a local-interaction model of a multiplayer game. We will consider two different forms, one extending the framework of local-interaction models developed so far, and a second based on spatial proximity. These two forms by no means exhaust the possibilities for multiplayer local-interaction models, but they are a natural place to begin.

The extension proceeds as follows: given a graph G, such as the one appearing in figure 7.1, consider the group defined by the set of all individuals connected to some player j by an edge, together with player j herself. Call this the *group associated with* j.[2] So, for example, in figure 7.1 the group associated with player 13 consists of players 8, 12, 13, 14, and 18. The group associated with player 5, on the other hand, consists solely of players 4, 5, and 10. Whether all groups have the same number of players thus depends on the actual structure of the graph.

Given these induced group definitions, game play proceeds in the following way: each *group* plays the associated multiplayer game (synchronously), with

---

[2] Note that this is not the same thing as the *neighborhood* of player j. The neighborhood of a player, whether it be the interaction or update neighborhood, never includes that player.

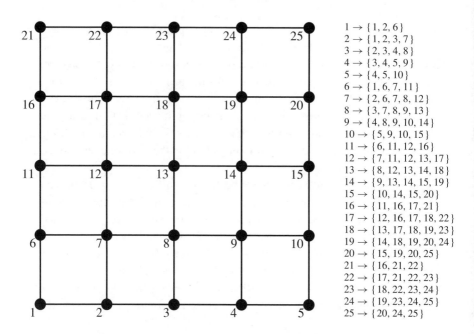

Figure 7.1 A basic von Neumann graph G and the induced groups.

each *player* receiving a score equal to the sum of the individual payoffs for each multiplayer game he participates in. Notice that, when a player has a large group associated with them, that player will be likely to receive a score higher than those of players with smaller associated groups. Why? A player j has a large associated group when j is connected to a number of players $p_1, p_2, \ldots, p_n$ via edges. Not only will j receive a payoff from the *single* game he plays with $p_1, p_2, \ldots, p_n$, but also j will receive a payoff from the group associated with p_1, the group associated with p_2, and so on.

Once the interaction phase has finished, each individual modifies his strategy using a learning rule applied to his update neighborhood. (As before, the learning rule used by a player remains fixed throughout.) The update neighborhood for a player is defined, as before, using another graph, which may include individuals with whom he does not play a game.

Note that, when individuals update strategies via imitative learning, this introduces a natural bias towards the strategies used by people in larger groups. While one might wish to avoid incorporating such a bias, doing so would require excluding many natural learning rules. *Imitate-the-Best* would have to be omitted, as would *Imitate Proportional to Success*. Even the learning rule which chooses a new strategy on the basis of the average payoff received by all members in a player's update neighborhood who use that strategy suffers

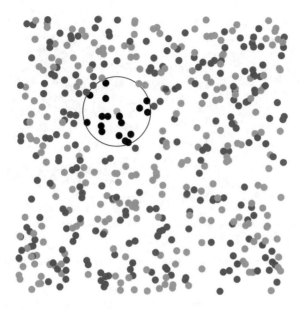

Figure 7.2 A proximity model of local interactions.

from such a bias. Such a bias seems difficult to avoid without concentrating overmuch on artificial learning rules; hence, no further worry about such bias will appear below.

The second model to consider for multiplayer games is a spatial-proximity model. In this model, each player j is located at a particular position (x_j, y_j) in the plane. Each player also has an interaction radius ρ_j, which can be thought of as how far away j is willing to travel in order to gather his neighbors together in order to play a game. The group associated with j, in this case, corresponds to all individuals located within the circle having center (x_j, y_j) and radius ρ_j. Figure 7.2 illustrates the interaction radius (highlighted in black) for the light-colored individual in the middle, with all members belonging to the group colored black.

In the proximity model, each group, as before, plays a multiplayer game with each individual receiving a score equal to the sum of the individual payoffs for each game he participates in. After each round of interaction, each player engages in strategic learning by applying a learning rule to all the individuals falling within his update neighborhood. The update neighborhood for a player j is determined by an update radius ρ'_j, which need not equal the interaction radius.

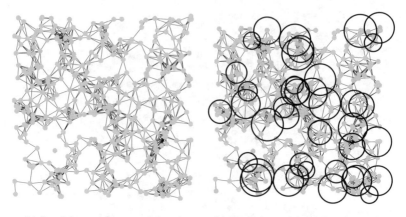

(a) Promixity model as a graph-based   (b) Proximity model with forty interaction
    local-interaction model   radii included

Figure 7.3 How a proximity-based local-interaction model can be viewed as a graph-based local-interaction model.

Thus far, nothing differentiates the proximity model from the graph-based local-interaction models: every proximity model corresponds to a local-interaction model given the right sort of underlying graph (see figure 7.3). What *does* differentiate the proximity model from a local-interaction model is that, at the end of each update phase, each individual migrates to a new spatial position, with the membership of their interaction and update neighborhoods changing accordingly. The method of migration is simply a random walk: each player moves to a new point selected at random within the unit square centered upon his current position. The cumulative effect of individual migration thus tends to make groups transient entities.

7.2 Cooperation

The key strategic feature of the two-player prisoner's dilemma is the following: the best *collective* result obtains when both you and I Cooperate and, no matter what you do, it is always in my interest to Defect. The multiplayer prisoner's dilemma has the same basic form, the key difference being that, instead of my payoff depending solely upon your strategy and my strategy, in the multiplayer case, my payoff depends on my strategy and what proportion of the *group* I belong to chooses to Cooperate.[3]

---

[3] This particular form of the multiplayer prisoner's dilemma is due to Fletcher and Zwick (2000).

Let c_i denote the limit of the payoff received by Cooperators as the proportion of Cooperators in the group approaches zero, and let d_i denote the limit of the payoff received by Defectors as the proportion of Cooperators in the group approaches zero. In addition, let m denote the rate of increase of payoffs both to Cooperators and to Defectors as the proportion of Cooperators in the group increases. The last assumption – the common rate of increase in payoff – makes sense if we think that the payoffs received both by Cooperators and by Defectors are solely the result of the efforts of Cooperators. Defectors, by definition, siphon off resources from the group without contributing anything to the common pool, so the payoff Defectors receive *should* increase solely according to the number of Cooperators present. By the same argument, though, the payoffs received by Cooperators should also increase solely according to the number of Cooperators.[4]

Suppose that each player in the group has the strategy of either Cooperate or Defect, and let p denote the proportion of Cooperators in the group. Each Cooperator then receives a payoff of $mp + c_i$ and each Defector receives a payoff of $mp + d_i$. Figure 7.4 plots the payoffs received by Cooperators and Defectors as the proportion of Cooperators increases from 0 to 1 for $c_i = 0$ and $d_i = \frac{1}{4}$. If everyone Cooperates, all receive a payoff of 0.5; if everyone Defects, all receive a payoff of 0.25. As in the two-player case, the state in which All Cooperate is preferable to the state in which All Defect. At the same time, because the black line representing the payoff to Defectors always lies above the gray line representing the payoff to Cooperators, it is always in the interest of an individual to Defect rather than Cooperate – no matter how many people in the group Cooperate.

What of the requirement that the state in which everyone cooperates must be the collectively optimal outcome? Upon inspection of the graph in figure 7.4, one may wonder whether it is possible for the gain received by a single Defector to be so large that it offsets the corresponding loss incurred by all the other Cooperators in the group. If this were possible, we would not have a pure generalization of the two-player prisoner's dilemma.

The collective optimality of Cooperate requires that moving from the state in which everyone cooperates to the state in which everyone cooperates, except for one defector, produces a *decrease* in the overall payoff. A violation of the

---

[4] Why assume, though, that payoffs increase linearly with the number of Cooperators? This is just the simplest starting assumption. It would be interesting to consider cases for which "economies of scale" exist in the production of goods by Cooperators. In this case, the temptation to be a Defector would decrease as the number of Cooperators grew.

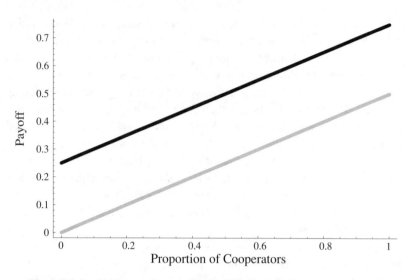

Figure 7.4 A multiplayer prisoner's dilemma. The black line represents the payoff curve for Defect, the gray line the payoff curve for Cooperate ($m = \frac{1}{2}$, $c_i = 0$, and $d_i = \frac{1}{4}$).

collective optimality means, of course, the opposite. Formally, if s (a positive integer) denotes the size of the group, a violation of the collective optimality of Cooperate occurs[5] when

$$(s-1)\left(m \cdot \frac{s-1}{s} + c_i\right) + m \cdot \frac{s-1}{s} + d_i > s(m+c_i),$$

which is nothing more than $d_i > m + c_i$. Notice that d_i is the payoff received by a Defector when the proportion of Cooperators in the population is zero, and that $m + c_i$ is the payoff received by a Cooperator when everyone in the population cooperates. This means that the only way a violation of the *collective optimality* of Cooperate can occur is if the parameters d_i, c_i, and m are chosen so that it is no longer the case that *individuals prefer* the state in which everyone cooperates to the state in which everyone defects. In short, the payoff scheme we've identified generalizes both of the core features of the two-player prisoner's dilemma.

Now consider our most basic social network: a simple cycle or ring such that each person is connected to one individual on his left and right. Suppose

---

[5] Strictly speaking, a violation of the collective optimality of All Cooperate includes the possibility that some mix of cooperators and defectors produces as good a collective result as the state All Cooperate. I do not consider this possibility in the following.

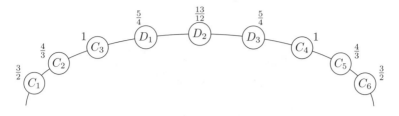

Figure 7.5 A cluster of three Defectors surrounded by Cooperators. Total payoffs
are indicated for the prisoner's dilemma with $m = \frac{1}{2}$, $c_i = 0$, and $d_i = \frac{1}{4}$.

that everyone Cooperates except for one lone Defector. Suppose also that the
values of m, c_i, and d_i are $\frac{1}{2}$, 0, and $\frac{1}{4}$, respectively. If everyone learns using
Imitate-the-Best, what happens?

Given this social structure, all of the groups consist of three persons (each
player, plus his immediate neighbors on the left and right). A group consisting
entirely of Cooperators yields a payoff of $mp + c_i = \frac{1}{2} \cdot 1 + 0 = \frac{1}{2}$ to each
member of the group. A group containing one Defector and two Cooperators
yields a payoff of $\frac{1}{2} \cdot \frac{2}{3} + \frac{1}{4} = \frac{7}{12}$ for the Defector and a payoff of $\frac{1}{2} \cdot \frac{2}{3} + 0 = \frac{1}{3}$
for each Cooperator.

From this, we can calculate the total payoffs for each person in the population. The lone Defector plays three games: one for the group associated with
his neighbor on the left, one for the group associated with himself, and one
for the group associated with his neighbor on the right. All of these groups
contain exactly one Defector and two Cooperators, so his total payoff is $\frac{7}{4}$. The
Cooperators adjacent to the lone Defector likewise play three games; however,
only two of the games involve groups containing a single Defector. One game
is played among a group containing only Cooperators. Each of these two Coop-
erators thus receives a payoff of $\frac{1}{3} + \frac{1}{3} + \frac{1}{2} = \frac{7}{6}$. All other Cooperators receive
a payoff of $\frac{3}{2}$. Under *Imitate-the-Best*, the two Cooperators adjacent to the
lone Defector will switch to defecting in the subsequent generation, creating a
cluster of three Defectors.

After the first generation, the distribution of strategies is that indicated in
figure 7.5. What happens now that there is a cluster of defectors present in
the population? In order to calculate the payoffs for each player under this
configuration of strategies, we need to know the payoffs both for Defectors and
for Cooperators under every possible composition of groups. If we use $W_D(G)$
to denote the payoff received by a Defector in the group G, and $W_C(G)$ to
denote the payoff received by a Cooperator in the group G, these payoffs are

as follows:

$$W_D(\{\,D,D,D\,\}) = m \cdot 0 + d_i = \tfrac{1}{4}$$
$$W_D(\{\,C,D,D\,\}) = m \cdot \tfrac{1}{3} + d_i = \tfrac{5}{12}$$
$$W_D(\{\,C,C,D\,\}) = m \cdot \tfrac{2}{3} + d_i = \tfrac{7}{12}$$

$$W_C(\{\,C,D,D\,\}) = m \cdot \tfrac{1}{3} + c_i = \tfrac{1}{6}$$
$$W_C(\{\,C,C,D\,\}) = m \cdot \tfrac{2}{3} + c_i = \tfrac{1}{3}$$
$$W_C(\{\,C,C,C\,\}) = m \cdot 1 + c_i = \tfrac{1}{2}.$$

The total payoffs received by all players in figure 7.5 are indicated in the figure.[6]

Under *Imitate-the-Best*, the cluster of Defectors will not expand any further. Although the two Defectors on the edge (D_1 and D_3), with payoffs of $\tfrac{5}{4}$, have received higher payoffs than have the Cooperators adjacent to them (C_3 and C_4), neither of those Cooperators will switch to defection. Why? Because, in each of *their* update neighborhoods, there exists another Cooperator (C_2 and C_5, respectively) who has received a payoff of $\tfrac{4}{3}$. One can increase the size of the cluster of Defectors from 3 to 4, or even larger, and the same result holds: the cluster of Defectors will not spread further. Although the final configuration of strategies depends upon the initial state of the population, we can state what it will qualitatively look like: it will consist of clusters of Defectors of size 3 or more, surrounded by clusters of Cooperators of size 4 or more.[7]

If interaction and update neighborhoods differ in size, though, the story changes. Suppose that the update neighborhood contains the two nearest players on the left and right of each agent, and consider the case of figure 7.5 again. The two Defectors who receive payoffs of $\tfrac{5}{4}$ will switch to cooperating because both of them have a Cooperator who earned a payoff of $\tfrac{4}{3}$ belonging to their update neighborhood. In this case, clusters of Defectors who share a border with three or more Cooperators will shrink, as Defectors on the boundary switch to cooperating. Figure 7.6 illustrates the spread of Cooperate for two different cases with unequal sizes of interaction and update neighborhoods.

On a two-dimensional lattice, we find that some of the qualitative behavior identified in chapter 3 continues to hold in the multiplayer case. Figure 7.7

---

[6] Remember that, although each player is incident on two edges, each player actually receives the payoff from *three* games.

[7] There have to be four or more adjacent Cooperators in order to insure that boundary Cooperators like C_4 are adjacent to Cooperators like C_5 who have earned payoffs of $\tfrac{4}{3}$.

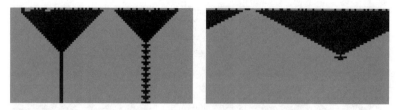

(a) Interaction radius = 1, update radius = 2   (b) Interaction radius = 1, update radius = 3

Figure 7.6 The prisoner's dilemma on a ring. The initial strategy distribution had approximately 75 percent of the population cooperating. Gray indicates the strategy Cooperate, black the strategy of Defect.

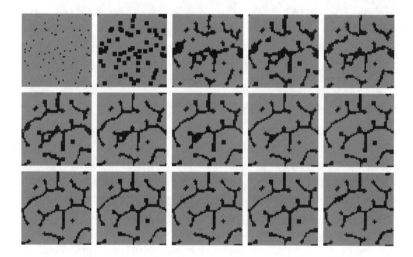

Figure 7.7 The multiplayer prisoner's dilemma ($m = \frac{1}{2}$, $d_i = \frac{1}{7}$, and $c_i = 0$) played on a 50×50 lattice, with the Moore (8) neighborhood both for group structure and for updating, and *Imitate-the-Best*. The initial strategy distribution assigned Cooperate to 97.5 percent of the population.

illustrates how populations containing a mix of Cooperate and Defect can be stable under *Imitate-the-Best*. Likewise, figure 7.8 shows how, for a slightly different payoff function (one increasing the desirability of defecting), the population quickly slides into the Hobbesian war of all against all.

In general, though, it is much more difficult for Cooperate to spread in the two-dimensional case. Out of 1000 simulations using random initial conditions, the Moore (8) neighborhood for determining group structure, and the Moore (24) neighborhood for strategic updating, only twenty-seven converged

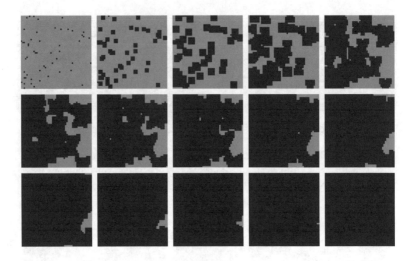

Figure 7.8 The multiplayer prisoner's dilemma ($m = \frac{1}{2}$, $d_i = \frac{1}{4}$, and $c_i = 0$) played on a 50 × 50 lattice, with the Moore (8) neighborhood both for group structure and for updating, and *Imitate-the-Best*. The initial strategy distribution assigned Cooperate to 97.5 percent of the population.

to the state of All Cooperate. Of these, sixteen began with conditions favorable to Cooperate, with over 90 percent of the population initially cooperating.[8]

If the benefit of defecting is not too large, it is possible for Cooperators to drive Defectors to extinction, as figure 7.9 illustrates. In order for this to happen, though, a properly shaped cluster of Cooperators of the right size must be present. The cluster has to be "properly shaped" in order for there to be one Cooperator who receives a high enough payoff to prevent adjacent Cooperators from switching to Defect. For example, it isn't enough for there to be a connected region of twenty-five Cooperators: twenty-five Cooperators in a line surrounded by Defectors will all switch to defecting in the next generation. However, if the twenty-five Cooperators happen to be arranged in a 5 × 5 grid (and the Moore (8) neighborhood determines the group structure), the central Cooperator will receive a payoff of $9 \cdot (m + c_i)$, preventing the rest of the Cooperators from switching to Defect.

The proximity model of the multiplayer prisoner's dilemma proves very hostile to the emergence of cooperation. Consider the following environment:

---

[8] The remaining eleven also began with conditions favouring Cooperation, only not so much. All but one of the eleven had more than 80 percent of the population cooperating, and in the one exception Cooperators constituted 76 percent of the initial population.

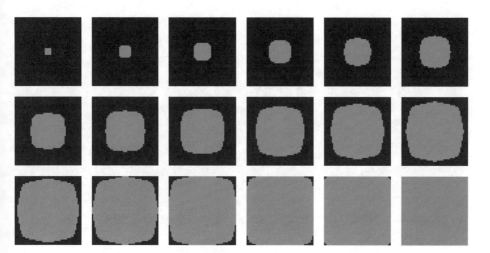

Figure 7.9 The spread of Cooperate in the multiplayer prisoner's dilemma ($m = \frac{1}{2}$, $d_i = \frac{1}{7}$, and $c_i = 0$) with unequal sizes of interaction and update neighborhoods.

400 individuals, each with an interaction radius of 4 and an update radius of 8, positioned at random on a torus of width 40 and height 40. (As before, the learning rule used was *Imitate-the-Best*, and the payoff parameters were $m = \frac{1}{2}$, $d_i = \frac{1}{4}$, and $c_i = 0$.) After each interaction and update phase, individuals move from their current position to a new location somewhere within the unit square centered upon them. Out of 1000 simulations beginning in a state with 80 percent of the population consisting of cooperators, *not a single model* converged to the state of All Cooperate. All simulations converged to the state All Defect.

It is possible for Cooperate to drive Defect to extinction, but Cooperators need to be given a significant head start in order for this to occur (and even then it happens infrequently). Figure 7.10 shows a plot of time-series data for one simulation in which this happened. Beginning with 97.5 percent of the population cooperating, within seventy generations Cooperate had managed to drive Defect to extinction. It is worth noting, though, that what we have here amounts to little more than an existence proof of the possibility of Cooperate coming to dominate. The odds strongly favor the state All Defect over All Cooperate.

The story changes slightly if the attractiveness of defection is reduced. Using the same parameters as before, but with an intercept value of $d_i = \frac{1}{6}$ for the payoff function, the state of All Cooperate emerges roughly 26 percent of the time when the initial distribution of strategies had 80 percent of the population

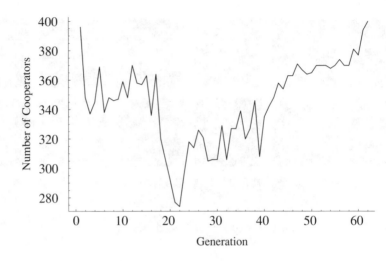

Figure 7.10 Time-series data for the number of Cooperators present in a proximity model of the multiplayer prisoner's dilemma ($m = \frac{1}{2}$, $d_i = \frac{1}{4}$, $c_i = 0$).

cooperating.[9] If the initial frequency of Cooperate is increased to 95 percent, the state of All Cooperate occurs 97 percent of the time. If the population begins in a state in which everyone cooperates, save for a single Defector, then the Cooperators were able to drive out the Defectors 100 percent of the time in simulations.

7.3 Trust

The problem of trust, as represented in the two-player Stag Hunt, can be generalized in several different ways.[10] In the form considered here, let S denote the maximum payoff to stag hunters, which is obtained when everyone in the group hunts stag, and let H denote the payoff to hare hunters. If n_S^j denotes the number of individuals in subgroup j who hunt stag, and n_H^j denotes the number of individuals in subgroup j who hunt hare, then the payoff to Stag Hunters is $S \cdot n_S^j / (n_S^j + n_H^j)$ and the payoff to hare hunters is H. In the ordinary two-player Stag Hunt, it is always better for one person to hunt stag if the other person does; here, it is only in a player's interest to hunt stag if a certain percentage of the group hunts stag.[11] Why assume that the payoff to stag hunters increases linearly in proportion to the number of stag hunters in

---

[9] That is, 262 times out of 1000 simulations.
[10] See also Skyrms (2003).
[11] The critical threshold being when $n_S^j / (n_S^j + n_H^j) > H/S$.

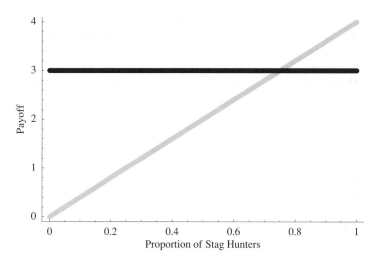

Figure 7.11 A payoff function for the multiplayer Stag Hunt.

the group? As with the multiplayer prisoner's dilemma, linearity provides the simplest starting assumption. Figure 7.11 illustrates the payoff function for the multiplayer Stag Hunt with $S = 4$ and $H = 3$.

What are the dynamics, using *Imitate-the-Best*, on a simple cycle where each person is connected to one player on the left and right? Let the values S and H be fixed. An isolated stag hunter surrounded by hare hunters receives a total payoff of S. For each of the three games he plays, he receives a payoff of $S/3$. The surrounding hare hunters all receive a total payoff of $3H$. Provided that $S/3 < H$, an isolated stag hunter will switch to hunting hare in the next generation.

If we have an isolated group of two stag hunters, both stag hunters will switch to Hunt Hare if $\frac{5}{9}S < H$. In this case, each stag hunter plays three games, one in which he is the only stag hunter (receiving a payoff of $S/3$), and two in which two thirds of the group are stag hunters (receiving a payoff of $2S/3$, for each game). Hare hunters, as before, receive a total payoff of $3H$. Similarly, it is easy to show that an isolated group of three stag hunters will be driven out if $\frac{7}{9}S < H$, and an isolated group of four stag hunters will be driven out if $\frac{8}{9}S < H$. Groups of five or more stag hunters aren't any less susceptible to being driven out by hare hunters than are groups of four, unless the graph which determines the update neighborhood differs from the graph determining the interaction group structure.

Suppose that players update their strategy by looking at their two nearest neighbors both on the left and on the right. In this case, we can predict what

Table 7.1. *Simulation results*

von Neumann		Moore (8)	
Stag Hunters (s)	Models	Stag Hunters (s)	Models
$s \leq 100$	0	$s \leq 100$	355
$100 < s \leq 200$	106	$100 < s \leq 200$	520
$200 < s \leq 300$	374	$200 < s \leq 300$	102
$300 < s \leq 400$	327	$300 < s \leq 400$	19
$400 < s \leq 500$	136	$400 < s \leq 500$	4
$500 < s \leq 600$	44	$500 < s$	0
$600 < s \leq 700$	8		
$700 < s \leq 800$	2		
$800 < s \leq 900$	3		
$900 < s$	0		

will happen by reversing the above inequalities. That is, the center player in a group of three stag hunters receives a payoff of $\frac{7}{3}S$, so, if $\frac{7}{3}S > 3H$, the bordering hare hunters will switch to hunting stag in the next generation. In a group of four adjacent stag hunters, both of the innermost stag hunters receive a payoff of $\frac{8}{3}S$, so the bordering hare hunters will switch if $\frac{8}{3}S > 3H$. Since it is a defining feature of the Stag Hunt that $S > H$, the presence of four adjacent stag hunters is thus enough to guarantee that Hunt Stag will dominate on a cycle with an expanded update neighborhood, unless the benefit of hunting stag is very slight indeed.

What happens in two dimensions? Simulations provide a first glimpse into the answer to this question. If we begin with a 50×50 lattice in a randomly selected state with equal numbers of stag hunters and hare hunters, we find that it never converges to a state containing only stag hunters, but it also never converges to a state containing only hare hunters. The evolutionary dynamics under *Imitate-the-Best* instead carry the population to a polymorphic state containing a mix of the two strategies. The results for a series of 1000 simulations for the von Neumann and Moore (8) neighborhoods are shown in table 7.1.

Yet it is possible for the state All Hunt Stag to emerge. Figures 7.12(a) and (b) illustrate how, from initial conditions under which slightly more than 50 percent of the players hunt stag, a global state of trusting behavior evolves. What explains the difference between the simulation results above and the results of figure 7.12?

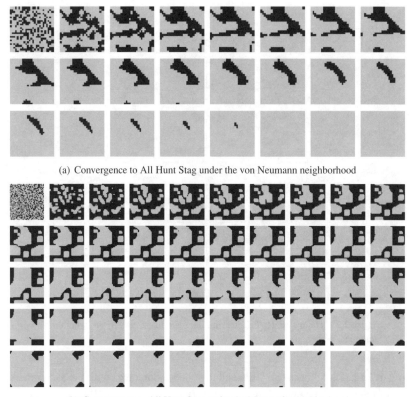

(a) Convergence to All Hunt Stag under the von Neumann neighborhood

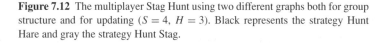

(b) Convergence to All Hunt Stag under the Moore (8) neighborhood

Figure 7.12 The multiplayer Stag Hunt using two different graphs both for group structure and for updating ($S = 4$, $H = 3$). Black represents the strategy Hunt Hare and gray the strategy Hunt Stag.

Consider the case in which the von Neumann neighborhood determines both the group structure and the update neighborhoods for all players. In this environment, a hare hunter always receives a payoff of $5H$.[12] Hare hunters switch to hunting stag if they are next to a stag hunter who earns a payoff strictly greater than their own. How likely is it that a random assignment of strategies to players brings this about?

Figure 7.13 illustrates the problem. The central stag hunter s is connected to a hare hunter h, the player whose probability of switching to Hunt Stag we want to determine. Although we know that h's payoff does not depend on the strategy

---

[12] Remember that a player always appears in one more game than the number of edges she is incident on.

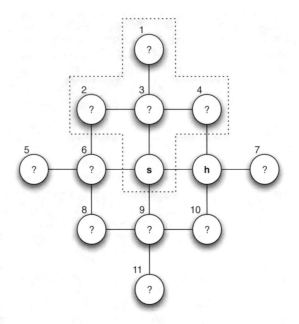

Figure 7.13 The figure used in determining the number of ways in which a hare hunter can be replaced.

of any of her neighbors, we still need to concern ourselves with the assignment of strategies to her immediate neighbors (labeled 4, 7, and 10 in the diagram) because the strategy followed by *these* players affects the composition of three of the groups in which s participates (the dashed line indicates one of the five groups). Because there are eleven players appearing among the five groups for whom the strategies are indeterminate, there are $2^{11} = 2048$ assignments of strategies to consider.

One can easily calculate the payoffs earned by s for every possible assignment of strategies to the eleven other players. Once this has been done, it is then possible – in some cases – to determine how many payoffs exceed $5H$, given the relative size of S and H. The qualification "in some cases" is needed because, for example, if all we assume is that $S > H \geq 0$, we cannot say, with certainty, whether *any* particular assignment of strategies will cause h to adopt hunting stag. However, if we know that $S > \frac{5}{4}H \geq 0$, we *can* say, with certainty, that 50 out of the 2048 possible assignments of strategies to players will cause the hare hunter to change.

To see this, consider the following strategy vector:

$$\vec{s}_1 = \langle 1, 1, 0, 1, 0, 1, 1, 1, 1, 1, 1 \rangle,$$

where the ith component of $\vec{s}_1$ denotes the strategy assigned to player i in figure 7.13 (we use "1" to denote Hunt Stag and "0" to denote Hunt Hare). Given this vector, s finds himself interacting in five groups:

$$g_1 = \{\text{Stag, Stag, Hare, Stag, Stag}\}$$
$$g_2 = \{\text{Stag, Hare, Stag, Stag, Stag}\}$$
$$g_3 = \{\text{Stag, Stag, Stag, Stag, Stag}\}$$
$$g_4 = \{\text{Stag, Stag, Stag, Stag, Hare}\}$$
$$g_5 = \{\text{Hare, Stag, Stag, Stag, Hare}\}.$$

The payoffs earned by a stag hunter in these five groups are $4S/5$, $4S/5$, S, $4S/5$, and $3S/5$, respectively. The *total* payoff earned by the stag hunter equals the sum of these, i.e., $4S$. Thus, if we know that $S > \frac{5}{4}H \geq 0$, we know that the hare hunter h of figure 7.13 will switch to hunting stag.

Consider, though, the following strategy vector:

$$\vec{s}_2 = \langle 1, 1, 0, 1, 0, 1, 0, 1, 1, 1, 1 \rangle,$$

which equals $\vec{s}_1$ in all respects except for the strategy assigned to player 7. According to this vector, the payoffs to the five groups are $4S/5$, $4S/5$, S, $3S/5$, and $3S/5$, respectively. This gives s a total payoff of $19S/5$. If all we know is that $S > \frac{5}{4}H \geq 0$, we cannot say, with certainty, that the adjacent hare hunter will switch to hunting stag. Some values of S and H do facilitate this (like $S = \frac{26}{19}$ and $H = 1$), but others do not (like $S = \frac{195}{152}$ and $H = 1$).

As the relative difference between S and H increases – that is, as the rewards for trusting behavior become greater – the number of strategy assignments which cause h to imitate s's strategy increases. For example, if $S > \frac{3}{2}H \geq 0$, then 394 of the 2048 possible assignments lead to the certain adoption of Hunt Stag by h; if $S > \frac{7}{4}H \geq 0$, then 884 assignments lead to the certain adoption of Hunt Stag; and if $S > 2H \geq 0$, then the number of vectors which cause h to switch rises to 1430. This makes sense: increasing the relative difference between S and H reduces the risk involved in choosing to hunt stag. Once $S > 2H \geq 0$, the corresponding two-player Stag Hunt would count Hunt Stag as the risk-dominant strategy!

Although the strategy of Hunt Stag does rather poorly in a world containing 50 percent or fewer stag hunters, once the percentage of stag hunters is increased to 60 percent, All Hunt Stag emerges much more easily. Although *no* simulations based upon the von Neumann network converged to the All Hunt Stag state when only 50 percent of the population initially hunted stag, 850

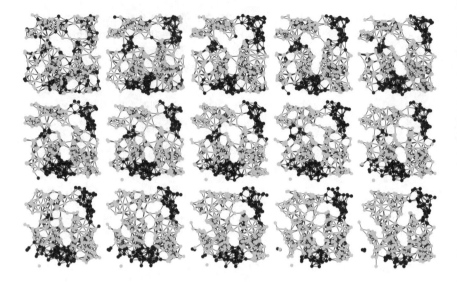

Figure 7.14 The multiplayer Stag Hunt, with a proximity model. Edges indicate transient group structure.

out of 1000 simulations converged to All Hunt Stag when the initial conditions were that 60 percent of the players were stag hunters.[13]

Turning our attention to the proximity model of the multiplayer Stag Hunt, let us begin by considering the case in which we have a population of 250 players spread out uniformly over a 40×40 world. We assume that the interaction (and update) radius for each player is 4.25, which means that each player interacts with roughly eight other players each generation. The typical *group* size, then, is approximately nine.

Simulations show that, from an initial state containing roughly equal numbers of stag hunters and hare hunters, with strategies distributed at random, and payoff parameters of $S = 4$ and $H = 3$, Hunt Stag is typically driven to extinction. Out of 1000 simulations, only 40 converged to All Hunt Stag; the remaining 960 converged to All Hunt Hare. However, if the update radius is larger than the interaction radius,[14] then, from uniform initial conditions All Hunt Stag evolves 32 percent of the time. However, if under the initial conditions 60 percent of players are stag hunters, then All Hunt Stag evolves just over 70 percent of the time.

---

[13] The lattice used was 50×50, with payoff parameters of $S = 4$ and $H = 3$.

[14] In this case, the interaction radius was 4 and the update radius was 8.

7.4 Fairness

The standard story behind two-player divide-the-cake refers to an entity other than the players: both players submit their requests to a referee who doles out the cake, provided that the requests are compatible. There are, then, two different versions of multiplayer divide-the-cake: one that does not explicitly include the referee among the players, and one that does.

In the form which leaves the referee implicit, each of the N players belonging to group j has a strategy s_i that represents the amount of the resource they would like.[15] Their requests are submitted to a referee (who is not a member of the group), and the referee awards s_i to player i, provided that $s_1 + \cdots + s_N \leq C$, where C is the total amount of cake available. If the sum of all the requests exceeds C, no player receives anything.

In the form which explicitly includes the referee, one player from the group takes on the role of referee and collects the requests from the remaining individuals. If the sum of the requests is less than or equal to C, the referee gives each player the amount requested and *keeps the remainder of the cake (if any) for himself*; if the sum of the requests exceeds the amount of cake available, then no one, including the referee, gets anything. Which player is taken to be the referee? For multiplayer local-interaction models, the referee is the player upon which the group is centered; for proximity models, the player is the individual whose interaction radius defines the group.

In a group of size N, the egalitarian norm of fairness dictates that all group members ought to receive C/N. In the case of goods that cannot be infinitely subdivided, the egalitarian norm dictates that all group members ought to receive $\lfloor C/N \rfloor$, the greatest integral amount less than or equal to C/N. In a three-person group with a cake size of 10, this means that each person should receive three slices of cake.

I mention the expected outcome under the egalitarian norm for the three-person group because, for a population whose interaction group structure is determined by a simple cycle, each player has three interactions every round and each group contains three persons. Figure 7.15 illustrates the evolution of one such population under *Imitate-the-Best* from random initial conditions, with a cake size of 10, and no referee.[16] With the exception of one small "blinker" of Demand 4 located at the center, the rest of the population has adopted the strategy of Demand 3 – the behavior which accords with the egalitarian norm!

---

[15] The strategy used by a player is the same across all groups. In some cases it might make sense for a player to condition their strategy on the group they are interacting with. I do not consider that possibility here.

[16] The group structure was determined by a simple cycle, as was the update neighborhood.

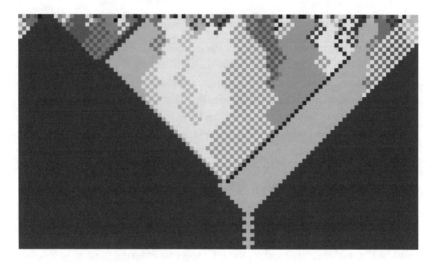

Figure 7.15 Multiplayer divide-the-dollar, in one dimension, with a cake size of 10. Each player interacts with his immediate neighbors on the left and right, and learns from the same individuals.

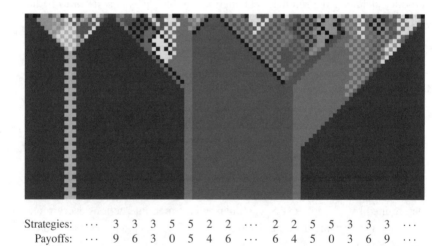

| Strategies: | ⋯ | 3 | 3 | 3 | 5 | 5 | 2 | 2 | ⋯ | 2 | 2 | 5 | 5 | 3 | 3 | 3 | ⋯ |
| Payoffs: | ⋯ | 9 | 6 | 3 | 0 | 5 | 4 | 6 | ⋯ | 6 | 4 | 5 | 0 | 3 | 6 | 9 | ⋯ |

Figure 7.16 How two strategies can block the spread of the egalitarian solution.

The egalitarian norm proves surprisingly robust and generally tends to drive other strategies to extinction. However, as figure 7.16 shows, in the absence of mutation this does not always happen. The phenomenon illustrated is similar to those discussed in chapter 5, where two strategies, through fortutious positioning, manage to prevent a region from adopting fair behavior even though *all* individuals within that region are receiving less than they would if they switched to fair division.

In figure 7.16, almost all players who follow the egalitarian strategy of Demand 3 receive a payoff of 9. Individuals in the center of the non-egalitarian region follow the strategy Demand 2 and generally receive a payoff of 6. (The exception to the "generally" occurs at the boundary, which we'll discuss shortly.) The two individuals bounding the region on the left and right each follow the strategy Demand 5. The outermost person who asks for five slices receives nothing: one of his interaction groups contains two Demand 3 and one Demand 5, another group contains one Demand 3 and two Demand 5, and the third contains two Demand 5 and one Demand 2. All of these groups have jointly incompatible demands. Yet the reason why this boundary player doesn't switch strategies is that his update neighborhood includes another person who follows Demand 5, and *that* player receives a sufficiently high score to prevent him from switching. The table at the bottom of figure 7.16 shows how the particular arrangement of strategies serves to block the spread of egalitarianism.

If individuals experiment with new strategies, the population tends towards the egalitarian solution. It doesn't uniformly adopt the egalitarian solution because, in a group of size three with a cake of size 10, if one person switches from Demand 3 to Demand 4, everyone continues to receive a payoff (the requests in the set of demands {3, 3, 4} are mutually compatible). However, this creates a temporally unstable arrangement: the person who switched to Demand 4 now receives a higher total payoff than do his peers. As a result, his peers will switch to asking for four slices of cake in the following round. In that round, the new followers of the strategy Demand 4 will find that switching strategies wasn't such a good idea: the conflict generated when everyone in a group asks for four slices means that they will earn a lower payoff than will be received by their neighbors who ask for three slices. As a result, they will switch back to the strategy of Demand 3, and the cycle will begin all over again.

There thus exists a tension between egalitarianism and optimality when they are not simultaneously satisfiable. The evolutionary dynamics under *Imitate-the-Best* drives the population towards states in which a compromise between the two competing aims is struck. Yet, if the cake size permits distributions that simultaneously satisfy egalitarianism and optimality, then the evolutionary dynamics on the simple cycle, with mutation, will arrive at that state. For example, figure 7.17 illustrates how, when groups have three members each, a cake size of 12 yields a Pareto-optimal outcome when all members ask for four slices.

Introducing the referee into the game structure modifies the dynamics considerably. Whereas the non-referee case, with mutation, tends to evolve to a state as close to the egalitarian split as possible, rather different behavior occurs

Figure 7.17 The simultaneous satisfiability of egalitarianism and optimality with a cake size of 12 and a mutation rate of 1 percent.

when a referee is present. Figure 7.18 illustrates several hundred generations of one simulation beginning from random initial condititions with a cake size of 10. As before, the group structure for interactions was determined by a simple cycle, as was the update neighborhood.

The greatest change concerns the patterns of mutual invasion between regions of Demand 5 and a polymorphic region containing both Demand 4 and Demand 6. Figure 7.19 provides magnified views of two such sections. In figure 7.19(a), the region on the left is occupied solely by Demand 5 and the region on the right by individuals following Demand 4 or Demand 6 (the two individuals on the border follow Demand 6).

Consider the payoffs received by the players following Demand 5. Players f_3 and f_4 both earn a total score of 10 because they appear – *not* in the role of referee – in two groups where their partner also asks for five pieces of cake. Both f_3 and f_4 receive a payoff of 5 from these interactions. When f_3 takes on the role of referee, the group for which he acts as referee contains f_4 and f_2; since these two players both ask for five pieces of cake, there is nothing left over, and hence f_3 doesn't receive anything. The same holds true when f_4 acts as referee.

Player f_2 receives a payoff of 5 from his interaction with f_4 when f_3 acts as referee. When f_2 acts as referee, it is for an interaction between f_3 and f_1, and he receives nothing because all of the cake is distributed. Lastly, f_2 interacts with g_1 with f_1 acting as referee. Since the demands of f_2 and g_1 are incompatible, f_2, f_1, and g_1 all receive nothing from this interaction. Thus f_2 earns a total score of 5.

Player f_1 receives a payoff of 5 from his interaction with f_3 where f_2 acted as referee. He also doesn't receive anything from refereeing the interaction between f_2 and g_1. When f_1 interacts with g_2, with g_1 as referee, f_1 again receives nothing because the strategies of f_1 and g_2 are incompatible. Thus f_1 earns a total score of 5.

By similar reasoning, player g_1 earns a total score of 6, and g_2 also a total score of 6. The modest player m_1 earns a total score of 8, and m_2 a total score of 10. The reason why m_2 earns a higher score than m_1 is that m_2 referees an

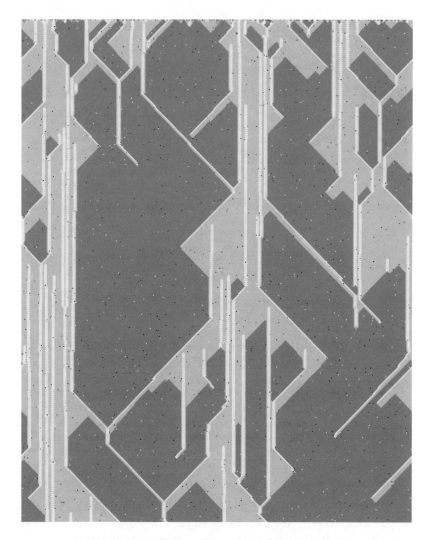

Figure 7.18 Multiplayer divide-the-dollar, with a cake size of 10 and an explicit referee. Group structure and update neighborhoods are determined by a simple cycle.

interaction between two modest players. Since not all of the cake is distributed, m_2 keeps the leftovers.

From this, it follows that f_1 will adopt the strategy Demand 6 in the next generation and g_2 will adopt the strategy Demand 4. All other players will continue to employ the same strategies as before. The 4–6 polymorphism thus advances one place into the region occupied by Demand 5.

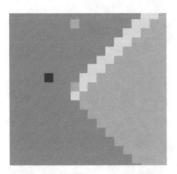

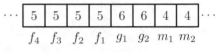

| ··· | 5 | 5 | 5 | 5 | 6 | 6 | 4 | 4 | ··· |

$f_4 \quad f_3 \quad f_2 \quad f_1 \quad g_1 \quad g_2 \quad m_1 \quad m_2$

(a) How mutation can stop the advance of the 4–6 polymorphism.

(b) A diagram for a frontier analysis of (a). Strategies are indicated in the box, with names assigned to the player listed below.

(c) How mutation can trigger the advance of the 4–6 polymorphism.

Figure 7.19 A close-up of expanding regions for multiplayer divide-the-dollar.

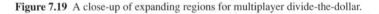

The reason why the dynamics of figure 7.18 is so complicated is that mutation can both serve to stop the advancement of the 4–6 polymorphism and create the conditions that allow it to occur. In figure 7.19(a), the outermost Demand 6 mutates to Demand 4. Yet, because the advancement of the 4–6 polymorphic region depends upon there being two players asking for Demand 6 on the boundary, this tips the dynamics in favor of Demand 5, which then proceeds to invade the region occupied solely by Demand 4. Likewise, if a player in the middle of a Demand 4 region mutates into one who asks for 5, this, too, initiates an invasion of the Demand 4 region by Demand 5.

How can mutation trigger the advance of the 4–6 polymorphism? If a player in the middle of a Demand 4 region mutates into one who asks for six slices of cake, this will create, in the next generation, a stable island of three individuals, all of whom ask for six slices of cake. This island of three individuals can lead to a standoff between the 4–6 polymorphic region and the region of Demand 5, as seen in the top part of figure 7.19(c). Chance mutations, though, can transform the stable island of three players following Demand 6 into the formation of strategies required for an invasion of the Demand 5 region. This happens in the bottom half of figure 7.19(c).

In two dimensions, similar behavior obtains. When the game does not explicitly include the referee, the population evolves to a state as close as possible to the egalitarian solution. If the group structure is determined using a von Neumann graph that wraps at the edges, then each interaction group contains five players. The egalitarian solution (which, in this case, is also efficient) is Demand 2, and that is exactly what evolves in figure 7.20(a).

If the game does explicitly include the referee, a slightly different outcome emerges. Although each group officially has five players, the effective size of the group is four because one of the players acts as the referee. With a cake of size 10, and a group of size four, it is no longer possible to distribute the good in an egalitarian fashion to all four players without some cake being left over. If all four players in a group follow Demand 2, it is in the interest of at least one of the players to switch to Demand 3 or Demand 4. Given this, we would expect a polymorphic population consisting primarily of Demand 2, with some players following Demand 3 and Demand 4 as well. As figure 7.20(b) illustrates, this outcome is exactly what we find.

Lastly, let us consider the proximity model of divide-the-cake. We keep the cake size fixed at 10 and consider, for simplicity, the version which does not explicitly include the referee. However, instead of positioning individuals uniformly along an $N \times N$ world, as in previous proximity models, we use the following method for initially positioning players: player i will initially be located at (r_i, θ_i), in polar coordinates, where $r_i \in [0, 40]$ and $\theta_i \in [0, 2\pi)$, both drawn from a uniform distribution.

The reason for considering this distribution is the following question: when group sizes differ, is it possible for individuals who use *Imitate-the-Best* to adjust their demands so that they take into account group size? Positioning players according to the above rule causes the local population density around the origin to be higher than that at the periphery. If *Imitate-the-Best* is capable of providing local adaptations to context, we would expect individuals towards the center of the model to ask for fewer slices of cake than individuals at the periphery.

Previous proximity models treated the world as a torus, so that during the random walk players who walked off one "edge" appeared on the other side. If we implemented the random walk in the same way, in this model, any initial

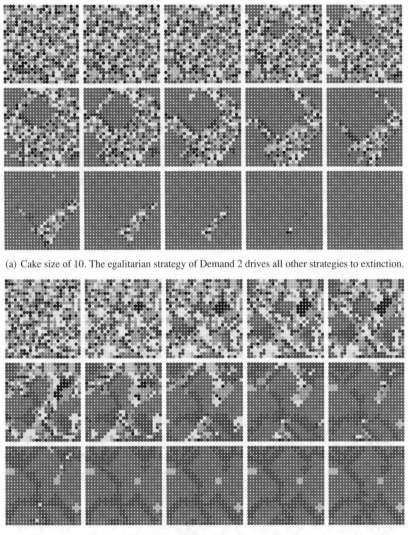

(a) Cake size of 10. The egalitarian strategy of Demand 2 drives all other strategies to extinction.

(b) Cake size of 10, with referee. The darkest color represents the strategy Demand 3 and the lightest patches are Demand 4.

Figure 7.20 Multiplayer divide-the-dollar in two dimensions, with group structure and update neighborhoods determined by the von Neumann graph.

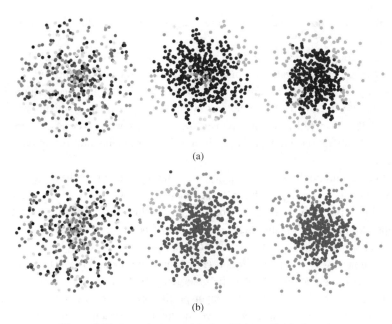

(a)

(b)

Figure 7.21 A proximity model of multiplayer divide-the-cake.

difference in the population density would eventually disappear via diffusion. Consequently, for these simulations we treat the world as an unbounded infinite plane.

In figure 7.21, we see that *Imitate-the-Best* is capable of providing local adaptations to context. In figures 7.21(a) and (b), individuals towards the center adopt more modest strategies than those followed by individuals at the periphery. In both cases, we see that evolution tends imperfectly towards the egalitarian solution. In figure 7.21(a), players towards the center ask for one slice of cake, and individuals on the periphery ask for four slices of cake. In figure 7.21(b), players towards the center ask for two slices of cake, and individuals on the periphery ask for five slices of cake. Among strategically myopic players, naïve, selfish maximization of payoffs can produce behavior close to the egalitarian ideal.

7.5 Conclusion

In this chapter, I have taken a small first step towards generalizing three of the games considered in previous chapters to more realistic – and interesting – multiplayer forms. Given the limitations on what I've been able to discuss, it would be imprudent to attempt to draw any sweeping conclusions. Yet some apparent trends can be tentatively identified.

First, cooperation is much harder to obtain in the multiplayer case. Although the strategy of Cooperate can survive and, indeed, come to be followed by the majority of the population, the attractiveness of Defect cannot be too high. If the attractiveness of Defect is not too high, then the same mechanisms which facilitate the spread of cooperation in the ordinary two-player case, namely unequal interaction and update neighborhoods, work in the multiplayer case as well.

Second, although trusting behavior is also harder to obtain in the multiplayer case, it is slightly *easier* to obtain than cooperation. Once the frequency of Hunt Stag in the population exceeds 60 percent, the evolutionary dynamics leads the population to the All Hunt Stag state roughly 85 percent of the time.

Third, fair behavior obtains about as readily in the multiplayer case as in the ordinary two-player case. It is true that including the referee as an explicit player in the game complicates the emergence of fairness. In a way, this is to be expected: identifying one player as the referee breaks the symmetry condition that holds both in two-player divide-the-cake and in the version of multiplayer divide-the-cake without the referee. We should not be surprised that slightly different outcomes will be generated once players are no longer perfectly symmetric. Nevertheless, what is surprising is that, even here, we do not move too far away from the egalitarian outcome.

8

Philosophical reflections

8.1 The problem

In the last five chapters we have seen multiple examples of how structured interactions in a population of self-interested, boundedly rational agents tend to promote moral behavior. Although this does not hold universally for all structures and all games,[1] it does seem that it holds often enough for it to be more than a mere coincidence. The central philosophical question, then, is what, if anything, does this imply for our understanding of morality and moral theories?

It is not immediately clear that the results discussed in chapters 3–7 affect our understanding of morality at all. Perhaps the best encapsulation of the general problem evolutionary explanations of morality face – and why they might not illuminate our understanding of morality – can be found in the following observation:

> ... it's important to demonstrate that the forms of behaviour that accord with our sense of justice and morality can originate and be maintained under natural selection. Yet we should also be aware that the demonstration doesn't necessarily account for the superstructure of concepts and principles in terms of which we appraise those forms of behaviour.
>
> *(Kitcher, 1999)*

As moral agents, we care about the superstructure of concepts and principles that we use to describe and evaluate our behavior and the behavior of others. We want, for example, to understand the difference between guilt and shame,

---

[1] See, in particular, the discussion in chapter 6 on the ultimatum game, where the effect of local interactions tends to promote behavior more akin to that of *homo economicus*.

and between regret and remorse, and we want to know the circumstances under which feeling one or the other is warranted. We want to know what actions are praiseworthy, what actions are blameworthy, and what actions are morally neutral. If there are extenuating circumstances that can transform in our assessment a normally blameworthy act into one that is praiseworthy (or at least morally neutral), we want to know what those circumstances are and why they have this transformational capacity. It is this superstructure of concepts and principles which requires both illumination and explanation. Yet, Kitcher alleges, it is exactly this superstructure which is unaccounted for in typical evolutionary models.

Let us introduce some terminology to express the concern in a slightly different form. Say that an individual "thinly" conforms with a principle of morality if, while behaving in the manner required, the individual fails to hold sufficiently many of the beliefs, intentions, preferences, and desires to warrant application of the term "moral" to his or her action. (We may also need to require that the rest of society, or a suitable proportion of society, also shares sufficiently many of the right beliefs, intentions, preferences, and so on.) For example, when someone acts morally we typically require that she intended to act morally, that she preferred to act morally over acting immorally, that she was in the "right state of mind," that she possessed "the appropriate feelings," and so on. Furthermore, let us say that an individual "thickly" conforms with a principle of morality if she holds sufficiently many of the beliefs, desires, and so forth to warrant describing her action as a "moral action." (As before, we may also need to impose a requirement on the beliefs, intentions, preferences, and so on held by the rest of society.)

In introducing these terms, I am explicitly borrowing (and mildly corrupting) the language of Clifford Geertz, who himself took the term "thick description" from an earlier work by Gilbert Ryle (1971). Ryle's point was simply that, without context, we cannot ascribe meaning to certain kinds of communicative signals accurately. The classic example is that, when a person winks at us, we cannot be sure whether the person is attempting to flirt, to signal agreement, to indicate approval, or so on, without knowing the full context behind the gesture. Geertz (1973) adopted the term "thick description" from Ryle because, in Geertz's view, *all* of human behavior was subject to the same interpretive problem. Part of the task of an anthropologist, for Geertz, was to seek out and provide thick descriptions of human behavior.

In my usage, a thick description of behavior that conforms to a moral principle is, minimally, a description that attributes to a person the right combination of intentional and emotional states in order for the behavior to be considered a moral action. In addition, the person has to perform the behavior for the right reasons.[2] The description is "thick" in one sense because it provides a rich, robust account of the current mental state of the individual agent. However, the description is also thick in Geertz's sense, insofar as thick descriptions of behavior conforming to a moral principle will often need to reference the social context, since moral beliefs and theories refer to social norms, intersubjective beliefs, or common knowledge that such-and-such is the case.

Note that the problem of providing thick (versus thin) descriptions of behavior is different from the problem of distinguishing between moral *action* and moral *behavior*. Moral behavior is simply behavior that produces the brute outcomes mandated by some moral principle, such as fair division in perfectly symmetric situations, or cooperation instead of defection under certain circumstances; similarly, moral action is action that conforms to moral principles. Does mere moral behavior exist? There is good reason to think so, at least under a sufficiently broad conception of morality. Consider *lex talionis*, the rule of "eye for an eye, tooth for a tooth," which states that you should do unto others as they have done unto you. If *lex talionis* embodies a moral principle, then TIT-FOR-TAT produces behavior that conforms to it. According to results from experiments done by Milinski (1987), stickleback fish use TIT-FOR-TAT as a rule governing predator-inspection visits. Since stickleback fish lack much of the higher-order cognitive machinery required for the intentional states underlying action, this is an example of arguably moral behavior but not moral action. However, even if it *were* a moral action (suppose that stickleback fish possess the appropriate intentional states for us to legitimately speak of them performing actions), there would still be something missing. The "something missing" is, of course, the rich set of concepts, emotions, and principles which underlies moral reasoning and, more importantly, motivates moral agents to act the way they do. The distinction between thick and thin descriptions draws attention to the fact that one can behave, and act, in ways that comply with the demands of moral principles, yet still fall short in important ways.

One of the difficulties of the analysis provided in chapters 3–7 is that it shows only how an evolutionary process can produce a social state in which individuals *thinly* conform with moral principles. Under the cultural-evolutionary interpretation of the replicator dynamics, and cultural-evolutionary interpretations of the local-interaction models, the repeated choices of individuals lead, in many cases, to arguably moral action. Why moral action? Since the agents in these models are making explicit choices, what they do admits an intentional explanation, so what they do is an action. Nevertheless, we are not given an

---

[2] To eliminate the problem of deviant causal chains, we may also need to require that the reasons cause the action in the right way.

account of the rich content of our moral life. For example, the evolution of the behavior called "fair division" in chapter 5 shows only that demanding half dominates because[3]

> ... demanding half realizes a higher average return than the alternatives ... Hence there is no clear analogue for, and no apparent need for, the kinds of righteous indignation and punishment that moral agents visit upon those who violate morality's constraints. Nor is there any need for a propensity for feelings of guilt when we 'unfairly' demand more than half — recognition of the lost returns should suffice to bring us back on track.
>
> *(D'Arms, 2000, p. 298)*

In summary, the problem is this: can game-theoretic analyses (either evolutionary or traditional) explain how and why individuals *thickly* conform with moral principles? Then, if we assume that we have shown (or that it can be shown) that natural selection favors moral behavior, wherefrom does our moral psychology derive?

8.2 Gestures towards a solution

Ultimately, I must admit skepticism as to whether evolutionary game theory *on its own* is capable of providing thick descriptions of moral behavior. The reason behind this scepticism is simply that fine-grained accounts of individual psychology are not the sort of thing which falls within the domain of the theory. In the original biological setting, evolutionary game theory analyzed problems in which frequency-dependent fitness introduced a strategic element into evolution. In the cultural setting, evolutionary game theory examines repeated interdependent decision problems played in populations of boundedly rational individuals. In both settings, the theory tracks only changes in the frequencies and distributions of strategies and, perhaps, other relevant properties. Under either interpretation, evolutionary game theory addresses only the *strategic* aspect of the superstructure, not the *psychological* aspect.

There are two natural approaches to the problem, which build upon previous work. Both of these approaches aim at providing thick, or, at least, *thicker*, descriptions of behavior conforming to moral principles. The first approach proceeds by expanding the class of games to include ones with richer strategy

---

[3] Do note that I am somewhat distorting the intended interpretation of this quote by including it here, since D'Arms was, strictly speaking, only criticising Skyrms' replicator-dynamics model of divide-the-cake. However, I feel that no harm is done in the distortion because D'Arms's point applies equally well to my discussion of fairness.

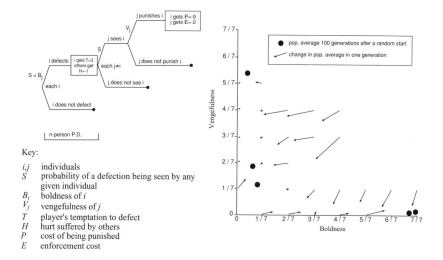

Figure 8.1 Axelrod's norms game.

sets. That is, one considers games whose strategies include the adoption of certain attitudes by the agent. Axelrod (1986) provided a canonical example of this approach.

Axelrod introduced the "norms game," illustrated in figure 8.1. The game consists of several different stages. To begin, each individual agent in the population has the opportunity to defect in an ordinary N-player prisoner's dilemma. If an individual defects, he receives a reward T, imposes a small cost H on all other players, and incurs a small chance of being seen. If the defector is spotted, then the person who spotted the defector may choose to punish the defector. If punishment occurs, the punisher incurs a small "enforcement cost" E and the defector incurs a sizable cost P as punishment.

An individual strategy in the norms game is an ordered pair (b, v), with $0 \le b, v \le 1$, where b and v denote the *boldness* and *vengefulness* of a player, respectively. Bold players are more likely to defect when given the opportunity, and vengeful players are more likely to punish. The two values b and v are most naturally interpreted as probabilities of defecting and punishing, respectively, given the opportunity to do either.

The results of Axelrod's simulation are shown in figure 8.1. A point on the graph represents the average boldness and vengefulness of the entire population. Arrows indicate the direction in which the evolutionary dynamics pushes the population at a given point. The large black dots indicate points at which one of Axelrod's simulations terminated. From the diagram, one can see that

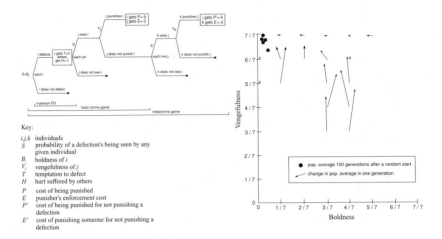

Figure 8.2 Axelrod's metanorms game.

"vengeful" strategies, that is, ones willing to punish observed defections, can grow to dominate the population under certain conditions while, at the same time, boldness falls almost to nothing. This would seem to provide the evolution of a norm against defecting: people's willingess to defect drops (that is, the mean boldness falls) and their willingness to punish grows (that is, the mean vengefulness climbs).

However, that is not the only evolutionary outcome. Inspection of the diagram reveals that another possibility produced by evolution is the state in which vengefulness *increases* almost to unity, and boldness falls nearly to zero. This state corresponds to the Hobbesian state of nature: hardly anyone is willing to punish defectors, and virtually everyone is willing to defect if given the opportunity. The evolutionary story appears inadequate given how sensitive the evolution of norms is to the initial conditions of the population.

Part of the problem with this evolutionary story, according to Axelrod, is that it fails to include a very common social occurrence: the punishment of people who fail to enforce a norm. Consequently, he introduced a "metanorms" game, in which people who witness defection, yet fail to punish, can themselves be punished. Figure 8.2 illustrates the metanorms game, with the results of the simulation. The result here is that, when one allows people to be punished for failing to enforce a norm, the norm for punishing can very quickly become pervasive, as the diagram shows.[4]

---

[4] However, Galan and Izquierdo (2005) argue that the results of Axelrod's simulations are unreliable: running simulations for longer times and modifying key parameters allow some of

Suggestive as Axelrod's results are, they, and the entire approach they illustrate, nevertheless suffer from the same failing as has been attributed to evolutionary explanations by D'Arms and Kitcher. It doesn't matter that the strategy labels are "punish" and "enforce a norm," for the model still admits a *purely behavioral* interpretation. All the model shows is that strategies requiring players to be willing to incur an expense to impose costs on defectors, in certain circumstances, will be favored in certain evolutionary contexts. Insofar as the psychological makeup of the agents is concerned, there could be a variety of reasons and motivating factors for why they choose to incur an expense to impose costs on defectors. We don't want an account of evolutionary pressures that shows how people will come to act *as if* they are punishing defectors; we want an account of why people *really punish*. We want an account of why people care about justice, and an explanation for the feelings of moral outrage that drive people to engage in retribution. Since the first approach to the problem cannot provide this, it is time to set it aside and look elsewhere.

The second approach to the problem proceeds by enriching the conception of boundedly rational agents to include nonstrategic, psychological elements. It involves making explicit connections between evolutionary game theory and psychology, and hence means that one no longer attempts to explain the origins and nature of morality using just evolutionary game theory.[5] One promising example of work in this direction is that of Gerd Gigerenzer, Reinhard Selten, and the researchers at the Center for Adaptive Behavior and Cognition in Berlin. "Bounded rationality," as understood by Gigerenzer, refers to the use of "fast and frugal heuristics," which are used by agents of limited cognitive ability to make decisions. One can think of such heuristics as relatively reliable algorithms, where the reliability of the algorithm stems from its exploitation of structural features of the decision problem. In chapter 1, I referred to the use of such heuristics as one motivation for considering the use of learning rules such as *Imitate-the-Best*. We now have reason to revisit the topic.

Gigerenzer provides a useful example of such heuristics in action. Consider the task of catching a fly ball in baseball. The standard computational approach associated with "perfect rationality" requires the individual to (a) estimate the relative velocity of the fly ball and the position from which it was launched, (b) solve the complex differential equation describing its trajectory, (c) run toward

---

the claims to be overturned. This does not affect my central claim, though, which is that Axelrod's approach to providing thick descriptions of conformity with moral principles cannot work, in principle.

[5] This explains my scepticism on page 270. It is not that I am suddenly repudiating all of the work done in previous chapters. Rather, I am explicitly acknowledging the explanatory limits of what may be done using those tools alone.

the location where the fly ball is predicted to land, and (d) revise continuously *en route* the prediction of where the ball is going to land because factors such as the ball's spin may affect its trajectory, yet will be difficult for the outfielder to estimate from his position on the ground. Clearly, this procedure requires an incredible amount of computational power. A simpler approach – the fast and frugal approach – consists of the following rule: estimate where the ball will land, then begin to run toward that position keeping the angle between one's eye and the ball constant. Doing so will result in the outfielder catching the ball. The desired effect, catching the ball, is achieved with less computational overhead.

Recall D'Arms's criticism about evolutionary explanations for the moral principle of the equal split: when we don't ask for half of the cake, "recognition of the lost returns should suffice to bring us back on track." Yes, such recognition *should* suffice, but such recognition need not occur, at least not explicitly, nor as often as required for agents to link poor performance with particular strategies. We may recognize that we aren't doing "as well as we'd like," but yet be unable to pin our failure to any particular act in any particular context. In the real world, our interactions rarely come with specified payoff matrices that we are shown ahead of time, and we rarely have the rules of the game explained to us in detail. Our inability to correlate poor performance with the following of certain strategies becomes more plausible once we recognize that the game of life is significantly more complex and involves many more people than the simple games typically studied.

Nonetheless, it is a fact that we are capable of identifying general rule-governed relations and patterns, even when we cannot articulate the rule which governs them. In *One for All*, Russell Hardin (1997) relates an experiment in which people were subjected to electric shocks while listening to a sequence of nonsense syllables. When the shock was correlated with the presence of a certain syllable, people would develop an anticipatory response to the impending shock, although they were unable to articulate exactly why they were anticipating it. Given that we can recognize such relations and patterns, yet not be able to identify the true underlying rule or process generating those relations, it makes sense that boundedly rational agents will, in interdependent decision contexts, set out rules for themselves to follow, if the strategic choice recommended by the rule is sufficiently well correlated with successful payoffs.

Thus, I wish to suggest, the solution to the main problem is as follows: evolutionary game theory, together with experimental psychology and recent work in the theory of bounded rationality, can explain some of the structure and content of our moral theories by working in tandem. Evolutionary game theory allows us to identify certain types of behavior in interdependent decision problems that maximize the long-run expected utility of individuals. Given this, there is then a further question as to what motivational structures exist for actually *producing* this behavior in boundedly rational individuals. As I see it, morality, broadly construed, plays two parts in the production of this utility-maximizing behavior. First, the moral sentiments – the "morally relevant" emotions, moods, interpersonal affective stances, and attitudes – motivate us to act. Second, the content of moral theories instructs us how to act once we have been motivated to do so. The outcomes produced by acting in accordance with moral theory are such that they tend to maximize our expected utility over the lifetime of the individual.[6]

This is not to say that acting in accordance with moral theory *always* maximizes one's expected utility in the long run. Life is complicated and, because the moral sentiments and the content of moral theories are only heuristics, there is a lot that can go wrong. However, given that the kinds of interdependent decision problems people face in society are ones that often preclude full rational deliberation – because people lack information about the game, the exact payoff structure of the other person, people's past behavior, the likelihood that they (or I) can get away with certain sorts of behavior, and so on – it is the best that we can do. It is precisely *because* we cannot engage in full rational deliberation about what to do, and because we face choices of this kind all the time, that it is useful to rely on the heuristics governing social behavior which are embedded in morality.

The above conception of boundedly rational agents using morality as a heuristic in strategic contexts can be thought of in the following way: moral heuristics govern the search for effective strategies (i.e., behaviors) in the game of life. This invokes a conception of heuristics as composed of three parts:

> There are at least three important types of building blocks of which simple heuristics are composed ... (a) there are building blocks to guide information search; (b) different heuristic building blocks determine how to stop search; (c) other building blocks are used to make a decision based on the information gathered. All of these building blocks can be influenced (or implemented) by processes involving emotions ... individual learning ... and social learning.
>
> (*Sadrieh* et al., *2001, pp. 93–94*)

---

[6] One might be inclined, I suppose, to view this as providing a kind of evolutionary foundation for a variant of rule utilitarianism. However, there is one extremely important difference between the view espoused here and that held by classical rule utilitarians: namely, there is no guarantee that the rules obtained generate the greatest good for the greatest number (whatever that means). At best, what I am assured of is that I will probably obtain the "greatest good" for *myself* subject to the constraints placed by other people.

An example of how moral principles function as heuristics governing a search is indirectly provided by Braithwaite's solution to the core problem in *Theory of Games as a Tool for the Moral Philosopher*:

> Suppose that Luke and Matthew are both bachelors, and occupy flats in a house which has been converted into two flats by an architect who had ignored all considerations of acoustics. Suppose that Luke can hear everything louder than a conversation that takes place in Matthew's flat, and vice versa . . . Suppose further that each of them has only the hour from 9 to 10 in the evening for recreation, and that it is impossible for either to change to another time. Suppose that Luke's form of recreation is to play classical music . . . and that Matthew's amusement is to improvise jazz on the trumpet . . . Suppose that the satisfaction each derives from playing his instrument for the hour is affected, one way or the other, by whether the other is playing . . . Suppose they put to me the problem: Can any plausible principle be devised stating how they should divide the proportion of days . . . [that they play] . . . so as to obtain maximum production of satisfaction . . . ?
>
> *(Braithwaite, 1954, p. 8)*

Braithwaite, after discussing some additional assumptions, eventually recommends that Luke and Matthew divide their playing times in the ratio of 17 to 26. But consider this solution for a minute. Why does not Braithwaite simply recommend that Luke *kill* Matthew, thereby removing his noisy neighbor entirely and enabling himself to enjoy his classical music whenever he wishes? Or, if Braithwaite is Matthew's friend, why not recommend the reverse?

The point is that, for Braithwaite, recommending that Luke kill Matthew so that Luke may obtain increased enjoyment of classical music is not even considered an option. Yet there is no *a priori* reason why this possibility should be excluded, given the nature of the fundamental conflict of interest underlying this decision problem. Luke's killing Matthew *is* a real option and it does, at least in principle, belong to the feasible set. However, we would consider there to be something very deeply wrong with an individual who treated that outcome as actually belonging to the feasible set. The reason why, for Braithwaite, the theory of games is merely a tool for the moral philosopher – not a wholesale replacement for moral theory – is that Braithwaite assumes that the shape of the feasible set is already determined by a moral perspective. That is, one first takes the set of physically possible outcomes and passes them through the filter of a moral theory to obtain the feasible set. As Gigerenzer and Selten (2001, p. 5) note, "a key process in bounded rationality is limited search." Moral theories facilitate limitation of the search for solutions to interpersonal decision problems by virtue of the shape they impose on the feasible set.

Moral theories also include heuristics that guide information searches. If I am told that Jones killed Sam, my moral training compels me to ask, before passing judgment, whether certain standard exculpating conditions obtain. Did Sam attack Jones with murderous intent? This is nothing more than a guided information search. Moral theories also include heuristics that tell us when to terminate an information search. If I find out that Sam attacked Jones without provocation and with murderous intent (and suitable means to carry out the assault), and that Jones defended himself without using excessive force, our moral theories tell us that, *ceteris paribus*, we need not continue collecting information before making a judgment as to the moral worth of Jones's action. Sam's death might be a regrettable outcome, but Jones did no wrong. Lastly, moral theories include general heuristics that lead us to make a decision on the information gathered. If *A* killed *B* under such-and-such (roughly specified) conditions, then *A* acted out of self-defense and is not morally culpable.

The thought that morality might best be understood as evolved heuristics is not entirely new. Allan Gibbard hints at such a view in *Wise Choices, Apt Feelings*:

> We avoid cheating and fraud, more or less. On the whole we probably gain more from these plain scruples than we would from close, egoistic calculations that probed the limits of what we could do with impunity.
>
> *(Gibbard, 1990, p. 258)*

Gibbard and I are in agreement here. However, I think we can be a bit more explicit than just saying "we probably gain more" in explaining how it is that the heuristics help us. To reiterate the mantra, following heuristics to avoid cheating and fraud tends to maximize my expected utility in the long run, given my preferences (and the preferences of other people) and the way social interactions are structured.

On a number of points, though, Gibbard and I part company. First, Gibbard suggests that many of the heuristics which operate were fixed by natural selection at the *biological* level. Regarding the psychological mechanisms which motivate individual action, he writes (italics mine) that

> We should not imagine a sly, unconscious general-purpose calculator, assessing advantage and then producing the most advantageous feelings for a person's circumstance. The picture should rather be one of specific psychic mechanisms, some of them emotional. Each mechanism responds to special sorts of cues in special ways. *Natural selection itself is the prime general-purpose calculator, but it calculated long ago, blind to current novelties. It produced a set of heuristics, a set of useful rules for reproducing as a hunter–gatherer.*
>
> *(Gibbard, 1990, p. 259)*

The extent to which one agrees with the above quote depends considerably on the extent to which one agrees with the general research program of evolutionary psychology. I do not doubt that much of our psychological life has been shaped considerably by evolutionary pressures; the question is simply whether the evolutionary pressures which shaped our *moral* life are primarily biological or cultural pressures. Gibbard plumps for biological evolution as the source of the heuristics, whereas I favor cultural evolution.

That said, Gibbard does circumscribe the role of biological evolution. Even if our capacity to make judgments of fairness has evolved,

> [n]o unique standard of fairness is wired into our brains, if my story is right. Judgments of fairness are shaped in part by complex workings of normative discussion.
>
> *(Gibbard, 1990, p. 262)*

Here, though, I suspect that normative discussion plays a less significant role in our judgments of fairness. I think our sense of fairness is fairly well calibrated to track behaviors and outcomes that satisfy our preferences to the greatest extent possible subject to constraints. The theories and principles which we use to explain *why* an outcome is fair might very well be shaped by normative discussion (theories have to come from somewhere), but the reason why those theories have the form that they do is not due to discussion. Moral theories have the form they do because it is a *fact* that social beings such as us, who have preferences of a certain kind, maximize our long-run expected utility by behaving in ways that conform to certain moral principles.

There are two other points of divergence between my view and Gibbard's, which I would like to discuss briefly. The first concerns the type of adaptive problem for which evolution has developed an solution, and the second concerns the notion of stability which underlies the view. Let us consider each of these in turn.

What is the core adaptive problem our moral nature addresses? According to Gibbard, the "key to our moral nature ... lies in *coordination* broadly conceived" (Gibbard, 1990, p. 26). More generally, "[s]ystems of normative control in human beings ... are adapted to achieve interpersonal coordination" (Gibbard, 1990, p. 64). Problems of interpersonal coordination are certainly important for understanding human nature, but not all interpersonal decision problems are problems of coordination, even under the broad conception of coordination urged by Gibbard.[7] The key to our moral nature, rather, lies in the fact that we all face repeated interpersonal decision problems – of many types – in socially structured environments.

---

[7] Consider the simplest case: two-player, two-strategy symmetric games. One can show that every one of these games (without payoff ties) falls into one of three different categories: those which are like the prisoner's dilemma, those which are like coordination games, and those which are like the Hawk–Dove game discussed in chapter 2 (see Weibull, 1995, p. 30).

Now let us turn to the notion of stability. For Gibbard, judgments of fairness are shaped by normative discussion. Certainly other aspects of moral theory will be shaped by normative discussion as well. How are we to understand the process of normative discussion?

> Normative discussion must tend toward all accepting the same norms, and acceptance of norms must tend to guide action. Selection pressures could develop and maintain these tendencies only if, in the context of others' having them, having these tendencies oneself enhanced one's fitness. The tendencies, in other words, would have to constitute an evolutionarily stable strategy.
>
> *(Gibbard, 1990, p. 76)*

Our moral nature, by virtue of being shaped by normative discussion, will thus tend towards behaviors that constitute evolutionarily stable strategies.

Although I have discussed evolutionarily stable strategies at various points in this book, the primary notion of stability has been a kind of dynamic stability. This was deliberate, for I think that formal game-theoretic notions of stability are of little use for helping to explain and understand our evolved moral nature. This is a heretical view, admittedly, but one I think capable of being supported by argument.

Gibbard, as indicated above, disagrees. So does Ken Binmore, who states that "[s]tability tells us that social contracts need to be equilibria in the game of life" (Binmore, 2005, p. 14). (The notion of "equilibria" Binmore refers to is that of a Nash equilibrium.) There is a straightforward relationship between evolutionarily stable strategies and the set of Nash equilibria: the set of evolutionarily stable strategies is a subset of those strategies which are in Nash equilibrium with themselves (see Weibull, 1995, pp. 27 and 37). Consequently, the argument will proceed in two parts: first, an argument for why we should not use the concept of a Nash equilibrium as the primary analytical tool for explaining and understanding our moral nature; and second, an argument for why we should try to explain our moral nature by invoking a general notion of dynamic stability.

Let us assume that our moral nature is an evolved response to handling interpersonal decision problems. Why should the concept of a Nash equilibrium not be the primary analytical tool for understanding our moral nature? While a great many of the decision problems we face in society involve two people, other decision problems involve many more, and the notion of a Nash equilibrium is less useful in these cases. Suppose that we are all faced with an N-player decision problem, and that some assignment of strategies to players is a Nash equilibrium. The defining feature of a Nash equilibrium is that each person's strategy is a best response to the strategies held by the others. That is, so long as no one else deviates, it is not in my interest to change what I do. But why should we consider only the prospects of isolated *individual* deviations from equilibrium play? Both Bonnie *and* Clyde might decide to renege on their part to play in society. Once society reaches any considerable size, the possibility of regular coordinated deviations from equilibrium play is a fact of life we will have to face.

A second reason is that we have no guarantee that a Nash equilibrium in the game of life even exists. It is well known that games with infinitely many strategies can have no Nash equilibrium. How many strategies does the game of life have?

A third reason is that, even if a Nash equilibrium exists for the game of life, we have no guarantee that we would be able to *find it*. Prasad (1991, 1997) shows, in a series of extremely clever arguments, that there are games in which it is possible for us to know *that* a Nash equilibrium exists while, at the same time, the problem of *determining* the Nash equilibrium is noncomputable! Thus, even if we set aside the question of whether we humans are boundedly rational or not,[8] it is possible that even a perfectly rational agent would be unable to figure out what the Nash equilibrium is in the game of life.[9]

Let us now turn to the second argument: why a general notion of dynamic stability is more useful for explaining and understanding our evolved moral nature. This amounts to a shift away from the search for evolutionarily stable strategies. Because the set of evolutionarily stable strategies is a subset of strategies that are in Nash equilibrium with themselves, all of the arguments mentioned above apply here, as well.

Yet there is an important pragmatic reason why we should be more concerned with dynamic stability: in practice, nothing is evolutionarily stable. One proves the existence of evolutionarily stable strategies by fixing, once and for all, the space of possible strategies for an artificial game. In the real world, though, evolution is open-ended and strategy spaces are unbounded. There will always be something better coming along in the future. Or, as the joke says, to a first approximation all species are extinct.

But that's perfectly fine. On the view I have sketched here, a notion of dynamic stability – or even a notion of being "relatively stable" such as "unlikely to be driven out within a reasonably long time frame" – suffices for explaining how our moral sentiments and moral theories could have evolved.[10] Lest one

---

[8] We are.

[9] Provided that the computational abilities of a rational agent are restricted to the realm of recursive functions of positive integers (i.e., to the realm of things traditionally viewed as computable under the Church–Turing thesis).

[10] I am deliberately avoiding a discussion of what I take to be the right formal stability concept, since it would take us too far afield. For an informal sense of what I mean, think back to how

think that we need something more substantive than a weak notion of stability on which to base morality, keep in mind that there is nothing "weak" about being relatively stable. As so many geopolitical conflicts serve to illustrate, stability in heterogeneous populations where there are many competing ends can be notoriously difficult to achieve. The costs of failing to achieve it can be extremely high, as evidenced by so many recent examples of genocide.

8.3 Artificial virtue

One may find it difficult to see how the view which treats moral principles as heuristics that maximize our long-run expected utility can account for *all* of morality. Indeed, one may feel inclined to argue that many of our moral principles have little, if anything, to do with maximizing our long-term expected utility. There is much to say about this. To begin, one must appreciate the flexibility of the contemporary notion of expected utility maximization. Provided that people have a consistent and coherent set of preferences governing their choice of behavior, it is always possible to define a utility function f over outcomes such that, if people choose in a manner consistent with their preferences, we can say that they are acting as if they were maximizing their expected utility. Since these preferences may range over anything, including the benefits obtained by other people and their overall well-being, the notion of long-term expected utility maximization can encompass purely *altruistic* behavior as well as purely selfish behavior. This objection thus rests on nothing more than a very serious misunderstanding of the standard theory of expected utility.

A more important concern involves the transition from the kinds of simplistic models considered in previous chapters – and the kinds of simplistic moral principles to which they give rise – to the rich and subtly nuanced intuitions embodied in contemporary moral theory. The game of divide-the-cake is a very simple game, and the moral principle it gives rise to is a very simple principle. Our contemporary moral life, though, contains a vast array of complex interrelating intuitions. Even assuming that the story told so far does account for the origins of moral principles like "share equally in perfectly symmetric situations," how did we get here from there?

The science of morality is only in its infancy, so any attempt at gesturing towards an answer will always leave itself open to the criticism of figure 8.3.

---

many of the results discussed in chapters 3 through 7 amounted to essentially showing that a behavior did well enough to tend to dominate in the population, while resisting being driven out.

"I think you should be more explicit here in step two."

Figure 8.3 A standard criticism of theories about the evolution of morality (Harris, 1981).

Even so, there is no reason why we should not make the attempt. No matter how complete a story one puts forward, there will always be some questions that remain unanswered.

In this section, I wish to sketch how the view of morality defended previously can, in principle, be extended to account for much of the rich content of our current moral life. I shall do so by invoking Hume's distinction between the natural and artificial virtues. It should be noted that my concern here is not to make sense of what Hume meant by these terms, but rather to show how the framework developed enables us to speak of natural and artificial virtues in a way that, although not Hume's, is certainly Humean. Much of what I say here shall be speculative but the general spirit is, I think, correct – at least in broad outline.

Recall Hume's distinction between the natural virtues and the artificial virtues from the *Treatise*:

> ... our sense of every kind of virtue is not natural; but ... there are some virtues, that produce pleasure and approbation by means of an artifice or contrivance, which arises from the circumstances and necessities of mankind.
>
> *(Treatise, Book III, Part II, Section I, p. 477)*

The natural virtues, for Hume, are those which "produce pleasure and approbation" from means *other than* the "circumstances and necessities of mankind." That is, the source of approbation for natural virtues derives from natural affection, or other sentiments, which we possess simply as a result of being human, and is not culturally or socially constructed. Why do we blame a father when he neglects his child? According to Hume, it is because it "shews a want of natural affection."

Artificial virtues, on the other hand, do not derive from such natural affections. Consider, for example, the virtue of honesty with respect to property, which Hume includes among the artificial virtues. The reason why we feel approbation for this virtue is simply because we know that respect for personal property is necessary, given the circumstances of mankind. Human societies of any significant size and scale would not be possible without honesty with respect to property.

Hume was writing without the benefit of having Darwin's theory of evolution ready to hand. Yet, given that we have this advantage, we might seek to ground the distinction between natural and artificial virtues somewhat differently. To do so, let us return to one of the central themes underlying this book: interdependent decision problems.

It is a basic fact of humanity that all of us, each day, face a variety of interdependent decision problems. This was a basic fact of existence even before there were *homo sapiens*. We evolved from social primates who themselves faced interdependent decision problems. One of the lessons of evolutionary game theory is that the animal kingdom is rife with interdependent decision problems, even if the animals which face these problems lack the cognitive machinery to conceptualize and represent these problems to themselves as such.

However, and this seems to me to be the crucial point, some of the interdependent decision problems we must contend with are ones inherited from our evolutionary history, whereas other problems are ones we have created for ourselves. Call these decision problems of the first and second type, respectively. This presents one important departure from Hume's view. In distinguishing between the natural and artificial virtues, Hume based this distinction upon whether the approbation we feel when contemplating those virtues arose "from the circumstances and necessities of mankind" or not. Yet this fails to distinguish between types of virtues, for *all* interdependent decision problems derive from the circumstances and necessities of mankind; we are social beings, after all. What we can do, though, is differentiate interdependent decision problems thrust upon us by our evolutionary heritage from those which were not. From this, we can then recover a distinction between natural and artificial virtues, which, albeit not Hume's, is most certainly Humean in spirit.

Recall that, for Hume, character traits are the objects of moral evaluation. Certain positive traits are considered virtuous, and certain negative traits are considered vices. What is a character trait? Roughly, a character trait is a psychological disposition that tends to cause people to act in certain ways. Actions consist, in part, of behavior, and some behaviors are responses to inter-dependent decision problems. Possessing certain character traits, then, can be interpreted as adopting (or holding) certain strategies for use in interdependent decision problems.

Character traits that generate behavior for interdependent decision problems can then be divided, roughly, into two categories on the basis of the kind of interdependent decision problem they are most commonly invoked to solve. This presents a second revision of Hume's view. Whereas, for Hume, the distinction between natural and artificial virtues concerned the origin of the *character traits* themselves, in my view the distinction between natural and artificial virtues derives from the source of the problem in which they are most commonly invoked.

It is the case that my distinction between natural and artificial virtues be-comes somewhat blurred, for some virtues may be invoked in more than one class of decision problem. This should not be seen as problematic, though, because reasonably clear cases of both types do exist. Consider the virtue of paternal beneficence. This character trait is most typically invoked in decision problems of the first type, and hence classified as a natural virtue (in my sense of the term), which is in agreement with Hume. The virtue of honesty with respect to property is exclusively invoked in decision problems of the second type, and hence classified as an artificial virtue (in my sense of the term), also in agreement with Hume.

We now have all the tools we need to sketch a story about the evolution of morality. Back when *homo sapiens* was emerging as a species, our evolutionary heritage had saddled us with a variety of interdependent decision problems each of us had to solve. Evolution had already crafted solutions, of one form or another, to these problems. These solutions were embodied in emotions and other cognitive machinery,[11] and generated adaptively beneficial behavior.

As we evolved, and our cognitive abilities increased, this changed the nature of the interdependent decision problems we faced. Consider the notion of personal property. Before we had the ability to make use of found objects as tools or clothing, there was no need for the concept of personal property: the notion of a particular object *belonging* to someone had no role to play in our cognitive space.[12] However, once we became tool users, and possession of

---

[11] Perhaps even in the form of the evolved psychological mechanisms that evolutionary psychologists speak of, although one need not be committed to this.

[12] Notice that there is an important difference between property rights, in the sense of objects that belong to a person, and property rights, in the sense of space or territory that a person has claim to. Many animals that are not tool users exhibit territoriality.

effective tools conferred corresponding fitness benefits on a person, a new class of interdependent decision problems was suddenly created. How was one to determine which person had a claim to use which tool? This problem forced itself upon our ancestors, even before they could articulate it or recognize it as a problem.

The growth of our cognitive capacity – and the creation of new interdependent decision problems – was accompanied by the growth and development of language. We became capable of describing the world around us, as well as our own mental life. We became able to attribute beliefs, desires, dispositions, and so on, to ourselves and other people. We could then express what we wanted and communicate our desires to others. Negotiation became possible, as well as misleading, misrepresenting, and a host of deceptive practices.

At some point, our language became sufficiently expressive to describe in a rudimentary fashion the small societies humans lived in, and the kinds of behavior people performed in these societies. People, acting as pattern-recognition machines, already knew, in some form or another, what forms of behavior were conducive to stable, mutually beneficial societies. At this point, if not earlier, key elements of the language of morality entered, including the concept of punishment, shame, threats to the common good, social roles, as well as the notions of duty and obligation.

Earlier, I said that the distinction between natural and artificial virtues was best viewed as deriving from the distinction between interdependent decision problems inherited from our evolutionary history, versus problems created by ourselves. As the short, purely fictional, discussion above makes clear, even *this* dividing line is not so clear. Is the interdependent decision problem which the virtue of honesty with respect to property solves a problem inherited from our evolutionary history, or one created by ourselves? Can it be said to be both?

Regardless, the following seems clear: once we have acquired the ability to theorize about morality, about what we value, and to articulate *why* we value what we value, we have arrived at the crucial dividing point between natural and artificial virtues. The natural virtues are seen by us *as* virtues due to our evolutionary heritage. We do not choose to value parental beneficence, we simply do. We are, so to speak, hard-wired for it. But when I identify myself as a British citizen, or as a member of the European Union, or of the human race *in toto*, rather than with exclusively local allegiances, I am making a choice about what I value. Artificial virtues, like nationalism, are of use in realizing desired outcomes we have chosen, either explicitly or implicitly. Are these virtues seen by us *as* virtues due to their usefulness in realizing some ulterior motive? Or are these ulterior motives realized because we first long to possess the associated virtue? Both may be true.

Recall E. O. Wilson's famous observation from *On Human Nature* (1988) that "genes hold culture on a leash." We might make a similar observation regarding the relationship between natural and artificial virtues. Consider the view that there is nothing like an essential human nature; rather, who we are is entirely a product of choices we make. This view of humanity is intoxicating, for it suggests that all aspects of life, including who we are, and what we value, may be re-shaped. Yet how does this re-shaping occur? As the product of individual choices.

Therein lies the rub. All choice relies upon preexisting preferences. Where do these preferences come from? Some are acquired, some are not. Likewise, some of the things we view as virtues are learned – these are the artificial virtues – and some are not – these are the natural virtues. Given that we cannot change the natural virtues, for they are hard-wired into us, the extent to which the artificial virtues may be shaped by choice is constrained by the natural virtues. Do we know the extent to which the natural virtues constrain the artificial virtues? No, we do not. But, like all empirical questions, this admission of ignorance is nothing more than a call to action.

8.4 Evidential support

So much for just-so stories and what might be viewed by some as philosophical flights of fancy. Let us return to the hard facts. Do we have evidence that peoples' moral beliefs have been shaped by evolutionary considerations? Do we have evidence that moral principles can be understood as heuristics in the way articulated above? The evidence is still far from certain, but in closing I want to discuss the results of two experiments, which are highly suggestive.[13]

Experiments have found that people favor following different moral rules in different contextually specified distribution problems. In their classic 1984 paper "On dividing justly," Yaari and Bar-Hillel presented subjects with distribution problems phrased according to one of the following categories:

(1) differences in needs,
(2) differences in tastes,
(3) differences in beliefs.

---

[13] These two experiments barely scratch the surface of a vast topic. However, even to attempt a decent discussion of the empirical evidence for the evolution of morality would require an entire second volume on its own. For a start, see de Waal (1996, 1998, 2005), Shermer (2004), and Ridley (1996).

In the first category, subjects tended to favor Rawls's maximin principle, which divides goods so as to make the position of the worst-off individual as good as possible. When faced with a choice in category (2), subjects increased their use of the utilitarian distribution principle and decreased their use of the maximin principle. This occurred even though the problems presented in categories (1) and (2) had the *same* mathematical representation.

The connection between maximin rules and need-based distribution problems makes good evolutionary sense. If someone will die unless they obtain a minimum amount of a good, and you don't know ahead of time that you won't receive the short end of the stick, then, from the point of view of survival, you should favor distributing that good according to a maximin rule. (This may also be viewed as an application of the decision principle of Disaster Avoidance.) In cases of distributing goods solely according to the pleasure conferred, it makes more sense to adopt a distribution rule like the utilitarian one, since you will then experience as much pleasure as possible compatible with the constraints imposed by the presence of other people. Different moral principles can thus serve as heuristics that provide solutions to distribution problems according to various contextual cues.

What about people's conception of fairness? Do we have evidence suggesting that this may be shaped by an evolutionary process? In a 1993 paper, "Focal points and bargaining games," Ken Binmore and others ran a series of experiments examining this question. Subjects were randomly assigned to one of four groups and put through an initial "training phase" during which they played a repeated asymmetric Nash demand game against a computer opponent (see figure 8.4). Although subjects were told that the purpose of the training was merely to familiarize them with the operation of the computer interface, the computer opponent was actually programmed to try to condition the subject to play one of four equilibrium outcomes selected by a bargaining theory.

People were trained to play one of four equilibrium outcomes: the Equal Increments solution, the Kalai–Smorodinsky solution, the Nash bargaining solution, and the Utilitarian solution. The Equal Increments solution is obtained by following the line $y = x$ up to the point where it intersects the Pareto frontier. (It also corresponds to Rawls's maximin criterion in the case in which the players are treated symmetrically.)

The Kalai–Smorodinsky solution is obtained via the following procedure.

1. Identify the "utopia point" (m_1, m_2), where m_1 is the maximum possible payoff for player 1, and m_2 is the maximum possible payoff for player 2. The utopia point thus corresponds to the ideal distribution ignoring all considerations imposed by the shape of the feasible set.

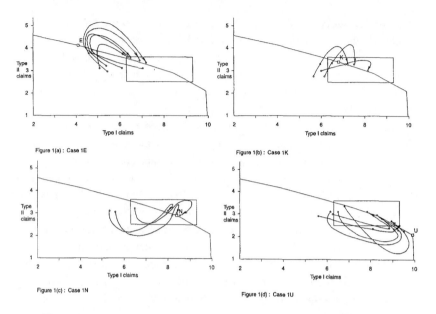

Figure 1(a) : Case 1E

Figure 1(b) : Case 1K

Figure 1(c) : Case 1N

Figure 1(d) : Case 1U

Figure 8.4 Outcomes from the bargaining experiment of Binmore *et al.* (1993).

2. Draw the line ℓ connecting the disagreement point to the utopia point.
3. The point where ℓ crosses the Pareto frontier is the Kalai–Smorodinsky solution.

The intuition behind the Kalai–Smorodinsky solution is that each player should proportionally scale back his or her demands from the best that they can hope for until they reach a feasible point.

The Nash bargaining solution is slightly more difficult to describe than the Kalai–Smorodinsky solution. To begin, let F denote the feasible set of the bargaining problem. We'll assume that F is bounded and convex.[14] The Nash solution is obtained via the following procedure.

1. Since the utility function for each player is unique only up to a positive affine transformation, rescale each player's utility function to move the disagreement point to the origin. Call the new feasible set resulting from the rescaling F'.

---

[14] A set S is convex if, given any two points p_1, $p_2 \in S$, the line connecting p_1 and p_2 lies entirely within S. There is no real loss of generality in assuming that F is convex because, if it isn't, but we allow randomization when assigning outcomes, then the set of expected utilities, taking into account randomization, is convex.

2. The Nash solution is that point $(n'_1, n'_2) \in F'$ such that the product $n'_1 n'_2$ is the greatest of all products $n_1 n_2$, where $(n_1, n_2) \in F'$.

The reason why the Nash solution warrants consideration is that it is the provably *unique* solution satisfying several very natural desiderata.[15]

Lastly, the Utilitarian solution simply chooses that point from the feasible set which maximizes the sum of the payoffs to both players. The primary reason for considering the Utilitarian solution is that it has, together with the Equal Increments solution, the greatest aura of legitimacy among philosophers.

It need not be the case that all four points recommend different solutions to a bargaining problem. Indeed, in the symmetric game of divide-the-cake considered in chapter 5, all four solutions agree on their recommendation. Binmore *et al.* studied the particular asymmetric game shown in figure 8.4 because that game has the property that the above-mentioned four solution points disagree.

After subjects had completed the training period, they played against each other for real money. Figure 8.4 shows aggregate statistics and paths for groups of subjects. On each path, three points are shown: the initial point that a particular group of subjects had been conditioned to play by the training period, the point subjects had arrived at midway through the experiment, and the final point arrived at when the experiment was terminated. Note the following.

1. It was possible to condition subjects to conform, more or less, to any one of the four equilibria.
2. After conditioning, subjects initially continued to play (for a short while) as they had been conditioned to play.
3. The two equilibrium points with the greatest amount of support in the philosophical literature – the Equal Increments point and the Utilitarian point – are extremely unstable. That is, subjects rapidly deviate from them when given the opportunity.
4. The final outcome subjects arrive at depends upon their initial conditioning.

At the end of the experiment, Binmore asked subjects to say whether they thought that the outcome of the bargaining game was fair (see figure 8.5). Subjects exhibited a strong tendency to identify as fair *whatever outcome was arrived at by their group at the end of the experiment*. The moral of the story, then, is this: people's conception of fairness (which I take to be reflected in the strategies they play) is flexible and can be made to conform to salient

---

[15] Namely, that the solution to the bargaining problem should be invariant under choice of utility function, on the Pareto frontier, and independent of irrelevant alternatives, and should satisfy a symmetry condition.

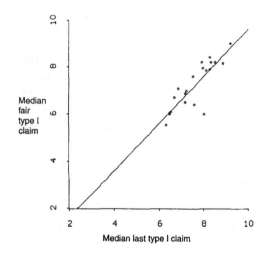

Figure 8.5 Comparison of the medians of the last claims made by player 1 in each experiment with the medians of the claims said to be "fair" for player 1 (from Binmore *et al.*, 1993).

"focal points."[16] Moreover, perceptions of fairness are connected to the general behavior followed by the group to which they belong.

8.5 Conclusion

In this book, I have attempted to show how boundedly rational individuals who face decision problems in structured environments, and who make choices using rules like *Imitate-the-Best*, would learn to behave morally. I have argued that such individuals would learn to cooperate in the prisoner's dilemma, trust in the Stag Hunt, share equally in resource-allocation problems, and even (in some limited cases) behave fairly while adopting punitive behavior for unfair offers in the ultimatum game. I have also argued that many of these tendencies persist when we move from considering two-player games to N-player games. The results are not conclusive, of course, but they are, I believe, better than merely suggestive.

---

[16] Notice that this provides some degree of support for Gibbard's claim that "judgments of fairness are shaped in part by complex workings of normative discussion." Although I suspect it's unlikely that this experimental environment approximates anything close to what Gibbard would consider normative discussion, it does show how judgments of fairness can be shaped.

In this chapter, I have attempted to show how the results discussed in the rest of the book can be used to support a conception of morality that exists harmoniously with the evolutionary account. In doing so, I've attempted to respond to the criticism that previous evolutionary explanations of morality fell short in several important respects.

For Braithwaite, the theory of games was a tool for the moral philosopher because it allowed the moralist to recommend solutions to interdependent decision problems in cases where no moral principle served to settle the debate clearly. For us, I suggest, the theory of evolutionary games can be a tool for the moral philosopher in a rather different sense. Rather than recommending particular solutions to problems, evolutionary game theory, coupled with the theory of bounded rationality and recent work bridging the gap between psychology and economics, provides what appears to be a radical restructuring of the foundations of moral theory. According to the view I've suggested, the recommendations, constraints, and obligations imposed by moral theories are real and binding – but also somewhat arbitrary. If we were different kinds of creatures, and if our societies were structured differently, our lives would be composed of very different interdependent decision problems. Consequently, the moral theories which legislate certain actions as a means of solving those problems would also be different.

This means that our moral beliefs are simultaneously relative to our evolutionary history and our cultural background, but at the same time objectively true. Insofar as our moral beliefs provide solutions to interdependent decision problems, we cannot say that any one solution is better than any other – in an abstract sense – because, detached from our preferences, there is no absolute standard from which to judge. Given our preferences, and from our own personal point of view, there can be an objective moral theory that prescribes the best way of satisfying those preferences.

Yet is the restructuring described here really so radical? At the end of the day, I don't think so. This account is, I believe, Humean. What it does show, though, is just how much work must be undertaken in order to unpack Hume's "certain proposition" that "[T]is only from the selfishness and confin'd generosity of men, along with the scanty provision nature has made for his wants, that justice derives its origin."[17] And, as for the origin of justice, so for the rest of morality.

---

[17] *A Treatise of Human Nature*, Book III, part II, section II.

Select bibliography

Axelrod, R. (1984). *The Evolution of Cooperation*. New York: Basic Books.

Binmore, K. (1994). *Playing Fair*, volume 1 of *Game Theory and the Social Contract*. Cambridge, MA: Press.

(1998). *Just Playing*, volume 2 of *Game Theory and the Social Contract*. Cambridge, MA: The MIT Press.

(2005). *Natural Justice*. Oxford: Oxford University Press.

Skyrms, B. (1996). *Evolution of the Social Contract*. Cambridge: Cambridge University Press.

(2004). *The Stag Hunt and the Evolution of Social Structure*. Cambridge: Cambridge University Press.

Ullman-Margalit, E. (1978). *The Emergence of Norms*. Oxford: Oxford University Press.

Weibull, J. W. (1995). *Evolutionary Game Theory*. Cambridge, MA: The MIT Press.

References

Alexander, J. McKenzie (2000). "Evolutionary explanations of distributive justice." *Philosophy of Science* **67**: 490–516.

(2003). "Random Boolean networks and evolutionary game theory." *Philosophy of Science* **70**: 1289–1304.

Alexander, J. and B. Skyrms (1999). "Bargaining with neighbors: is justice contagious?". *Journal of Philosophy* **96**(11): 588–598.

Allais, M. and O. Hagen, eds. (1979). *Expected Utility Hypotheses and the Allais Paradox*. Dordrecht: D. Reidel.

Allais, M. F. C. (1953a). "La psychologie de l'homme rationnel devant le risque: la théorie et l'experience." *Journal de la Société Statistique de Paris* **94**: 47–73.

(1953b). "Le comportement de l'homme rationnel devant le risque: critique des postulats et axiomes de l'école americaine." *Econometrica* **21**, 4: 503–546.

(1953c). "L'extension des théories de l'equilibre économique général et du rendement social au cas du risque." *Econometrica* **21**, 2: 269–290.

Axelrod, R. (1984). *The Evolution of Cooperation*. New York: Basic Books.

(1986). "An evolutionary approach to norms." *American Political Science Review* **80**, 4: 1095–1111.

Axelrod, R. and W. D. Hamilton (1981). "The evolution of cooperation." *Science* **211**, 27: 1390–1396.

Barlow, N., ed. (1887). *The Autobiography of Charles Darwin*. New York: Norton.

Bell, D. E. (1982). "Regret in decision making under uncertainty." *Operations Research* **30**: 961–981.

Bereby-Meyer, Y. and I. Erev (1998). "On learning to become a successful loser: a comparison of alternative abstractions of the learning process in the loss domain." *Journal of Mathematical Psychology* **42**: 266–286.

Bicchieri, C. (2006). *The Grammar of Society: The Nature and Dynamics of Social Norms*. Cambridge: Cambridge University Press.

Binmore, K., A. Shaked, and J. Sutton (1985). "Testing noncooperative bargaining theory: a preliminary study." *The American Economic Review* **75**, 5: 1178–1180.

(1988). "A further test of noncooperative bargaining theory: reply." *The American Economic Review* **78**, 4: 837–839.

293

Binmore, K., J. Swierzbinski, S. Hsu, and C. Proulx (1993). "Focal points and bargaining." *International Journal of Game Theory* **22**: 381–409.

Björnerstedt, J. (1993). "Experimentation, imitation, and evolutionary dynamics." Mimeo. Department of Economics, Stockholm University.

Björnerstedt, J. and J. Weibull (1999). "Nash equilibrium and evolution by imitation," in K. J. Arrow, E. Colombatto, and M. Perlman, eds., *The Rational Foundations of Economic Behavior*. New York: St. Martin's Press.

Bögers, T. and R. Sarin (1993). "Learning through reinforcement and replicator dynamics." *Journal of Economic Theory* **77**, 1: 1–14.

Braithwaite, R. B. (1954). *Theory of Games as a Tool for the Moral Philosopher*. Cambridge: Cambridge University Press. (An inaugural lecture delivered in Cambridge on December 2, 1954.)

Curley, E. (1994). *Leviathan*. Indianapolis, IN: Hackett Publishing Company, Inc., Introduction.

D'Arms, J. (2000). "When evolutionary game theory explains morality, what does it explain?" *Journal of Consciousness Studies* **7**, 1–2: 296–299.

D'Arms, J., R. Batterman, and K. Górny (1998). "Game theoretic explanations and the evolution of justice." *Philosophy of Science* **65**: 76–102.

Darwin, C. (2004). *The Descent of Man*. London: Penguin. (Second edition originally published 1879.)

Dawkins, R. (1976). *The Selfish Gene*. Oxford: Oxford University Press.

de Groot, A. D. (1965). *Thought and Choice in Chess*. The Hague: Mouton.

de Waal, F. B. M. (1996). *Good Natured: The Origins of Right and Wrong in Humans and Other Animals*. London: Harvard University Press.

(1998). *Chimpanzee Politics*. Baltimore, MA: Johns Hopkins University Press.

(2005). *Our Inner Ape: A Noble, Nasty, and Naughty Heritage*. New York: Riverhead.

Durrett, R. and S. Levin (1994). "The importance of being discrete (and spatial)." *Theoretical Population Biology* **46**: 363–394.

Eddington, A. (1924). *Mathematical Theory of Relativity*. Cambridge: Cambridge University Press.

Ellison, G. (1993). "Learning, local interaction and coordination." *Econometrica* **61**: 1047–1071.

(2000). "Basins of attraction and long run equilibria." *Review of Economic Studies* **67**: 17–45.

Epstein, J. A. (1998). "Zones of cooperation in demographic prisoner's dilemma." *Complexity* **4**, 2: 36–48.

Falk, R. (2000). "The gene – a concept in tension," in P. Beurton, R. Falk, and H.-J. Rheinberger, eds., *The Concept of the Gene in Development and Evolution. Historical and Epistemological Perspectives*. Cambridge: Cambridge University Press, pp. 317–348.

Fisher, R. A. (1930). *The Genetical Theory of Natural Selection*. Oxford: Oxford University Press.

Fletcher, J. A. and M. Zwick (2000). "*N*-Player prisoner's dilemma in multiple groups: a model of multilevel selection," in C. C. Maley and E. Boudreau, eds., *Artifical Life VII Workshop Proceedings*. Cambridge, MA: MIT Press, pp. 86–89.

Foster, D. and H. Peyton Young (1990). "Stochastic evolutionary dynamics." *Journal of Theoretical Biology* **38**, 219–232.

Friedman, M. (1953). "The methodology of positive economics," in *Essays in Positive Economics*. Chicago: University of Chicago Press.

Galan, J. M. and L. R. Izquierdo (2005). "Appearances can be deceiving: lessons learned re-implementing Axelrod's 'evolutionary approach to norms'." *Journal of Artificial Societies and Social Simulation* **8**, 3.

Gale, J., K. G. Binmore, and L. Samuelson (1995). "Learning to be imperfect: the ultimatum game." *Games and Economic Behavior* **8**: 56–90.

Geertz, C. (1973). *The Interpretation of Culture: Selected Essays*. New York: Basic Books.

Gibbard, A. (1990). *Wise Choices, Apt Feelings*. Oxford: Oxford University Press.

Gigerenzer, G. and R. Selten, eds. (2001). *Bounded Rationality: The Adaptive Toolbox*. Cambridge, MA: The MIT Press.

Gigerenzer, G., P. M. Todd, and the ABC Research Group (1999). *Simple Heuristics That Make Us Smart*. Oxford: Oxford University Press.

Güth, W., R. Schmittberger, and B. Schwarze (1982). "An experimental analysis of ultimatum bargaining." *Journal of Economic Behavior and Organization* **3**: 367–388.

Güth, W. and R. Tietz (1990). "Ultimatum bargaining behavior: a survey and comparison of experimental results." *Journal of Economic Psychology* **11**: 417–449.

Hardin, R. (1997). *One for All: The Logic of Group Conflict*. Princeton, NJ: Princeton University Press.

Harris, S. (1981). *What's so Funny about Science?* Los Altos, CA: W. Kaufmann.

Harsanyi, J. and R. Selten (1988). *A General Theory of Equilibrium Selection in Games*. Cambridge, MA: The MIT Press.

Henrich, J., R. Boyd, S. Bowles *et al.* eds. (2004). *Foundations of Human Sociality: Economic Experiments and Ethnographic Evidence from Fifteen Small-scale Societies*. Oxford: Oxford University Press.

Huberman, B. A. and N. S. Glance (1993). "Evolutionary games and computer simulations." *Proceedings of the National Academy of Sciences of the United States* **90**: 7716–7718.

Kalai, E. and M. Smorodinsky (1975). "Other solutions to Nash's bargaining problem." *Econometrica* **43**: 513–518.

Kandori, M., G. J. Mailath, and R. Rob (1993). "Learning, mutation, and long run equilibria in games." *Econometrica* **61**, 1: 29–56.

Kauffman, S. (1993). *The Origins of Order*. Oxford: Oxford University Press.

Kavka, G. S. (1986). *Hobbesian Moral and Political Theory*. Princeton, NJ: Princeton University Press.

Kitcher, P. (1999). "Games social animals play: commentary on Brian Skyrms' *Evolution of the Social Contract*." *Philosophy and Phenomenological Research* **59**, 1: 221–228.

Lewis, D. (1969). *Convention: A Philosophical Study*. Reprinted 1994, Oxford: Blackwell.

Lindgren, K. and M. G. Nordahl (1994). "Evolutionary dynamics of spatial games." *Physica D* **75**: 292–309.

Loomes, G. and R. Sugden (1982). "Regret theory: an alternative theory of rational choice under uncertainty." *Economic Journal* **92**: 805–824.

Luce, R. D. and H. Raiffa (1957). *Games and Decisions: Introduction and Critical Survey*. New York: John Wiley and Sons, Inc.

Maynard Smith, J. (1982). *Evolution and the Theory of Games*. Cambridge: Cambridge University Press.

Maynard Smith, J. and G. Price (1973). "The logic of animal conflict." *Nature* **246**: 15–18.

Milgram, S. (1967). "The small world problem." *Psychology Today* **2**: 60–67.

Milinski, M. (1987). "Tit for tat in sticklebacks and the evolution of cooperation." *Nature* **325**: 433–434.

Morris, S. (2000). "Contagion." *Review of Economic Studies* **67**: 57–78.

Moss, L. (2003). *What Genes Can't Do*. Cambridge, MA: The MIT Press.

Nash, J. (1950a). "Equilibrium points in *N*-person games." *Proceedings of the National Academy of Sciences of the United States* **36**: 48–49.

(1951a). *Essays on Game Theory*. Reprinted 1996, Cheltenham: Edward Elgar Publishing.

(1951b). "Non-cooperative games." *Annals of Mathematics* **54**, 2: 286–295.

Nash, J. F. (1950b). "The bargaining problem." *Econometrica* **18**: 155–162.

Newell, A. and H. A. Simon (1972). *Human Problem Solving*. Englewood Cliffs, NJ: Prentice-Hall, Inc.

Nowak, M. and K. Sigmund (1993). "A strategy of win–stay, lose–shift that outperforms tit-for-tat in the Prisoner's Dilemma game." *Nature* **364**: 56–58.

Nowak, M. A. and R. M. May (1992). "Evolutionary games and spatial chaos." *Nature* **359**: 826–829.

(1993). "The spatial dilemmas of evolution." *International Journal of Bifurcation and Chaos* **3**, 1: 35–78.

Nydegger, R. V. and G. Owen (1974). "Two-person bargaining: an experimental test of the Nash axioms." *International Journal of Game Theory* **3**, 4: 239–249.

Page, K. M., M. A. Nowak, and K. Sigmund (2000). "The spatial ultimatum game." *Proceedings of the Royal Society of London B*. **267**: 2177–2182.

Prasad, K. (1991). "Computability and randomness of Nash equilibrium in infinite games." *Journal of Mathematica Economics* **20**: 429–442.

(1997). "On the computability of Nash equilibria." *Journal of Economic Dynamics and Control* **21**: 943–953.

Ridley, M. (1996). *The Origins of Virtue*. London: Penguin Books Ltd.

Roth, A. E. (1995). "Bargaining Experiments". In J. Kagel and A. Roth, eds., *The Handbook of Experimental Economics*. Princeton, NJ: Princeton University Press, chapter 4, pp. 253–348.

Rousseau, J.-J. (1755). *Discourse on the Origin of Inequality*. Oxford: Oxford Paperbacks, 1999 edition. Franklin Philip, translator.

Ryle, G. (1971). "The thinking of thoughts: what is 'le penseur' doing?" In *Collected Papers of Gilbert Ryle*. London: Hutchinson.

Sadrieh, A., W. Güth, P. Hammerstein *et al.* (2001). "Group report: is there evidence for an adaptive toolbox?," in G. Gigerenzer and R. Selten, eds., *Bounded Rationality: The Adaptive Toolbox*. Cambridge, MA: The MIT Press, chapter 6, pp. 83–102.

Sarkar, S. (1998). *Genetics and Reductionism*. Cambridge: Cambridge University Press.

Sen, A. (1967). "Isolation, assurance, and the social rate of discount." *Quarterly Journal of Economics* **81**: 112–124.

Shermer, M. (2004). *The Science of Good and Evil*. New York: Times Books, Henry Holt and Company, LLC.

Simon, H. A. (1957). *Models of Man: Social and Rational*. New York: John Wiley & Sons, Inc.

Skiena, S. (1990). "Graph isomorphism," section 5.2 in *Implementing Discrete Mathematics: Combinatorics and Graph Theory with Mathematica*. Reading, MA: Addison-Wesley, pp. 181–187.

Skyrms, B. (1992). "Chaos in game dynamics." *Journal of Logic, Language, and Information* **1**: 111–130.

(1993). "Chaos and the explanatory significance of equilibrium: strange attractors in evolutionary game dynamics," in *Proceedings of the 1992 PSA*, volume 2, pp. 374–394.

(1996). *Evolution of the Social Contract*. Cambridge: Cambridge University Press.

(2004). *The Stag Hunt and the Evolution of Social Structure*. Cambridge: Cambridge University Press.

Skyrms, B. and R. Pemantle (2000). "A dynamic model of social network formation." *Proceedings of the National Academy of Sciences of the United States* **97**, 16: 9340–9346.

Taylor, P. D. and L. B. Jonker (1978). "Evolutionary stable strategies and game dynamics." *Mathematical Biosciences* **40**: 145–156.

Thaler, R. H. (1988). "Anomalies: the ultimatum game." *Journal of Economic Perspectives* **2**, 4: 195–206.

Vanderschraaf, P. and J. McKenzie Alexander (2005). "Follow the leader: local interactions with influence neighborhoods." *Philosophy of Science* **72**: 86–113.

von Neumann, J. and O. Morgenstern (1944). *Theory of Games and Economic Behavior*. Princeton, NJ: Princeton University Press.

Watts, D. J. (1999). *Small World: The Dynamics of Networks between Order and Randomness*. Princeton, NJ: Princeton University Press.

Watts, D. J. and S. H. Strogatz (1998). "Collective dynamics of 'small-world' networks." *Nature* **393**, 4: 440–442.

Weibull, J. W. (1995). *Evolutionary Game Theory*. Cambridge, MA: The MIT Press.

Wilson, E. O. (1988). *On Human Nature*. Cambridge, MA: Harvard University Press.

Wuensche, A. and M. J. Lesser (1992). *The Global Dynamics of Cellular Automata: An Atlas of Basin of Attraction Fields of One-Dimensional Cellular Automata*, volume 1 of *Santa Fe Institute Studies in the Sciences of Complexity*. New York: Addison-Wesley.

Yaari, M. E. and M. Bar-Hillel (1984). "On dividing justly." *Social Choice and Welfare* **1**: 1–24.

Young, H. Peyton (1993). "The evolution of conventions." *Econometrica* **61**, 1: 57–84.

(1998). *Individual Strategy and Social Structure: An Evolutionary Theory of Institutions*. Princeton, NJ: Princeton University Press.

Index